THE ABINGDON PREACHING ANNUAL 2006

The ABINGDON PREACHING ANNUAL 2006

**COMPILED AND EDITED BY
THE REVEREND DAVID NEIL MOSSER, PH.D.**

ASSISTANT EDITOR RONDA WELLMAN

Abingdon Press
Nashville

THE ABINGDON PREACHING ANNUAL 2006

Copyright © 2005 by Abingdon Press

This book is printed on acid-free paper.

ISBN 0-687-34286-4
ISSN 1075-2250

05 06 07 08 09 10 11 12 13 14—10 9 8 7 6 5 4 3 2 1

MANUFACTURED IN THE UNITED STATES OF AMERICA

CONTENTS

❧❧❧❧

Contents

Contents

JULY

Contents

Contents

Contents

III. APPENDIX

INTRODUCTION

The edition of the *Abingdon Preaching Annual* (*APA*) you now hold in your hands is a piece of writing that has a long history. We have listened to and heard our readers' important suggestions to improve on the *APA*'s ease of use and effectiveness for preachers. We have certainly taken your comments to heart. Because we know all too well that the previous *APA*s were often unwieldy for preachers to work with on an already over-crowded workspace, we are now publishing the 2006 *APA* in a hardback format. We trust that this new feature will allow pastors to work with the *Annual* and other reference materials simultaneously. The hardback for-mat allows the *Annual* to lay open on a desk while preachers are also free simultaneously to consult other reference materials. In addition, we have made the 2006 *APA* noticeably larger, making this book easier to use.

Another suggestion from our readers alerted us to the reality that not all preachers preach from the lectionary. Of course we knew this fact, but as we thought about how to be helpful to those both inside and outside "the lectionary family," we resolved to include not only a longer lec-tionary text sermon but also a nonlectionary sermon that might fit each season of the Christian year. Thus, rather than the previous *APA* formats that included three 600-word sermon briefs, we have chosen two ser-mons—one lectionary and one nonlectionary—each about one thousand words long. This length allows our capable writers more expansiveness. This change also offers readers useful sermons both inside and outside of the lectionary rubric. As your editors, we are eager to make the *APA* as helpful to our readers as possible. We value your insights and have tried to format a book that will make the preaching in our churches more effec-tive and faithful.

We trust that these format changes will give preachers more flexibility and options in using the *APA*. Many preachers have recently turned from the lectionary exclusively to preaching series of sermons on faith topics. With this in mind, many of the nonlectionary sermons included are part of an ongoing series of sermons. Some of the sermon series are on individual topics such as the life of Moses, the journey in the wilderness, prayer, generous living, and the Holy Spirit. One of our contributors has taken the biblical Epistle of Ephesians and explored it homiletically. Taken together with a text for each liturgical day of the year, we have assembled a collection of thirteen sermon series for those who want to depart for a season from the lectionary.

The 2006 APA will introduce classic sermons as well as special sermons for a church anniversary, weddings, the renewal of marriage vows, the occasion of a church building consecration/dedication, Sunday school promotion or Christian Education Sunday, and baccalaureate or graduation services. Because many pastors are called upon to preach at funerals or memorial services, we have incorporated into the APA some sermons you might find helpful, including an unexpected or sudden death, a suicide, and the death of a child. We hope that these sermons can assist preachers when faced with tragic circumstances in which the gospel of comfort and strength is most desperately needed by family and friends of the deceased person.

Another feature of the 2006 APA is a CD-ROM that Abingdon Press has created for those who employ computer technology in the creation of Sunday's sermon. Of course, this is in addition to the print edition and has a wealth of new and usable resources for Sunday morning worship. Included in the CD-ROM are additional, stand-alone illustrations for each Sunday and more pastoral and presermon prayers. We have also included on the CD-ROM a bibliography of suggested biblical materials such as commentaries and other resources to go with each liturgical day. *The Abingdon Preaching Annual* has been a resource that preachers have come to use and trust. We hope the improvements we have made for this year's edition will continue to serve the needs of pastors and preachers.

One additional comment seems in order. Often, people think that a book like the APA is one that preachers simply raid for sermons late on Saturday night. However, nothing could be further from our intent in gathering the materials for the APA. We recognize that every preacher stands in a unique place within his or her congregation. For many preachers, exegeting a biblical text is more or less a uniform task. We read the text, place it in its biblical context, and try to apply the message of that text to the people for whom we labor as pastors.

However, every preacher also stands in an absolutely unique position with regard to the congregation within which he or she preaches. You know the people (in many cases well enough even to know their pets), and for this reason preachers exegete not only the biblical texts from which they preach but also the congregation to whom they preach. We, as their pastors, know their dreams and aspirations as a people of God. Not only this, but we also know where our people hurt and the deepest questions of human existence that they each bring to worship every week. Thus, we read the biblical texts, and we read our people.

Books like the *APA* are intended to be a springboard to help you, the preacher/pastor, bring to your people each week the best of your own thinking about the Bible and apply it to your own unique circumstance. Preachers, who try to offer "canned" sermons to their own congregations without tailoring it to suit their needs, will find a "flatness" to their preaching. Consequently, we urge you to ponder these sermons in the *APA*, but make them your own by inserting your own thought and personality into the sermons that this group of fine preachers offers you here.

My prayer is that you will find stimulation and faithfulness from what you find in this book. I also pray that your interaction will help you become a better preacher after having conversed with the writers in this book.

David Mosser

I. GENERAL HELPS

CHURCH AND CIVIC CALENDAR 2006

JANUARY	FEBRUARY	MARCH
S M T W T F S	S M T W T F S	S M T W T F S
1 2 3 4 5 6 7	1 2 3 4	1 2 3 4
8 9 10 11 12 13 14	5 6 7 8 9 10 11	5 6 7 8 9 10 11
15 16 17 18 19 20 21	12 13 14 15 16 17 18	12 13 14 15 16 17 18
22 23 24 25 26 27 28	19 20 21 22 23 24 25	19 20 21 22 23 24 25
29 30 31	26 27 28	26 27 28 29 39 31

APRIL	MAY	JUNE
S M T W T F S	S M T W T F S	S M T W T F S
1	1 2 3 4 5 6	1 2 3
2 3 4 5 6 7 8	7 8 9 10 11 12 13	4 5 6 7 8 9 10
9 10 11 12 13 14 15	14 15 16 17 18 19 20	11 12 13 14 15 16 17
16 17 18 19 20 21 22	21 22 23 24 25 26 27	18 19 20 21 22 23 24
23 24 25 26 27 28 29	28 29 30 31	25 26 27 28 29 30
30		

JULY	AUGUST	SEPTEMBER
S M T W T F S	S M T W T F S	S M T W T F S
1	1 2 3 4 5	1 2
2 3 4 5 6 7 8	6 7 8 9 10 11 12	3 4 5 6 7 8 9
9 10 11 12 13 14 15	13 14 15 16 17 18 19	10 11 12 13 14 15 16
16 17 18 19 20 21 22	20 21 22 23 24 25 26	17 18 19 20 21 22 23
23 24 25 26 27 28 29	27 28 29 30 31	24 25 26 27 28 29 30
30 31		

OCTOBER	NOVEMBER	DECEMBER
S M T W T F S	S M T W T F S	S M T W T F S
1 2 3 4 5 5 7	1 2 3 4	1 2
8 9 10 11 12 13 14	5 6 7 8 9 10 11	3 4 5 6 7 8 9
15 16 17 18 19 20 21	12 13 14 15 16 17 18	10 11 12 13 14 15 16
22 23 24 25 26 27 28	19 20 21 22 23 24 25	17 18 19 20 21 22 23
29 30 31	26 27 28 29 30	24 25 26 27 28 29 30
		31

FOUR-YEAR CHURCH CALENDAR

	2006	2007	2008	2009
Ash Wednesday	March 1	February 21	February 6	February 25
Palm Sunday	April 9	April 1	March 16	April 5
Good Friday	April 14	April 6	March 21	April 10
Easter	April 16	April 8	March 23	April 12
Ascension Day	May 25	May 17	May 1	May 21
Pentecost	June 4	May 27	May 11	May 31
Trinity Sunday	June 11	June 3	May 18	June 7
Thanksgiving	November 23	November 22	November 27	November 26
First Sunday of Advent	December 3	December 2	November 30	November 29

TEXT GUIDE*
THE REVISED COMMON LECTIONARY (2006—YEAR B)

Sunday	First Lesson	Psalm	Second Lesson	Gospel Lesson
1/1/06	Isa. 61:10–62:3	Ps. 148	Gal. 4:4-7	Luke 2:22-40
1/8/06	Gen. 1:1-5	Ps. 29	Acts 19:1-7	Mark 1:4-11
1/15/06	1 Sam. 3:1-10, (11-20)	Ps. 139:1-6, 13-18	1 Cor. 6:12-20	John 1:43-51
1/22/06	Jonah 3:1-5, 10	Ps. 62:5-12	1 Cor. 7:29-31	Mark 1:14-20
1/29/06	Deut. 18:15-20	Ps. 111	1 Cor. 8:1-13	Mark 1:21-28
2/5/06	Isa. 40:21-31	Ps. 147:1-11, 20c	1 Cor. 9:16-23	Mark 1:29-39
2/12/06	2 Kgs. 5:1-14	Ps. 30	1 Cor. 9:24-27	Mark 1:40-45
2/19/06	Isa. 43:18-25	Ps. 41	2 Cor. 1:18-22	Mark 2:1-12
2/26/06	2 Kgs. 2:1-12	Ps. 50:1-6	2 Cor. 4:3-6	Mark 9:2-9
3/5/06	Gen. 9:8-17	Ps. 25:1-10	1 Pet. 3:18-22	Mark 1:9-15
3/12/06	Gen. 17:1-7, 15-16	Ps. 22:23-31	Rom 4:13-25	Mark 8:31-38
3/19/06	Exod. 20:1-17	Ps. 19	1 Cor. 1:18-25	John 2:13-22
3/26/06	Num. 21:4-9	Ps. 107:1-3, 17-22	Eph. 2:1-10	John 3:14-21
4/2/06	Jer. 31:31-34	Ps. 51:1-12	Heb. 5:5-10	John 12:20-33
4/9/06	Mark 11:1-11	Ps. 118:1-2, 19-29	Phil. 2:5-11	Mark 14:1–15:47
4/16/06	Acts 10:34-43	Ps. 118:1-2, 14-24	1 Cor. 15:1-11	John 20:1-18
4/23/06	Acts 4:32-35	Ps. 133	1 John 1:1–2:2	John 20:19-31
4/30/06	Acts 3:12-19	Ps. 4	1 John 3:1-7	Luke 24:36b-48
5/7/06	Acts 4:5-12	Ps. 23	1 John 3:16-24	John 10:11-18
5/14/06	Acts 8:26-40	Ps. 22:25-31	1 John 4:7-21	John 15:1-8
5/21/06	Acts 10:44-48	Ps. 98	1 John 5:1-6	John 15:9-17
5/28/06	Acts 1:15-17, 21-26	Ps. 1	1 John 5:9-13	John 17:6-19

*This guide represents one possible selection of lessons and psalms from the lectionary. For a complete listing see *The Revised Common Lectionary.*

Sunday	First Lesson	Psalm	Second Lesson	Gospel Lesson
6/4/06	Acts 2:1-21	Ps. 104:24-34, 35b	Rom. 8:22-27	John 15:26-27; 16:4b-15
6/11/06	1 Sam. 8:4-11, (12-15), 16-20, (11:14-15)	Ps. 138	2 Cor. 4:13-5:1	Mark 3:20-35
6/18/06	1 Sam. 15:34-16:13	Ps. 20	2 Cor. 5:6-10, (11-13), 14-17	Mark 4:26-34
6/25/06	1 Sam. 17:(1a, 4-11, 19-23), 32-49	Ps. 9:9-20	2 Cor. 6:1-13	Mark 4:35-41
7/2/06	2 Sam. 1:1, 17-27	Ps. 130	2 Cor. 8:7-15	Mark 5:21-43
7/9/06	2 Sam. 5:1-5, 9-10	Ps. 48	2 Cor. 12:2-10	Mark 6:1-13
7/16/06	2 Sam. 6:1-5, 12b-19	Ps. 24	Eph. 1:3-14	Mark 6:14-29
7/23/06	2 Sam. 7:1-14a	Ps. 89:20-37	Eph. 2:11-22	Mark 6:30-34, 53-56
7/30/06	2 Sam. 11:1-15	Ps. 14	Eph. 3:14-21	John 6:1-21
8/6/06	2 Sam. 11:26-12:13a	Ps. 51:1-12	Eph. 4:1-16	John 6:24-35
8/13/06	2 Sam. 18:5-9, 15, 31-33	Ps. 130	Eph. 4:25-5:2	John 6:35, 41-51
8/20/06	1 Kgs. 2:10-12; 3:3-14	Ps. 111	Eph. 5:15-20	John 6:51-58
8/27/06	1 Kgs. 8:(1, 6, 10-11), 22-30, 41-43	Ps. 84	Eph. 6:10-20	John 6:56-69
9/3/06	Song 2:8-13	Ps. 45:1-2, 6-9	Jas. 1:17-27	Mark 7:1-8, 14-15, 21-23
9/10/06	Prov. 22:1-2, 8-9, 22-23	Ps. 125	Jas. 2:1-10, (11-13), 14-17	Mark 7:24-37
9/17/06	Prov. 1:20-33	Ps. 19	Jas. 3:1-12	Mark 8:27-38
9/24/06	Prov. 31:10-31	Ps. 1	Jas. 3:13-4:3, 7-8a	Mark 9:30-37
10/1/06	Esth. 7:1-6, 9-10; 9:20-22	Ps. 124	Jas. 5:13-20	Mark 9:38-50
10/8/06	Job 1:1; 2:1-10	Ps. 26	Heb. 1:1-4; 2:5-12	Mark 10:2-16
10/15/06	Job 23:1-9, 16-17	Ps. 22:1-15	Heb. 4:12-16	Mark 10:17-31
10/22/06	Job 38:1-7, (34-41)	Ps. 104:1-9, 24, 35c	Heb. 5:1-10	Mark 10:35-45
10/29/06	Job 42:1-6, 10-17	Ps. 34:1-8, (19-22)	Heb. 7:23-28	Mark 10:46-52
11/5/06	Ruth 1:1-8	Ps. 146	Heb. 9:11-14	Mark 12:28-34

*This guide represents one possible selection of lessons and psalms from the lectionary. For a complete listing see The Revised Common Lectionary.

Sunday	First Lesson	Psalm	Second Lesson	Gospel Lesson
11/5/06	Ruth 1:1-8	Ps. 146	Heb. 9:11-14	Mark 12:28-34
11/12/06	Ruth 3:1-5; 4:13-17	Ps. 127	Heb. 9:24-28	Mark 12:38-44
11/19/06	1 Sam. 1:4-20	1 Sam. 2:1-10	Heb. 10:11-14, (15-18), 19-25	Mark 13:1-8
11/26/06	2 Sam. 23:1-7	Ps. 132:1-12, (13-18)	Rev. 1:4b-8	John 18:33-37
12/3/06	Jer. 33:14-16	Ps. 25:1-10	1 Thess. 3:9-13	Luke 21:25-36
12/10/06	Mal. 3:1-4	Luke 1:68-79	Phil. 1:3-11	Luke 3:1-6
12/17/06	Zeph. 3:14-20	Isa. 12:2-6	Phil. 4:4-7	Luke 3:7-18
12/24/06	Mic. 5:2-5a	Luke 1:47-55	Heb. 10:5-10	Luke 1:39-45, (46-55)
12/31/06	1 Sam. 2:18-20, 26	Ps. 148	Col. 3:12-17	Luke 2:41-52

*This guide represents one possible selection of lessons and psalms from the lectionary. For a complete listing see *The Revised Common Lectionary*.

LITURGICAL COLORS

If the gospel can be proclaimed visually, why should it not be? Color helps form general expectations for any occasion. Traditionally, purples, grays, and blues have been used for seasons of a penitential character such as Advent and Lent, although any dark colors could be used. White has been used for events or seasons with strong christological meaning such as the Baptism of the Lord or the Easter Season. Yellows and golds are also possibilities at such times. Red has been reserved for occasions relating to the Holy Spirit (such as the Day of Pentecost or ordinations) or to commemorations of the martyrs. Green has been used for seasons such as the Season after Epiphany or the Season after Pentecost. The absence of any colored textiles from Maundy Thursday to the Easter Vigil is a striking use of contrast. Colors and textures can be used most effectively in textiles for hangings on pulpits, on lecterns (if any), for the stoles worn by ordained ministers, or for ministerial vestments.*

Advent: Violet (purple) or blue

Christmas: Gold or white for December 24-25. White thereafter, through the Baptism of the Lord. (Or, in the days between January 6 and the Sunday of the Baptism, green may be used.)

Ordinary Time (both after Epiphany-Baptism and after Pentecost): Green

Transfiguration: White

Lent Prior to Holy Week: Violet. Black is sometimes used for Ash Wednesday.

Early Holy Week: On Palm-Passion Sunday, violet (purple) or [blood] red may be specified. For the Monday, Tuesday, and Wednesday of Holy Week, the same options exist, although with variations as to which color to use on each day.

* James F. White, *Introduction to Christian Worship* (rev. ed.; Nashville: Abingdon Press, 1990), 85-86.

Triduum: For Holy Thursday, violet (purple) or [blood] red may be used during the day and changed to white for the evening Eucharist. Then the church may be stripped.

Good Friday and Holy Saturday: Stripped or black; or [blood] red in some churches on Good Friday.

Great Fifty Days: White or gold. Or gold for Easter Day and perhaps its octave, then white for the remainder of the season until the Vigil of Pentecost.

Day of Pentecost: [Fire] red

Annunciation, Visitation, and Presentation of Jesus: White

Commemoration of Martyrs: [Blood] red

Commemoration of Saints not Martyred: White

All Saints: White

Christ the King: White**

** Laurence Hull Stookey, *Calendar: Christ's Time for the Church* (Nashville: Abingdon Press, 1996), 156-57.

CLASSICAL PRAYERS

Morning Prayer

Almighty and most merciful Father; We have erred, and strayed from thy ways like lost sheep. We have followed too much the devices and desires of our own hearts. We have offended against thy holy laws. We have left undone those things which we ought to have done; And we have done those things which we ought not to have done; And there is no health in us. But thou, O Lord, have mercy upon us, miserable offenders. Spare thou those, O God, who confess their faults. Restore thou those who are penitent; According to thy promises declared unto mankind In Christ Jesus our Lord. And grant, O most merciful Father, for his sake; That we may hereafter live a godly, righteous, and sober life, To the glory of thy holy Name. Amen.

Eucharistic

Make this Bread the precious Body of thy Christ, . . . And that which is in this Chalice, the precious Blood of thy Christ. . . . Transmuting them by thy Holy Spirit . . . So that they may be to those that partake, unto sobriety of soul, unto remission of sins, unto communion of thy Holy Spirit, unto fulfilment of the Kingdom of the heavens, unto boldness toward thee, not unto judgement, nor unto condemnation.

An Orthodox Prayer

I praise Thee, O God of our Fathers, I hymn Thee, I bless Thee, I give thanks unto thee for Thy great and tender mercy. To Thee I flee, O merciful and mighty God. Shine into my heart with the True Sun of Thy righteousness. Enlighten my mind and keep all my senses, that henceforth I may walk uprightly and keep Thy commandments, and may finally attain unto eternal life, even to Thee, Who art the source of life, and be admitted to the glorious fruition of Thy inaccessible Light. For Thou art my God, and unto Thee, O Father, Son and Holy Spirit, be ascribed glory, now and ever and unto ages of ages. Amen.

A General Thanksgiving

Almighty God, Father of all mercies, we, thine unworthy servants, do give thee most humble and hearty thanks for all thy goodness and loving-kindness to us, and to all men; [*particularly to those who desire now to offer up their praises and thanksgivings for thy late mercies vouchsafed unto them.*] We bless thee for our creation, preservation, and all the blessings of this life; but above all, for thine inestimable love in the redemption of the world by our Lord Jesus Christ; for the means of grace, and for the hope of glory. And, we beseech thee, give us that due sense of all thy mercies, that our hearts may be unfeignedly thankful; and that we show forth thy praise, not only with our lips, but in our lives, by giving up our selves to thy service, and by walking before thee in holiness and righteousness all our days; through Jesus Christ our Lord, to whom, with thee and the Holy Ghost, be all honour and glory, world without end. *Amen.*

Prayer of Saint Francis of Assisi

Lord, make me an instrument of your peace.
Where there is hatred, let me sow love;
Where there is injury, pardon;
Where there is doubt, faith;
Where there is despair, hope;
Where there is darkness, light;
Where there is sadness, joy.
Divine Master,
grant that I may not so much seek
To be consoled as to console;
To be understood as to understand;
To be loved as to love;
For it is in giving that we receive;
It is in pardoning that we are pardoned;
It is in dying that we are born to eternal life.

A Prayer of Saint Chrysostom

Almighty God, who hast given us grace at this time with one accord to make our common supplications unto thee; and dost promise that when two or three are gathered together in thy Name thou wilt grant their requests; Fulfil now, O Lord, the desires and petitions of thy servants, as may be most expedient for them; granting us in this world knowledge of thy truth, and in the world to come life everlasting. Amen.

Serenity Prayer

God, grant me the Serenity
To accept the things I cannot change;
Courage to change the things I can;
And Wisdom to know the difference.

(Reinhold Niebuhr)

An Orthodox Evening Prayer

O eternal God! Ruler of all creation! Who hast vouchsafed that I should live even down to the present hour, forgive the sins I have committed this day by deed, word or thought. Cleanse, O Lord, my humble soul of all corporal and spiritual stain. And grant, O Lord, that I may during this night have a peaceful sleep, so that on rising from my humble bed, I should continue to praise Thy holy Name throughout all the days of my life, and that I be victorious over all the physical and spiritual enemies battling against me. Deliver me, O Lord, from all vain thoughts that defile me, and from evil desires. For Thine is the Kingdom, and the Power, and the Glory of the Father, and of the Son, and of the Holy Spirit, now and ever, and unto ages of ages. Amen.

Prayer from Saint Augustine

You are great, O Lord, and greatly to be praised: great is your power and to your wisdom there is no limit. And man, who is a part of your creation, wishes to praise you.... You arouse him to take joy in praising you, for you have made us for yourself, and our heart is restless until it rests in you.... Lord, let me seek you by calling upon you, and let me call upon you by believing in you, for you have been preached to us. Lord, my faith calls upon you, that faith which you have given to me, which you have breathed into me by the incarnation of your Son and through the ministry of your preacher.

A Collect for Peace

O God, from whom all holy desires, all good counsels, and all just works do proceed; Give unto thy servants that peace which the world cannot give; that our hearts may be set to obey thy commandments, and also that by thee, we, being defended from the fear of our enemies, may pass our time in rest and quietness; through the merits of Jesus Christ our Saviour. *Amen.*

"Morning Prayer," *The Book of Common Prayer* (New York: Thomas Nelson and Sons, 1928), 6.

"Eucharistic," from *The Divine Liturgies of Our Fathers among the Saints: John Chrysostom and Basil the Great* (ed. J. N. W. B. Robertson; London: David Nutt, 1894), 303.

"An Orthodox Prayer," http://www.orthodoxphotos.com/readings/prayers/thanksgiv ing.shtml.

"A General Thanksgiving," *Book of Common Prayer*, 33.

"A Prayer of Saint Chrysostom," *Book of Common Prayer*, 20.

"An Orthodox Evening Prayer," http://ocf.org/OrthodoxPage/prayers/evening.html.

"Prayer from Saint Augustine," *The Confessions of Saint Augustine* (trans. John K. Ryan; New York: Doubleday, 1960), 43.

"A Collect for Peace," *Book of Common Prayer*, 31.

CLASSICAL AFFIRMATIONS OF FAITH

The Apostles' Creed (ca. 700 c.e.)

I believe in God, the Father Almighty,
  creator of heaven and earth.
I believe in Jesus Christ, his only Son, our Lord,
  who was conceived by the Holy Spirit,
  born of the Virgin Mary,
  suffered under Pontius Pilate,
  was crucified, died, and was buried;
  He descended to the dead. [or "He descended into hell"]
  On the third day he rose again;
  he ascended into heaven,
  and is seated at the right hand of the Father,
  and will come again to judge the living and the dead.
I believe in the Holy Spirit,
  the holy catholic church,
  the communion of saints,
  the forgiveness of sins,
  the resurrection of the body
  and the life everlasting. Amen.

The Nicene Creed (325 c.e.)

We believe in one God,
  the Father, the Almighty,
  maker of heaven and earth,
  of all that is, seen and unseen.
We believe in one Lord, Jesus Christ,

the only Son of God,
eternally begotten of the Father,
God from God, Light from Light,
true God from true God,
begotten, not made,
of one Being with the Father;
through him all things were made.
For us and for our salvation
    he came down from heaven,
    was incarnate of the Holy Spirit and the Virgin Mary
    and became truly human.
    For our sake he was crucified under Pontius Pilate;
    he suffered death and was buried.
    On the third day he rose again
    in accordance with the Scriptures;
    he ascended into heaven
    and is seated at the right hand of the Father.
    He will come again in glory
    to judge the living and the dead,
    and his kingdom will have no end.
We believe in the Holy Spirit, the Lord, the giver of life,
    who proceeds from the Father and the Son,
    who with the Father and the Son
        is worshiped and glorified,
    who has spoken through the prophets.
We believe in one holy catholic and apostolic church.
We acknowledge one baptism
    for the forgiveness of sins.
We look for the resurrection of the dead,
    and the life of the world to come. Amen.

The Athanasian Creed (ca. 500 c.e.)

Whosoever will be saved, before all things it is is necessary that he hold
    the Catholic Faith.

Which Faith except everyone do keep whole and undefiled, without
    doubt he shall perish everlastingly.

And the Catholic Faith is this: That we worship one God in Trinity, and
    Trinity in Unity, neither confounding the Persons, nor dividing the
    Substance.

For there is one Person of the Father, another of the Son, and another of the Holy Ghost.

But the Godhead of the Father, of the Son, and of the Holy Ghost, is all one, the Glory equal, the Majesty co-eternal.

Such as the Father is, such is the Son, and such is the Holy Ghost.

The Father uncreate, the Son uncreate, and the Holy Ghost uncreate.

The Father incomprehensible, the Son incomprehensible, and the Holy Ghost incomprehensible.

The Father eternal, the Son eternal, and the Holy Ghost eternal.

And yet they are not three eternals, but one eternal.

As also there are not three incomprehensibles, nor three uncreated, but one uncreated, and one incomprehensible.

So likewise the Father is Almighty, the Son Almighty, and the Holy Ghost Almighty.

And yet they are not three Almighties, but one Almighty.

So the Father is God, the Son is God, and the Holy Ghost is God.

And yet they are not three Gods, but one God.

So likewise the Father is Lord, the Son Lord, and the Holy Ghost Lord.

And yet not three Lords, but one Lord.

For like as we are compelled by the Christian verity to acknowledge every Person by himself to be both God and Lord,

So are we forbidden by the Catholic Religion, to say, There be three Gods, or three Lords.

The Father is made of none, neither created, nor begotten.

The Son is of the Father alone, not made, nor created, but begotten.

The Holy Ghost is of the Father and of the Son, neither made, nor created, nor begotten, but proceeding.

So there is one Father, not three Fathers; one Son, not three Sons; one Holy Ghost, not three Holy Ghosts.

And in this Trinity none is afore, or after other; none is greater, or less than another;

But the whole three Persons are co-eternal together and co-equal.

So that in all things, as is aforesaid, the Unity in Trinity and the Trinity in Unity is to be worshipped.

He therefore that will be saved must thus think of the Trinity.

Furthermore, it is necessary to everlasting salvation that he also believe rightly the Incarnation of our Lord Jesus Christ.

For the right Faith is, that we believe and confess, that our Lord Jesus Christ, the Son of God, is God and Man;

God, of the Substance of the Father, begotten before the worlds; and Man, of the Substance of his Mother, born in the world;

Perfect God and perfect Man, of a reasonable soul and human flesh subsisting;

Equal to the Father, as touching his Godhead; and inferior to the Father, as touching his Manhood.

Who although he be God and Man, yet he is not two, but one Christ;

One, not by conversion of the Godhead into flesh, but by taking of the Manhood into God;

One altogether; not by confusion of Substance, but by unity of Person.

For as the reasonable soul and flesh is one man, so God and Man is one Christ;

Who suffered for our salvation, descended into hell, rose again the third day from the dead.

He ascended into heaven, he sitteth on the right hand of the Father, God Almighty, from whence he shall come to judge the quick and the dead.

At whose coming all men shall rise again with their bodies and shall give account for their own works.

And they that have done good shall go into life everlasting; and they that have done evil into everlasting fire.

This is the Catholic Faith, which except a man believe faithfully, he cannot be saved.

The Creed of Chalcedon (451 c.e.)

Therefore, following the holy fathers, we all with one accord teach men to acknowledge one and the same Son, our Lord Jesus Christ, at once complete in Godhead and complete in manhood, truly God and truly man, consisting also of a reasonable soul and body; of one substance (homoousios) with the Father as regards his Godhead, and at the same time of one substance with us as regards his manhood; like us in all respects, apart from sin; as regards his Godhead, begotten of the Father before the ages, but yet as regards his manhood begotten, for us men and for our salvation, of Mary the Virgin, the God-bearer (Theotokos); one and the same Christ, Son, Lord, Only-begotten, recognized in two natures, without confusion, without change, without division, without separation; the distinction of natures being in no way annulled by the union, but rather the characteristics of each nature being preserved and coming together to form one person and subsistence, not as parted or separated into two persons, but one and the same Son and Only-begotten God the Word, Lord Jesus Christ; even as the prophets from earliest times spoke of him, and our Lord Jesus Christ himself taught us, and the creed of the Fathers [the *Nicene Creed*] has handed down to us.

"The Apostles' Creed" and "The Nicene Creed" are from *The United Methodist Hymnal* (Nashville: The United Methodist Publishing House, 1989), 882 and 880.

"The Athanasian Creed" and "The Creed of Chalcedon" are from *The Book of Common Prayer* (New York: Oxford, 1979), 864-65.

CONTEMPORARY AFFIRMATIONS OF FAITH

A New Creed (United Church of Canada)

We are not alone,
   we live in God's world.

We believe in God:
   who has created and is creating,
   who has come in Jesus,
     the Word made flesh,
     to reconcile and make new,
   who works in us and others by the Spirit.

We trust in God.

We are called to be the Church:
   to celebrate God's presence,
   to live with respect in Creation,
   to love and serve others,
   to seek justice and resist evil,
   to proclaim Jesus, crucified and risen,
     our judge and our hope.

In life, in death, in life beyond death,
   God is with us.
We are not alone.

   Thanks be to God.

The Korean Creed

We believe in the one God, maker and ruler of all things, Father of all
men, the source of all goodness and beauty, all truth and love.

We believe in Jesus Christ, God manifest in the flesh, our teacher, example,
and Redeemer, the Savior of the world.

We believe in the Holy Spirit, God present with us for guidance, for comfort,
and for strength.

We believe in the forgiveness of sins, in the life of love and prayer, and in
grace equal to every need.

We believe in the Word of God contained in the Old and New
Testaments as the sufficient rule both of faith and of practice.

We believe in the Church as the fellowship for worship and for service of
all who are united to the living Lord.

We believe in the kingdom of God as the divine rule in human society,
and in the brotherhood of man under the fatherhood of God.

We believe in the final triumph of righteousness, and in the life everlasting.
Amen.

A Modern Affirmation

We believe in God the Father,
    infinite in wisdom, power, and love,
    whose mercy is over all his works,
    and whose will is ever directed to his children's good.
We believe in Jesus Christ,
    Son of God and Son of man,
    the gift of the Father's unfailing grace,
    the ground of our hope,
    and the promise of our deliverance from sin and death.
We believe in the Holy Spirit
    as the divine presence in our lives,
    whereby we are kept in perpetual remembrance
    of the truth of Christ,
    and find strength and help in time of need.
We believe that this faith should manifest itself
    in the service of love
    as set forth in the example of our blessed Lord,
    to the end
    that the kingdom of God may come upon the earth. Amen.

World Methodist Council Social Affirmation

We believe in God, creator of the world and of all people;
> and in Jesus Christ, incarnate among us,
>> who died and rose again;
> and in the Holy Spirit,
>> present with us to guide, strengthen, and comfort.

We believe;
God, help our unbelief.

We rejoice in every sign of God's kingdom:
> in the upholding of human dignity and community;
> in every expression of love, justice, and reconciliation;
> in each act of self-giving on behalf of others;
> in the abundance of God's gifts
>> entrusted to us that all may have enough;
> in all responsible use of the earth's resources.

Glory be to God on high;
and on earth, peace.

We confess our sin, individual and collective,
> by silence or action:
>> through the violation of human dignity
>>> based on race, class, age, sex, nation, or faith;
>> through the exploitation of people
>>> because of greed and indifference;
>> through the misuse of power
>>> in personal, communal, national, and international life;
>> through the search for security
>>> by those military and economic forces
>>> that threaten human existence;
>> through the abuse of technology
>>> which endangers the earth and all life upon it.

Lord, have mercy;
Christ, have mercy;
Lord, have mercy.

We commit ourselves individually and as a community
> to the way of Christ:
>> to take up the cross;

to seek abundant life for all humanity;
to struggle for peace with justice and freedom;
to risk ourselves in faith, hope, and love,
    praying that God's kingdom may come.
Thy kingdom come on earth as it is in heaven. Amen.

"A New Creed" from *Voices United: The Hymn and Worship Book of the United Church of Canada*, United Church Publishing House, 2003 reprint, p. 918. Used with permission.

"The Korean Creed," *The Book of Worship for Church and Home* (Nashville: The Methodist Publishing House, 1964), 180.

"A Modern Affirmation," *The United Methodist Hymnal* (Nashville: The United Methodist Publishing House, 1989), 885.

"World Methodist Council Social Affirmation" adopted by the World Methodist Council, Nairobi, Kenya, 1986. Used with permission of the World Methodist Council.

II. SERMONS AND WORSHIP AIDS

JANUARY 1, 2006

❧❧❧

First Sunday after Christmas Day

Readings: Isaiah 61:10–62:3; Psalm 148; Galatians 4:4-7; Luke 2:22-40

I'm Only Human
Isaiah 61:10–62:3

We are created as children of God, in God's own image. When we live our lives in Christ we become joint heirs of all God's promises. Such truth gives us confidence and hope for the living of these days. The Old Testament prophet Isaiah quotes God: "You shall be a crown of beauty in the hand of the LORD."

There are some things that really irritate me. One of these is people who make excuses for not doing what they could do if they had a different attitude. These are individuals, young and old, who use their unique situations to justify not doing something they should and can do.

You have heard such excuses. Perhaps you have used them yourself: "I'm too young"; or, "I'm just one person"; or, "I'm too busy"; or, "I'm too old." The prophet Jeremiah said, "Ah, Lord GOD! Truly I do not know how to speak, for I am only a boy" (Jeremiah 1:6).

Excuse me! When did being human or too young or too old become an excuse for mediocrity or poor performance or substandard behavior? People use such excuses as "I'm only human" when they are exhausted or exasperated or they have royally fouled things up and are trying to justify their behavior. "Well, I'm only human." We use excuses as a way of justifying something we have done or not done: We slept late and are late for school, we ate the last piece of chocolate cake, we have been immature. Come now and let us reason together about this business of being "only human." After all, God said, "You shall be a crown of beauty in the hand of the LORD." To be human is one of God's many blessings.

3

I know a man who travels all over the country teaching health care executives how to move their organizations toward excellence. As a child he had a hearing and speech defect and the outlook for his life was not good. Today, however, loaded down with hearing aids, he speaks at leadership conferences all over the world. My friend is only a human being in a defective body. I know people who live in perfect bodies who are living defective lives. It is amazing what my friend is doing, because he is "only human."

The youth in our church encouraged support of the Heifer Project International. This money purchased reproductive cattle, sheep, and chickens that were shipped to third-world countries where they are having a significant effect. I thought the children would be lucky to raise $500, but they raised $7,500, and they are only youth!

An eighth grader in her school science project called into question the 1995 environmental soil testing study in our area. This prompted many new tests and brought to the community's attention concerns about the land on which we live and the water that flows below it that we drink. To some, this student is only a kid!

No matter how young you are, or how old you are, when you are only human people have the ability to envision things and then make them happen. Dreams do come true. You are only human and you can make things happen. The church has historically taught us that we are tainted with what is called "original sin," which is our fallen nature. It is true that our nature is basically selfish and bent toward evil. Thus we are called by the Christian faith to "a more excellent way," "a better way," "to God's way." But it takes a decision on our part to pursue the excellent way. We can make excuses for ourselves till the cows come home, but when we stand to the full height of our humanity we give evidence of God's divine image. Perhaps the ultimate sin is to limit God.

Life is not easy, and often we are challenged beyond our abilities, but God has made us a little lower than the angels. We are "God's masterpiece." We are "a crown of splendor in the LORD's hand, a royal diadem in the hand of [our] God" (NIV). The Christian way of life leads to abundance in this life and eternal life in the next, but it is not easy. It takes effort and discipline, but anything worthwhile takes effort and is not easy.

Do you think marriage is easy? You must not be married. Do you think holding down a job is easy? You must not be working. Do you think tithing and being an active member of the church is easy? You must not be tithing or an active member of the church.

Listen, you are only human, which makes you "a little less than the angels," which makes you "a royal diadem in the hand of God." To be "only human" makes you God's child. So you don't want to say, "I'm only a youth" or "I'm only a student" or "I'm only a senior citizen" or "I'm only a housewife," or "I'm only a human." Say, instead: "I am human! I am human! I am God's child! I am saved by Jesus Christ! I am not a victim! I am a victor! I am a crown of splendor in the Lord's hand."

Today I ask you to stop using your *humanness* as an excuse for mediocrity. Instead, stand up to the full measure of your *humanity*. After all, you are only human! (Henry E. Roberts)

Divine Persona

First in a Series of Four: Prayer

Luke 11:1-4

Psychiatrist Gerald May begins his book *Addiction and Grace* with a bold statement: "I am convinced that all human beings have an inborn desire for God" (*Addiction and Grace* [San Francisco: Harper & Row, 1988], 1). Although we in the church live with such hope, the universality of May's statement often is counter to our experience.

The intensity of our desire for a relationship with God is manifested in our prayer life. Prayer is our human response to the awareness of God. The disciples' request that Jesus teach them to pray resonates with our own passion for prayer. We thirst for the same relationship with God. Jesus' prayer encourages his disciples to think of God metaphorically. When you pray, said Jesus, address God as you would your parent.

Developing a meaningful image of God is crucial. Our series on prayer begins with our image of God and moves through some of the challenges postmodern people encounter in their relationship to God. In the end, we hope to be able to make a greater investment in prayer.

Jesus' investment in prayer was both personal and private. Luke offers frequent references to Jesus praying, and almost always in isolated places. Matthew introduces the Lord's Prayer with instructions from Jesus to "go into your room and shut the door and pray to your Father who is in secret" (Matthew 6:6). As Jesus does, we also can have an intimate relationship with God in prayer.

Our image of prayer from scripture and church history is that it is personal and private. In the postmodern church, the model for prayer remains the contemplative life, sheltered from cultural influences. Spirituality, especially prayer, we see juxtaposed to culture.

Our church culture brings together several generations, each with different perspectives and different expectations. The collision of these generations creates at least four postmodern cultural challenges to a healthy prayer life.

The tragedy of 9/11 has drawn America into a world of chaos. Safety and security are tenuous. Our sense of identity has also changed. We no longer see ourselves as primarily from white European ancestry, nor are we isolated. The world has come to live as our neighbor.

Technological advances contribute to our global community. We live in an instant culture with satellite communications, computers, and mobile phones. We even follow our wars instantly on television. Fast food and credit are ways of our fast-paced life. We are an impatient people.

Technology is at the core of our culture and our expectations for the future. With space stations, moon explorations, and trips to Mars, there seem to be no limits to what technology can provide. Americans believe medical research will ultimately find a cure for all disease. Education has been the door to social improvement for the last fifty years. Our culture believes there is no problem too large for human resourcefulness. We believe human resources through technology will be able to solve all future problems.

Socially, however, relationships are changing. Families are scattered and shattered. We build relationships on how they personally benefit us.

Our prayer life is affected by the cultural impact of perceived universal chaos, instant gratification, unequivocal trust in human ingenuity through technology, and relationships grounded in personal gratification. In an instant society, we expect prayer to produce instant results. Prayer, however, runs counter to our egocentric society. Prayer is about our relationship to God and other people. "Father, hallowed be your name. Your kingdom come.... And forgive us our sins, for we ourselves forgive everyone indebted to us" (Luke 11:2, 4). Prayer is about a covenant relationship with God and with all of God's creation.

Our high-tech culture approaches prayer with skepticism. In this chaotic and confusing world, human resourcefulness offers more hope than "a god" who has created this mess. Yet Gerald May is right, there is still part of our soul that believes God is the ultimate answer.

The biblical story is about translating the mysterious creator God into an intimate friend. Our creation stories in Genesis personalize God, making the creator walk the garden with Adam and Eve. Moses tried to personalize the God of the burning bush.

Jesus is God's response, the incarnation of God and the reflection of the *divine persona*. Jesus said, "Whoever has seen me has seen the Father" (John 14:9). In Christ, the image of and relationship with God became concrete.

If we relate to God through human characteristics, it becomes possible for us to imagine God as a friend. But if our experience lacks positive relationships, it may be difficult to develop a trusting relationship with God through prayer. How can one imagine a loving God when life has offered mainly abuse, trauma, and isolation in relationships?

The most common prayer, the Lord's Prayer, is an intimate communication with a friend, which can be difficult for postmodern people. How can we use intimate language as toward a parent when we have no model of parental love? How can we pray that we will forgive others when our personal needs have not been met? God's created world seems chaotic rather than peaceful. How can such a God be trusted more than human ingenuity?

A major postmodern obstacle to our response to the awareness of God is our image of God. To imagine God as a divine person—as a friend— narrows the gap between the divine and the human. Only with a divine friend will a trusting relationship in prayer be possible and our soul's sincere desire satisfied. (Dan L. Flanagan)

Worship Aids

Call to Worship

Leader: Lord, you are before us as creator and as the great "I Am."

People: You also walked with Adam and Eve in the garden of Eden.

Leader: You warned us through the prophets.

People: And walked with us in the person of Jesus Christ.

Leader: In Christ you call us to a personal relationship.

People: A relationship as friend, and as Savior. Amen.

Invocation

Out of a world of conflict and confusion, Lord, we gather seeking your peace. May we find comfort in your presence. As our Savior, we lay our lives before you. As our friend, your presence gives us strength. We celebrate your faithfulness in song and word. In your Spirit, may we then be moved to respond in faithfulness as our lives are lived in relationship with you. Amen.

Benediction

Our friend, Jesus the Christ, calls us. May we live our lives in relationship with the God who loved us so much to become one of us. (Dan L. Flanagan)

JANUARY 8, 2006

❧❧❧

Baptism of the Lord

Readings: Genesis 1:1-5; Psalm 29; Acts 19:1-7; Mark 1:4-11

Affirmation and Assurance
Mark 1:4-11

Did Jesus come into the world with full knowledge of his identity and destiny from the very beginning? The idealized image of Jesus with which I grew up saved him from the human struggle of not knowing everything from the outset. This early orientation in the faith was heavy on the divinity of Jesus and light on his humanity.

The Bible clearly tells us that "we do not have a high priest who is unable to sympathize with our weaknesses, but we have one who in every respect has been tested as we are, yet without sin" (Hebrews 4:15). Since all of us can recount a journey of struggle with identity and destiny, we can assume that Jesus struggled with "not knowing" everything about his identity and destiny.

We know practically nothing of what he was thinking or doing from early infancy to age thirty. Only Luke saves us from knowing absolutely nothing of the first thirty years of his life. Luke tells us that Jesus "grew and became strong, filled with wisdom; and the favor of God was upon him" (Luke 2:40). Luke also tells us that Jesus' family went every year to Jerusalem for the festival of the Passover. He then recites the lovely story of how Jesus went to Jerusalem for Passover with his family when he was twelve. When they were a day out of Jerusalem on the way back home, they discovered that Jesus was not with them. Jesus' parents then retraced their steps and after three days found him in the temple "sitting among the teachers, listening to them and asking them questions. And all who heard him were amazed at his understanding and his answers" (Luke 2:46-47). After his parents chided him for treating them with such disregard, he said to them: "Why were you searching for me? Did you not know that I must be in my Father's house?" (Luke 2:49). They did not understand what he meant. Jesus went home with his family where Luke tells us

9

"Jesus increased in wisdom and in years, and in divine and human favor" (Luke 2:52). We know nothing more about his life until he emerges from obscurity at age thirty and is baptized by his cousin John the Baptist.

We do not know what other affirmations or signs he received during those hidden years, but on the occasion of his baptism he received a divine affirmation that must have given him strength and courage for the rest of his life.

All four Gospels give essentially the same account. "And just as he was coming up out of the water, he saw the heavens torn apart and the Spirit descending like a dove on him. And a voice came from heaven, 'You are my Son, the Beloved; with you I am well pleased'" (Mark 1:10-11). The three Synoptic Gospels give the distinct impression that this was not an experience seen and heard by present observers, but that it was private to Jesus. The Gospel of John says that John the Baptist saw the Spirit descend on him as a dove from heaven, and it remained on him (John 1:32). This sign certified to John that Jesus was indeed the Son of God.

We do not know what other signs of role and identity came to Jesus as he withdrew (as he often did) to pray alone, but Jesus seemed to have a great need for this means of communing with "the Father." The next notable affirmation came in the Transfiguration experience, which was attended by Peter, James, and John. Here the voice from the cloud addresses the three: "This is my Son, the Beloved; listen to him!" (Mark 9:7). At Jesus' baptism the voice of God addresses Jesus. At the Transfiguration the voice of God affirms Jesus' identity to the three disciples. We do not know at what point Jesus' identity became clear to him, but apparently it was already clear before the Transfiguration. Jesus has a firm grasp on his identity and he moves with increasing confidence in his unfolding destiny.

In the garden of Gethsemane he was deeply distressed over the direction in which his destiny was unfolding. He prayed to God: "Remove this cup from me; yet, not what I want, but what you want" (Mark 14:36). We are not privy to any additional dialogue between Jesus and "the Father" on that occasion, but he leaves the garden with his commitment intact and walks into the control of his enemies.

What manner of person is this Messiah, whose earthly life is freighted with a full dose of humanity, and yet who is so obviously equally divine? Here is an individual who is plagued by the struggles such as are common to us all, yet he remains without sin. Jesus' questions and hesitations are not counted as sin, but as a legitimate process by which Jesus lives out, and dies with loyalty to God intact.

We each struggle with our identity. We all want to know God's will for our lives, and we pray for faith and courage to fulfill it. We want to know more than we need to know, more than is in our best interest to know. Perhaps we want to know more than it was ever intended in the scheme of things that we should know. We want to know before it is timely for us to know. We lust after knowledge, when the best we can do is trust.

No one describes our dilemma more graphically than the writer of Ecclesiastes: "I have seen the business that God has given to everyone to be busy with. He has made everything suitable for its time; moreover he has put a sense of past and future into their minds, yet they cannot find out what God has done from the beginning to the end" (Ecclesiastes 3:10-11).

I do not know of any person of great spiritual stature who has not experienced periods of frustration and depression from not having a clear sense of direction. How should we deal with the pain of this inevitable struggle? We had best remember Jesus who has already been down our road. Jesus knows what the landscape looks like when we are caught up in the struggle for identity and destiny. Jesus is the pioneer who has gone before us and is therefore not only our Savior but also our model for coping.

Martin Luther was plagued by depression all of his life. When conflicts and doubts assailed him, he would say to himself over and over, "I am baptized." Remembering the spiritual high points in our lives can give us strength to go on. God does not come by every day to reassure us. Faith is the bridge between God's reassuring visits. Remember what God last said to you and hold on to that until once again God speaks. (Thomas Lane Butts)

Praying to an Absent God

Second in a Series of Four: Prayer

Luke 11:5-8

In our first sermon in this series on prayer we established the necessity of developing a relationship with God as person or friend. For many of us such an image of God is challenging.

From the time we first think about God, we are taught that God is perfect in every way. Then life experiences challenge these assumptions about God. How are we to understand God's role in suffering, evil, and natural disasters?

God's faithful servant Job asked similar questions: "From the city the dying groan, and the throat of the wounded cries for help; yet God pays no attention to their prayer" (Job 24:12). God's silence angered Job. "And what profit do we get if we pray to him?" (Job 21:15). The prayers of the writer of Lamentations find a similar void, "Though I call and cry for help, he shuts out my prayer" (Lamentations 3:8). In the midst of his passion, Jesus cried out on the cross, "My God, my God, why have you forsaken me?" (Mark 15:34). Each of us has been in the wilderness, struggling with an absent God.

Our society demands a broadband God who responds to our needs immediately. Any delay in response causes frustration in our relationship with God. There may also be frustration in discerning and accepting God's response. However, a healthy prayer life is less about understanding and more about experiencing God.

Whereas my seminary training was heavy on theology, spiritual practices have become an increasingly significant part of the seminary experience. A student entering Duke Divinity School recently made it clear that she wanted her seminary experience to form her as a person of prayer (L. Gregory Jones and Willie James Jennings, "Formed for Ministry: A Program in Spiritual Formation," *Christian Century* 117, no. 4 [February 2, 2000]: 124-28). For this student, as it should be for all of us, prayer is a way of life rather than an isolated call for divine crisis intervention. Prayer is not simply a part of life. It *is* life.

Persistence in prayer is a common theme of the Gospels. In the eighteenth chapter of Luke, the story of the importunate widow suggests persistence is a characteristic of the faithful. After teaching his disciples how to pray, Jesus urges the disciples to be persistent as a man seeking bread from a friend at midnight. In the midst of our frustrations with God, we are called to maintain a relationship with God in prayer.

Leonard Sweet talks about changing his prayer life by deleting a comma. Instead of the intercessory mode of "Please, God," his prayers are now of the form "Please God," or, how can God's purposes be fulfilled in our lives? (Leonard Sweet, *Learn to Dance the SoulSalsa* [Grand Rapids: Zondervan, 2000], 101). If our emphasis is "Please God," rather than "Please, God," our prayers become a celebration of our relationship with a divine friend, rather than enticing God to meet our expectations.

A Native American tradition illustrates divine presence. On the night of a boy's thirteenth birthday he is placed in a dense forest to spend a night. Following an anxious and sleepless night, as the sun rises the boy sees the figure of a man standing just a few feet away, armed with a bow and arrow. It is the boy's father who has been there all night long (Sweet, *Learn to Dance the SoulSalsa*, 23). Like the Native American father, our God is relational and compassionate.

My favorite analogy for the relationship between God and God's creation is the flowing stream. A stream is ever changing, displaying power, caressing its banks, and gently redirecting itself as it moves forward. The water helps shape the bed and banks of the river while the riverbed gains its texture from the water. God is like the water, seeking to fill the spaces of its universe, remolding the riverbed by moving through it with a natural flow. God guides us in a similar way, gently calling us to reshape our lives in accordance with the ever flowing stream. Our relationship to God is as mutual as the water and its channel, and evident over time.

Some of the channel material and outside forces deter the flow of the stream. But the natural flow of the stream is a gentle, ever changing, eternal relationship between the water and the ground.

The postmodern person wants to build dams and create diversions. We want to control the flow of life so that it responds to our immediate needs. Whereas our part of the river may appear chaotic, the river's flow maintains integrity. When we view God as totally beyond creation it is easy to characterize God as indifferent. When we turn inward and search for God within our own souls and experience, our relationship with God changes.

I have always been intrigued with Paul Tillich's description of God as "the ground of being." Only recently have I come to understand it as foundational for my spiritual practices. The "ground of being" is inherently a natural relational image. We are never separate from our ground. God, then, becomes our springboard for relating to the rest of creation.

A healthy prayer life should move us to the deepest parts of our souls. Prayer moves us to a place where God is always present and standing with us in the midst of the tumultuous influences outside ourselves. It is also a place where the future is created gently in a dynamic relationship between the creator and the created.

The persistence in prayer called for by scripture flows naturally from our soul's encounter with God. We persist in prayer to "Please God," to celebrate a relationship that is the ground of our being and the hope for our future. (Dan L. Flanagan)

Worship Aids

Call to Worship

God is faithful and compassionate. God provides peace in the midst of life's storms. It is God who guides us and creates new paths. Thanks be to God!

Invocation

In the beginning, you created and you continue to create out of chaos, O God. In the midst of chaos, it is difficult for us to hear your voice. In our time of worship may we hear words of encouragement and understand how you offer new opportunities. You never abandon us. Our songs and worship are lifted to you in praise, and in thanksgiving. Through you we see all things anew! Amen.

Benediction

We have reconnected with God. It is we, and not God, who was absent. Let us go forth celebrating God's faithfulness and our renewed relationship with our creator. (Dan L. Flanagan)

JANUARY 15, 2006

᪐᪐᪐

Second Sunday after the Epiphany

Readings: 1 Samuel 3:1-10 (11-20); Psalm 139:1-6, 13-18; 1 Corinthians 6:12-20; John 1:43-51

On Earth as It Is in Heaven
1 Corinthians 6:12-20

What is your hope? What is your dream? Toward what are you moving, with every step, day, breath, production, and reproduction?

One current popular perspective upon the terrorism of September 11, 2001, which hurled innocent civilians one hundred stories to their death on the concrete of lower Manhattan—some of them flapping their arms in gruesome attempts, as they fell, to fly out of the clutch of this hideous, sinful insult to humanity—is that the treachery of these murderous individuals should not be understood in religious terms, or analyzed in theological categories, or approached in a spiritual sense. Another is this: only a religious, theological, spiritual, and, finally, eschatological perspective upon this mutilation of meaning can bring anything like light, salt, healing, and truth.

This act of terrorism was done skillfully, imaginatively, willfully, and with a clear eye as to the potential ongoing consequence of the action. It was done with a clear desire to take innocent life, and much innocent life—thousands of lives and more. It was done with a clear longing to provoke waves of anger, fear, bitterness, and resentment across a largely apolitical land. It was done with the hope that it would provoke, as it has, a large-scale military response, to further harm and hamper our already testy relations with Islamic nations. It was done with the fervent prayer that all the world would see these sights televised, as has happened. It was done with intention to mark indelibly in the memories of American children the sights and sounds and smells of frightful, unexpected death. Whatever sin we are, as a people, to confess, and whatever guilt we are, as a nation, to bear, none of it deserved the murder of many innocent human beings on that September day.

Our church admonishes us not to let the sun go down on our anger. Our tradition cautions us about seven deadly sins, of which anger is one. Our experience shows us that anger, often expressed in hatred, is always misdirected to some degree. It is more than kicking the dog after a bad day, or disrupting the school board after a bad year. Anger seizes us and controls us if we are not careful. We begin to look for and to use scapegoats if we are not careful. Anger is a great challenge for religion.

Religiously trained men carried out these assassinations. The brand of Islam from 9/11 is about domination. Jesus is about empowerment. The 9/11 religion, however odd a form of Islam it may be, makes great space for domination. Domination of women by men. Domination of younger by older. Domination of poor by rich. Domination of people by God. You may assert, correctly, that Christianity has done the same. But there is a world of difference.

This Islamic religion is the result of a certain theology, a picture of God. In this brand of Islam God is high not low, heavenly not earthly, powerful not weak, majestic not rude, orderly not human, dominant not servile. Reverence for this God produces the Alhambra but not Teresa of Avila in her mud cart; the Taj Mahal but not Mother Teresa with her untouchables; disciplined prayer but not with women and men together. In short, this kind of Islam is God without Jesus.

Which brings us straight to eschatology. Eschatology is the term in our tradition used to refer to the last things, to the ultimate horizons, to death, judgment, heaven, and hell. Advent, for centuries, was the four-Sunday period during which sermons were given on the four horsemen of the Apocalypse—death, judgment, heaven, and hell. Coming toward the manger, the ancient church scoured its life with the scalding and smarting tonic water of eschatology. Dust you are and to dust you return. God shall separate the sheep from the goats. Depart from me you evildoers—I never knew you. Death, judgment, hell. And, "Thy kingdom come . . . on earth as it is in heaven." Oddly, and with no apparent point of interest expressed from the slavering news media, it is this liturgical tradition, advent teaching upon eschatology, which explains the autumn horror.

The murderers of 9/11 lived with a certain hope. There is no life apart from hope of some kind. They had theirs and you have yours, and the two are as different as a fish is from a bicycle. They had a religious, theological, and spiritual eschatology. They had a dream. More than anything else, we are identified, named, defined by our dreams.

As I understand it, they dreamed of death and instant translation to a paradise of sensual wonders. Beautiful women would minister to their every need. Their heroic deeds in the flesh would be rewarded with sumptuous feasts and eternal honors. The brutal sacrifice of life, theirs and others, would be a passkey into heavenly bliss. Their eschatological dream, as they murdered thousands on 9/11, was not for heaven on earth, but for some earthly delight in heaven. They looked forward to a kind of Valhalla according to Hugh Hefner.

They dreamed of destruction on earth as a means of attaining pleasure in heaven. Friends, this is a well-known and well-worn form of eschatology. Read the book of Enoch, the apocalypse of Peter, and the paraphrase of Shem. We find shadows of it even in the New Testament, both on the apocalyptic and on the gnostic fringes. Read through the Revelation to John. To some degree, both Christianity and Islam are related to ancient Zoroastrian Persian dualisms, which viewed the created order with pessimism and disdain. Earth is simply a forecourt, at best of heaven and at worst of hell. Even my beloved Paul of Tarsus sometimes slips into this mode, although it is contrary to his own primary teaching.

Our hope is affirmed every Sunday from the time of our youth. Our eschatology could not be clearer. Our dream—simple but not easy. We pray it on Sunday: "on earth as it is in heaven."

Whatever else we must do and say in the aftermath of human disaster, let it be done and said with the dream that Jesus gave us, with the hope that Jesus taught us, with the desire that Jesus shared with us—"Thy kingdom come … on earth as it is in heaven." (Robert Hill)

A Time-challenged God

Third in a Series of Four: Prayer

Exodus 3:1-2, 5-10

Hear the words of Bill Gates: "In terms of allocation of time resources, religion is not very efficient. There's a lot more I could be doing on Sunday morning" (Anita Mathias, "Learning to Pray," *Christian Century* 117, no. 10 [22 March 2000]: 342).

For the postmodern person, spirituality is anachronistic. A culture with strong faith in technology does not have the patience to wait for God. God's response to our prayers may seem time challenged, or even nonexistent. A culture focused on efficiency, profitability, and instant gratification is not likely to be drawn to a compassionate God of history.

The biblical story tells of a covenant God with a covenant people. "I am the God of your father, the God of Abraham, the God of Isaac, and the God of Jacob" (Exodus 3:6). Although the covenant came through one person, Abraham, it was a covenant for all human descendants. "I will make of you a great nation, and I will bless you, and make your name great, *so that you will be a blessing*" (Genesis 12:2). The biblical pattern is that God works through individuals for the benefit of all people.

God's blessings to the whole usually come at a price for the one called. Moses, for example, was content tending his flock when God called. "I have observed the misery of my people who are in Egypt; I have heard their cry on account of their taskmasters. . . . So come, I will send you to Pharaoh to bring my people, the Israelites, out of Egypt" (Exodus 3:7, 10). After four hundred years of frustration, God's intervention must have been a joyous occasion for Israel. But their complaints for the next forty years wandering in the desert are clearly recorded in scripture and during the Babylonian exile.

The God of the New Testament is also time challenged. The disciples of Jesus spent fifty days behind closed doors for fear of their lives until God responded to their prayers with the gift of the Holy Spirit. To this day the Christian church also awaits a promised second coming of Christ.

Whereas the biblical story is about waiting for God, it is also about our inability to discern God's presence. Elijah was looking for God in the dramatic events of wind, earthquake, and fire when he discovered God in silence. Jesus wept over a city because its people were unable to recognize the time of God's visitation, and seemed angry with Philip who asked Jesus to show him God. "Have I been with you all this time, Philip, and you still do not know me? Whoever has seen me has seen the Father" (John 14:9).

The power of the covenant God comes in community. Prayer is, and should be, a personal communion with God. It is also a common experience in the covenant community, an experience of communion with other people.

A Hebrew word for prayer, *avodah*, means "to be of service" and "to work or take action for a higher purpose." Prayer has a social component. When we pray to invite God to change our environment, we also must be ready to be changed. Abraham, Moses, and Jesus each discovered that in relationship with the divine, prayer is not a passive experience. Prayer moves us to a higher purpose.

In some ways there are similarities between today's younger generations and those entering adulthood in the politically charged 1960s and 1970s. Many were, and still are, skeptical that a relationship with God would bring about racial equality, eliminate poverty, and bring world peace. These socially active baby boomers wanted to change the world and they were impatient waiting for God to do it.

Our covenant God is a God of change, and the covenant people are called to be the agents of change. Abraham, Moses, and Jesus were change agents, instruments within the covenant community for God to heal the world.

We live with the tension between self-care and social responsibility. In his book *Let Your Life Speak*, Parker Palmer argues that self-care is never a selfish act. It is simply good stewardship to discover and nurture the gifts God has given us to fulfill our social responsibility. Whereas fulfilling one's role in God's healing of the world can be satisfying, it can also be agonizing.

Parker Palmer's agony came in the form of depression—twice. Palmer's discovery during his depression seems valuable for our spiritual life. A counselor observed that Palmer viewed depression as the hand of the enemy trying to crush him. "Do you think," said the counselor, "you could see it instead as the hand of a friend, pressing you down to ground on which it is safe to stand?" (Parker Palmer, *Let Your Life Speak* [San Francisco: Jossey-Bass, 2000], 66).

Our personal struggles may offer a way of reconnecting us with God, the ground of our being. God as *ground* is a wonderful image of renewal and safety as we gain strength to reenter the social arena. Jesus' prayer at the garden of Gethsemane, for example, was Jesus' attempt to ground himself to give him strength to face the cross.

Our most frequent prayers may seek God's intervention. We may come away from this intercessory prayer wondering why God has not responded, or unable to discern God's response.

Yet our biblical history assures us that God is faithful to the covenant community. We may enter prayer hoping for personal healing and discover that the real power in prayer is in community. Prayer is an activity of personal reflection that ultimately connects us with God and with other people. It is an activity that calls us beyond ourselves to a higher purpose.

Whereas often our human vision is myopic and time constrained, God's vision lacks limits and seeks the good of God's creation. Our prayer life reconnects us with our ground of being and calls us into community and toward the larger vision to heal the world. (Dan L. Flanagan)

Worship Aids

Call to Worship

Leader: The God of new beginnings has called us to this place.

People: We come to celebrate the new life that God offers all people.

Leader: Be patient. Be attentive. The creator God is here.

People: In our singing and in our praying and in the silence, God is here.

Invocation

We come in awe of the incredible mystery before us. In the beginning, God created—and continues to create. God promised Abraham land and a multitude of descendants. Through Moses God led Israel out of Egypt. In Christ, God's grace is available to all. Your footprints are throughout history, Lord, demonstrating your faithfulness to us today. Amen.

Benediction

We have celebrated the grace of God evident throughout history. May God's grace empower us to be instruments of healing in the world! (Dan L. Flanagan)

JANUARY 22, 2006

እድእድእድ

Third Sunday after the Epiphany

Readings: Jonah 3:1-5, 10; Psalm 62:5-12; 1 Corinthians 7:29-31; Mark 1:14-20

Gone Fishing?
Jonah 3:1-5, 10; Mark 1:14-20

One of my favorite movies is a slapstick comedy titled *Gone Fishin* starring Danny Glover and Joe Pesci as two fools whose only passion in life is to fish. They do some fishing, they battle some alligators, they wreck some boats, but the interesting thing is they never catch a fish the entire movie! It reminded me of a famous parable: There once was a fishing village on the shore of a great lake stocked full of fish. The fishermen of the village diligently debated and discussed what fishing is, how best to do it, which equipment to use. They invested millions in boats and gear and a fishing headquarters, hired a staff, and sent emissaries around the world to search other lakes and rivers for fish.

One day, a little child stood up in their meeting and asked, "You all claim to be great fishermen—how come you've never caught a fish?" Indeed, no one in the village had ever actually caught one. They had never even been fishing.

Sadly, many churches and many Christians go for years without bringing a single soul to Christ. We are not called to be keepers of the aquarium—Jesus calls us to be "fishers of people," to catch folk up in God's grace, love, and salvation.

We are not the first to have had reluctance to share our faith with strangers. The book of Jonah, one of the oldest books in the Bible, tells the familiar story of a reluctant evangelist. Rather than heeding God's call to reach out to the strangers in Nineveh, Jonah fled in the other direction. Ironically, in his reluctance to be a "fisherman" for God, he became fish bait! Even after the great fish spewed Jonah back onto shore, even after Jonah went and converted the people of Nineveh, he still had no compassion for them.

21

I hope our problem is not a lack of compassion or a lack of desire. Maybe we truly want to be "fishers" for Jesus but need some specific direction for the task.

Perhaps the lessons my fishing father taught me about actual fishing can be applied to evangelism: Foremost, fishing requires patience. As a child, I had little patience. If I failed to get a nibble immediately, I would pull my bait out of the water and cast to another spot. It had to be a quick fish to get on my hook!

The unconverted may have no experience of God's love or may even have had a negative experience with religion. They may be highly resistant to an invitation to hear the gospel. Great patience is required to convey Christ's love to a person whose only exposure to church were fire and brimstone sermons.

There is a right time to fish. There are certain times of the day when the tides and temperatures are conducive to fishing. Likewise, there are right and wrong times to evangelize. Right now is not always an appropriate time to talk about our faith with others. If we embarrass someone, they will not be receptive to the gospel. We are wise and polite to wait for a suitable opportunity when our message will meet open ears.

If we listen, people will give us hints about when the time is right. They may ask our advice about a problem or for our opinion about world events, whereupon we can then say, "You know, my belief in God gives me strength in facing that sort of thing."

There is a right place to fish. You cannot catch fish in a baptismal font. You must leave the church building and go where the fish are. Jesus did. He didn't hide out in the synagogue. Jesus went into the streets and marketplace, into the villages and homes of the common people. Likewise, we must develop friendships with those who are not Christians. We must reach out to people in need wherever they are.

Just as fishing requires the right lure, so does fishing for believers. My dad had a whole tackle box full of shiny colored lures. But he was always quick to tell me that nothing beats the real thing: live bait. The world offers all kinds of glitzy lures, but they are often artificial. People are sometimes lured by money, success, and popularity, or by the pleasures of drugs and alcohol. Addiction to drugs is appropriately referred to as "being hooked." It is easy to get hooked by attractive artificial lures.

Christ alone has the real thing. Jesus is not artificial; he is living, he is real. Jesus offers us true and lasting love, joy, and peace. Authentic faith is what the world is hungry for, and this is what we need to offer others.

If you know God as a real and genuine power in your life, share that with others. In a world full of artificiality, people respond to a sincere word about your experience with God.

Finally, serious fishermen mourn over the loss of a fish. They regret having one get away. But even if they come home without fish, the true fishermen are glad they tried. Moreover, they will try again.

People really do want to hear about salvation and hope, about life and love given through Jesus. We need not be timid with our valuable message. The most selfish thing in the world is to discover the joy and peace of God's love and then refuse to share it with others.

Sharing the good news of God's love means offering a word of hope, a word of forgiveness, a word of love, a gospel of grace to folk beyond our church walls. We must cast beyond the gunnels of our own boat. When Jesus called his disciples, they had to leave their boats and their fishing village and journey to new places. When God called Jonah, he had to reach out to strangers in Nineveh. Where is God calling you to cast your net? (Lance Moore)

Investing in Prayer

Fourth in a Series of Four: Prayer

Psalm 63:1-8

The relationship between the author of Psalm 63 and God is clearly intimate: "Your steadfast love is better than life." Among the key elements in a healthy prayer life, the relationship with God is most important. Our relationship to God must be like that of a personal friend. Our experiences of an absent God assume God is somehow separate and distant from us. If, however, we can reimage God to be our ground of being rather than totally other, our relationship with the one who created us becomes more intimate and constant.

Prayer has a social component too. Self-renewal through the one who created the world and us moves us to a higher purpose, thus, a call from God. God's call is an instrument in the healing of the world.

Whereas the God of Genesis proclaims all creation to be good, in our postmodern culture spirituality and culture are in conflict. An improved spiritual life requires a different image of God and of ourselves than our culture promotes. Our biblical story reminds us of the faithfulness of our covenant God, a time-tested foundation for life. Without a strong basis in faith, if technology ultimately fails us our culture may be facing tremendous personal and social crises.

Prayer, too, is risky. We are transformed by prayer and moved to a higher calling to change the world.

My first experience with desert spirituality came in a two-year project in spiritual formation. Generally, I enjoyed experimenting with different types of prayer. I found centering prayer very difficult whereas scriptural meditation was more satisfying. There are a variety of ways to invest in prayer. One style of prayer is not superior to another, but one style may be more comfortable than another style.

Rote prayers, the most common style of prayer, can be public or private. "The Jesus Prayer" is a traditional prayer that repeats this phrase: "Lord Jesus Christ, Son of God, have mercy on me, a sinner." The prayer, or mantra, is repeated in rhythm. Breath prayer is a more personal expression in mantra form. Rote prayers are common in public worship. The Lord's Prayer, the most common rote prayer, is almost universally used in Christian worship.

There are a number of prayers designed to enhance one's relationship with God. The traditional centering prayer focuses on one word such as "God" or "love." For *Star Trek* followers, centering prayer is similar to the Vulcan mind meld—when Spock puts his hand to one's head and reads his thoughts—as the mind of God becomes one with our mind in prayer by discarding foreign thoughts and focusing on a single word.

Intercessory prayers invite God to change something. Intercessory prayer can be of a personal nature, seeking something for the one praying, or it can be of a social nature. We may pray for the well-being of another person, or for greater clarity of purpose, namely, to move ourselves in line with God's vision.

Praying the scriptures, or *lectio divina*, encourages us to live in the scripture, to allow the scripture to move us. In short, the scripture prays for us.

Silence may be the most powerful form of prayer. Quakers use silence well, often going extended periods of time without speaking. In the silence, if we listen intently as did Elijah, God will encounter us in surprising ways.

Movement may be the least appreciated form of prayer. The movement of our bodies praises God, expresses suffering, or simply communicates openness. Activities such as dance, singing, celebrating the Eucharist, or even work can be forms of prayer. The activity of walking a labyrinth helps one "live" the journey and our movement becomes prayer.

Prayers of thanksgiving are uplifting, not only for God but also for us. Psalm 63, for example, recognizes the power of divine relationship and divine grace. Giving thanks to God in prayer often motivates us to give thanks for other people and other things in our lives.

Finally, there are the prayers of higher purpose, which may feel more like prayers of resistance. God does call us to special tasks just as God called Abraham, Moses, and Jesus. In these prayers of response we offer ourselves to God for higher purposes.

We may be intentional about just one form of prayer, or several forms of prayer, but prayer is not an isolated practice. If prayer is a human response to our awareness of God, then prayer is manifested in every aspect of our lives. No matter what we are doing, when we are aware of God, we are praying.

We began this series with an observation by Gerald May that all human beings have an inborn desire for God. The psalmist's intimate relationship with God led the writer to exclaim, "Your steadfast love is better than life." A healthy prayer life is possible only if we relate to God as intimately as the psalmist. God is not merely totally other, but the very foundation of our lives and of all creation. Our relationship with God brings us into relationship with all creation.

Ultimately, prayer moves us to a higher plane. The power and intent of prayer is fulfilled in community. This community is engaged in the healing of the world.

The highlight of our prayer life comes when we recognize that God desires us as much as we desire God. God's faithfulness is related in scripture and experienced in life. Postmodern culture challenges our spirituality. But God's desire, and ours, is for relationship—an intimate divine/human relationship and a relationship with all of God's creation. (Dan L. Flanagan)

Worship Aids

Call to Worship

Leader: It is good to give thanks to you, O God.

People: Your love is better than life itself.

Leader: Your faithfulness is to all generations.

People: We sing for joy at the works of your hands.

Invocation

Our life is about investment, O Lord. We invest in friends and family. We invest in work and school. We invest in leisure. We feel your creative Spirit within us calling us to invest in our relationship with you. Help us know how to respond to your call. Help us accept the relationship you offer us. Amen.

Benediction

Having been renewed in worship, we now face life with the reassurance of our friendship in the Lord, through Jesus Christ. May that relationship help us change the world. (Dan L. Flanagan)

JANUARY 29, 2006

Fourth Sunday after the Epiphany

Readings: Deuteronomy 18:15-20; Psalm 111; 1 Corinthians 8:1-13; Mark 1:21-28

A Savior Who Disturbs and Disrupts
Mark 1:21-28

Jesus has a message. Jesus is an individual not with just words to fill an hour but with a message that can make the difference between life and death; a message that has the power to heal and make us whole. This is how Mark presents Jesus at the beginning of his ministry.

Several years ago I was present for the launching of a political campaign for a friend who was running for a state office. On the day of his official announcement, my friend selected certain sites that symbolized the issues of the campaign. He spoke at a college to articulate his position on education. He spoke at a factory to talk about jobs and the economy. The point he was making was that he was embarking on an important campaign and where he chose to speak was as important as what he had to say.

According to Mark, Jesus chose a special place from which to speak. Jesus went to the synagogue where the people of God came to hear God's word for their lives. There was a lot of talking in the synagogue, but when Jesus spoke something was different. The Bible says he spoke "as one having authority." There is something powerful about people who speak with authority—whose message is as much in their heart as it is in their mind.

Once two men recited the twenty-third psalm. One was a well-known actor, the other an old and rather unsophisticated minister. The actor's rendering of the psalm was beautiful and commanding. Everyone enjoyed hearing the rich words of the beloved psalm spoken in his clear baritone. All the inflections and pauses were perfect.

Then the old minister spoke. He stumbled a bit and the words were broken with unnatural punctuations of silence. But when he finished there were tears in the eyes of the listeners. Something had happened and it was the actor who gave the interpretation: "I know the psalm," he said, "but this man knows the shepherd." That is the difference authority makes.

Have you ever noticed how, when someone speaks with authority, there will be those who hear and rejoice and there will be those who want to resist what is being said? There are always those who are invested in hearing the same old message, no matter how tired it becomes, rather than listening to something new and daring and challenging.

Jesus, speaking with authority, creates a crisis. In today's text, the man with the unclean spirit cries out, "What have you to do with us, Jesus of Nazareth? Have you come to destroy us? I know who you are, the Holy One of God." Such is the threat of a new word that invites us to live in a different way.

I wonder if this ancient scene is not lived out in the church again and again? Jesus came to a world that was immersed in religion. But it was a very tired religion. It was a religion that had everything completely under control and that offered a God who did things exactly as they wanted them done. There was no mystery, no surprise, and no conversion. Confronted with Jesus, they felt torment. "Don't destroy us, Jesus!" they seemed to cry out.

When Christ comes to us the doors of life are flung open to wonder and amazement. When you meet Jesus you know that great chunks of life exist that cannot be wrapped snugly inside a blanket of rational explanation. It is easy to feel disoriented by Jesus' strange ethics, Jesus' way of including everyone, Jesus' dislike of religious convention.

We do not have a clinical name for the condition of the man healed by Jesus that day in the synagogue. All we know is that the man was healed and the people were amazed. And it was all so long ago.

But this text suggests that there may be times when, like the ancient man in today's story, we too are in the grip of an evil spirit. A spirit that robs life of its joy and reduces everything to rational explanation. A spirit that keeps everything under control, tied down, neat and safe. Today I believe the gospel invites us to be healed by the authority of God. It takes the authority of God to keep our minds open to wonder, to be ready for the tug of God's spirit on our spirits. It takes radical healing to be open to the grace of a new day or to feel your knees quiver at the sight of a mother loving her child, or have your mind confounded by the grace of forgiveness.

The authority of God commands us to imagine a new world. This imagination is so needed. Like the ancient people in today's scripture lesson, we are tired of the same old ways of thinking and being. We have had the words with us so long that they have gone flat in our souls: "Love your neighbor"; "Care for the least"; "Show mercy to all." We know this language well enough. But something is lacking between the words and the deeds. We need the authority of God to set us free to begin the exciting and dangerous work of imagining a new world. Perhaps it would be better to say that we need the authority of God to free us to use our imaginations in a new way. It takes imagination to create weapons of destruction and it takes imagination to create communities of healing. It takes imagination to rob people of their dignity through corrupt systems and it takes imagination to offer everyone the opportunity to live as a child of God.

The question is: Will we submit our imaginations to God's authority? When we do, there will be resistance. Someone will cry out, "Don't torment us!" But be of good cheer. We follow the one whose authority is such that it cannot be silenced. And, undergirded by that authority, we are invited to go forth and engage the work of creating a new day, a new world. It is the most exciting work any people could ever be asked to be about. It all begins today, in this place, before the authority of these wonderful words from Mark's Gospel. (Chris Andrews)

Tell Me the Stories of Moses

The writer of Exodus was a master storyteller. In the language of history and metaphor, the writer helps the Hebrew people remember their history. In that same language, the writer helps us understand how God moves in our lives.

If good preaching is good storytelling—as it often is—these texts are a fertile field for the preacher. The six messages, which follow, provide a sample of what a preacher can do with Exodus texts. One could probably identify at least a dozen more. May you develop many more relational messages out of this foundational book.

The Story of Moses: Auspicious Beginnings

First in a Series of Six: Moses

Exodus 1:1-2, 10

The story of Moses' birth takes place amid tragedy. A king arose in Egypt, a pharaoh, who was threatened by the Hebrew people. Even after the Hebrews were forced into hard labor, Pharaoh was still troubled. We do not know why. Perhaps it was sheer numbers. Perhaps it was the

Hebrews' faith in God. Perhaps it was their tenacity of spirit. Perhaps it was their obvious and unwavering confidence in a Lord of history!

Pharaoh may have been an emotionally insecure man. The storyteller wants us to understand that the number of Hebrews was sufficient to threaten those in power.

The result: Pharaoh issued a terrible decree. He ordered that all male infants born of the Hebrew women were to be thrown into the Nile River and drowned. His executive order was given to the Hebrew midwives. The midwives, however, refused. They simply could not or would not comply with such a command. So Pharaoh called them before him in the palace. "Why have you done this," he cried, "and allowed the boys to live?" (1:18).

The midwives used clever tactics in their response. They replied, "Because the Hebrew women are not like the Egyptian women; for they are vigorous and give birth before the midwife comes to them" (1:19).

And the storyteller says, "So God dealt well with the midwives" (Exodus 1:20). God looked favorably upon these family servants. The message is clear. Sometimes it is important for the people of God to be shrewd. The Hebrew midwives exhibited a bright, quick-witted handling of the situation.

Moses' mother kept him securely guarded and quiet when he was a very young infant. But once he was three months old, something had to be done. She decided to hide the child.

She built a small basket of reeds from the river. She cemented the reeds together with some kind of tar or pitch. She placed her son in the basket and set it quietly afloat among the tall grasses along the edge of the Nile. She assigned the family baby-sitter to watch over him. Capture this picture in your mind's eye: a tiny child floating in the Nile and an older sister perhaps fifteen or twenty yards away keeping watch. The setting has an inherent beauty all its own. If the infant Moses could have spoken at this point in our story, he probably would have spoken of the miracle of an older sister who loved him and who stood watch over his basket in the river.

One day the daughter of the pharaoh (the princess of the land) came to bathe in the Nile. She heard the sound of the baby crying. Moses' sister was assuredly alarmed at this development. She probably thought, "Oh, no. We're done. We are discovered!"

But the baby Moses captured the heart of the princess. In one special moment a daughter of Pharaoh broke the pattern of cruelty that had been ordered in Egypt. The princess knew the edict of her father. But she also knew the innocence of this small child. Her heart claimed him. She would take him home.

Next comes what may be the most fascinating part of the initial story. Moses' sister went to the princess and asked, "Would you like me to find someone to nurse and care for the child?" The princess was delighted. Miriam left at once to get her mother. She brought her back to the princess.

Note what happened next! The princess said, "Take this child and nurse it for me, and I will give you your wages" (Exodus 2:9). Here is a statement to warm the heart of every mother! (This might even be a good preacher's text for Mother's Day!) A mother paid by the state for watching and raising her own child!

Moses' mother raised him in the palace of the Egyptian king. Evidence indicates that she was the one who saw God at work in all of this. The whole scenario could have been coincidence, of course. It could have been blind luck. But Moses' mother knew better.

This Hebrew mother faithfully told her son of their God. In the midst of a pagan palace of pagan religions, she spoke of God. She told him the stories of Abraham, Isaac, Jacob, and Joseph. And during quiet palace nights, she would even whisper in Moses' ear the sacred name of Yahweh.

Moses knew the sacred name before he was able to talk. His mother told her son who he was and whose he was. Who whispers the name of Jesus to the children today? Who will tell today's children the stories of Jesus, the stories of faith and hope?

In the midst of plenty and of privilege, who will keep the name of God alive? In the midst of a host of secular gods, prolific lures, and growing materialistic expectations, who will say, "Remember that you are a child of God. Remember that God alone is your strength"? In the midst of the trappings of luxury and expansive lifestyles, who will whisper the sacred name in the ear of every child?

The story of Moses is one of auspicious beginnings. The message of the storyteller seems clear. God is intimately involved and present in our lives. God is present in the cleverness of the Hebrew midwife. God is present in the softened heart of an Egyptian princess, in the quick thinking of an older sister, and in the religious fervor of a mother. (Let us take note that all of these principals are women! It took at least four good women to build one great man!)

31

God is present. That's the gospel in the story. God is working out a purpose in history, just as God always has and always will. (Brian K. Bauknight)

Worship Aids

Call to Worship

Leader: Come before the Lord in holy worship!

People: We come as we have so many times before. Is today going to be different?

Leader: Open your hearts to God's spirit and let him renew your life.

People: We are ready. We are willing. We give ourselves to the renewing spirit of God.

Invocation

We gather as your people, O God, as we have done many times before. We ask that today be different. Electrify our spirits, transform our minds, renew our energy. Fill us with the energy of your love that we might be about the work of transforming the world in the name of Jesus. Amen.

Benediction

We have heard your word, O Lord. It is a powerful word and has changed our lives. In your spirit we go forth to live and work that life might be renewed and people redeemed. Be with us now and always. (Chris Andrews)

FEBRUARY 5, 2006

❧❧❧

Fifth Sunday after the Epiphany

Readings: Isaiah 40:21-31; Psalm 147:1-11, 20c; 1 Corinthians 9:16-23; Mark 1:29-39

The Purpose-Driven Life
Mark 1:29-39

One of the most popular books in recent years is Rick Warren's *The Purpose-Driven Life*. In its first sixteen months of publication it sold ten million copies in English and three million in twenty other languages. Throughout the book the author asserts that the meaning of life is not about you, it's about God.

Some religious leaders and professors have criticized the book because it "looks and smells too much like American culture." Some say that it's just another self-help guide, serving up "bite-sized portions for ready consumption and immediate application."

Regardless of one's attitude toward the book, its runaway success is strong evidence that people today are desperately looking for something that will help them find the purpose for their lives.

The French have a phrase—*raison d'être*—which means reason or justification for existence. It is when we discover our reason for being that life takes on wonder and joy and fulfillment.

Jesus knew his *raison d'être*. Jesus did nothing accidentally, but always purposefully. In the scripture text today, Jesus was thrust into a whirlwind of activity, preaching and healing in the early days of his ministry. Rather than trying to escape the demands on his time and energy, Jesus plunged himself into the task.

Jesus was even eager to expand his ministry: "Let us go into the next towns, that I may preach there also, because for this purpose I have come forth" (v. 38 NKJV).

The clear-eyed statement of purpose would become familiar to the disciples as they heard Jesus repeatedly affirming his reason for being and the purpose of his life. They must have thrilled with anticipation when they heard Jesus say that he had come that they might have life more abundantly (John 10:10 NKJV).

The disciples were surely perplexed when Jesus told them that he could not pray for the Father to save him from the cross, because "for this purpose I came to this hour" (John 12:27 NKJV). What were they to make of his assertion that he had not come to judge the world but to save the world? (John 12:47 NKJV).

Even to Pilate, the one who would deliver him to the executioners, Jesus revealed the purpose for his existence: "For this cause I was born, and for this cause I have come into the world, that I should bear witness to the truth" (John 18:37 NKJV).

Perhaps Christ's most comprehensive statement of purpose was the humble statement that "the Son of Man did not come to be served, but to serve, and to give His life a ransom for many" (Matthew 20:28 NKJV).

Today's text finds Jesus busy at that purpose—serving and giving himself; and it also enlightens us to some of the power points of such a purpose-driven life.

A genuine serving and giving purpose always begins at home. The very first healing miracle that Jesus performed was for Peter's mother-in-law, and it was done in quiet privacy with only a few friends and family present (vv. 29-31). Jesus embodied his own teaching that those who are faithful in small things will receive greater responsibility.

The purpose-driven life attracts people like a magnet. The whole city was gathered at the door and the disciples told Jesus, "Everyone is looking for you" (v. 37). The world is drawn to the focused person of purpose, especially one who is dedicated to serving and giving.

The purpose-driven life takes time to refresh and recharge. Long before daylight Jesus went to a solitary place for prayer and meditation (v. 35). Even the Lord himself, with the noblest purposes ever known by human kind, needed private time before public ministry.

In a speech at the Crystal Palace in London, Benjamin Disraeli once said, "The secret of success is the constancy of purpose." The overwhelming global success of the Christian message and the Christian church becomes even more incredible when one considers that the public ministry of Christ lasted for fewer than three years. One reason for this astounding result has to be the purpose-driven life of Christ.

When, with his last breath, Jesus cried, "It is finished," it was not the wail of defeat, but the shout of victory. The modern equivalent of those ancient words of closure would be, "Mission accomplished." Jesus had completed his purpose, he had been true to his *raison d'être*. Jesus had given himself in service and love.

Albert Schweitzer was one of the most outstanding individuals of modern times. The world remembers him as the selfless doctor of Lambaréné, where in his jungle hospital he labored for half a century in the service of suffering African humanity.

He turned his back on many opportunities for greatness in order to serve in obscurity. He was one of the world's leading interpreters of the music of Johann Sebastian Bach. He was a scholar of theology who shook the seminaries with a revolutionary interpretation of Jesus, a world-famous virtuoso of the organ, and a respected philosopher of history. He was honored with the Nobel Peace Prize and became even more renowned with his principle of "the reverence for life."

Once in a talk to boys in an English school, Schweitzer said, "I don't know what your destiny will be. But one thing I know: the only ones among you who will be really happy are those who will have sought and found how to serve." Schweitzer's purpose-driven life was one of unselfish service, and his message to the young schoolboys is one for all of us to hear. (Bill Austin)

The Story of Moses: An Incredible Theophany

Second in a Series of Six: Moses

Exodus 2:11–3:9

Similar to the story of Jesus, we have no stories from the boyhood of Moses. The storyteller moves us quickly from infancy to adulthood. We read a summary of his childhood under Pharaoh's daughter (2:10) and are moved immediately to this statement: "One day, after Moses had grown up" (2:11).

Moses was forced into exile from Egypt. Having been observed in the act of striking and killing an Egyptian taskmaster, he traveled to the land of Midian. Most historians believe the area lay along what is now the eastern coast of the Gulf of 'Aqabah. There Moses assumed the life of a shepherd. He married and had several children. Moses' life was comfortable and relaxed. He grew old in this land, and eventually attained the traditional age of retirement. Old age apparently felt good to Moses. He retained good health and vigor as he approached his ninth decade of life. Moses said to himself, "My life has been good. I am satisfied."

The storyteller sets the stage for us in strikingly understandable images. A settled comfortable life with children and grandchildren was pleasing. However, God had another plan. God intruded with a *theophany*. A theophany is an experience where God unexpectedly interrupts or encroaches upon the ordinary affairs of life. The intrusion is absolutely unsought. This unsolicited incursion of God into the flow of life is exactly what happened to Moses.

One day Moses was tending his sheep near the foot of a sacred mountain. As he looked into the distance, he saw something burning. The fire did not seem to spread. Neither did it go out. And it did not consume that which was burning. The fire simply burned.

The well-known burning bush shrub provides exciting color to many home landscapes each fall. This simple shrub transforms into glorious colors of red and orange for a few weeks. The plant derives its name, of course, from the story of Moses in Exodus 3. In that story, a bush was on fire, but it was not consumed.

Moses decided that he must go and check out this strange sight. His life was radically transformed by that decision. Have you ever made a quick decision that significantly reoriented the flow of your life?

As he approached the bush, he heard his name being called: "Moses, Moses!" (3:4). Right away Moses no doubt assumed he was in some trouble. Bushes do not call out our names, even burning bushes.

"Remove the sandals from your feet," the voice commanded. "The place on which you are standing is holy ground," it continued (3:5). We can safely assume that Moses kicked off his shoes rather quickly. Moses' name was called. The command was given. Off came his shoes.

Somewhere I heard a lecturer suggest that those who go shoeless on a regular basis have an average increased life expectancy of up to three years. Perhaps kicking off your shoes under your desk during the day or under the pew in Sunday worship has longevity benefits!

Slowly Moses became aware of who spoke to him. There is no evidence in scripture to suggest that Moses was a particularly religious man up to this point in time. He was not irreligious, nor could he even be considered agnostic. He was probably a passively religious person in his shepherd's lifestyle.

Gradually Moses recalled the name of the God that his mother whispered in his ear as a small child in the palace of the Pharaoh. Moses thought to himself, "This must be the God of my mother and of my people." Childhood stories and sacred memories came flooding back. Moses fell to his knees. In a theophany, in an unexpected interruption of life by God, we kneel!

God continued the message: "I have observed the misery of my people who are in Egypt; I have heard their cry on account of their taskmasters. Indeed, I know their sufferings" (3:7).

Moses listened. He remembered images of the pitifully wretched conditions of slavery that he had seen so many years ago—images of his people trampling clay for bricks in the mud pits, images of taskmasters with huge whips cracking regularly over the people's backs. If Moses had dared, he might have retorted, "Well, God, it is about time. After all, it has been more than four hundred years!"

"I know their sufferings," said the voice. "I have heard their cry." These words may well affirm the single most dominant part of God's nature: God does hear the cry, the hurt, and the pain of God's people. God has a special "ear" for the oppressed.

God knows the aching heart of every human being. This is part of the good news in the message of our Exodus storyteller. God knows your occasional fear of dying, the times of emptiness or loneliness, the uncertain sexuality, the hidden abuse in a marriage or a family, or the bouts with depression. God knows.

Is not the nature of the God revealed in Jesus Christ right here? Is not the word from the burning bush an anticipation of the very nature of Jesus Christ?

Moses undoubtedly responded positively to this good news. He seemed to say, "Thank you, Lord. Thank you for hearing the cry of your people. But, now, what are you going to do about it?"

At this point the real measure and impact of the theophany becomes clear in the story: God offered a startling observation: "Wrong question, Moses. It is not what am *I* going to do about it; rather, I am calling *you*."

"Me, Lord?"

"Yes, you, Moses. I'm sending you to confront the oppressor, to speak strong words to Pharaoh, to lead my children out of Egypt."

"Whoa! Wait just a minute, Lord. Me? You want me to lead people out of Egypt and across the desert?" Moses began to comprehend the radical dimensions of this theophany. (Brian K. Bauknight)

Worship Aids

Call to Worship (Isaiah 40:27-30)

> Leader: Why do you say, O Jacob, and speak, O Israel, "My way is hidden from the LORD, and my right is disregarded by my God"?

> **People: Have you not known? Have you not heard? The LORD is the everlasting God, the Creator of the ends of the earth.**

Leader: He does not faint or grow weary; his understanding is unsearchable. He gives power to the faint, and strengthens the powerless.

People: Even youths shall faint and be weary, and the young will fall exhausted;

Leader: But those who wait for the LORD shall renew their strength, they shall mount up with wings like eagles,

People: They shall run and not be weary, they shall walk and not faint.

Pastoral Prayer

> God of grace and God of glory,
> on thy people pour thy power;
> crown thine ancient church's story;
> bring her bud to glorious flower.
> ("God of Grace and God of Glory,"
> *The United Methodist Hymnal* [Nashville:
> The United Methodist Publishing House,
> 1989], 577)

Lord, if we know our hearts, we truly long to be what you have in mind for us. We yearn and strain to bring our bud to glorious flower. We believe that you have a purpose for us and that you will not be satisfied until that purpose is realized. If we are on the right track in fulfilling that purpose, give us strength and perseverance to run the race and win the prize. If we are not centered on your divine will and purpose, "Grant us wisdom, grant us courage, for the facing of this hour." In the name of Christ our Lord we pray. Amen.

Benediction

We know that God causes all things to work together for good to those who love God, to those who are called according to his purpose, and we know that his purpose is that we become conformed to the image of his Son. Go, therefore, living lives that shall define and demonstrate this holy purpose in and before the world. May the grace of God, the example of his Son, and the power of his Spirit enable you to fulfill the great dream he has for you. Amen. (Bill Austin)

FEBRUARY 12, 2006

❧❧❧

Sixth Sunday after the Epiphany

Readings: 2 Kings 5:1-14; Psalm 30; 1 Corinthians 9:24-27; Mark 1:40-45

The Drive-Up-Window God
2 Kings 5:1-14

I was recently pondering some of the most important life-changing symbols of the modern culture for me. I was evaluating the effects of modern invention on my hurried life as a minister and parent of small children. Keep in mind, of course, that I have never lived in a world without electricity, indoor plumbing, television, telephone, or air and automobile travel. Obviously, the computer is among the most favored inventions. (It is, after all, difficult for many of us to imagine functioning without a handy keyboard and World Wide Web at our fingertips.) The top of my list, however, was another modern marvel—the drive-up window. This may seem strange, but who among us does not employ this modern convenience in some fashion at least once a week? For me, it is much more often. I order at least a meal a week by speaking into a little box affixed to a giant menu. I scarcely remember the last time that I actually went inside the bank. I am much more likely to do my banking via a small tube, tunnel, and glass window connected to a human only by a scratchy intercom. Perhaps, most conveniently, I only fill my car with gasoline at stations that offer an option to pay at the pump, the service station equivalent to a drive-up window. I even find myself annoyed when businesses do not offer this convenience. It would be nice to pick up my forgotten gallon of milk at the grocery drive-up or to order my large latte at a window on the side of the coffee shop. The convenience of purchasing a product or acquiring a service from the ease of my driver's seat is a luxury that I would not easily give up.

I cannot help but recognize, however, the detrimental effects of the drive-up craze. There are some things in life that cannot best be experienced in a hurried drive-up fashion. Among those things is our faith. Yet,

39

I am increasingly aware of our human tendency, intensified by modern invention, to want our faith experiences to be as quick and simple as a stop at the nearest drive-up window to grab a burger or cash a check. Although the incident involving Naaman in today's scripture seems to be neither quick nor easy, there is a hint of that very human desire for easy faith that seems to be such a threat to modern Christians.

First Kings 5 relays the story of Naaman, the Aramean army commander suffering from leprosy. It is one of ten stories that are part of the Elisha cycle in 1 and 2 Kings. The stories in the Elisha cycle demonstrate the power of the prophet versus the power of the royal office (Thomas G. Smothers, "1 and 2 Kings," in *Mercer Commentary on the Bible* [ed. Watson E. Mills and Richard F. Wilson; Macon, Ga.: Mercer University Press, 1995], 315.) Naaman experienced this power firsthand. He was, after all, a highly regarded person to the Aramean royalty. He was well respected by his countrymen as well as by the king. Yet respect and success were not enough for Naaman, as he suffered from the incurable debilitating ailment of leprosy. We do not know what leprosy treatments had been tried by Naaman to this point, but given his willingness to take the advice of an Israelite slave girl, Naaman was probably feeling hopeless and desperate.

After hearing about the prophet in Samaria, Naaman secured the king's permission and blessing and set off for Israel. The king sent a letter ahead to the king of Israel to notify him of Naaman's journey. Naaman arrived in Israel and was sent to Elisha, the prophet. Up to this point in the story Naaman seems to be a person so driven by his desperate desire for healing that he will do anything—including precarious travel and potentially dangerous interaction with a foreign government. The verses that follow, however, depict a person much less willing to go the extra mile. After being told to go dip in the Jordan River, Naaman lost his temper wondering why the prophet would not just simply call on God and lay hands on Naaman himself for healing. Naaman was angered that he should come all this way to dip himself in the Jordan when there were better waters in his homeland. He was so angered that after all of his journey for healing, nearing the finish, he left in a rage.

Although Naaman was willing to make quite an effort to get to Elisha for his healing, in the end he wanted an easy fix. He wanted Elisha to wave his hand and heal him without anything more than travel required of Naaman. His dip in the Jordan required Naaman to have faith that this God of Israel could actually heal him. This requirement proved to be too much for Naaman who was almost willing to forgo his healing rather than go down to the Jordan. His wise servants, however, reminded him that he would have been willing do to something great for his healing. Why should he sacrifice this possibility of healing because it was not what he expected—to go out on faith and do something that seemed too simple? Naaman finally agreed and was healed.

So often, faith seems too simple. God does not always require us to go a great distance or do a great task to experience God's touch. On the contrary, it is usually not what we can do at all. God requires us to have a simple faith. At the same time, simple faith can be the greatest challenge because simple faith is not usually easy. What Naaman desired was a "drive-up-window" healing. He expected just to make the journey. Elisha would perform the healing and Naaman would conveniently receive it. God required more as God always does.

We are probably not seeking a leper's healing like Naaman. Our generation is, however, seeking to experience God like never before. We want a tangible experience with Christ. Naaman's story should remind us that that experience may require more of us than we realize. We cannot, for example, merely attend a worship service or spiritual event, buy a book, or listen to religious music. Doing those things is not enough without faith and a true desire to encounter Christ. It is when we are willing to dip in the Jordan that God intersects our life. The modern convenience of the drive-up will probably only continue to grow. Let us remember that when it comes to our faith and relationship with our Lord and Savior, we are called to do more than roll down the window of our soul. We are called to actively seek our God and embrace the opportunity to meet God wherever we can. (Tracey Allred)

The Story of Moses: Arguing the Mission

Third in a Series of Six: Moses

Exodus 3:10–4:20

Have you ever carried on a lively debate with God? Have you ever tried to change God's mind on some matter? Have you argued with God about some issue or circumstance in your life? Moses' first step in his journey of discipleship is to do exactly this. He argues with the God of the ages!

Moses quickly becomes defensive in this extraordinary calling he has received. Moses is convinced he cannot respond. He plays the game of "Yes, but" with God. Any time we feel called or compelled to do something we would rather not do, we are tempted to "Yes, but" the person making the request. Moses plays the "Yes, but" game with God for the next segment of our story. He "Yes, buts" God at least five times.

First, Moses asks a simple question: "But . . . who am I that I should go to Pharaoh, and bring the Israelites out of Egypt?" (3:11). Probably Moses was simply thinking, "Hey, I am too old for this job. I've just gotten my pension check into a direct deposit cycle in my bank account! I'm enjoying my AARP discounts. I am not ready for a whole new mission in life." Moses was about eighty years old when the call of God came. This is hardly the time when we think of a whole new vocation in our lives!

God simply says, "I will be with you, Moses." God does not acknowledge Moses' argument. Neither does God acknowledge Moses' age or stage in life. God simply calls.

Moses suggests a second argument. He asks God for God's name.

The *name* of God was closely intertwined with the *nature* of God in the ancient mind. Thus, the writer of Psalm 23 says, "He leads me in right paths *for his name's sake*" (Psalm 23:3, emphasis mine).

Moses was actually asking how he could offer the definitive nature of their God to the Israelites. "If I go, and they ask me about you, what shall I say?" seems to be Moses' question.

The response of the voice from the bush is one of the most mysterious in all of scripture. God says, "I am who I am." Therefore, Moses is to tell the people that "I am" has sent him.

We are not able to probe the mystery of God's nature. God preserves God's mystery for all time. God is not about to open up the full mystery of Being to Moses in this moment of Moses' life.

Perhaps God is offering a "name" that is only finally completed in the person of Jesus. The Gospel of John may be a partial unfolding of the mystery of God's words to Moses in Exodus: Jesus uses various images to suggest Jesus' identity (John 6:35, 8:12, 10:7, 15:1, 10:11, 11:25).

Unflappable in his desire for some kind of permanent deferment, Moses raises a third argument. "But suppose they do not believe me or listen to me, but say, 'The LORD did not appear to you'" (4:1). In effect, Moses is saying, "What if I go to preach and nobody listens or even cares?" This is one fear of every preacher: "What if the people do not listen? What if they do not come? What if my words make no contact and no difference at all?"

God replies convincingly: "Moses, I will create signs and wonders before you. I will make the fruits of your ministry happen. I will make things happen in your wake." That's quite a promise.

Moses relentlessly hurls his fourth "Yes, but" at God. Emotions are running high. Moses trembles at the thought of what might be unavoidable. He says, "O my Lord, I have never been eloquent. . . . I am slow of speech and slow of tongue" (4:10). Moses pleads a new tact: "I mumble a lot, Lord. I can't think fast on my feet. And I don't always use good grammar."

God's response to Moses' self-imposed ineptness is wonderful: "I will be with your mouth" (4:12). We remember the promises to the disciples of the New Testament where they are told by Jesus that they will receive the words to speak when they stand before power and before enemies (see Matthew 10:19 and notice the remarkable resemblance to the Exodus text).

The fifth "Yes, but" exasperates the patience of God. Moses says, "O my Lord, *please send someone else*" (4:13). Here is a last desperate plea to avoid the interruption of a very pleasant existence. "I really do enjoy retirement, Lord. And those senior discounts at the fast-food counters and movie theaters are really nice. You don't really want me to go to Egypt, do you?"

With the fifth "Yes, but" the storyteller says, "Then the anger of the LORD was kindled against Moses" (4:14). God is frustrated with all of Moses' excuses—and ours! In the end, God tells Moses that Aaron will be called to be alongside of Moses. Moses will give Aaron the words of God to speak, and God will be with *both* of their mouths. In essence God says, "No more objections, Moses. Now go!"

Moses went in faith. Someone has said that faith is most simply "waiting for the rest of the story to unfold."

You may be called. You may even have a theophany! God may interrupt your life—either briefly, or for the long haul. You may "Yes, but" God a few times yourself. However, in the end, you will find yourself saying, "OK, Lord! Here I am. I have heard your call. I think I know your name and your nature. Here I am, Lord. Lead me to where the hurt is. Help me set your people free. And I will go." (Brian K. Bauknight)

Worship Aids

Invocation

O Lord, we enter this place today aware of your great gifts. We thank you for the gift of your creation and presence. We are thankful for your forgiveness and redemption. We are thankful for your willingness to meet us wherever we are. We thank you especially for the gift of your Son who personified all of your love for us. Accept this gift of our worship on this day. Anoint us with your presence. Amen.

Benediction

The Lord bless you this day as you reenter the world outside these walls. Be ever mindful of the gifts of God and of our calling to return to God our gifts. Accept the challenge to actively experience God in all that you do in this week. Amen.

Prayer of Confession

Eternal God, we enter into your presence with the desire and need for redemption. We are mindful of our sins of commission and omission. We are mindful of our failures to show our love to you and to follow your command to love others as we love ourselves. Forgive us, O God, of all of the things in our lives that separate us from you. Restore our souls. Lead us toward you and your way. Remind us of the ultimate act of forgiveness by the one who was without flaw. Amen. (Tracey Allred)

FEBRUARY 19, 2006

❧❧❧

Seventh Sunday after the Epiphany

Readings: Isaiah 43:18-25; Psalm 41; 2 Corinthians 1:18-22; Mark 2:1-12

Getting Ready for a New Thing
Isaiah 43:18-25

Sometimes things happen that change our lives forever. Think of events like that—marriage, the birth of the first baby, a significant achievement, or, on the negative side, a serious change in your health or that of someone dear to you. You may not even recognize it at the time, but your life history has just been split in two, like B.C.E. and C.E.

Sometimes these events come in with trumpets blaring, announcing to the world that things have changed. Sometimes they creep up on us quietly, and we recognize their significance only later.

Such things can occur on a vast scale too. In national life, sometimes they're related to catastrophes like September 11, 2001. Certain events become watershed events for communities, nations, and indeed for history itself.

Our Isaiah passage focuses on such a watershed event in the history of Israel. God said, "I am about to do a new thing." This statement was a bombshell in Israel's life, but probably the people had to work at seeing how it could come to pass. We may have to work at seeing that ourselves. The reason is that we've heard "new and improved" about this or that product for so long that we scarcely believe such promises even if they're God's promises. We've bought "new and improved" items and found them rather like what we've known before.

When God, however, said these words in the book of Isaiah, "I am about to do a new thing," God's message came in such a way that the people had to take notice. Likely the people were discouraged at their situation in the sixth century before Christ. These words came to a people in exile. They had been uprooted from their homes decades before and taken into captivity. They had lost members of their family in war at the

45

hands of the Babylonian army. They may have felt that all hope was gone and the good life was no longer possible.

God, however, smashed through those discouraging feelings. Prior to our text for today, God referred to the central event of Hebrew history, the exodus (Isaiah 43:16-17). The Hebrews viewed this event as the watershed event of their national life. The exodus, which had occurred centuries before, was the good old days to which Israel looked back. That was the event that had transformed a ragtag collection of slaves into a people on their way to the promised land.

Then, shockingly, God said, in essence, "Forget about it." Of course, God didn't actually mean, "Forget about it." What God was saying was that he was about to do something so significant that even the event of the exodus would pale in comparison. What I am about to do, God said, is going to be so wonderful that you're going to stop talking about and hoping for and trying to get back to the good old days.

People who fish know what it's like to get started out fishing and run into someone who says, "You should have been here yesterday. They were really biting." There's always someone around, it seems, to say all the good things are over. Things will never be as good as they were "back then."

A person in his fifties said, "After fifty, it's all downhill." He didn't mean that things got easier then, like riding a bicycle downhill. He meant there were no longer any "ups" to look forward to.

A town or a city can start feeling like that. When the employment situation gets shaky and people are unable to find jobs, a town or a city can start feeling like there are no longer any "ups." Things will never be good again.

A church can start feeling like that. Perhaps some in the congregation keep looking back on better days, those wonderful days "when Reverend So-and-So was here." Things were so wonderful then, they say; not like now, they imply; although, if truth be told, some of those same people even in those good days sometimes at least under their breath called the wonderful Reverend So-and-So just a "so and so"! The thought is that those wonderful good old days are gone—forever.

Let's not sugarcoat the situation. Bodies do wear out as we grow older, and the fountain of youth hasn't been found. Economic situations do change, and sometimes a community can't recover the jobs it once had. The situation with churches changes too. The community changes, and the reality is that the church is not going to be the same no matter how hard the church tries to employ the magic formula now that they thought made things so good back then.

Even so, we must affirm that God can still do "a new thing," a thing so wonderful that it makes us realize there are still good days ahead—different, but good.

"I am about to do a new thing," God said centuries ago. Is that a word for us? Yes, if we're discouraged. Yes, if we're remembering the good old days too vividly for our own good now and in the future.

How can it happen? Let us be clear that only God can bring this about. If "a new thing" happens and it's any good, God is going to have to do it. It's beyond human ingenuity. It's not, however, beyond God if we cooperate. The rest of this passage speaks to the need for God's people to praise God, call on God, live in faithfulness to God, and repent of their sins before God. That is God's call to us today. God wants to do "a new thing" in our lives, but God has so structured life that we need to work with him to let it happen. We must do that rather than remembering the great things of the past so much that we can't see that God has plans for us now. God "is about to do a new thing." Will we let God? (Ross West)

The Story of Moses: A Miraculous Fairway

Fourth in a Series of Six: Moses

Exodus 14:1–15:21

I recently saw an advertisement for a roller coaster in an amusement park. The ad read, "Two minutes and fifteen seconds of the biggest thrill this side of a bungee cord." Such description cannot begin to compare with the Red Sea crossing in Exodus. There are many miracles and wonders in the Bible. Few are as dramatic as this one. One has to wonder whether even Moses expected this much drama from his efforts!

A very quiet and shy minister was visiting a parishioner in a nursing home. He sat opposite her wheelchair and they talked for some time. Finally, as he prepared to leave, she asked him if he would pray for her. Specifically, she asked him to pray that she would walk again. The minister felt a distinct uncertainty inside, but he obliged. He prayed for her life and health, and for God's healing power so she could walk again.

When he finished praying, there was a strange light in the woman's eyes. "Pastor," she said, "would you please help me stand up?" The minister was stunned at her request but could only oblige her. She took his hands and stood up, haltingly at first, but then with growing strength. Soon she was moving her feet, walking, jumping up and down, and shouting—attracting the attention of every other resident and staff member in the area.

The minister was not sure what to do. He backed out of the room, turned toward the corridor, and walked with increasing haste toward the door. Once outside, he raced to his car, got in, grabbed a tight hold on the steering wheel, looked up toward heaven, and said, "Lord, don't you ever do that to me again!"

Do you suppose Moses felt something like that as the waters parted the Red Sea at his command? The Red Sea crossing presents a story that is always exciting in the telling and retelling. It has a way of binding us in its spell.

Our twenty-first-century mentality seems to need to explain a miracle. In many ways, we need to explain away a miracle. We seemingly need reasons for the wonder. Ours is an age that seems to need explanations. We cannot merely accept that which defies rational interpretation. We attempt to master the sacred with our minds.

In this story, as before, we must remember that the storyteller is preaching. He is giving us a lot more than word pictures about winds blowing water around. In relating the story of crossing the Red Sea, the storyteller is preaching.

We *may* ask this: "What is his message?"

We learn that journeying with God is an adventure. In eastern Pennsylvania, an ecumenical retreat center features many beautiful hiking trails. At the head of one of those trails is a marvelous sign. It reads simply, "The Great Walk." The trail fits that description precisely. So does the journey of Christian discipleship! Once you put yourself in God's hands, be ready for adventure! That is exactly what Moses did. Moses not only put himself, but a whole nation into the hands of God.

The storyteller in Exodus is looking back. And he is saying, "To be God's people is genuinely exciting." To really be God's people is authentically exciting. If you put your hand into the hand of God, be ready for things to happen!

It is possible to miss the adventure, even when you are right in the middle of it. But the adventure is real; it is sure. In part, adventure is what caused the Bible to be written. The Bible is the written record of God's active accompaniment of God's people. The promise is sure: more adventure always lies ahead.

The storyteller also proclaims this particular event as a central act of God in history. Regardless of the specific details, this is a major decisive event in God's overview of history. The story of the Red Sea crossing is to the Hebrew scriptures what the story of Easter is to the New Testament.

The climactic Easter event gives rise to genuine mystery and abiding wonder. Easter is the definitive saving event of the New Testament story. The barrier of death is broken. All of the remainder of the gospel story now makes sense.

Similarly, the Red Sea crossing is an event cloaked with mystery and abiding wonder. It is the story of the deliverance of a people out of bondage. The exodus is the singular saving event upon which the rest of the Hebrew Bible is built.

We don't know with objective accuracy what happened at the Red Sea in the thirteenth century B.C.E. We only know that an abiding covenant was the result. God promised to be faithful to a people for all time.

The storyteller also proclaims that we are held in God's hand at all times. Life is not without pain or suffering or even dying. Life is not without setbacks or doubts or uncertainty. All of these things are part of living. They do not happen as a part of God's plan, but they are a part of living on this planet.

The message is steadfast and consistent. When the enemy is chasing us (the enemy of death or pain or hurt or disappointment) and when the churning unknown lies before us like a vast ocean (family, health, financial stability), God is still with us. We have a sign that God is faithful and present.

Life is not without setbacks, doubt, and uncertainty. Such issues are part of living. But God remains close to us and with us in each new situation. Specifically—in the exodus story's imagery—God will be with us even when the enemy is in hot pursuit and when the future looks bleak. God will sustain us, uphold us, and then graciously receive us at the end of our journey. (Brian K. Bauknight)

Worship Aids

Call to Worship

God says, "Call to me and I will answer you, and will tell you great and hidden things that you have not known" (Jeremiah 33:3).

Invocation

O God, you have brought us great blessings in the past. Today we call on you to prepare us to receive from you the great blessings you have for us now and in the future. In Jesus' name, Amen.

Benediction

Open our eyes and ears, O Lord, to the new things you have in store for us. Help us not hold the past in our hands so tightly that we cannot receive from you the blessings you have for us now and in the future. In Jesus' name, Amen. (Ross West)

FEBRUARY 26, 2006

❧❧❧

Transfiguration Sunday

Readings: 2 Kings 2:1-12; Psalm 50:1-6; 2 Corinthians 4:3-6; Mark 9:2-9

Denial to Confidence

2 Kings 2:1-12

My daughter called, with hesitation and a hint of fear in her voice. With one infant not yet walking, she confided: "I think I'm pregnant. We didn't want another one this soon." Through questioning, I discovered she had taken a home pregnancy test four times! Each result was positive. Upon talking to her doctor's office on Monday, the nurse asked which brand of kit she had used. The nurse said, "Oh, that's the most reliable one. After four tests, you are pregnant—and in denial!"

We may know a truth, be told about it not once, or even twice, but four times, and still not accept it! My daughter was in denial and so was Elisha. Reliable sources, the prophets from Bethel and Jordan, warned Elisha that this was the day that Elijah was to be taken away. Elisha responded, "I know; keep silent."

Denial of the truth, even when it is from a person of integrity or an unbiased source, indicates there are some things we do not want to face. Why not? Is it selfishness? Fear? Loss of control? Or perhaps lack of confidence?

Elijah was Elisha's mentor. For years Elisha followed Elijah, watching and learning from him. He saw Elijah perform miracles, settle debates, bring reconciliation. Elijah had spent many years training and preparing Elisha for this very time: the time when Elisha would pick up the mantle of leadership.

The first twelve verses of chapter 2 reflect so many virtues and emotions: fear, confidence, selfishness, commitment, timidity, courage, and mourning. Even what we think of as negative can be positive when fulfilling God's purpose. Elisha's fear was well founded. As a leader for Israel, history shows that this nation is not easy to lead—they backslide and test

God; they test their leaders. The fear may be justified, but soon it is replaced by courage and a confidence that Elisha witnessed in Elijah.

The courage and confidence comes from a faith in what Elijah believed and taught, and how God moved through his life. Courage and confidence comes from a belief in the vision and promises God gives.

In Elisha's case, his confidence is seen in two distinct ways. First, he will not allow Elijah out of his sight. Just as he had done for many years, he was Elijah's shadow. Even in the face of death and separation, he did not run or hide. In the second place, Elisha found the courage to ask for a double portion of Elijah's spirit. It is almost like asking, on a person's deathbed, if you can have their car. Today, we allow the family and the attorneys to take care of a person's estate after the person's death. Here is Elisha, not only asking for a portion, but a double portion of something more valuable than any material object.

Often, we find ourselves in a position to perform, or take on a leadership role. Even if it is not the first time, many of us feel a bit insecure. We ask ourselves, Do I know what I am doing? What if individuals who do know what they are doing challenge me? I wonder why so-and-so wasn't chosen; she knows so much more than I do. I wonder where the best place to start is?

Elisha, at first fearful and in denial, moved on in courage and purpose once he accepted the truth. For us, the trick seems to be the committed, faithful acceptance of the truth. Know, in your heart and mind, that whatever task is before you, God has equipped you to handle it. Too often we put off making decisions because of our fear and insecurity. What if Elisha had said, "Elijah, can you wait just a minute? I need to call my pastor or my friend and check with them about what I should do." Our fear may mean that we do nothing; we let opportunities pass us by. Sometimes, it is just better to act rather than become paralyzed by indecision. You know the analogy: to get anywhere you have to take the first step.

Elisha stepped out boldly. In faith, his action did not mean that he did not feel sorrow when Elijah went away. It did not mean that he had all the answers immediately. It did not mean that he would not make mistakes. What it did mean was that he had faith—faith in God, faith in Elijah, and faith in himself that he was following God's purpose for his life. He allowed for change to take place in himself, not in his circumstances or his surroundings. Scripture continues to show us that Elisha did receive a double portion of Elijah's faith—he performed twice as many miracles as his mentor.

I urge you to reevaluate yourself and a task of which you are fearful. Remember Elisha and how he learned from watching and following someone more knowledgeable and wiser. Remember that if God calls you to a task, God will give you the tools and grace to handle it. Remind yourself that everything you do can be a sacrifice to God. And finally, accept that the victory comes when you believe that you are not only equipped to handle it, but that God has made it possible for you to excel in this endeavor! (Raquel Mull)

The Story of Moses: Morning by Morning

Fifth in a Series of Six: Moses

Exodus 16

Within several weeks after leaving Egypt, the people were murmuring and muttering against Moses on several counts. Some people love to murmur in the church. Do you know anyone who murmurs? It is part of the liability of leadership that people murmur from time to time.

The people murmured against Moses. Moses must have had a difficult time with all of it. Surely it was not easy keeping this ragtag procession going in the wilderness. It felt very much like trying to keep a whole host of balls in the air at one time.

I once heard that life is like a chicken trying to lay an egg on an escalator. Just as she settles in, the bottom drops out. Moses must have known that feeling. The first weeks in the desert were simply awful.

The providing nature of God permeates the biblical narratives. The Israelites complained against Moses when the Egyptians were chasing them. They complained when they were thirsty. And then they complained that they were hungry.

Certainly this incident reflects thickheadedness and hard-heartedness on the part of the people. They simply would not trust Moses to be leading by God's will in this matter. They had crossed the Red Sea on dry land, and seen the Egyptian army drown in the sea. Yet they did not understand.

I imagine that Moses turned to God in prayer. He prayed, not in frustration with God, but in frustration with the people's complaints. He might have prayed something like this: "O Lord, what shall I do? How do I handle this situation? I have run out of ideas." Most of us have prayed that kind of prayer at least some of the time in our lives. "O Lord, what do I do now?"

God responded to Moses. God would act. But God said that action would come in a very special way. God would act so as to both feed the people *and* teach them something about the meaning of discipleship. Here, in the story of Moses from 3,300 years ago, we have an episode in which God tries to form disciples.

Thus we come to the story of the manna. What was this manna? Our storyteller tells us that it was a "fine flaky substance" and "the taste of it was like wafers made with honey." Moses told the people simply, "It is the bread that the LORD has given you to eat." A friend once offered his own guess. He said that the manna was an ancient form of grits—both are described as "fine, flaky substance" and both are absolutely no good as leftovers!

But there was a catch to this wondrous gift of God. This is what the Lord commanded: "Gather as much of it as each of you needs, an omer to a person according to the number of persons ... in [your] tents."

"Gather as much as you need for each person in your household!" That was the divine command. There was to be no greed, and no hoarding. If one person was stronger than another, he or she was not to collect more manna purely on the basis of extra strength. Each person was to collect an omer for each member of the family. An omer was about one and one-half quarts.

Some of us remember the periods of rationing during the days of World War II. Rationing is actually a very biblical notion!

We are becoming painfully aware that unnecessary accumulation through power and/or greed clearly means serious deprivation for others. The earth supplies an abundance of enough for each of its inhabitants. But there is no overabundance for some without major life-threatening shortages for others.

The Israelites, of course, did not always comply with the restriction. Some of them took more than they needed, and tried to store it for the next day—in case there was no manna on that day. But overnight the manna became foul and rotted. It did not last. The people were forced to learn to trust the providence of God.

God, through Moses, was training them to trust—day by day, morning by morning.

What is the message in this? That food will always be available? Perhaps. But surely there is a greater message. The story tells us that the only enduring value in life is faith and trust in God.

For this reason of trust Jesus teaches us to pray, "Give us this day our daily bread" (Matthew 6:11). Some have tried to rework the phrasing to read, "Give us this day enough bread for tomorrow." But I am convinced that such renderings destroy the original intent of the prayer. The disciple is to petition God each day for that day's provisions. And tomorrow we petition God for tomorrow's provisions.

The story concludes when the people create a symbol of God's trustworthiness. "And Moses said to Aaron, 'Take a jar, and put an omer of manna in it, and place it before the LORD, to be kept throughout your generations.'"

Here a jar of manna was to be a symbol on the altar of the Lord for all the years to come. When the children of the Israelites asked, "What does that jar mean?" they were to be told the story of how God provides.

What symbol works today so that when our children ask, "What does that figure on the altar mean?" we may similarly respond, "It is a sign that God is faithful. God provides enough for all."

If we can conquer greed, and if we can learn to live more simply, and if we can learn to trust, there will be an abundance of enough for all God's children, day by day, morning by morning, throughout the journey of our lives. (Brian K. Bauknight)

Worship Aids

Call to Worship

Leader: Great Spirit! You lived first, and you are older than all need, older than prayer.

People: All things belong to you—the two-legged, the four-legged, the wings of the air, and all green things that live.

Leader: We are lifting our voices to you, Great Spirit.

People: Forgetting nothing you have made, the stars of the universe and the grasses of the earth. Hear our praise.

All: As long as the sun shines and the waters flow, this land will be here to give life. Help us worship you by caring for Mother Earth and one another.

(Adapted from Black Elk, Oglala Sioux)

Invocation

(In the way of the Diné, we face east—greeting the new day.) Creator God, our faces and hearts face east as we greet the new day. We lift our face to the light, which you have sent to warm us. We are reminded of your power because you set the sun in the sky as well as the moon and the stars. We are thankful for your mercy as we are given another day of life. Each day is a new beginning and is full of new opportunities. Be with us as we seek your face and gather to worship you. In Jesus' name, Amen.

Benediction

Go in peace. Happily may you walk. Happily with abundant showers, may you walk. Happily with abundant plants, may you walk. Happily on the trail of pollen, may you walk. Empowered by the gift of the Holy Spirit, may you walk in beauty. (Raquel Mull)

MARCH 1, 2006

※ ※ ※ ※

Ash Wednesday

Readings: Joel 2:1-2, 12-17; Psalm 51:1-17; 2 Corinthians 5:20*b*–6:10; Matthew 6:1-6, 16-21

By What Authority?
Matthew 6:1-6

The other day, a Saturday, I stopped at a convenience store for a paper. Three of us waited while a new cashier grappled with the mysteries of her computerized register. Her customer was not pleased. He asked for a pack of cigarettes, which she haltingly produced. The computer did not cooperate. She apologized. He fumed. At last the register totaled his bill. He did not have, or could not locate easily in his jeans, enough money. Angry, nettled, and embarrassed, he hurled the cigarettes back, scooped up what money he had, and raged on out. His pickup truck squealed as he shouted and gestured a form of valediction. Our service provider returned to her struggles. The day *inched* forward. Somewhere, however, the question lingered about our angry customer: Who died and left him boss? By what authority does one hurl judgment at another? And what one of us has not done so?

The Gospel of Matthew was composed to meet the needs and answer the questions of the third-generation church. Now Jesus has gone. Now Paul has died. Now those whom Jesus gathered have gone. Now those whom Paul inspired have died. Tell us, Matthew, the good news in truth about living together as a church. Tell us about your passion for compassion. And tell us, too, about children and their place in life; about marriage and divorce; about money and its ills and blessings; about heaven; about leadership; and, so today, about authority. What Jesus has said Matthew has noted in ways that are helpful to his church.

At the end of the first century, when this Gospel was written, the still new Christian church, spread out across the Mediterranean, needed answers to big questions, including this one: Who will have authority in the church and of what kind will that authority be? Matthew teaches

57

about authority a dozen times in the course of his Gospel. Today we traverse the path of one point in his teaching.

My Saturday continued, unaware that its unsuspecting contours would later be fitted to the flow of a narrative sermon. Using the historic present, I park for a moment to be inspired again by the spire of a church. I return to thoughts about Matthew. Here is how our Gospels came to life: Faced with the care of widows and orphans, Matthew remembers Jesus' teaching about the poor and the young.

Faced with the need to raise another generation with discipline and compassion, Matthew remembers Jesus' teaching about a house built upon the rock.

Faced with inevitable dilemmas related to money and resources, Matthew remembers Jesus' parables and sayings about God and mammon.

Faced with the desire to share his own fierce passion—saving the lost, reaching the outsider, welcoming the stranger, churching the unchurched—Matthew remembers Jesus' own parables and manners and patterns of welcome.

Faced with the vital questions of how to arrange and manage the affairs of a nascent organism, a church body, Matthew remembered that Jesus had something to say as well about authority, and that Jesus had run his own risks in the face of authority. Authority raises a religious question.

I lollygag. The paper bought at the outset of the day lies unread. I skim—now a habit—the last two paragraphs of each editorial. A Yale teacher is wondering about authority. Can one nation act alone and unilaterally?

War and peace. Ah, yes. In most of our churches, people of faith have usually assumed one of two traditional positions in the face of armed conflict, or as is often the case, a kind of wisened situational combination of the two: pacifism or just war. Often, too, the chief job of the pastor in such a time is to help the congregation think clearly, and also to maintain space for a variety of views within one body. The pacifist position depends upon Matthew, in verses such as chapter 5:38 "You have heard that it was said, 'An eye for an eye and a tooth for a tooth.' But I say to you, Do not resist an evildoer. But if anyone strikes you on the right cheek, turn the other also." The activist position does too, in verses such as Matthew 10:34-38, "Do not think that I have come to bring peace on earth; I have not come to bring peace, but a sword. . . . Whoever does not take the cross and follow me is not worthy of me." How shall we think about this?

You remember that there have been five basic criteria, from Augustine to Aquinas to us, in the so-called just war theory: just cause in response to serious evil; just intention for restoration of peace with justice, not self-enrichment or devastation of another; last resort; have legitimate authority; have a reasonable hope of success, given the necessary constraints of discrimination and proportionality.

Our current course as a country moves in a third way, apart from both the pacifist and activist positions in the history of Christian thought. Our policy now is not a response but a preemption; not a restoration but a dislocation; not a last but an initial resort; not an act based on a communal authority, but a nearly unilateral act. We are told that this is a new age, that patience must be balanced with realism about the threat at large, that in due time we shall be shown the proof for the need of this new doctrine. But let us be clear: preemption, destruction, initiation, usurpation—these have little basis or foothold in the history of Christian thought, to this point. We are left, as disciples of Jesus Christ, either to redefine the expanse of Christian ethics developed over two thousand years or to reconsider our current debate. Let me ask us in the coming week to assess what we think is true by the mysterious measure of today's scripture: "By what authority?"

There is a form of authority that is not authoritarian at all. It is the authority of service, to which we are drawn as to our truest home. "Whoever wishes to become great among you must be your servant.... For the Son of Man came not to be served but to serve" (Mark 10:43-45). (Robert Hill)

The Story of Moses: An Extraordinary Offering

Sixth in a Series of Six: Moses

Exodus 35:4–36:7

The wandering nation of people needed a designated space for worship. They were God's people. They wanted to honor God with an appropriate setting for community worship. Something must be created that would reverence God, provide adequate sacred space, and yet still be portable for the unknown wanderings ahead.

A worthy tabernacle would also be made of quality products: jewels and other precious stones, durable hardwoods, fine linens, and such. Where could such valuable materials be found? Moses decided to receive an offering.

The call went out for voluntary gifts. The people responded enthusiastically. Gifts came pouring in. The size and number of the gifts suddenly seemed to overwhelm the project managers. They went to Moses with a most unusual request. "Tell the people to stop, Moses. We have enough to do the job. We have more than enough. We are being inundated with offerings," they seemed to say.

Moses listened to the artisans' story. Then he went to the people with this stunning proclamation: "No man or woman is to make anything else as an offering for the sanctuary." In effect, Moses said, "Stop bringing your offerings. We already have more than enough to do the job."

What becomes important is the *why* of the story. Why did the people respond so completely and so generously? What was the amazing secret of this offering? We can learn from what happened in this desert offering more than three millennia ago!

First, there seems to be a great love for the holy place. Translated into our time, this means a great love for the church. Whatever else may be in doubt, people seem to have an innate, God-given love for the holy place. A great love for the "church" thrived in the desert, in the hearts of the Hebrew people. They found joy in giving, and they knew God had a serious claim on their lives. They knew an innate durability in the holy place. The ancient Hebrews gave abundantly, generously, because they knew they were investing in something that would last.

Second, the story suggests that the trust level was very high. Integrity was in place. Through a multitude of experiences, confidence had grown. The God of Moses was clearly among them. Integrity is very important to the church. Integrity was present in the desert. Thus, resources came in abundance.

Third, the capacity to give was present. Who would have believed that wandering nomads in the desert could make such an offering? Perhaps they had plundered the Egyptians before leaving. Maybe they had collected some precious valuables along the way. The point is this: their capacity to give was greater than they knew. But Moses knew.

We sometimes cry "poor" today. We have cried "poor" for so long that we have talked ourselves into believing that we *are* poor. The capacity to give is present for most people. Very few congregations are overextended. A great teacher of stewardship once said, "Not one church in a hundred has any real notion of its power." The offerings began to pour in.

Fourth, this offering was a freewill offering. The storyteller makes this abundantly clear. Key phrases are used throughout. Consider all of the phrases in one short story—some of them used several times.

"Everyone whose heart was stirred."

"Everyone whose spirit was willing."

"A willing heart."

"Everyone . . . whose hearts made them willing."

"A freewill offering to the LORD."

Paul writes, "Each of you must give as you have made up your mind, not reluctantly or under compulsion" (2 Corinthians 9:7). His words form the foundation of what happens to us and to what happened in the desert long ago.

Authentic believer giving is not a tax or a tax deduction. Neither is it dues or some legalism. Giving is not what I "owe" my church. Giving is not a safe passage to heaven. Giving is a freely offered response to the goodness of God in my life. Giving among the community of believers has a whole different standard from the world.

Benjamin Franklin offers a valuable testimony in his autobiography. His witness demonstrates the power of good growth giving in the human spirit. In this setting, Franklin is listening to the preaching of George Whitfield.

> [During the sermon] I perceived he intended to finish with a Collection, and I silently resolved he should get nothing from me. I had in my Pocket a handful of Copper Money, three or four silver Dollars, and five Pistoles in Gold. As he proceeded I began to soften, and concluded to give the Coppers. Another Stroke of his Oratory made me asham'd of that, and determin'd to give the Silver; and he finish'd so admirably, that I empti'd my Pocket wholly into the collector's Dish, Gold and all. (Benjamin Franklin, *The Autobiography of Benjamin Franklin* [New Haven: Yale University Press, 1964], 177)

Is this not one clear picture of the way God works—a rustling in the heart? Is this not a graphic illustration of our storyteller when he says, "The hearts of the people were stirred"?

Finally, the story proclaims this important truth: "There is enough to do what God wants us to do." Notice that these words come from the craftsmen, the artisans. These are *not* the words of Moses. Moses was a learner in this situation.

One of my favorite phrases is "abundance of enough." That is the nature of God's blessing. God does not often give us everything we want; but God does give us everything we need. Probably not a lot of cushion! Probably not a surplus! But God will supply an abundance of enough.

Some eternal principles are at work in this story. We hear a simple promise from the author of faith. If we stand on the promise and use theologically appropriate methods, the gifts will be present. (Brian K. Bauknight)

Worship Aids

Call to Worship

Sing to God, all people of the earth, sing praises to the Lord! Proclaim the power of God, whose majesty is over all the land and whose power reigns above the skies. Praise be to God!

Pastoral Prayer

O Lord our God, we praise you above all creatures and all things. We lift prayers of thanks for the amazing fact that you loved us enough to give yourself fully for us. Now we have the challenge of trying to live fully for you. Help us in the task of discipleship. Be our spiritual teacher; remove our thick clouds of ignorance. Help us, O God, to live by the pattern and example given to us by Jesus Christ. Give us an eagerness and joyful desire to obey your command to make disciples of all nations. Send us out with renewed courage to proclaim the faith and hope within us to a world that needs both so that we may become your body in the world. Amen.

Benediction

May God guide you this week into the places and unto the people where your voice is needed. In that moment, may you speak the good news, in the name of the Father, and of the Son, and of the Holy Spirit. (Lance Moore)

MARCH 5, 2006

First Sunday in Lent

Readings: Genesis 9:8-17; Psalm 25:1-10; 1 Peter 3:18-22; Mark 1:9-15

Overcoming the Circumstances of Your Life
Mark 1:9-15

This scripture reveals that God can make something out of nothing.

Those of us who grew up in rural Alabama always joked, "Thank God for Mississippi," because we laughed that there would be one state below us on any social measurement. Most of us might consider growing up in Yazoo City, Mississippi, as a disadvantage, but not Zig Ziglar, the popular author. He grew up in Yazoo City. As he often said: "You can go anywhere in the world from Yazoo City, Mississippi."

Jesus was not from Yazoo City, but he was from Nazareth. Nazareth received the same kind of respect from the rest of Israel that any small rural town yet receives from the big cities. Nathaniel, one of the future disciples of Jesus, even asked when Philip told him about Jesus: "Can anything good come out of Nazareth?"

Jesus proved that an individual can go anywhere from Nazareth. The message of the first chapter of Mark tells us clearly that when you know yourself to be a child of God, you can overcome your circumstances.

Let us recognize that life is difficult, for many of us come from "Nowhere, U.S.A." Let us also recognize that many have overcome their circumstances and so can you. And third, know that God is saying to you as God said to Jesus: "You are my child, whom I love, with you I am well pleased."

Fred Dawson in the book *When Black Folks Was Colored* tells of the 1906 hurricane that all but leveled the city of Pensacola, Florida. At the time, he and his family were living in a south Alabama community raising cotton and nearly starving to death. Most of the other black families were packing up and moving north. Dawson's family packed up and moved south to Pensacola to help rebuild the city after that major hurricane. They became significant landowners. Fred Dawson learned early on

63

that it is not so important where you come from, but who you are that makes the difference.

Years ago when I was in college I drove to a community just south of Monroeville, Alabama, to preach every other weekend at the Bermuda Methodist Church. I had a friend who now lives in Monroeville who recently told me an amazing story:

He and his sister grew up in a shack of a house in Bermuda, Alabama. His father was a two-mule farmer, his mother a part-time beautician. The children would walk out of their house to catch the school bus for the eight-mile trip to school. While they waited for the bus, sometimes on a cold day they would see black children walking on the road to their run-down black school about four miles away. What they didn't know was that some of those black kids had already been walking for thirty minutes in the rain and cold and would still be walking long after the school bus would pull up to the white school. One day his sister asked, "Why can't they ride the bus with us?" And no one ever came up with an answer that would make sense back in the 1940s.

My friend, now in his 70s, has moved to Monroeville and recently met a very impressive lady, Mrs. Jones (not her real name), when she joined the local Kiwanis Club. It is new territory for a woman to be a member of the formerly all-male club, but what is even more unusual is that Mrs. Jones, the retired librarian at a junior college, is black. She has three children—one a medical doctor at a state university, another a college professor in California, and a daughter who is the senior editor of the editorial page of a prestigious national newspaper. What is even more amazing is that Mrs. Jones was one of those black children who sixty years ago walked past my friend's house to her black school. It is not so important where you come from, but who you are and where you are going that makes a difference.

Martin Luther King, Jr. was a middle-class, black, Baptist preacher, but his message of Christian love and nonviolent social change saved this nation from a revolution in the 1960s. I heard him preach one time and I was stirred deep within. But when I was in college, there was so much negative press about him that I just didn't know what to believe about him. None of us knew who he really was. Now we realize from a perspective of history that it is not so important the color of your skin, but the character of your soul, that makes a difference.

When the world asks, "Can anything good come out of Nazareth?" the stories of the Lord of the church and of God's people of all the years answer back: "You can overcome the circumstances of your birth." The heavens opened when Jesus was baptized with God's affirmation. Some people couldn't see it while Jesus was here on earth, and some still can't. But eyes of faith see wondrous things happen all the time. Believe and you will begin to see things happen in your life. Listen and you will hear: "You are my child, whom I love, and with you I am well pleased."

Yes, we may start off in a place called Yazoo City, Mississippi, or a place called Nazareth, but hear this: it doesn't matter where you start out and it doesn't matter what obstacles you have to overcome. You can become a winner, a hero, a Christian, God's special child, by listening today to the mystery beyond us. Listen and you will hear: "You are my child, whom I love, and with you I am well pleased." (Henry E. Roberts)

Wilderness Time: A Time for Learning

First in a Series of Six: Lent

Mark 1:12-15

Jesus' wilderness time "immediately" followed his baptism and the powerful affirmation of who he was: "You are my Son, the Beloved; with you I am well pleased" (Mark 1:11). The Synoptic Gospels say that the Spirit who descended on him at his baptism drove him out into the bleak, lonely, and dry Judean wilderness for forty days of testing (see Genesis 7:2, Exodus 24:18, 1 Kings 19:8).

Wilderness time is a part of our lives too. We cannot live and love and engage life in meaningful ways without sometimes ending up in the wilderness. Wilderness times are those times when we feel we are tested to our limits, and we describe those times in wilderness terms: dry, desolate, lonely, trying, difficult, agonizing. We speak of hunger, thirst, and longing in the wilderness. This series explores this difficult spiritual territory.

We first recognize that wilderness time is a time for learning.

One of those e-mail lists making the rounds a few years ago listed significant things children have learned about life. Here are just a few of them:

"You can't trust dogs to watch your food for you."

"Don't sneeze when somebody is cutting your hair."

"You can't hide a piece of broccoli in a glass of milk."

"When your mom is mad at your dad, don't let her brush your hair."

"No matter how hard you try you cannot baptize a cat."

These are the kinds of accelerated learning experiences we call "learning the hard way." So it is with the hard time in the wilderness. A lot can be learned in the wilderness, but one lesson stands out. The wilderness can be a time of accelerated learning about priority—what really matters in our lives. Patrick Morley in his book *The Man in the Mirror* relates the lack of a clear sense of priority to a trip to the grocery store on an empty stomach without a shopping list. Nearly everything looks delicious and you wander through the aisles without a plan, loading up the shopping cart with goodies. After the shock of the bill at checkout, there is the shock of your spouse when you arrive home with sacks of snacks and food for only three real meals in the whole bunch! (Brentwood, Calif.: Wolgemuth & Hyatt, 1989, 163).

Life presents us with many options—a myriad of ways to use our resources, time, abilities, and influence. Without a clear sense of what is most important, we can spend it all and at the end of the day find that we have not taken care of what matters most.

Jesus' time in the wilderness—coming just before he was to begin his public ministry—was a time for sorting out what mattered most and to get clear about God's will for his life. The longer accounts in Matthew and Luke tell us that Jesus was tempted by wealth, fame, and power to deviate from his mission. As we follow Jesus into the wilderness, we can see that our own wilderness time can be an important time of testing our values, looking at what is most important, and making decisions about our life's priorities.

A few years ago, a young man I knew was in the wilderness, suffering from an aggressive form of cancer. During the time of his surgeries and treatments, it was my privilege to be his pastor and to spend time with him in that wilderness. He said, "I have learned that what I thought was very important before doesn't seem very important now, and what I took for granted and thought I could put off for another day has risen to the top of my list of priorities."

As painful as wilderness experiences are, they can yield more spiritual growth than the good times. They can be times of learning about ourselves, about God, about what is most important, and about where life is headed. Without that time of stocktaking and learning—whether in the wilderness or not—life can just go along without much thought. Here are some good wilderness questions: What important relationships and friendships have I been putting off to some future time? What is God calling me to do with my life and with all the resources God has given me? What in my life right now do I take for granted?

A businessman visiting the pier of a coastal village noticed a small boat with just one fisherman pulling up to the dock. Inside the small boat were several large yellowfin tuna. He complimented the fisherman on the fish and asked how long it took to catch them. "Only a little while," the fisherman replied.

"Why didn't you stay out longer and catch more fish?"

"I have enough to support my family's needs."

The businessman then asked, "But what do you do with the rest of your time?"

The fisherman said, "I sleep late, fish a little, play with my children, take a siesta with my wife, and stroll into the village each evening where I sip wine and play guitar with my friends. I have a full and busy life."

The businessman scoffed, "I am a Harvard MBA and could help you. You should spend more time fishing and with the proceeds buy a bigger boat. With the proceeds from the bigger boat you could buy several boats and eventually have a whole fleet of boats. You would cut out the middleman and sell directly to the processor, eventually opening your own cannery. You would control the product, processing, and distribution. You would need to leave this small village and move to Mexico City, then Los Angeles, and eventually New York City where you would run your expanding enterprise."

The fisherman asked, "But, how long will all this take?"

The MBA replied, "Fifteen to twenty years."

"But what then?" the fisherman asked.

The American laughed and said, "That's the best part. When the time is right, you would announce an initial public offering and sell your company stock to the public and become very rich; you would make millions."

"Millions?" the fisherman asked. "Then what?"

The American said, "Then you would retire and move to a small coastal fishing village where you would sleep late, fish a little, play with your kids, take a siesta with your wife, and stroll to the village in the evenings where you could sip wine and play guitar with your friends."

What is most important? Where is your life headed? These are good wilderness questions! (Tim K. Bruster)

Worship Aids

Call to Worship

As our Lord Jesus spent forty days in the wilderness discerning and clarifying the direction of his life, may the forty days of Lent be a time of discernment and clarity in our own lives. Let us follow Jesus into the wilderness and there learn from him what is most important in our own lives.

Prayer of Confession

Our gracious God, Jesus taught us love you with all our heart, soul, mind, and strength. He taught us to love our neighbors as ourselves. He taught us to trust you completely. We confess that we have often failed to learn, and what we have learned we have often failed to put into practice. Forgive us, we pray, in the name of Jesus. Amen.

Words of Assurance

Hear the good news: God is evermore ready to forgive than we are to acknowledge our need for forgiveness. Receive God's gift of forgiveness in Christ and walk in newness of life. (Tim K. Bruster)

MARCH 12, 2006

Second Sunday in Lent

Readings: Genesis 17:1-7, 15-16; Psalm 22:23-31; Romans 4:13-25; Mark 8:31-38

Laughing at God
Genesis 17:1-7, 15-16; Mark 8:31-38

Most families have a first ancestor, a patriarch or matriarch who founded the clan. It may be the ancestor that first came to these shores from another continent. Whether that ancestor came over on the Mayflower or in the hold of a slave ship, you are probably proud of the courage and the ability to overcome great obstacles your renowned ancestor represents.

The Israelites had a renowned ancestor also. The Israelite nation considered themselves descendants of one ancestral couple, Abraham and Sarah. God promised Abraham and Sarah that they would receive two great things: land and children. Most of their lives they lived as childless, landless bedouins. Then an angelic visitor came to their tent when Abraham was ninety-nine and Sarah was ninety years old and repeated the promise of God. "You will have land and you will have children." It was a farfetched, impossible, unlikely, humorous promise. Abraham thought the idea was so ridiculous he bowed down before the angelic visitor and laughed his head off. It seemed laughable, except it was the plan and the promise and the program of God.

Generations before Abraham, we have a similar example of the way the plan and program of God seemed laughable. Consider the story of Noah and his ark. Noah built a huge boat on dry land. Think of the laughs his neighbors were having on Noah. We can read the Bible as the story of how people reacted to the seemingly laughable ideas of God. All through the Bible God seemed to have laughable, impossible, impractical plans and most people didn't get it. The Bible is also the story of the few who did.

Generations after Abraham and Sarah the Israelites had multiplied to be a great nation, but they were oppressed into slavery in Egypt. One bright sunny day Moses came to Pharaoh's palace. Moses said, "Pharaoh, I just got a message from God. God says, 'Let my people go!'" Can you imagine the snickering in the back room? "Moses arrived with this crazy idea; God wants us to give up our free labor? Ridiculous! Laughable!"

The exodus is one long comedy. Remember the ten plagues? We read them with such a long and serious face. The plagues are comedy routines. Frogs and gnats and hail and storms are funny! God seems to be toying with the Egyptians, making fun of them. If we have eyes to see, the whole exodus story is full of laughs. Early on, it is the Egyptians laughing at Moses' freedom idea. Later, it is God's last laugh on Egypt.

Later the Israelites were on the doorstep of the promised land. The first fortified city they approached was Jericho. Archaeologists say Jericho may be the longest continuously occupied city on earth. Human occupancy at Jericho goes back uninterrupted for ten thousand years. When the Israelites arrived at Jericho, it had been inhabited for 7,500 years. What did the Israelites do? Be prepared to laugh. They marched around the city in silence led by priests rather than soldiers. Imagine the guards in Jericho's towers watching this goofy parade every day. Imagine their laughter at these people from the desert. Then, on the seventh day, the Israelites made their circuit and didn't stop. The priests blew their horns and the laughter of the guards of Jericho was drowned out by the sound of the walls falling down. It seemed laughable, crazy, impossible, and impractical. It was also God's big idea.

Centuries later, a prophet and healer named Jesus made his way around Galilee saying, "If you want to save life, you must lose it. If you give it away, you'll find it." It sounds like a ridiculous paradox. Jesus said other things that must have struck people as hopelessly idealistic. He said not only, "Love your neighbor" (Sometimes that's pretty laughable, isn't it?) but also, "Love your enemy. Pray for those who persecute you." Such instructions are contrary to the conventional survival wisdom in a dog-eat-dog world. They seem to be laughable instructions except that they are the program, the promise, and the agenda of God.

What if someone came to us today and said, "Beat your swords into plowshares and your spears into pruning hooks?" What if someone came to us today and said, "Take your bombers and make school classrooms, make your tanks into medical clinics and your guns into the implements of agriculture?" Why, we would accuse that person of being impractical, crazy, laughable, and maybe even traitorous. But the Bible tells us that God's mighty dream is for us to beat our swords into plowshares. What if some prophet were to come among us in North America and Europe and say, "It is the will of God that you lower your standard of living 50 percent for the sake of the poor and for the sake of the planet"? We might think that person hopelessly naive, the program laughable. And yet, wouldn't it be consistent with the biblical admonition to care for creation and for our neighbors?

Often God is calling us to do things that seem altogether out of character. God asks us to do things that would make our neighbors and coworkers laugh their heads off. God still asks God's people to do incredibly foolish, naive, and laughable things.

Love your neighbor and your enemy. Pray for those who abuse you. God's plan, God's program, God's agenda is frequently so different from our own and so different from what is expected in our world. Yet which program really works? God's? Or the world's? Yes, all of human history has been the story of people who laughed at God's program of justice, love, and compassion. We keep on laughing and God keeps on inviting us to be those rare people that get with the program. Amen. (Carl L. Schenck)

Wilderness Time: A Time of Challenge

Second in a Series of Six: Lent

Mark 1:12-15; 2 Corinthians 4:8-11

In these forty days of Lent we remember Jesus' time of testing in the wilderness and that we each have our own times of wilderness testing. Each wilderness experience that comes our way presents us with difficulties and struggles. Mark says that there were wild beasts in the wilderness with Jesus. Aren't our wilderness times complete with wild beasts? Fear crouches in the brush nearby, ready to pounce and strangle. Temptation slithers around waiting for the opportunity to strike. Despair circles overhead, waiting to land and devour. Wilderness times have their wild beasts! They are times of challenge. Our faith, our values, our trust in God, what we believe, are all tested in the wilderness.

We call this testing temptation.

When I turned forty, one of my "friends" sent me a card that said, "As you grow older, don't worry about avoiding temptations. Temptations will avoid you." Would that it were true! We never outgrow temptation. Saint Anthony spoke the truth when he said, "Expect temptation with your last breath." Temptation is a very real part of life and it is especially challenging in wilderness times—those times of spiritual dryness, loneliness, despair, fear, disappointment, low self-esteem, and bitterness. In those times, we are more susceptible to the power of temptation. Each temptation in the wilderness presents us with a corresponding challenge.

In the wilderness, the temptation is to stray from the values we hold dear—the challenge is to hold fast to them and live by them.

In the wilderness, the temptation is to take shortcuts, to avoid struggle, to find the easy way through—the challenge is to move through the struggle and take the hard way. The right way, the way to life, is often the hard and narrow way (see Matthew 7:13-14). The challenge is to persevere and move through the struggle—to take the hard way.

In the wilderness, the temptation is to listen to voices that would lead us away from God—the challenge is to listen to our living and life-giving God. Radio, television, and the Internet fill our ears with thousands of voices, representing many understandings of what is ultimately important, what gives meaning and purpose to life, and what principles guide life. With all the voices, it is increasingly difficult—especially for children and young people—to discern the good from the evil. So often the evil that tempts us and leads us to give allegiance to someone or something other than God is portrayed as ugly with a scary voice. In reality, the evil that presents itself in our lives doesn't come with pointy tails, horns, cloven hooves, or a menacing scowl. That would be repulsive. Rather, evil generally presents itself as something good and is generally the twisting of something good and life-giving into something evil and destructive of life. Money, power, influence, sex, security, winning, fame—all are good and yet all can be twisted to become evil and destructive.

In the wilderness, the temptation is to substitute "stuff" in the place of God to make us feel better—the challenge is to live knowing that God is sufficient. One of the great temptations we face is the temptation always to have more. Happiness is just around the corner if only we have more things, or more wealth, or the finer things of life.

In the wilderness, the temptation is to give up—the challenge is to persevere. The life-giving way is to rise to meet the challenges head-on and persevere in doing what's right, in being faithful to God, in trusting God, in listening to God, and in loving others as God loves us. The good news is that God strengthens us to meet the challenges. Paul wrote out of his own experience, "We are pressed on every side by troubles, but not crushed and broken. We are perplexed because we don't know why things happen as they do, but we don't give up and quit. We are hunted down, but God never abandons us. We get knocked down, but we get up again and keep going" (2 Corinthians 4:8-9, *The Book* [Wheaton, Ill.: Tyndale House, 1984]). Perseverance is so often the key to meeting the challenges of the wilderness.

Meeting the challenge of the wilderness each time helps us prepare for meeting the challenge the next time. We struggle with our temptations in the wilderness and out of that struggle comes character. James 1:2-4 tells readers, "My brothers and sisters, whenever you face trials of any kind, consider it nothing but joy, because you know that the testing of your faith produces endurance; and let endurance have its full effect, so that you may be mature and complete, lacking in nothing."

In the stories of the Desert Fathers there is one story concerning Abbot John the Dwarf. Abbot John prayed to the Lord that all passion be taken from him. His prayer was granted. He became impassible. In this condition he went to one of the elders and said: "You see before you a man who is completely at rest and has no more temptations."

The elder surprised him. Instead of praising him, the elder said: "Go and pray to the Lord to command some struggle to be stirred up in you, for the soul is matured only in battles."

Abbot John did this, and when the temptations started up again, he did not pray that the struggle be taken away from him. Instead, he prayed: "Lord, give me strength to get through the fight" (Thomas Merton, *The Wisdom of the Desert* [New York: New Directions, 1960], 56-57).

Whereas temptation seems to be only a trap that leads to difficulties and even devastating tragedy, there is another side to temptation. If we pay attention, it presents us with the opportunity to learn about ourselves as we imagine the consequences of yielding to the temptation. We mentally work through the consequences without having to live through them. The benefit is obvious—only if we act on the temptation do we create negative consequences for ourselves and others.

We learn from Jesus that we meet the challenges of the wilderness by meeting God daily. Jesus, the Son, was ready to meet the challenges in the wilderness because Jesus had met daily with God, the Father. Jesus was thoroughly versed in the will and way of God for his life. When we meet God daily before the wilderness time comes our way, then we are more prepared for the challenges of the wilderness. (Tim K. Bruster)

Worship Aids

Pastoral Prayer

God, our Strength and Redeemer, in this gathered community there are some who are struggling in the wilderness at this moment. Give them peace and strength to sustain them through this difficult time and the assurance that you are present even in the most desolate wilderness. In the name of our Lord Jesus Christ, who is no stranger to our wilderness times, Amen.

Prayer of Confession

God of mercy and grace, we confess that when temptation has come our way we have often failed to meet its challenge. We have strayed from what we know to be right. We have taken the easy way instead of the way that leads to life. We have sought our security in mere possessions, status, and wealth instead of placing our trust in you. Forgive us, we pray, in the name of Jesus. Amen.

Words of Assurance

God "does not deal with us according to our sins, nor repay us according to our iniquities. For as the heavens are high above the earth, so great is his steadfast love toward those who fear him; as far as the east is from the west, so far he removes our transgressions from us" (Psalm 103:10-12). Thanks be to God. (Tim K. Bruster)

MARCH 19, 2006

❧❧❧

Third Sunday in Lent

Readings: Exodus 20:1-17; Psalm 19; 1 Corinthians 1:18-25; John 2:13-22

Fools for Christ
1 Corinthians 1:18-25

The news is constantly filled with scandals. The scandals in the tabloids as I write will be replaced by a whole new set by the time you read this—news of Hollywood, corporate America, Washington, or even ecclesiastical scandal. The Bible, too, is full of scandals and fools. We need not repeat the long litany of nefarious characters and flawed heroes that make up the pantheon of biblical personalities, from Jacob the cheat all the way to the chosen twelve disciples, one of whom was a coward and another a traitor.

Yes, we might wonder about God's discernment of character. God seems to need a better personnel manager or casting director. Another of God's scandalous choices was Paul. Paul started out as a persecutor of Christians. He assisted in the stoning of Stephen. Paul seemed no good. When God told Ananias that he was to anoint Paul as his "chosen instrument," Ananias said, in effect, "Lord, you must be mistaken." It seemed foolish, scandalous.

Perhaps that is why later, when Paul was writing to the church at Corinth, he reminded them: things that seem like low foolishness to us may be high wisdom to God. Paul then pointed out the most apparently foolish, scandalous thing God had ever done: God had come into the world as a peasant carpenter from the backwater town of Nazareth.

Next in this Corinthian letter, Paul calls Jesus a "stumbling block to the Jews." He meant that the idea of God coming as a peasant was such a scandalous thing the Jews couldn't believe it. They were expecting a powerful king; instead, they got a baby in a barnyard surrounded by animals and stench. This was a scandal.

The very word Paul used for this, translated in English as "stumbling block," is the Greek word *skandalon*, from which we get our English word *scandal*.

Jesus was born into scandal: from his parents' disgraceful marriage, to a smelly barn, then escaping to Egypt. Jesus grew up in a place of which they said, "Nothing good comes from there," then became a friend to prostitutes, tax collectors, and working-class roughnecks. Jesus was indeed a stumbling block, a scandalous offense to those who wanted a pure Messiah. Jesus fulfilled the prophecy of Isaiah 8:14 (NIV): "He will be a stone that causes [people] to stumble."

The Israelites overlooked the prophecies. They expected a military ruler, a king, a superhuman. Instead they got a baby in a manger, and finally a bleeding, beaten figure dying ignominiously on a cross.

The message of scripture is clear: God chooses the scandalous. God uses the weak and the meek. God redeems the sinful. This fragile vessel of flesh is God's tool of choice. Again, Paul wrote: "We have this treasure in jars of clay to show that this all-surpassing power is from God and not from us" (2 Corinthians 4:7 NIV). It is to God's glory that the foolish and weak are used to achieve a grand purpose. Nowhere is this more clear than in the concept of incarnation, of God coming into mortal flesh to touch us and die for us.

A doctor in Atlanta has a remarkable record of success in healing. The hospital chaplain had a chance to discover why. He told me of one particular patient who had a horrible infection on his feet. His feet were disfigured, nasty, and pus-covered. The doctor came in, and with a gentle bedside manner, unwrapped the bandages. The chaplain was almost overwhelmed by the infection's odor. But the doctor was unfazed. He gently touched and massaged those horrid feet as he inspected the progress of healing. He did this daily until the man was completely healed. This doctor didn't remain in the sterility of his office. He became involved with the flesh of his patients.

We have a God who comes into a scandalous and brutish world to touch and heal our wounds. The first part of that incarnation story is Jesus' birth and ministry of healing; the second part is what we remember during Lent. It is a journey that culminates with Holy Week, commemorating a painful and shameful torture upon a Roman cross. Even the triumphal ride into Jerusalem, which we celebrate on Palm Sunday, was an earthy and scandalous occurrence. Jesus did a very undignified thing. He poked fun at both his worshipers and his detractors. He rode humbly on the back of a baby donkey. Imagine if our president rode in the inaugural parade on one of those little go-carts that clowns drive. But with that silly donkey ride, Jesus fulfilled the messianic prophecies and taught us something about humility. Scandalous.

The associated word Paul uses in this passage is *foolishness*. "For the message about the cross is foolishness to those who are perishing.... God decided, through the foolishness of our proclamation, to save those who believe" (1 Corinthians 1:18-21). Are we willing to appear foolish for the sake of the cross and the gospel?

I was once asked to play a part in a lighthearted Christmas skit in which the animals of the manger scene discuss the coming of the Christ Child. I had the role of a talking donkey, in a costume with ears. The children greatly enjoyed seeing their pastor in a different persona. But after it was over, an irate parishioner showed up in my office. This, she insisted, had been undignified and disgraceful for the office of the pastor to be portrayed as a donkey. Shameful. I simply said, "Well, I guess you are also embarrassed by the fact that our Savior rode a baby donkey into Jerusalem." I am proud to be a part of a long lineage of "fools" who have been criticized for proclaiming the gospel in new, "scandalous," ways—from Saint Francis of Assisi (a self-proclaimed "fool for Christ"); to the troublemaking Martin Luther; to the shunned John Wesley, who preached while standing on his father's tombstone; to "Crazy" Mike Warnke, Christian comedian. Most of the characters of the Bible, the Christian martyrs, and the reformers of the church could be called "The Fools for Christ Club." Are you willing to be a member? (Lance Moore)

Wilderness Time: A Time of Dependence

Third in a Series of Six: Lent

Mark 1:12-15; Hebrews 4:14-16

Wilderness time is a time of complete dependence on God. This is such an important part of the wilderness experience. When the people of God were in the Sinai wilderness, God gave them what they needed and God gave them only what they needed for the day. God could have provided at once the manna and everything else the Israelites needed for their wanderings in the wilderness. But, God didn't do that. God gave them only enough for the day. This lesson taught the Israelites not just dependence, but habitual dependence on God. Each new day brought them a new reminder of their utter dependence on God.

Remember that Jesus taught us to pray in the Lord's Prayer, "Give us this day our daily bread." Jesus was telling us that every day we should acknowledge who the source of everything is. Jesus was telling us to acknowledge every day our dependence on God.

I remember one man and his family in a church I served many years ago. He and his wife had three children, two boys and a young disabled girl with many medical needs. He quite suddenly lost his job and was unemployed for some time. He shared with me that during that time he learned to live daily in a way he never had before. The church as a body and various members of the church individually helped that family for several months as they struggled along. They literally did not know where the next meal was coming from sometimes. Each day was a new day and God provided through the generosity of God's people. I remember he told me that the Lord's Prayer had new meaning for him—for the first time in his life, he really understood what it meant to pray, "Give us this day our daily bread."

God gives us what we need in the wilderness. When our strength, our emotional resources, and other sources of what we need are at an end, then we learn to be dependent on God. God renews our strength, so "[we] shall run and not be weary, [we] shall walk and not faint" (Isaiah 40:31).

The Bible is full of images that call to mind our dependence on God. It is good to meditate on these images—whether in the wilderness or not.

Shepherd. God is characterized time and again as our shepherd. Jesus referred to himself as the Good Shepherd. Scripture constantly characterizes us as being more like a sheep than any other creature. One of the reasons sheep must have a keeper is that after centuries of domesticated herd life they lack the instincts to defend themselves against a wolf or coyote or other predators. Sheep are completely dependent on a shepherd who protects them from the dangers around them and even from themselves.

Most of us are taught that dependence is bad and independence is good. We don't like to think of ourselves as dependent on anyone—or anything else, for that matter. In the wilderness, however, we have needs that we can't meet with our own resources. What is called for in the wilderness is dependence—dependence on God, who is able to meet our needs.

Vine. Jesus said, "I am the vine, you are the branches" (John 15:5). That means our strength and our sustenance comes from outside ourselves. It comes from our connection to *the Source.*

There is a grapevine at Hampton Court Palace near London that was planted in 1768. Some of its branches are two hundred feet long, and its single root is at least two feet thick. Because of skillful cutting and pruning, that one vine produces more than six hundred pounds of black grapes every year. And although some of the smaller branches are two hundred feet from the main stem, they bear plenty of fruit because they are joined to the vine and allow the life of the vine to flow through them. We, like the branches, are dependent on Jesus Christ for life in all its fullness. We draw our life from him.

The apostle Paul learned so well that his strength for the wilderness was from outside of himself that he said, "I can do all things through [Christ] who strengthens me" (Philippians 4:13).

High Priest. The writer of Hebrews teaches us that Jesus Christ is our great High Priest and that we have a high priest who is able to sympathize with our weaknesses and who in every respect has been tested as we are, yet without sin. He then says, "Let us therefore approach the throne of grace with boldness, so that we may receive mercy and find grace to help in time of need" (Hebrews 4:16).

Christ understands our loneliness and despair. Christ understands the wilderness. Whatever wilderness we find ourselves in, Christ understands. Why? Because Jesus has been there too—in every respect tested as we are.

A few years ago, a *Fort Worth Star-Telegram* newspaper reporter posed as a homeless man and spent time on the streets. There he came to understand and then to communicate to others the plight of the homeless and the services available to them as well as the needs they have. Because he experienced what they experienced, he understood in a powerful way who they were and the demands and challenges of their lives. So it is with Jesus. Jesus walked where the outcasts walk. That is part of the message of the cross. Jesus walked where we walk. When it is time for us also to walk the *via dolorosa,* the way of suffering, Jesus walks with us.

In the wilderness times, in times of our greatest need, we will receive strength from beyond ourselves. That strength comes from God.

A boy and his father were walking along a road when they came across a large stone. The boy said to his father, "Do you think if I use all my strength, I can move this rock?"

His father answered, "If you use all your strength, I am sure you can do it."

The boy began to push the rock. Exerting himself as much as he could, he pushed and pushed. The rock did not move. Discouraged, he said to his father, "You were wrong, I can't do it."

79

The father placed his arm around the boy's shoulder and said, "No, son, you didn't use all your strength—you didn't ask me to help." (David J. Wolpe, *Teaching Your Children About God* [New York: Henry Holt, 1993], 214)

Wilderness time is time when we must use all our strength—and God is our strength! (Tim K. Bruster)

Worship Aids

Call to Worship

Leader: Since, then, we have a great high priest who has passed through the heavens, Jesus, the Son of God, let us hold fast to our confession.

People: For we do not have a high priest who is unable to sympathize with our weaknesses, but we have one who in every respect has been tested as we are, yet without sin.

Leader: Let us therefore approach the throne of grace with boldness, so that we may receive mercy and find grace to help in time of need (Hebrews 4:14-16).

Invocation

Almighty God, boldly we approach your throne of grace. Joyfully, we come knowing you always welcome us. Humbly, we acknowledge before you and one another our need. Eagerly, we seek your mercy and grace, which are sufficient for our every need. Grant us open hearts, minds, and lives that we might gratefully receive. We pray in the name of Jesus, our great High Priest. Amen.

Benediction

Go in peace, for you do not go alone. God goes with you. Go in peace, for when your path leads into the wilderness, remember that Jesus Christ has been there before you. Go in peace to bless others along the way and to receive their blessing. Amen. (Tim K. Bruster)

MARCH 26, 2006

Fourth Sunday in Lent

Readings: Numbers 21:4-9; Psalm 107:1-3, 17-22; Ephesians 2:1-10; John 3:14-21

The Unconditional Love of God
John 3:14-21

The single most revolutionary concept in the New Testament is embodied in two verses in John's Gospel: John 3:16-17. It reverses so much of what had been taught for hundreds of years that it is little wonder that Jesus attracted the intense hostility of the religious establishment. Of course, the idea of God's love was not absent from the Jewish concept of God, but it was not central. It is there in what we know as the Old Testament, but it is circumscribed and pushed to the margins. In truth, the idea of the universal, unconditional love of God, which is so central to the Christian faith, still gets marginalized, even with all that we know in Christ.

We have all heard it, sometimes we have said it, and even in the absence of the words, we have thought it. This is the words and music to the idea: "Of course God loves and God is love, but . . . " Then all that follows the "but" belies what preceded it. Of course God loves everybody . . . well, almost. He loves all of us, but not all of "them." When we begin to reflect on the realities of life, the exceptions to God's universal love begins. We exclude individuals we do not like who are beyond our love and we assume they are therefore beyond God's love. We exclude whole groups who in our view of reality do not qualify. It was not just the Jews who made God local and exclusive. We do it also. Furthermore, the Jews, our forebears in the faith, should not be judged by a standard that was not in place in their time, and which was not to become extant for hundreds of years. The most dramatic revelation of God's love was yet to come. They had glimpses of what it might be in their messianic dreams, but their ambitions of political domination and personal power distorted their hopes and dreams for a messiah. Of all the images of a messiah only one came close to what really happened. Isaiah's "suffering servant" pointed in the right direction, but was only a hint. The Jews expected a messiah who would confirm their exclusivism, destroy their enemies, and give them power over all nations.

It did not happen that way. The birth and growth of Jesus hardly matched the extravagant and dramatic expectations they had nurtured through the years. Jesus came preaching of a kingdom undergirded by the power of love instead of the love of power. They had pretty well figured out the nature of God and written rules to guide human beings in the worship of a God they conceived. When Jesus came preaching and teaching about a God who is like a "father," things simply got out of hand. God got too big. Their theological understandings did not fit anymore. New areas of mystery developed for which they had no traditional explanation. God as "Father," who loves everybody, even those other people, this was just too much! Jesus had to go.

If God loves us all as a father loves a child then so many of our attitudes and practices of worship are misdirected. Prayer and acts of worship designed to placate God miss the point altogether. The gospel of Jesus and the whole thrust of New Testament faith teach us that God is "for us." God is already on our side. We do not have to design and practice ways of gaining God's favorable attention. We already have God's favorable attention. There is no need to beg God to love us, understand us, and help us. We need only trust God. To beg and plead and cajole belies our fear that God does not love us as a father. This behavior is a symptom of mistrust.

The most elusive and sought after commodity in this life is unconditional love and acceptance. It is that most precious of all conditions, which, when we find it, everything else is secondary. It empowers us and gives us a sense of meaning and worth. It is the "pearl of great price" for which we would give all that we have. Indeed, there is so little of it in the places we look. When we find some glimmer of it in another person, we want to possess that person. We marry for it. We pretend to be someone and something we are not in the hope of winning it for ourselves. People experience great disappointment in friendship, love, and marriage when their source of unconditional love and acceptance dries up. We want to be loved in that indescribable, mystical, and unconditional way. Think about how much of your life you have spent looking for that kind of love. Think about the scars you have from the crushing disappointment of thinking you had it, but you misjudged.

How ironic that we search and sacrifice, beg and plead for what is ours for free. The unending source of what we want is freely offered to us by God in Christ. We get temporary snatches of unconditional love from human beings, but it never lasts. It dries up or turns into something else. The greatest human disappointments come when we expect of human beings what can only be expected of God. Friends and loved ones ultimately fail and disappoint us. Their self-interest or lack of understanding or their mere human frailty leaves them unable to do and be for us what only God can do and be for us.

When you discover that you cannot handle all that happens to you in life alone; when your friends fail and loved ones leave you in one of the many ways in which someone can go away; when you feel all alone in the universe; take these two verses of scripture into your heart and find the comfort that comes when you trust them to be true. "For God so loved the world that he gave his only Son, so that everyone who believes in him may not perish but may have eternal life. Indeed, God did not send the Son into the world to condemn the world, but in order that the world might be saved through him" (John 3:16-17). (Thomas Lane Butts)

Wilderness Time: A Time of Doubt

Fourth in a Series of Six: Lent

Mark 1:9-15; Mark 9:24b

In wilderness time, just about everything is tested and called into question. Doubt is often part of the experience. Our cry in the wilderness is often the cry of the father recorded in Mark: "I believe; help my unbelief!" The cry of that father seeking healing for his son was not the first such cry, nor would it be the last. People of faith down through the ages— including the greatest Christian leaders—have experienced doubt in the wilderness time.

Unfortunately, we in the church have often dismissed or discounted doubts as the products of an immature faith, although sitting in any congregation on any Sunday morning are many people who hold unresolved issues of faith and belief. It is critically important that the church be a safe place where these doubts can be raised without the questioner being made to feel like a second-class Christian!

The important truth is that doubt is a part of our faith journey. Most Christians experience it at one time or another—especially in the wilderness times. Some Christians experience it a number of times throughout their lives. Doubt is part of the Christian's journey, but doubt is not a good destination—any more than the wilderness is a good destination. It is not intended to be a stopping place. Doubt calls us to action. It moves us on and moves us forward. There is a big difference between doubting and giving up. There is an immense difference between wrestling with faith and throwing it to the side. There is a big difference between moving through doubt and getting stuck there and becoming a cynic. The healthy way of understanding doubt is to understand it as part of the faith journey. The key to doubt being a journey and not a destination is caring about God and wanting to move to faith: "I believe. Help my unbelief."

The good news is that the doubt we experience in the wilderness times can actually be beneficial to us because doubt stimulates us and spurs us on to faith. Frederick Buechner wrote, "If you don't have any doubts you are either kidding yourself or asleep. Doubts are the ants in the pants of faith. They keep it awake and moving" (Frederick Buechner, *Wishful Thinking* [New York: Harper & Row, 1987], 20). Interestingly, God's most faithful servants have usually also been among the most doubtful.

We tend to think of doubt as the opposite of faith, but in reality apathy or staunch disbelief is the opposite of faith. Paul Tillich defined faith as "the state of being ultimately concerned." In other words, what we are most concerned about is what we really have faith in. We are called to be ultimately concerned with God—to have faith and trust in God. The opposite of being ultimately concerned is not caring at all. If I am ultimately concerned about God and my life in God, then my doubt will not destroy my faith, but deepen my concern and spur me on to resolve it.

Doubt is not the opposite of faith, but a part of it. As the poet Alfred, Lord Tennyson put it: "There lives more faith in honest doubt, believe me, than in half the creeds." If we look at the lives of those we consider most faith-filled down through the ages, it would be difficult to conclude that doubt is destructive of faith and is something to be avoided. Rather, we would have to conclude that one of the marks of a strong faith is a struggle with doubt. Perhaps that struggle is essential to a strong mature faith in the same way the struggle of a butterfly emerging from a cocoon is essential to the strength of the new creature.

So, if doubt is a part of the wilderness experience, what do we do with our doubts? First of all, we should not suppress them. Authentic faith begins with intellectual honesty, and doubt is the foundation of honesty. Ask the questions and continue to search. Don't let your doubts stop up the channels to God. Let doubts open the channels in new ways with new insights and understandings. Pray to God, "Lord, I believe, help my unbelief."

Second, we should stay involved with other Christians. We could learn a lesson here from the disciple Thomas, who voiced his serious doubts and yet continued to remain in the company of the other disciples as he worked through those doubts. Group support and sharing is a powerful way we can share our burdens and find support for moving through the periods of doubt.

Third, we should continue to seek Christ and faith in Christ. The issue for us is never, therefore, one of avoiding our doubts as if that will cure us of them. Rather, it is continuing in honest relationship to God. The prophet Jeremiah, speaking for God, says, "When you search for me, you will find me" (Jeremiah 29:13). Jesus said, "Ask, and it will be given you; search, and you will find; knock, and the door will be opened for you" (Matthew 7:7). When we do these things, our periods of doubts and questions can lead us to faith.

In the early days of John Wesley's ministry, when he was experiencing a particularly difficult time of doubts and uncertainties, he went to his Moravian friend Peter Boehler and laid his soul bare. Boehler told Wesley: "Preach faith until you have it, and then because you have it you will preach faith." In other words, act as though you have already moved past doubt to faith; then, as you act in faith, faith will come. (Tim K. Bruster)

Worship Aids

Pastoral Prayer

Gracious, loving God, you know our hearts better than we know them ourselves. You know our certainties and our doubts. Help us see through the pain and uncertainty of doubt to renewed and strengthened faith on the other side of doubt. Enable the doubt within us to stir us up and spur us on to deeper faith. Through Christ our Lord, Amen.

Benediction

Go, carrying your doubts with you until the time comes when you can lay them down and walk with a lighter load. Go with the assurance that God walks with you and helps shoulder all your burdens. In the name of the Father, the Son, and the Holy Spirit, Amen.

Prayer of Confession

Gracious God, doubt can be so troubling to us. Forgive us when we have failed to understand another's doubt and given them a safe place to share it. Forgive us when we have failed to allow another person to work through their doubt and so grow stronger. Forgive us, God, when we have made doubt a destination and have become complacent in seeking your presence, your will, and your way for our lives. Lord, we believe. Help our unbelief. In the name of Jesus we ask this. Amen.

Words of Assurance

Hear the good news. Our mighty God is far more willing and able to forgive than we are to ask. When we turn to God, he hears our prayers and forgives us. This is God's amazing gift of grace. (Tim K. Bruster)

APRIL 2, 2006

Fifth Sunday in Lent

Readings: Jeremiah 31:31-34; Psalm 51:1-12; Hebrews 5:5-10; John 12:20-33

No Place to Lay His Head
Psalm 51:1-12

The words of David in this venerable psalm remind us of our human frailty: the sacrifice acceptable to God is a broken spirit, a broken and contrite heart. The psalm reminds us vividly of the teaching of Jesus.

For instance, in the exuberance of youth, a scribe comes to Jesus and throws in his lot with the disciples: "I will follow you wherever you go." Jesus' response is startling. No encouragement, no congratulations, no thanksgiving. Jesus rebukes the scribe by telling him how homeless the Christ is in this world: "the Son of Man has no place to lay his head" (Matthew 8:19-22 NIV).

These words, dripping with nature imagery, cast in Aramaic grammar ("birds of the air"), proverbially arranged, and centering as they do on Jesus' favorite self-reference, "the Son of Man," surely come from the lips of Jesus of Nazareth. What a marvel, a miracle really, to hear his voice some two thousand years later! Yet, we know that we today need not only to hear what Jesus said, but also to know what this means for our life together. The verse "simply" reminds us that Christ is not at home in this world.

Christ is not at home in the lives of institutions, when people must forsake honesty for loyalty. The displacement of honesty by loyalty is inevitable in institutions. It goes with the territory. Of course, we must do our part to support meaningful, healthy institutions. It takes skill to run an institution: a family, a school, a church, a corporation, a government. But Christ is not always at home in institutions. Even—how painful this is—the church, for which Christ gave his life, sometimes places loyalty over honesty. I remember the old saw about a grandfather with his grandson at an ordination. They sat in the back of the large sanctuary; the boy slept for much of the service, but perked up when the bishop began to lay hands on the candidate. As a hush fell, the boy whispered, "What are they doing with their hands on his head?" Grandpa crustily replied, "They're taking out his spine." Christ is not at home where loyalty displaces honesty.

Christ is not at home in a world that denigrates diplomacy. No wonder we serve such a sleepless Savior, nowhere to lay his head has he, when the great world around us makes such little space for the wisdom of the serpent and the innocence of the dove.

In the 1990s, everything was negotiable. In this decade, nothing is negotiable. Both denigrate diplomacy. Diplomacy is the art of balancing the one with the other.

In the 1990s, everything was provisional, up for sale or rent. The long shadow of the White House of Never-ending Negotiation both reflected and shaped our culture. A night in the Lincoln bedroom—negotiable. Daily routines and deadlines—negotiable. Land in Arkansas—negotiable. Fate of the welfare poor—negotiable. Use of the Oval Office—negotiable. Personal morality—negotiable. The definition of *is*, *good*, *sex*, and other timely terms—negotiable.

In our time, the opposite is true. Nothing is for sale, but nothing is flexible either. The long shadow of the White House of Never-employed Negotiation, itself a creation of our revulsion at its predecessor, both reflects and shapes our culture. The goodness of lowering taxes—nonnegotiable. The subservience of the environment—nonnegotiable. The invasion of Iraq—nonnegotiable. The daily timetable—nonnegotiable. The death penalty—nonnegotiable.

In Christ, as Paul says, all is yes. In Adam, as Paul says, all is no. For us, upon this earth, in the ongoing invasion of Adam by Christ, yes and no are bedfellows. This is what makes life so real and difficult. It takes great balance to run a marriage, a family, a business, a church, a government, a world. It takes diplomacy. That is the kind of innocent wisdom and wise innocence that makes for a saving diplomacy.

Christ is not at home in a world of collateral damage. The biblical opposition voiced, over many months, to preemptory, unilateral, imperialistic, unpredictable military action continues. Such thought is outside the bounds of inherited Christian just war ethics. It is unreasonable when compared to the alternative of ongoing containment and potential retaliation. We cannot calculate the consequences of first strike, nonmultilateral, imperial invasion by one country of another. Such action would be "Pearl Harbor in reverse."

It is the Sleepless Savior, the Roving Redeemer, the Homeless Christ of this single sentence in our Holy Scripture—the Son of Man who has no place to lay his head—whose presence and wandering you can rely on when you also are sleepless, roving, and homeless; when, at night, you sing Psalm 51.

When you are crushed in institution life between honesty and loyalty—just there, not later when things get better, but right there—you have the best of company, the Son of Man who has no place to lay his head.

When you worry about a world that turns a deaf ear to the poetry of diplomacy, as we do today—just here, not when all is well later, but right here in our concern—we have the best of company, the Son of Man who has no place to lay his head.

When you lift your voice in sober concern about the collateral damage of war—just here, not after the armistice, but right here—we have the best of company, Jesus Christ, who has no place to lay his head. (Robert Hill)

Wilderness Time: A Time of Comfort

Fifth in a Series of Six: Lent

Mark 1:9-15; 2 Corinthians 12:7b-10

The wilderness is a difficult and often frightening place; so what sustains us in the wilderness? How do we cope? From where does our strength come? We sometimes believe that pure optimism is the key to making it through the wilderness. And there's no question that optimism can be powerful, but is optimism enough?

Think of the remarkable optimist who fell off a skyscraper. As he passed the twelfth floor horrified onlookers heard him shout, "So far, so good!" Optimism is great, but is it enough?

Or think of the two hunters who heard about a bounty offered for the hides of wolves that were decimating the farmers' livestock. They headed out to the wide-open spaces to shoot some wolves and make themselves rich. They had just fallen asleep out under the stars when a noise woke one of them. In the reflection of the campfire he saw the eyes of twenty-five wolves—teeth gleaming. He shook his friend and whispered hoarsely, "Wake up! Wake up! We're rich!" Optimism is great, but is it enough?

No, the optimism of our falling friend by itself is no match for the gravitational pull of the earth; nor is the optimism of our hunted hunter by itself a match for the wild beasts of the wilderness. Something more is needed! It is that "something more" that we focus on in the fifth sermon in the series on wilderness time. Mark's Gospel says, "And he was with the wild beasts." But then Mark says there was something more in the wilderness: "And the angels waited on him."

Almost anyone can tell you what an angel looks like: halo around the head, wings sprouting from the back, long flowing robe, perhaps a harp in the hands. But the Bible doesn't seem concerned about such descriptions. Why? Perhaps it is because you don't experience angels like you experience ornaments. You don't see angels like you see Christmas tree decorations. In nearly every instance, the Bible mentions angels simply for what they do, and not for what they look like. The Hebrew *malach* and the Greek *angelos* both mean "messenger." Angels are messengers of hope when God's message of hope is most needed. They are expressions of the inexpressible—the way we talk about God being present and bringing hope. Think of the role of angels in the Bible. They usually appear at the low points in the lives of those who receive their messages. They deliver their messages in the wilderness times: Abraham and Sarah unknowingly entertained three angels who gave them the message of hope that they would have a son (Genesis 18:1-15). Jacob wrestled all night with an angel as he struggled with God and with himself about his life and the fear he had of facing his estranged twin brother Esau (Genesis 33:24-30). An angel brought hope and strength to Elijah when he sat down under a broom tree just wanting God to take his life (1 Kings 19:5). An angel met the grieving women at Jesus' tomb and proclaimed the great message of hope: "He is not here; he has risen, just as he said" (Matthew 28:6 NIV).

These were terribly low times in these individuals' lives. These were times when God seemed far away and when the next moment seemed uncertain. They were times when both their need and their weakness to do anything about that need were very apparent. It was precisely in that moment of need and weakness that the messengers of God delivered their messages.

This is the good news that Paul discovered and recounted in the Epistle reading. Paul was tormented by some excruciating malady he called a "thorn in the flesh." When he prayed repeatedly for his awful "thorn in the flesh" to be removed, he received this answer from the Lord: "My grace is sufficient for you, for power is made perfect in weakness" (2 Corinthians 12:9). In our times of need and weakness, God's message of hope and comfort is spoken—most often in a language too deep for words and too profound to voice. In the times of greatest need, God's message of hope comes through when the soul is open to receive it, and sometimes even when the soul is not open. That is the good news of comfort in the wilderness. We are not alone in the wilderness. We have available to us God's sustenance and strength and we can leave the wilderness stronger people through God's working in our lives.

In the wilderness we are comforted not by mere optimism, but by hope—the hope that comes from knowing we are not alone; the hope that comes from knowing that the wilderness is not all there is; and the hope that comes from knowing that when our strength has gone God's strength is sufficient. Emily Dickinson, struggling to express the inexpressible, wrote, "Hope is the thing with feathers / that perches in the soul." Hope is not a thing that flies serenely above the storms, untouched by the demands and challenges we face. Rather, the power of hope lies in its presence in our everyday lives—it "perches in the soul." Hope stays within us singing its song in the bleakest wilderness.

There is also something else. If angels are simply messengers, can it be that most of the angels we meet are fellow human beings? Think of your darkest wilderness experiences. Were there people who were God's messengers of hope for you? That is one of the most beautiful ministries that God gives any of us—to become a ministering angel to help a brother or sister in the wilderness experience the comforting presence of God. Even in the worst wilderness imaginable, God calls us to be persons through whom the light and life and love of God flow into a wilderness world. John Henry Jowett said, "God does not comfort us to make us comfortable, but to make us comforters." (Tim K. Bruster)

Worship Aids

Psalter (Psalm 63:1-8)

Leader: O God, you are my God, I seek you, my soul thirsts for you; my flesh faints for you, as in a dry and weary land where there is no water.

People: So I have looked upon you in the sanctuary, beholding your power and glory.

Leader: Because your steadfast love is better than life, my lips will praise you.

People: So I will bless you as long as I live; I will lift up my hands and call on your name.

Leader: My soul is satisfied as with a rich feast, and my mouth praises you with joyful lips when I think of you on my bed, and meditate on you in the watches of the night;

People: for you have been my help, and in the shadow of your wings I sing for joy. My soul clings to you; your right hand upholds me.

Pastoral Prayer

Gracious and loving God, there are those who are dwelling in a dry, desolate, and lonely wilderness. As they struggle in the wilderness, help them know that they do not struggle alone. Help them know your presence and find comfort and strength to endure. And help us, O God, remember that you call us to be present in another's wilderness as those called to minister in Jesus' name. Amen.

Benediction

Go in peace, knowing that God comforts us and strengthens us for the wilderness times. And, having been comforted by God, go to comfort others in their wilderness times. In the name of the Father, the Son, and the Holy Spirit, Amen. (Tim K. Bruster)

APRIL 9, 2006

❧❧❧

Palm Sunday

Readings: Liturgy of the Palms: Mark 11:1-11; Psalm 118:1-2, 19-29

East to North
Mark 11:1-11

In the Diné way (Navajo), each day begins by facing east to greet the sun. Thanks is given for a new day, a new beginning. The direction of east is also symbolic for childhood, infancy. One is on the brink of a whole new life, a new day, a new adventure, or a new stage of life. Jesus is facing east—he is on the brink of a new period of his life, he is going to do things differently.

The people need Jesus. In the past, the crowds pressed in on him, they followed him, and chased after him. They laid in wait for him. Of course, the people who wanted to see him were the sick, the lame, the blind, and the possessed. Jesus, full of compassion, healed them and taught them. In Mark's healing stories, Jesus ordered the now whole people, the healed, not to say anything about him or what he has done. Jesus wanted absolutely no attention. Now, for the first time, Jesus prepares to meet the people in a more conspicuous manner.

It is a new way of doing things. Jesus even sends his disciples into the city before him to prepare for his visit. Before, he would try and come into a town quietly, drawing as little attention to himself as possible. Walking was the primary mode of travel. At this new stage of his life, he rides into town on a colt. Jesus has a procession, complete with fanfare and the ever present crowd. This time, he does not dodge the crowd; he enters into their midst. People are going before Jesus and following after him, shouting, "Hosanna!" What a change!

Jesus knows this is a new time in his life. It is the beginning of the end. In just a few days, he will be hanging on a cross. With new fortitude and determination, Jesus steps out. One can almost hear Jesus talking to himself, "I can do this. I will do this."

We reenact this scene in many ways in our own lives. We may not have a procession and be treated as royalty, but we face situations that demand fortitude and determination, an inner strength we did not really know we possessed. When we hear the word *cancer*, or find ourselves alone after the death of a spouse or loved one, we wonder how we will ever make it. Yet, at some point following these events, we make a choice and say to ourselves, "I can do this. I will do this."

Jesus rode into Jerusalem on the back of a colt that had never been ridden before. This was new for Jesus and the colt. As our population becomes more and more centered in the urban areas, much of the biblical example falls on deaf ears. Many of us, as city dwellers, do not know about unbroken colts—colts not "broken" to the saddle. Generally, horses and donkeys do not like people, or any kind of weight, on their backs. Their first reaction is to get rid of the burden on their backs. They kick. They buck. They bite. Rodeos still feature an event called bronco riding; people pay to watch a cowboy try and stay on an unbroken horse for eight seconds!

Horses spook very easily. They dislike things, like cloaks, flapping around them. Horses need to learn how to be led, to know the signals to turn left and right. Even in the present day, those horses that pull the wagons around Central Park have to learn not to be spooked by the painted lines on the street. This is a miracle! Jesus climbs on an unbroken colt—with cloaks flapping, crowds of people jostling and shouting, others throwing down cloaks and palm branches into his path—and rides into town.

Animals do have the ability to read humans. If a horse or dog senses that a person is nervous around them, they become nervous and jumpy. The colt, and the crowds, interpreted Jesus' determination and fortitude as confidence. I believe our lesson is, when faced with situations we do not like or want, to make the decision to do what is right and carry through with determination and fortitude. Too often, we play the "what if" game. What if the colt starts to buck or tries to run away because of the noise or the crowd? What if I fall off this beast? What if . . . ? Perhaps the better questions to ask are, "What if I don't do what is right? What if I allow my personal preferences, my comfort, influence my actions?"

This is the first time in Mark that Jesus foresees the future. He tells his disciples, "Go into the town and upon entering it, you will find a colt tied there." Even if he had the ability to do this before, this is the first time Jesus uses this gift. Scripture doesn't mention that his disciples questioned him, "How do you know?" Perhaps they know Jesus only speaks the truth, so if he says it, it must be true. Not only are we becoming more urban, we are becoming more cynical and sarcastic. We question everything and demand explanations. Faith is the opposite. "Now faith is the assurance of things hoped for, the conviction of things not seen" (Hebrews 11:1). Oh, that we would have that kind of faith!

This is a Sunday of great joy and hope as Jesus enters Jerusalem with his procession. We know what is before him—the crucifixion, and death before Easter. Our faith will be tested as we travel to Good Friday. As the Diné follow the direction of the sun, Good Friday will be north, the beginning of darkness, the twilight of our time on earth. As we move through this week, east to north, may your life be filled with determination, fortitude, and faith. Amen. (Raquel Mull)

Wilderness Time: A Time of New Beginnings

Sixth in a Series of Six: Lent

Mark 1:9-15; 2 Corinthians 5:14-19

In our last sermon in this series, we celebrate that the wilderness is a time of new beginnings. Another way to think of it is that wilderness times are temporary. I remember a retired pastor in a church I served telling me that one of his favorite phrases in scripture is found more than four hundred fifty times in the King James Version of the Bible: "It came to pass." That can be very good news, if you're contemplating wilderness time. Wilderness times come. But, they don't stay. They are not permanent. They pass. Wilderness time always comes to an end and is always followed by a new beginning.

According to Dante, written over the gates of hell are the words, "All hope abandon, ye who enter here!" Sometimes we imagine that those words are written over the gate to the wilderness and we are tempted to abandon hope. The good news of our Christian faith, however, is that the wilderness is never the final destination and hope is alive even in that desolate territory.

Wilderness times generally mark the end of one phase and the beginning of a new phase of our lives. Jesus' difficult and lonely time of testing in the Judean wilderness gave way to a new beginning—the beginning of his public ministry. It prepared him and strengthened him for it in a way that perhaps nothing else could.

New beginnings stand at the heart of the gospel message. No matter who we are or what we've done, no matter if the wilderness is of our own

95

making, God is present in the wilderness with us and can lead us through it and out of it. When we find ourselves in the wilderness of sin, guilt, and separation from God and from others, there is a way out of the wilderness and a new beginning. God provides that way in Christ.

The apostle Paul was an expert in new beginnings. He knew well the spiritual territory we call "the wilderness" because he spent a great deal of time there! Paul also knew the power of being made new and set free from the wilderness of a broken relationship with God and with others. Paul wrote, "So if anyone is in Christ, there is a new creation: everything old has passed away; see, everything has become new! All this is from God, who reconciled us to himself through Christ, and has given us the ministry of reconciliation; that is, in Christ God was reconciling the world to himself, not counting their trespasses against them, and entrusting the message of reconciliation to us" (2 Corinthians 5:17-19).

The good news of Christ is that no matter who you are or what you have done, there is always held out to you the chance for a new beginning. In Christ, we are new creations: "Everything old has passed away; see, everything has become new!"

Jesus told the story of a man who had two sons. One day the younger of the two went to his father and, in so many words, said, "I wish you were dead." He asked for his inheritance—not at all appropriate, since his father was very much alive! The father gave his younger son his share of the inheritance and the son ran away to a distant country, where he squandered it all. All that money his father had worked hard to earn and set aside for his son was just thrown away satisfying the son's every whim and desire and trying to buy friends. It was awful!

It didn't take him long to blow his inheritance and he found himself homeless and hungry. This young boy found himself doing the unthinkable. He wound up feeding pigs and was so hungry he even wanted to eat the pig slop. He was in the wilderness! When he came to his senses, he said, "How many of my father's hired men have food to spare, and here I am starving to death!" (Luke 15:17 NIV). So he decided to go home and beg his father for forgiveness. As he was approaching the familiar place that once had been his home, his father saw him. His father was so overjoyed and excited that he ran to his son, threw his arms around him, and kissed him.

Jesus taught us that God is like that loving father. If you're in the wilderness, feeling separated from God—and perhaps you even ran into that wilderness yourself—it may be difficult to believe, but God is like that father and will run to meet you and welcome you home with open arms, ready to give you a new beginning.

Ultimately, the wilderness never has the last word!

But, what about the greatest wilderness? What about death? The good news of our faith is that even the wilderness of death comes to pass. In Christ, Paul observed, "Death has been swallowed up in victory" (1 Corinthians 15:54). The good news of our faith is that even out of the wilderness of suffering and death, and even out of the wilderness of the death of someone we love, there is a new beginning. Death is swallowed up in victory through Jesus Christ. Death never has the final word.

I know a couple who lost their daughter in a tragic car accident. Out of that experience, they founded an organization to help parents who are grieving the loss of a child. Out of that terrible wilderness came a new beginning for that family and for many other families suffering the pain of losing a child in death.

The good news of our faith is that the wilderness never has the last word. When Jesus was on the cross, he was in the darkest wilderness of his life. Jesus was nailed to that cross to die as a criminal by that cruel Roman means of execution. As Jesus hung there, the life draining from him, he experienced the rejection, the anguish, and the loneliness of the darkest wilderness. Jesus cried out, quoting Psalm 22, "My God, my God, why have you forsaken me?" But, we know that the cross was not the end. We, who will walk the wilderness way with Christ through this Holy Week of services, know what we celebrate next Sunday. We know that death will never have the final word. We know that the wilderness "comes to pass." (Tim K. Bruster)

Worship Aids

Pastoral Prayer

God of new beginnings, help us hear the good news that in Christ the old has passed away and the new has come. Help us know that even the darkest wilderness gives way to light and life. We thank you that even when the wilderness is of our own making and we have purposely turned away from you, you await our return as a loving father awaits the return of a lost child. We pray through Christ our Lord. Amen.

Confession (from Psalm 51)

Leader: Have mercy on me, O God, according to your steadfast love; according to your abundant mercy blot out my transgressions.

People: Wash me thoroughly from my iniquity, and cleanse me from my sin.

Leader: For I know my transgressions, and my sin is ever before me.

People: Against you, you alone, have I sinned, and done what is evil in your sight.

Leader: You desire truth in the inward being; therefore teach me wisdom in my secret heart.

People: Wash me, O Lord, and make me clean.

Leader: Hide your face from my sins, and blot out all my iniquities.

People: Create in me a clean heart, O God, and put a new and right spirit within me.

Words of Assurance (from Psalm 103)

Hear the good news: Our gracious God forgives all your iniquity and crowns you with steadfast love and mercy; God is merciful and gracious, slow to anger and abounding in steadfast love; God does not deal with us according to our sins, or repay us according to our iniquities. For as the heavens are high above the earth, so great is the steadfast love of God; as far as the east is from the west, so far God removes our transgressions from us. Thanks be to God! Amen. (Tim K. Bruster)

APRIL 13, 2006

Holy Thursday

Readings: Exodus 12:1-4 (5-10), 11-14; Psalm 116:1-4, 12-19; 1 Corinthians 11:23-26; John 13:1-17, 31*b*-35

Peter the Denier
Exodus 12:1-4 (5-10), 11-14; John 13:1-17, 31*b*-35

The room was dark, giving it a gloomy feeling. We were gathered for a meal on the eve of Passover. Because the Lord was quietly pensive, we ate in silence. During supper, he stood, removed his robe and tied a towel around his waist like a servant. He poured water into a clay basin and began to wash the feet of each of us, drying them with the towel. "This is slave's work," I thought. I couldn't imagine the Lord, the One we believed to be the Messiah, doing the work of a common slave.

When he knelt at my feet, I asked, "Lord, are you going to wash my feet, too?"

He said, "You do not know now what I am doing, but later you will understand."

I said firmly, "You will never wash my feet."

The Lord's tone matched mine: "Unless I wash you, you will have no future with me."

"Then wash not only my feet, but my whole body," I said.

After washing my feet, the Lord said, "Not all of you are clean." I was perplexed by this.

He continued teaching, as he often did after performing a sign, "If I, your Lord and Master, wash your feet, you also ought to wash one another's feet. I have done this as an example for you."

At the time I thought, "How strange to tell us to wash one another's feet." Later I realized that he was not talking about foot washing, but about love. We were to follow his example and lovingly serve one another. As with everything the Lord did, foot washing pointed to a deeper truth.

After the foot washing we gathered around the table for supper. The Lord's face darkened with an expression I had never seen. He looked deeply distressed, as if in pain.

"I tell you truly, one of you will betray me," he said. I glanced at Andrew whose expression was a mixture of horror and sadness. "Who could he mean?" I thought. I turned to John, who was sitting next to Jesus, and whispered, "Ask him who he means."

John asked and the Lord said, "The one to whom I'm giving this piece of bread dipped in the dish." He handed the bread to Judas and said, "Do quickly what you must."

We thought Judas was simply leaving to buy more food. He was the treasurer and often left a meal early to buy food for the next day.

With Judas gone in the darkness of night, the Lord continued teaching, "Children, I am with you only a little longer. You will look for me, but where I am going, you cannot come."

Immediately I asked, "Lord, where are you going?"

He said, "You cannot follow me now where I am going, but you will follow afterward."

I was confused and afraid as I said, "Lord why can't I follow you now? I would lay down my life for you."

Shaking his head slowly from side to side, he answered, "Will you lay down your life for me? In truth, before the cock crows, you will have denied me three times."

The mystery of where Judas went was soon solved. After supper, we went with the Lord across the Kidron valley to a garden where he liked to pray. While we were praying, Judas emerged from the shadows leading a group made up of Roman soldiers, chief priests' guards, and some Pharisees.

The Lord turned and asked, "Whom are you looking for?"

They replied, "Jesus of Nazareth."

When the Lord said, "I am he," they stepped back and fell to the ground. He asked them a second time whom were they seeking. Their answer was the same. "You have found me. Now, let these men go," he said.

I couldn't allow the Lord to be arrested without a fight. I drew a sword from under my cloak and slashed at the man who was about to seize the Lord, cutting off his ear. The Lord rebuked me saying, "Put your sword away. Would you prevent me from drinking the cup the Father has given me?" Stung by these words, I stood frozen in place while they bound him. John violently jerked my arm and we ran for our lives.

We fled in terror and confusion, having no idea where the others went. When we realized the soldiers hadn't pursued us, we retraced our steps and followed the Lord and his arresters. They took him into Jerusalem to Annas, who shared the office of high priest with his father-in-law, Caiaphas.

John was admitted into the courtyard, since he was known to Annas. I remained outside the gate, crouching in the shadows, afraid of being recognized as a follower of Jesus. A short time later John came out and called, "Peter, where are you?" I emerged from hiding and followed.

As we passed a woman standing by the gate, she said, "Aren't you also one of Jesus' disciples?" I disagreed firmly saying, "I am not."

I disappeared into the crowd gathered in the courtyard, joining those huddled around a large fire in the cold dawn. I listened for news of what was happening to the Lord. Someone said that Annas was questioning him.

While warming myself by the fire, one of the temple police who had been at the arrest looked at me intently. I turned my face away. He said, "Aren't you also one of his disciples?" I answered, "I am not."

As I worked my way to the edge of the crowd, one of the slaves of the high priest who was also at the Lord's arrest said, "Didn't I see you in the garden with him?" I denied it vehemently by saying, "I was never there." No sooner had the words escaped, a cock crowed.

What have I done? I thought. *How could I deny my Lord? How could the words of betrayal have been spoken by my lips?* I didn't believe I was capable of such a cowardly act. But, in the end, *I denied him.*

I was devastated by the cowardice of my denials. I, who had sworn allegiance to the death, had crumbled in fear. The "rock" had been crushed; terror had triumphed over loyalty.

The Lord was crucified that same day. I didn't watch ... I couldn't watch. I was no longer Peter the Rock. In shame, I confessed my new name: Peter the Denier. (Robert Martin Walker)

Jesus Prepares the Disciples for His Death and Absence
John 13:1-17, 31*b*-35

We come now to John's account of the beginning of the end of Jesus' earthly life. This is the beginning of his passion. John establishes the mood of Jesus, which will permeate everything that happens for the next twenty hours (John 12–19:30). "Jesus knew that his hour had come to depart from this world and go to the Father" (John 13:1). He stayed focused and comforted in this knowledge until, on the cross, he said: "It is finished." And "then he bowed his head and gave up his spirit" (John 19:30b).

He wanted this final private session with the disciples. "He said to them, 'I have eagerly desired to eat this Passover with you before I suffer'" (Luke 22:14b). The public proclamation and the debates are over, and Jesus devotes himself to "his own in this world" because, unbeknownst to them, they are about to face the most shattering experience of their lives. He wants to prepare them for what is about to happen, as much as anyone can be prepared for such a terrible ordeal.

Time is of the essence. He has already said many things to them, much of which they have not understood. He said: "I still have many things to say to you, but you cannot bear them now" (John 16:12). He has spoken to them concerning his death, but they did not hear him because they did not want to hear that kind of news. It did not fit into their vision of what should be happening. It did not fit the messianic dream in which their minds had been marinated. After all he had said and done, after all they had hoped and dreamed, they could not face the possibility that death would be the final outcome. The idea of his absence from their world was completely unacceptable. Somehow Jesus had to help them face the stark reality of his death and give them something to hang on to until his resurrection.

There were problems that Jesus had to deal with in addition to time and apostolic imperviousness and denial. There was the attitude the disciples brought to the meeting. Luke gives us some insight into the reason for the mood of the disciples to which John does not refer. On the way to the meeting a dispute had arisen among the twelve as to which one of them was to be regarded as the greatest (Luke 22:24). This was probably continued contention resulting from an earlier occasion in which James and John had asked Jesus to give them places of eminence on his right and the other on his left (Mark 10:35-45). When the other disciples heard this they were indignant. It appears by the time of the Last Supper with Jesus the cancer of lust for power and prominence had spread to them all.

Like pouting children they arrived at the upper room with ill feelings and festering jealousy. They did not notice the basin, pitcher, and towel positioned there. It was customary that when people came as guests for dinner a servant (or slave) would wash the dirt and dust from the feet of the guests. Since they had no servant or slave to wait on them, it is likely their practice was to take turns at foot-washing duty. But not on this night. They had unsettled issues with one another. They went stubbornly to their appointed places at the table, not one of them willing to compromise his dignity by doing a menial task, which, in their collective misunderstanding, might lessen their chances of preference and prominence in this kingdom that was to come.

They began the meal with travel-stained feet because no one was willing to back down. Sensing the climate of anger and childishness, Jesus knew that he would not be able to accomplish what he had hoped with them unless he could empty the atmosphere of the palpable ill spirit of the twelve. Words would not work. He had to do something dramatic to get their attention. So, "During supper" (not "supper being ended," as rendered in the King James Version), "Jesus . . . got up from the table, took off his outer robe, and tied a towel around himself. Then he poured water into a basin and began to wash the disciples' feet and to wipe them with the towel that was tied around him" (John 13:3-5).

The disciples must have watched what Jesus was doing with a growing uneasiness. How embarrassed they must have been, but no one said anything until Jesus knelt down to wash the feet of Peter. The impulsive Peter asked in shock: "Lord, are you going to wash my feet?" Jesus answered: "You do not know now what I am doing, but later you will understand." Peter said: "You will never wash my feet." Jesus said, "Unless I wash you, you have no share with me." Peter said, "Lord, not my feet only but also my hands and head" (John 13:6-9). The wordless lesson got to all of them: he who is greatest among you must be servant of all.

One other pressing problem must be resolved before Jesus can get on with preparing them. Judas was sitting there. The implication in John (unlike the Synoptic) is that the deal with the devil had not been finalized, but that there had been preliminary negotiations. Jesus announced to them that one of the twelve would betray him, and the disciples began to question Jesus about who this might be. Jesus was troubled in spirit about this, which reads, angry at the betrayer. In answer to their question, Jesus said the betrayer is the one to whom he will give the bread he has dipped in the dish. He dipped the bread and offered it to Judas. Jesus said to Judas: "Do quickly what you are going to do" (John 13:27). The scene ends with Judas leaving. John's closing sentence in the scene is worthy of a sermon by itself. "And it was night" (John 13:30b).

The *New English Bible* characterizes the five chapters of John, chapters thirteen through seventeen, as "farewell discourses." Facing the death and absence of someone we love is painful beyond description. In a very short time life for the disciples was going to collapse into chaos. Darkness would come at midday and all would seem lost. It was against this that Jesus began to prepare his little company. There comes a time for all of us in which life cracks open at the seams—everything upon which we have counted falls to pieces. Few people get past mid-life without having their world crumble at their feet. This was what was about to happen to the disciples, and Jesus was giving them something to hang on to until the storm was over. How beautifully and with what great sensitivity Jesus comforts and prepares the twelve in these farewell discourses. Knowing Christians turn to this place in the Bible any time they face the death and absence of loved ones.

In the course of his discourse to the disciples Jesus offered a novel idea with which they had difficulty—and so do we. He said: "It is to your advantage that I go away, for if I do not go away, the Advocate (Holy Spirit) will not come to you; but if I go, I will send him to you" (John 16:7). How could this be? How could they (or we) be better for his leaving, especially in the manner in which he left? They were to understand later, but at the moment it left question marks hanging like fishhooks at their throats. Jesus was essentially saying, "This new power that has been arranged for you is waiting in the wings, and he will not come here until I get there." They would not understand until later.

Jesus was leaving because he had finished his work. The Bible teaches that he was born in "the fullness of time"—at the right time. Now he will leave in "the fullness of time"—at the right time. It was time for another level of development to take place. He must go and they would understand later.

I have a sign in my office that says: "When the pupil is ready the teacher will come." There is a paradoxical reverse to this saying: "When the pupil is ready the teacher will go." Students do not become teachers and disciples do not become leaders until the master is gone. Once one of the disciples marveled at what Jesus was doing and Jesus remarked: "These things you can do and greater things also when I go to the Father."

Jesus said that it was to their advantage that he was going away. "When I am gone I will be with you more substantially than when I was here. Turn me loose. Let me go." (Thomas Lane Butts)

Worship Aids

The Call to Worship

In the evening of the day before he died, Jesus acted out a profound example of humility and servanthood. When the disciples were too proud to wash one another's feet, Jesus "got up from the table, took off his outer robe, and tied a towel around himself. Then he poured water into a basin and began to wash the disciples' feet and to wipe them with the towel that was tied around him" (John 13:4-5). He who is the greatest among you must be the servant of all. How are you doing with that? (Thomas Lane Butts)

The Prayer of Confession

We confess, O Lord, that, like the disciples of old, we have let pride of place and lust for power slip in the back door of our lives and spoil our devotion to Jesus who was a servant-savior. Worse still, we have hidden these vices in euphemistic cloaks to make them appear good and welcomed them in the front door of our lives. Save us, O Lord, from these and all other sins of self that evade our commitment to the man who could have had it all, but who chose to be a servant instead—Jesus Christ, in whose name we pray. Amen. (Thomas Lane Butts)

The Benediction

Dear Jesus, in whose life I see
all that I would, but fail to be,
let thy clear light forever shine,
to shame and guide this life of mine.
("Dear Jesus, in Whose Life I See," *The United Methodist Hymnal* [Nashville: The United Methodist Publishing House, 1989], 468)

I bless you in the name of the Lord, Jesus Christ. Go now in peace and be not anxious or afraid. Amen. (Thomas Lane Butts)

APRIL 14, 2006

❧❧❧❧

Good Friday

Readings: Isaiah 52:13–53:12; Psalm 22; Hebrews 10:16-25; John 18:1–19:42

Joseph of Arimathea
Isaiah 52:13–53:12; John 18:1–19:42

As a member of the Sanhedrin, I had participated in audiences with the procurator of Judea several times.

This time was different.

This time, I wasn't approaching Pilate as a representative of the powerful ruling council. I was going as Joseph, a citizen of Jerusalem.

Walking up the polished marble steps of the procurator's palace, I reflected on how my friendship with Nicodemus led me here. I met Nicodemus after I was appointed to the Sanhedrin.

Nicodemus was a famous Rabbi. We soon became close friends, united by a deep devotion to the principles of Torah.

Early one morning a year ago, Nicodemus met me wearing a serious expression.

"Last night I met the Rabbi called Jesus," he said.

My face must have betrayed shock. To speak with Jesus without permission from the Sanhedrin was forbidden.

"Don't worry, Joseph. We met at night. Nobody saw us. The conversation was brief, but confusing. He spoke in riddles and I revealed my ignorance. But I will tell you this: he is a man sent from God."

"Do you realize what you are saying?" I said, worried for my friend. "You could be cast off the council, or worse, for speaking such blasphemy!"

He eventually became convinced that Jesus was the Son of God, the Messiah!

At first, I couldn't accept Nicodemus's radical change of heart. I was angry with him and tried to dissuade him from his belief in Jesus. Instead, over time, by listening to my friend's accounts of Jesus' teachings and works, I, too, became a believer.

By the time I joined Nicodemus as a secret believer, it was too late to save Jesus. Caiaphas, the high priest, had convinced the Sanhedrin that Jesus must be stopped. It was only a matter of time before Jesus was captured, tried, and executed.

Jesus died on a cross as the Passover lambs were being slaughtered. Nicodemus and I sat together in silence while he was crucified.

I realized what I had to do. So I went to the procurator's palace.

My legs were trembling when I reached the doors to the audience chamber. I could see Pilate on the far side of the room, perched on his throne, animatedly gesturing to one of the army of advisers who surrounded him.

After being announced, I walked toward Pilate as if approaching my own crucifixion. I knelt in front of the throne where Jesus had stood only hours before.

"I have come to beg a favor of the procurator, which I pray he will be gracious enough to grant. I would humbly ask His Highness to release the body of the man called Jesus of Nazareth to me for burial. He was crucified today."

Pilate grimaced. "I remember him well. Why should I give you his body? We usually leave the bodies for the dogs and birds."

"If it might please the procurator, our law says that one who is executed must be buried the same day. Also, if His Highness will indulge me one moment more, this is the Day of Preparation. Our Feast of the Unleavened Bread begins at sundown. If the body is not buried before daylight ends, our law prohibits burial until ..."

"Don't instruct me about your silly customs!" Pilate thundered. "I will grant your request, not because of your law, but because an innocent man deserves a decent burial."

"Thank you, Procurator. You are most generous. Thank you."

A centurion led me out of the palace and up the hill called Golgotha, the Place of the Skull. The bodies of the crucified lay crumpled in grotesque positions at the foot of the crosses on which they had died. Agonized souls, not yet dead, breathed in gasps.

I was led to a cluster of three crosses. Two men, more dead than alive, hung on the outside crosses. The middle cross was empty. An inscription in three languages nailed to it read: "Jesus of Nazareth, King of the Jews."

The centurion looked up at the two men panting for air, "They'll soon be joining this one," he said pointing to a body lying nearby. "I think this is the one you wanted."

I had only seen Jesus once, from a distance, and the bearded face was unrecognizable to me.

"Is this one Jesus?" I asked a weeping woman standing a few feet away. She looked at me, nodded, and returned to her grieving.

I hoisted the body onto my shoulder (it felt surprisingly light) and started the march to the garden where Nicodemus was to meet me. The tomb, which I had purchased several months ago as a family burial place, had been completed only a few days before.

As I gently laid the body outside the tomb's opening, Nicodemus emerged from the shadows.

"Is it really him?" I asked.

Nicodemus gazed at the body for several moments. Tears were streaming down his face when he finally said, "Yes, it is the Lord."

"We must work quickly," I said, because the sun was low on the horizon.

Nicodemus walked over to where he had been standing and began dragging a huge sack towards me. I went to help him.

"This weighs at least a hundred pounds. You must have spent a fortune on these spices!" I said.

"Nothing is too extravagant for the Lord's burial," he said.

Silently, we anointed Jesus' body with the lavish amount of spices and wrapped it in the linen cloths Nicodemus had brought. Our tears mixed with the myrrh and aloes as we lovingly prepared Jesus for burial.

When we finished, we carried him into the inner chamber of the tomb and laid a pure, white cloth over his head. Nicodemus rested his hand on Jesus' head for a brief time and closed his eyes in prayer.

Just as the sun was setting, we sealed the tomb by rolling the large, circular stone into the groove hewn for that purpose. It fit perfectly. Nothing will get in here, I thought.

Nicodemus and I walked into the soft light of evening, our arms around each other's shoulders, comforting each other in our loss. It was finished. (Robert Martin Walker)

Good Friday
John 18:1–19:42

What a day! Who in the world gave it the name "Good Friday"? Reading even the most sketchy and benign accounts of that day is enough to make even the strong shudder. No one there that day, including the

Romans who did the deed, would ever have agreed to call it "Good Friday." It was a terrible day by any standard of consideration.

Even dumb nature cried out against it. "When it was noon, darkness came over the whole land until three in the afternoon" (Mark 15:33). The stars hid their faces in shame and the sun refused to shine. The earth rebelled. There was an earthquake. Rocks split and graves opened and "the curtain of the temple was torn in two, from top to bottom" (Matthew 27:50-52). Good Friday? Nobody there that day thought so! It was a day of human infamy, when the very Son of God, who came in gentle love, was hurled back into the face of the Father who sent him. That day represents humanity at its worst, but God at God's best. Good Friday? There certainly did not appear to be anything good about it! Whatever good there may have been was not to be understood on that day—only later.

No one present that day would have ever dreamed—not in his or her wildest imagination—the significance that day would hold for all the world. No single day in the history of humankind has touched so many for so long. Its importance to Christians is equaled only by the resurrection three days later. In truth, one can hardly see how those two days can be separated. They are two events of one fabric. They are indivisible with a symbiotic relationship of meaning. Either day would be stripped of its meaning without the other.

It was just another day to many who were there. Pilate was anxious and hesitant because it was a political "hot potato" and he had used up his political capital with Rome. He was superstitious about the matter, but he otherwise had no personal investment in the outcome. It certainly was not the first time he had uttered those fateful words to a condemned man: "Ibis ad Crucem" ("You will go to the cross"), and it probably was not the last.

It was just another day for the Roman soldiers who happened to draw the duty of whipping and then crucifying a prisoner. They had done it before. They were obviously bored with the tedium of it all. They amused themselves by making sport of Jesus. They taunted him, placed an old purple cloak on him, and put a crown of thorns on his head. It was amusement to them. Only one of the execution squad sensed there was something special going on here. When the centurion who stood facing him saw how he died, he said: "Truly this man was God's Son!" But for all the other soldiers it was just "another day at the office." They had been there before. They would be there again.

It was just another day for the curious bystanders who came to gawk in some perverted amusement at the suffering and dying of the condemned. It was not their first time. It would not be their last.

It was important to the religious establishment that the problem of another disturber of "their peace" be silenced. To them Jesus was just another false messiah who was making trouble for them by getting the Romans upset. And he was disturbing their temple business of money-changing and selling sacrificial animals. There had been others. He had to go. Really, just another day.

It was not just another day to the family and followers of Jesus. It was the most terrible day of their lives. Not only did they lose a dear and special friend, their faith and hope was lost also. It was just another horrible day, like other horrible days, except many times worse. It certainly was not a "Good" day! They were much too grieved and upset to remember that he had said to them earlier that it was "good" that he was leaving— to their advantage even. He promised that he would be more substantially with them in his absence than when he was there. They did not understand this when he said it, and if it crossed their troubled minds on that Friday, it was no comfort.

It was three days before the significance of that Friday began to dawn on the followers and family of Jesus. It was not long before the Romans and the Jewish religious establishment began to sense there was more going on that Friday than "just another day." Unbeknownst to them, they had played into the hand and plan of the great God Almighty in a way they could never have dreamed. None of those who were instrumental in putting Jesus on the cross had any idea of what they were really doing. Jesus was speaking a word of fact as well as a word of forgiveness when from the cross he prayed: "Father, forgive them; for they do not know what they are doing." They did not know!

Soon the whole world would know. Soon the message of Jesus would spread like wildfire across the civilized world. Soon the day that his enemies thought was just another day, and his followers thought the most awful day imaginable, would take on a significance that would justify the title of "Good Friday." For two thousand years the significance of that day has continued to grow. Banks close. The stock exchanges close. Thousands of books have been written about it. Movies have been made and television specials run to tell again the story of that day. Special services are held in churches and people who otherwise do not tend to be religious take off their hats and bow their heads and remember.

Those of us who know how the story ends tend to forget that those who were there did not and could not have known. God is always doing things in our world and in our lives that we do not understand, the significance of which will dawn on us later. None of us are ever far from painful events, which we do not understand. There are things that happen that seem to us like the end of the world, but we later see how they blessed us and saved us in a manner we could not see at the time. Suffering in our lives has the potential of either crushing us or refining us. And, we do have some modicum of choice when our world turns dark at midday as to its ultimate effect on us. When we go into the tumbler, we have some choice about whether we come out crushed or polished. The God who turned the most awful day in history into Good Friday is still at work in our world and in our lives.

Today, as we walk the *via dolorosa* with Jesus and weep at the cross, we are kept from despair in the sure knowledge that there is an ending we do not see. When faith in the power and wisdom of God is the theme and mood of our lives, we can live with the pain of the moment.

Several years ago I listened in rapt attention to Dr. Tony Campolo describe a sermon preached by his pastor on Good Friday titled: "It Is Friday, but Sunday's Coming!" The disciples are lost in pain and shame. Mary is crying. The crowd is jeering: "He saved others, now let him save himself." The Jews are strutting and laughing. The Roman soldiers are shooting dice for his garments. Jesus is dying. What they do not know is that it is just Friday. Just Friday! But, Sunday is coming! Do you understand that? (Thomas Lane Butts)

A note: The thoughtful preacher will read himself or herself full of the excellent material on this subject available in good commentaries such as William Barclay's *The Gospel of John*, vol. 2 (Philadelphia: Westminster Press, 1975), part of the *Daily Study Bible* series, and the *Interpreter's Bible* and/or the *New Interpreter's Bible* published by Abingdon Press.

Worship Aids

Call to Worship

Think about the agonies of the world. The sufferings of Jesus did not end that day. The *via dolorosa* is two thousand years long, stretching all the way from then to now. Let us return to his day of suffering there so that we may better understand his suffering here. (Thomas Lane Butts)

The Prayer of Confession

Good Lord, Father and Mother of us all, hear our confession of sin as we look back in time and try to get some fix on why we are like we are. As we mingle with the cast of that doleful drama, we confess that we find ourselves to be so much like many of them. We confess to being detached bystanders. We confess to being like Judas the betrayer and like the disciples on the run. So much of us is strewn up and down the *via dolorosa*—and at the front of the cross too. Can we ever get over it all and make a fresh start? Help us, Lord! Amen. (Thomas Lane Butts)

The Benediction

> O LOVE Divine, what hast Thou done!
>   The' immortal God hath died for me!
> The Father's co-eternal Son
>   Bore all my sins upon the tree;
> The' immortal God for me hath died!
> My Lord, my Love is crucified!
> Behold Him, all ye that pass by,
>   The bleeding Prince of Life and Peace!
> Come, see, ye worms, your Maker die,
>   And say, was ever grief like His?
> Come, feel with me His blood applied:
> My Lord, my Love is crucified!
> ("O Love Divine, What Hast Thou Done" from
> vol. 2 of *The Poetical Works of John and Charles Wesley*
> [London: Wesleyan-Methodist Conference Office, 1869], 74)

APRIL 16, 2006

✼✼✼

Easter

Readings: Acts 10:34-43; Psalm 118:1-2, 14-24; 1 Corinthians 15:1-11; John 20:1-18; Mark 16:1-8

Rolling Away the Stones
John 20:1-18

The resurrection story is the foundation upon which our faith and hope is based. Christ has died. Christ has risen. Christ will come again. These familiar words have echoed through the ages, affirming our belief. We generally hear these words within the confines of a church, or in a gathering of the church. But what if we were reading this story for the very first time? Can you remember when you did not know the ending of the story?

We bring our assumptions and knowledge to this story, much like Mary. Mary came to the tomb fully expecting it to be as she left it. Instead she found the stone had been moved away, so she ran to find the disciples and tell them what had happened. "They have taken the Lord out of the tomb, and we do not know where they have laid him" (John 20:2). Scripture does not say she looked into the tomb, not like Peter and the other disciple. Mary assumed she knew what had happened by her first impressions.

Are we not guilty of that ourselves at times? I lived in the downtown area of Albuquerque, New Mexico. A man lived in a refrigerator box in the alley just one block away from my apartment. He was dirty, unshaven, and furtive. I was afraid of him and took great care to avoid that area when I ran. My next-door neighbor loved cats and gradually struck up an acquaintance with the "Kenmore man," who had a kitten. He even helped the man find a job. My neighbor told me, "Life is so strange. I am surprised that man would take the job of dishwasher and be grateful—a job completely below his education and ability." Imagine my shock when I learned the Kenmore man had a PhD in some field of physics! A divorce and subsequent depression had resulted in his current situation. We saw him two years later. He was still washing dishes but now had his own apartment and doing well. I based my assumptions on his appearance. As a minority, I expect that from others and was dismayed to see it in myself.

We also are guilty of making assumptions based upon our perceptions and stereotypes taught to us by family and Hollywood. If we assume we know how another person feels or thinks without giving that person the opportunity to speak for him or herself, we are wrong.

Mary saw the stone gone and accused "them" of removing Jesus' body. A first-time reader may need to be reminded of who "they" are. It is not unusual for people to expect certain actions from their enemies and blame them with hasty certainty. The distrust and animosity is based upon experience and past history, but not everyone shares in our history. Too often, our distrust colors our perceptions. We teach that same distrust to others, much like the politicians who spout rhetoric to divide and lure voters to their side.

When the disciples came running to see what Mary was talking and crying about, they were able to go directly into the tomb to see for themselves. Indeed, Jesus was gone. The stone no longer blocked their way or their vision. What is blocking our way to see Jesus?

A person reading this story for the first time would have great difficulty believing a person could be dead and is now alive. Our job, in making disciples for Christ, is to be like "them" and help remove any stone that may block others from accepting Christ as their Savior. For us, as Christians, it may also be the time to look honestly at a stone that may be blocking our way to complete transformation.

When we become Christians, we become new creatures. Many times I find there are areas in which we do not completely trust Christ. We set up our own stones. Let me use money as an example. We may trust Christ completely when it comes to time, how to raise our kids, respect for our spouses, prayer, dealing with enemies, and study of God's word. But when it comes to money, we hold back that portion of our lives. We may justify our actions by believing that God doesn't understand pensions and insurance; after all, they have only been in existence for the last fifty or so years. How can we trust God in our old age if we haven't prepared for it faithfully during our working life? How does God expect us to pay a tithe of 10 percent with rising utilities, mortgage, and other bills? We believe we know better how to manage our dollars than God does—God isn't even on the signature card!

Our stones take on many looks. They may be the stones of distrust, the pebbles of sexism, the boulders of homophobia, or the granite of selfishness. Anything that stands in the way of making disciples for Christ or sharing God's love with others, or prevents us from living life more abundantly, needs to be rolled away.

Mary embodies the transformation from weeping and sorrow to joy; from confusion to understanding. The same opportunities are open to us. We know the story, perhaps too well, because its familiarity results in complacency. We experience neither the confusion nor the joy of Mary. May we, in this hour, read with new eyes and hear with new ears the good news. May your rocks of certain unbelief and distrust roll away to reveal the joy anew, and may you be transformed. (Raquel Mull)

When God Created Salvation

First in a Series of Four

Matthew 28:1-10

What exactly is "March madness"? Sports fans know that this refers to the college basketball tournament that concludes with much competition all over the country. But March madness could also describe the violence that continues to take place in our world in the name of faith. I wish the absence of a particular school in the final four of a basketball tournament was the extent of the tragedy of March madness, but there's so much real tragedy and violence in the world and no sign of it stopping. What in God's name is happening in the world today? You see that's exactly the trouble. So much of it is happening in God's name and so much of it is wrong. There can be no disagreement; March madness has been a grim experience for us this year.

And if that's true, how is it that we can feel a sense of great and profound joy this Easter Sunday morning? Is it just religious March madness? Are we Christians just crazy? Insensitive to the suffering of others? In denial? Stupid? What is it with us Christians? This question can be answered in just three words—three powerful words that have made all the difference for us. *He Is Risen!* This is our good news! This is the source of our joy this morning. This is the reality of Easter! We are profoundly affected by the suffering in the world but we believe that the most profound answer to all of this is revealed to us in our scripture this morning when the simple dignity of the grieving of two women is interrupted by a stunning realization: He is not here! He is risen! Profound. The Easter reality! Why?

The resurrection is a profound revelation regarding creation. Remember, God created the world, the heavens, the planets, the birds, and the beasts, as well as humanity. Some have wondered: Did God create everything and "step out"? Is God even attending to our world and its problems today? Is God an absent God who phones it in and votes absentee with forwarding address unknown? Or is God like most of us, experiencing creation as an obstacle course to be completed a hurdle at a time, usually waiting until the night before? Does God stay up late figuring out what to initiate and how to respond to all of the complex actions, feelings, and prayers associated with the Middle East? The answer to these questions is that the Easter event makes clear that our God is a sovereign God who is always with us, who, while transcendent and unlimited by the tyranny of chronological time, has chosen to labor with us in history—shoulder to shoulder, deity to creatures.

The Easter reality is not just one revelation among many, for those of us who are Christians. It is the definitive revelation in which God has given us the good news. We instinctively need to know that there is life after death and that life overcomes. That's why this story is so important. At a time when there are so many fantastic narratives floating around on video and in movies, we need to be able to distinguish between that which is fiction and that which is real. We need to make sure that our children understand that this is our greatest story. Talk to many kids today about the guy who entered the city gates in triumphant fashion—you know, with the donkey—and they may say, "Oh yeah, I know that story—*Shrek.*" We might go on, "No, I'm talking about the otherworldly one that healed others, hid from the authorities, came back to life from death, and finally ascended into the heavens." Some kids today might say, "Oh yeah—E.T."

This morning we push away all of the good entertaining fictional stories to make room for the one greatest story ever told. The story that is not only true but also expresses a fundamental truth of our faith: that God raised the crucified Christ from the dead. All four Gospels agree that the tomb of Jesus was empty. Our faith was founded on the conviction not only that the tomb was empty but that God raised Jesus from the dead.

Karl Barth said that Christ is God's "Yes!" to humanity. I want to say this morning that the resurrection is God's "Nevertheless, yes!" to humanity. The ultimate victory of life over death puts the struggles of this world in perspective. We do not discount the pain, the sorrow, the sadness, and tragedy of the human condition. Instead, the resurrection affirms the importance of life by showing us that the barriers that seem so permanent and oppressive in the human drama will someday be eliminated. We will know eternity. We have concluded a century with two world wars and the stockpiling of nuclear arsenals capable of destroying the entire planet. Not long ago, we witnessed on live television the destruction of our World Trade Center in New York City. I would say that our so-called social sciences are not keeping up with our technology. We can synthesize DNA. Hooray! We cannot synthesize peace. We can make life. Super! But we cannot make life safe. Yet, the resurrection assures us that even when things look very bleak, God does not abandon us. In Christ, God in effect says, "Remember, I too knew dread in the garden of Gethsemane. I too knew rejection at the trial. I too knew suffering, agony, and death on the cross. But nevertheless, yes!" God will not allow death to be the final word. The resurrection is God's way of saying, "Nevertheless, yes!" to you and me.

This morning of all mornings we celebrate our confidence that God is God, that God has created and continues to create, and that God's love will provide for us in the future. We join with all creation in saying, "Christ the Lord has risen today! Alleluia and Amen!" (John Fiedler)

Worship Aids

Call to Worship

Leader: Mary Magdalene and the other Mary went to see the tomb.

People: Lord, we seek you as well.

Leader: But the angel said, "He is not here; for he has been raised."

People: He is Risen!

Leader: Christ the Lord is risen today!

All: Alleluia and Amen.

Prayer

God of the Cross and God of the empty tomb, we celebrate your great mysteries on this holy day. You have seen fit to raise us above the grim limitations of this life and give us joy. We give you great thanks for the blessings of new life through faith in you. In the name of the Resurrected One, Amen.

Benediction

Christ the Lord is risen today. Take this knowledge and go forth renewed and lifted up, victorious and bold. For God's love has vanquished all despair and we are set free. Amen. (John Fiedler)

APRIL 23, 2006

※※※

Second Sunday of Easter

Readings: Acts 4:32-35; Psalm 133; 1 John 1:1–2:2; John 20:19-31

A Plea for Unity
Acts 4:32-35; Psalm 133

I spoke with someone not long ago about our ever changing world and the challenge that is set before us as believers to keep up with the times. It often has been asked, What would be different in the world if you were in charge? For some the desire would be to eliminate crime, hatred, and prejudice. For others it might be the removal of pain and sickness. Still others might desire a world of peace and forgiveness.

In a world where wrong seems right and right seems wrong, unity among believers will help us keep our perspective. Our hearts will be in tune with God, as will our goals, in the desire that the entire world may know God. The psalmist knew of that when he wrote, "How good and how pleasant it is for brethren to dwell together in unity!" (Psalm 133:1 KJV). There was indeed a unity between Jesus and God, and we know that Jesus never lost sight of his purpose; that is, to die that we might live. Jesus was bold in his instruction to us to follow him, because to follow Jesus means more than traveling with him; it means being like Jesus. Our purpose as well is to die to self that we might live for Jesus. This is evident in the church of Acts, and is our model for how the church should conduct itself. Once we are clear on what unity means, all the other goals of the church become clear.

Luke, the physician and the writer of the book of Acts, gives us a glimpse of the New Testament church immediately following Pentecost. It was indeed a church of unity, love, and compassion. Luke makes it clear that the early church made unity a priority. They did not just talk about their love for one another, their love was evident according to verse 32, "The believers were one in heart and mind" and "shared everything they had" (NIV).

119

As we think back to our original question, What would I change if I were in charge of the world? I would like to see that degree of unity demonstrated among the church today. To be like-minded, having the same love, and being of one accord—such a commitment to unity within the body of Christ would only increase the impact of the church on the world, and perhaps create a newfound interest in the church.

One only has to read the headlines of the newspaper or turn on the television to see that the world is in search of something to believe in and somewhere to belong. People hunger for love and acceptance, and the church is called to be a haven of hope for those who are lost. The context from which our passage is found today reflects this very principle. Peter tells the crowd in Acts 2 that forgiveness through Jesus Christ is available, that the promise is for them, "for you and your children." Our text tells us that more than three thousand people received Christ as a result (Acts 2:41). Out of this gift of the Holy Spirit came a unity that was evident to all, to the extent that "the Lord added to their number daily those who were being saved" (Acts 2:47 NIV).

Beyond the impact such unity would have on the world, we must realize the impact it would have on the church itself. Luke tells us that no one lacked anything because no one claimed ownership of any possessions—everything was shared and therefore everyone's needs were met. Never do we look more like Christ than when we are giving. The church would benefit from accountability, consistency, and stability, all as a result of unity.

When unity is our goal, we find that our priorities will be correct as well; we will love the right things, do the right things, think the right thoughts, and dwell on things above. How often in the world do we lose sight of our priorities and emphasize the wrong things in life? With unity we find not only purpose and priorities but also a passion to please God. We will love a lost world, we will love one another, and we will love God with fervency. When unity becomes the driving force in our lives, the church will once again be all that God intended. (Jimmy McNeil)

When God Created Alienation

Second in a Series of Four

Genesis 3

Whatever happened to "happily ever after"? A middle-aged woman gets divorced and wonders what happiness might even be. A widower stares at the television in a nursing home and wonders where his life went. How many of you have been profoundly disappointed within the last year? Think about it. When is the last time you saw the meltdown of some major dream? Perhaps it's a concept that deserves to be put to death: personal happiness. Perhaps the cosmos has not been structured to foster our contentment or guarantee our happiness. Maybe that's the reason there is so little "happily ever after" and so much alienation.

The story of Adam and Eve in the garden of Eden is a story of temptation, inquest, judgment, and expulsion. Adam and Eve sin. They expressly do what God has forbidden them to do. Then they each pass the buck when God holds them accountable. Adam blames Eve. Eve blames the snake. It doesn't really matter. They all three get their punishment and then they are removed from paradise. The ground is cursed. Childbirth is made painful. Adam and Eve brought on the worst punishment themselves as a direct result of eating the forbidden fruit of the tree. It was what God did not intend for them (or so God said). Self-consciousness is the awareness by which we distinguish between the world and ourselves. We are no longer an integral part of all creation. Instead, we feel naked and ashamed. Our eyes have been opened in a way that estranges us from the world around us. Even if God had allowed them to remain in Eden, paradise was lost. No one can enjoy the garden when she or he is hiding all the time.

Of course, if you are a defense attorney you respond to God and maintain that the tree was not adequately zoned off—no warning signage whatsoever. You maintain your clients experienced damages—emotional distress from being deprived of their home and lifestyle. If you were shrewd, you would even maintain that God intended that Eve and Adam eat of the fruit. You would stipulate that the serpent was a theme-park employee acting on God's wishes while God was playing head games with your client. You would accuse God of leading Adam and Eve down a predictable path that led to their expulsion. In other words, you would claim that God created alienation.

Alienation, you will remember, is a turning away, an estrangement. The state of being an outsider or feeling isolated, alienation is also a sense of loneliness, which I believe is the plague of our time. I love Edward Hopper's painting *Nighthawks*. It is one of the best-known images of the twentieth century. It depicts an all-night diner with three customers lost in their own thoughts sitting on round bar stools. Fluorescent lights, a new invention for the early 1940s, emit an eerie glow, attracting lost souls like urban moths. And there's no door in sight. No way to get in. No way to get out. Just a seamless wedge of glass. Patrons under glass. You can see them but you cannot relate to them. Separate from one another. Separate from you. Remote. Alone in a crowd. Alienation.

Alienation is a crippling social disease because it makes you question whether life is even worthwhile. It makes you wonder why you go to work. It makes life seem absurd. Meaninglessness. In this country, with supposedly the highest standard of living in the world, the third leading killer of young adults behind car wrecks and cancer is suicide. Fortunately there are more constructive ways to stop the pain.

Remember, God never promised you a rose garden, but God does promise community. Community is the antidote for alienation. Authentic community is where you are welcome even if you did not sell anything this month, did not rack up any billable hours, or did not score a goal. Authentic community is where people stand with you during tough times. When you're hurting. When you don't feel attractive. One name for that community is "church." The witness of the church is its ongoing care of its members. Sunday school classes have a way of looking after one another even as the church staff also strives to care. But you have to make a conscious decision to get involved. Don't stand there looking wistfully at "Six Flags over Personal Happiness" and kicking yourself because you didn't get your hand stamped. Be an active part of the church. Don't let alienation deprive you of a wonderful church home. Don't hang on to some incident or comment from a previous (or present) pastor or staff person as a reason why you miss out on the blessings of church. You deserve better.

So much of our expulsion we bring upon ourselves. We are those people who think too much. We ate of the fruit of self-consciousness. We may put it in a blender and puree it into a smoothie but the results are the same: painfully self-aware. Shy. Afraid of life. Estranged from others because of what they might think of us. Walking in terror because our breath might stink, our twelve-hour deodorant might expire, our bodies might be in the wrong shape, striving to please a pagan god all the while our Creator God pads through the cool grass of Eden calling, "Where are you? What's gotten into you?" We are alienated from our own true nature. We have forgotten that we are God's own creatures and that God will take care of us.

Too many times we are casualties on the battleground of alienation. We feel like strangers in our own lives: hollow people leading hollow lives. There is an abundance of reasons for being reduced in such a fashion but our hope lies in another possibility: the new abundance promised in the community of Christ. (John Fiedler)

Worship Aids

Call to Worship

Leader: The Lord God calls us and asks, "Where are you?"

People: We are hiding because we are afraid.

Leader: What is it that you have done?

People: We have been tricked into doing wrong and no longer know you.

Prayer

O God, you have given us so many blessings and only a few admonitions. And yet we find ourselves fascinated by tempting possibilities to see for ourselves and create our own idols. Creator God, protect us from ourselves. When we do sin, ignore the blame we heap on others and forgive us for the wrongs we do. Remind us that we are never alone. In the name of Christ, Amen.

Benediction

Go into the world and know that you are neither cursed nor alone but rather you are heirs to the blessings of God's great kingdom. Amen. (John Fiedler)

APRIL 30, 2006

❦ ❦ ❦

Third Sunday of Easter

Readings: Acts 3:12-19; Psalm 4; 1 John 3:1-7; Luke 24:36b-48

I Had to See It to Believe It
Luke 24:36b-48

Could it really be true, we wondered? All day we had been hearing reports that Jesus was alive—but we were afraid to let ourselves believe it. After all, we had seen what they had done to him just two days before: the trials, the beating, and then the horrible death. We had watched from afar as they took his body down and gave it to Joseph for burial. But then, this morning, when Mary and Joanna and the others went to anoint Jesus' body with spices, Jesus' body was gone! Instead, the women saw two men in dazzling garments who told them Jesus had risen. They came running back to tell us, the disciples, and the others who were hiding in the upper room with us. At first, it seemed like an idle tale and we didn't believe them, so Peter got up and ran to the tomb himself. Peter, too, saw the empty linen cloths and came back amazed.

Later that day, two from among us were walking to Emmaus talking about all that happened. Suddenly, another person joined them on the road, asking them about what they were discussing. Our friends told him of Jesus' deeds and teachings, and then how Jesus had been handed over and put to death. They also told him about the strange events of the morning. Then, the man surprised them. Beginning with Moses and all the prophets, he interpreted the scriptures to them. When they arrived in the village, the person turned to go, but my friends invited him to stay the evening with them. They sat down to eat and the guest took the bread, blessed it, and broke it and gave it to them. Suddenly their eyes were opened and they realized that it was Jesus who was with them! Although it was late, they got up and hurried back to Jerusalem to tell us what they had experienced.

"The Lord has risen indeed and has appeared to Simon!" they cried.

I wanted to believe so desperately that it was true, but I still had my doubts. While we were still talking about this, suddenly Jesus appeared among us—right there before us! He spoke so calmly and gently: "Peace be with you."

Peace be with us, hardly! We were startled and terrified—we thought it was a ghost! Some of us still didn't understand that he had truly resurrected, others thought it was another spirit trying to deceive us. We couldn't say a word.

Jesus continued, "Why are you frightened, and why do doubts arise in your hearts?" As if he knew what we were thinking, as if he knew we needed proof, he said, "Look at my hands and my feet; see that it is I myself. Touch me and see; for a ghost does not have flesh and bones as you see that I have."

None of us had the courage to touch him to know for sure, but a sense of joy and amazement was beginning to dawn among us. Yet still we wondered, could we believe? Sensing this, Jesus spoke again.

"Have you anything here to eat?"

We gave him fish—and he ate it right in front of us. Surely a spirit couldn't eat bread with Simon and fish with us. Jesus proved to us he was real, and in that simple act, he reminded us of the miracle of the feeding of the five thousand with five loaves and two fish. Jesus had performed that miracle, could this be another one?

Then, just like Jesus had done with our friends on the road to Emmaus, he opened our hearts and minds to understand the scriptures. It was amazing. First he looked backward, talking about how everything written about him in the law of Moses, the prophets, and the psalms must be fulfilled. But then, Jesus also looked forward. He told us that repentance and forgiveness of sins through him was to be proclaimed to all the nations, beginning in Jerusalem and spreading from there. When I thought about it later, Jesus' words made perfect sense. After all, the annunciation of his birth had occurred here, as had his presentation in the temple. What better place for the church to begin than here as well. Although the forgiveness of sins would be preached to all, it was to begin with Israel then spread to others. Jesus told us it was our calling to tell everyone what we had seen and experienced. The responsibility for such a task seemed overwhelming, but then Jesus said, "You are witnesses of these things. And see, I am sending upon you what my Father promised; so stay here in the city until you have been clothed with power from on high."

By this time, we had learned to listen to Jesus, so we went back to Jerusalem to worship him and to reflect on what God was calling us to do. We knew that believing in his resurrection would change our lives and the lives of all of those who were touched by it.

As I've thought back on our time with Jesus, I've realized how fortunate we were. We heard him teach, saw the miracles, saw him resurrected from the dead. I don't know if I would ever have believed if I hadn't seen it for myself. I know many of you struggle to believe, wishing you had proof like we did. Your belief and obedience call for even greater faith. But know that you are blessed. Jesus said, "Blessed are those who have not seen and yet have come to believe." My prayer for you this morning is that you will receive Jesus' blessing with great joy, that in response you will worship God with all your hearts, and that you will be open to doing what God instructs you to do. Know that the same Spirit that empowered us empowers you today. And may you go in peace as you continue on the journey. (Tracy Hartman)

When God Created Doubt

Third in a Series of Four

John 20:19-29

It was the 1997 Super Bowl in New Orleans. Preparations were being made for the grand halftime extravaganza. The planners had invited a team of bungee jumpers to leap off of the rafters of the Superdome. Each jumper required a person who would control the bungee cord, progressively letting the line out after each rebound. The company putting on the show didn't have any trained personnel to handle the cords so they hired some locals and gave them a whopping two minutes training on handling the cords. Lora Patterson, a forty-one-year-old former circus aerialist performing that day, trusted that the company had made proper arrangements for her safety. She was mistaken and paid for this error with her life as the volunteer handling her cord let out too much slack, causing her to strike the forty-yard line as if she'd simply dived from the ceiling with no bungee cord at all.

Sometimes we trust when trust is not merited. Experience has taught us to be doubtful. We learn not to trust what people say. We have all heard "famous last words" such as: "That looks really great on you," coming from a department store sales clerk, or "The previous owner only drove it to church on Sunday" from a car salesperson. We learn not to open e-mails addressed to us from addresses we do not recognize that say, "about that report you requested." The fact is that experience teaches us to doubt.

Jesus had appeared to all of the disciples in the upper room, but Thomas had the misfortune to be away. When he returned to the group they were all so excited about their encounter with the risen Christ. But Thomas surveyed his colleagues and said, "Oh no you don't. You are not having fun at my expense." And then he makes the claim of the empiricist, "Unless I put my finger in the mark of the nails and my hand in his side, I will not believe." A week later Jesus appears again and he directly confronts Thomas' doubt by telling him to go ahead and touch the mark of the nails. Thomas does so and *then* believes. Jesus chides Thomas for believing only after Thomas has truly seen, stating that we are truly blessed when we believe without seeing.

The hermeneutic of suspicion or doubt is what developed into the scientific methodology that has served us so well as a civilization. Without it we would not be flying to faraway exotic places. Without science, we would still have polio and smallpox. Without science and its stubborn demand that we question our assumptions and recreate formulas under laboratory conditions, we wouldn't have that heart medicine that has made it possible for us to live longer. We couldn't care for the premature baby or give drugs to those afflicted with AIDS. Faith has no reason to fear science. All traditional beliefs now come under the white-hot scrutiny of scientific methodology. If a belief had been held for centuries, the irreverent reply of science was, "Then I doubt it." The heavy-handed authoritarian reply of the church toward the innovative men and women of the Enlightenment is a matter of record—and shame. When the church tries to take away freedom in the name of fostering belief, it usually ends up fostering anger and resentment. Copernicus was slapped down for suggesting that the earth revolved around the sun. It was only in October of 1992 that the Roman Catholic Church got around to confessing that its 392-year-old persecution of Galileo was misguided. Headlines had a field day with it: "Galileo acquitted, earth actually round says the pope."

It was inevitable that this hermeneutic of suspicion, this scientific methodology, would affect the interpretation of the scriptures as scholars struggled to delve into the scriptures—indeed, get behind the scriptures—and find their indisputable truth. They were seeking some undeniably factual dimension to the scriptures that would place modern Christians on firm footing. Yes, in a way they were trying to provide for belief without the necessity of faith. The doubters look with skepticism at accounts of virgin births, miracles, resurrections, and the like. If you feel that such doubt can help you hone your faith, help give it the postcritical edge, then by all means sharpen away. Just make sure that something remains when you are done. In other words, do not embrace the hermeneutic of suspicion so much that you lose your faith altogether. That happens to people and it is a great loss—too great. Because faith picks up where doubt leaves off.

Being in chronic doubt is like being a deer in headlights. It paralyzes you and prevents you from taking any leap of faith at all. In and of itself doubt can't bring about anything really profound. It has no power of its own. It can erode the power of a good idea. It can prevent the spread of bad ideas. But it does not replace bad ideas with good ones. That is another department. This is the realm of faith. The greatest effort in this life is to be chronically cynical about all of life's possibilities. You can doubt, but at some point you must make your stand. You have got to believe. Jesus tells Thomas to reach out his hand. The Greek word for reach is *fero*. It means to be carried, to be borne with the suggestion of force or speed. The Holy Spirit fills us like a sail and we are speedily sent crashing over the waves. It is exciting. That is the answer to doubt. That is what we need to do. Reach out toward Jesus. John Wesley had a prescription for those who doubt. He said if you do not have faith then act as if you do until you get faith. In other words, *fero*. Reach. Reach for the risen Christ. Reach for the Christ and know his power beyond all doubt. (John Fiedler)

Worship Aids

Call to Worship

Leader: Lord, in private moments we understand Thomas all too well.

People: For he demanded more than just somebody's word.

Leader: We are suspicious, we have doubts, and we want proof.

People: Yet you have called us to the life of faith.

Prayer

O God, you have called us to be wise as serpents in discerning that which is true and that which is false. We know that there are those who would willingly mislead us in this world. When we have doubt, transform it into faith. When we have no faith, give us the courage to act as if we do until we are blessed with its presence. In the name of him who revealed himself in his wounds, Amen.

Benediction

Go into a world full of doubt and mistrust and proclaim the truth of what God has done in Jesus Christ. Amen. (John Fiedler)

MAY 7, 2006

❧❧❧

Fourth Sunday of Easter

Readings: Acts 4:5-12; Psalm 23; 1 John 3:16-24; John 10:11-18

Sheep in Need of a Shepherd
John 10:11-18; Psalm 23

I have often heard that sheep are among the simplest of livestock. That is to say, sheep are quite vulnerable without a shepherd. They are vulnerable to their enemies such as wolves and the thieves mentioned in John 10. They are also vulnerable to themselves as they tend to wander from the flock. Although I have limited knowledge of sheep, it seems that a sheep that ventures from the watchful eye of the shepherd is bound for trouble. As dependent as they are on a watchful shepherd, I seriously doubt that sheep realize their dependence on the shepherd. They probably scarcely notice the shepherd's presence until they feel the pull of the staff when they are pulled from danger. At the other end of the spectrum, human beings are creation's most complex thinkers. We have the capacity to understand and process amazing quantities of facts and information. We can make complicated decisions. We are not very much like sheep. Yet, Jesus uses the parable of the good shepherd to teach his followers about the relationship offered and sought by God with God's creation. Jesus recognized an important tendency of humanity. Perhaps we are more like sheep than we realized.

The image and metaphor of the shepherd is a familiar one throughout scripture. It is utilized so often probably because it would have been easy to understand for contemporary recipients of the stories and teachings. Perhaps the best-known use of this metaphor is Psalm 23. "The Lord is my shepherd" is probably one of the best-known verses of scripture in the Old Testament. The image of God as our shepherd through the valley of the shadow of death is an image of comfort that indeed comforts many throughout life and death. In John 10, Jesus uses this metaphor as he attempts to teach his followers and the Pharisees about his role in their lives as well as his future with them. In the verses preceding today's passage, Jesus refers to himself as the gate that separates the sheep from danger. In verses 11-18, Jesus returns to the metaphor of himself as the good shepherd. The good shepherd is different from a hired worker because he is willing to lay down his life for the sheep. A person who is hired to watch the sheep is not invested in them like the shepherd and will likely desert them when danger approaches. Jesus suggests that as the good shepherd, he will not desert the flock and will indeed be willing to lay down his life. Jesus also alludes to the universal reality of his eventual sacrifice. In verse 16, Jesus acknowledges that there are more sheep that are not inside the sheep pen. These sheep also need him as shepherd and will be brought in to join the rest of the flock, and all will have the same shepherd. Finally, Jesus alludes to his own choice in laying down his life. Not only is it his choice to lay down his life, but his choice to take it up again. Through a postresurrection Christian lens, we can clearly see this allusion to Jesus' crucifixion and resurrection. Jesus indeed could have chosen to forego his death, but chose instead to face death and return from the dead.

As you can imagine, the religious authorities did not respond well to Jesus' depiction of himself as the good shepherd who has come to both lie down and take up his life for his sheep. Although some were challenged toward belief, others thought Jesus was crazy, and worse yet, blasphemous. I imagine there was another facet of this metaphor that would have been difficult for Jesus' listeners. We are accustomed to the concept of the Lord as shepherd and us as sheep. Jesus' listeners would have been less accustomed to this idea and would have had firsthand knowledge of the sheep and shepherd relationship. For Jesus to describe himself as the shepherd of the sheeplike people was probably difficult for the people to hear. They probably mistook his wise teaching for egotism. We have the advantage of knowing the rest of the story. We can see the gentle wisdom in Jesus' teaching. We know that he did just what he said and chose to lay down and take up his life for us.

I will admit, however, there is something a little disheartening about being described as a sheep. It is difficult to admit our likeness to animals that so depend on a shepherd for survival. We are much more accustomed to being shepherds in control than sheep so in need of leadership. Yet, when it comes to our relationship with God, Jesus understands our human tendencies better perhaps than we understand ourselves. When it comes to our faith, we are very much like sheep in need of a shepherd. Like sheep, we have the tendency to follow. Like sheep, we often confuse true leadership with the kind offered by hired hands (shepherds who are in it for the wrong reason). Like sheep, we are endangered by those who prey on our vulnerability, the spiritual wolves. Like sheep, we are perhaps most vulnerable to ourselves and our tendency to wander away from the care of the shepherd and the safety of the flock. We certainly need a good shepherd, like Jesus, who is willing to care and sacrifice for us. Accepting that we are indeed like sheep is the hardest part for many people. It is our human nature to want to be in control of our lives. Yet, to be a follower of Christ, we must accept our spiritual likeness to sheep and our need for a good shepherd. As we continue to ponder the great news of the resurrection, may we be ever aware that to fully experience Christ, we must allow Christ to be the shepherd of our lives. (Tracey Allred)

As God Creates the Kingdom of God

Fourth in a Series of Four

Revelation 21:1-14

This past week I saw that someone had painted a message on a silver traffic signal box mounted on a traffic-light pole. The message said, "Give up. It's not worth it." The author went to a great deal of trouble in defacing public property to share a message. He or she was making a general pronouncement on the futility of life. In the course of this sermon series so far, I have labored to be honest and name some problems we all face. I have learned that solutions offered in the absence of recognizing barriers are a rather fruitless affair, and one of our greatest challenges is lack of hope. In weak moments when we feel beaten down and discouraged in our lives, we may agree with this urban street philosopher. We may momentarily think that all is futile. But don't! Help is on the way! Help is on the way in the form of this beautiful message, today's scripture, written long ago.

John of Patmos, the author of the book of Revelation, penned this magnificent passage of expectation and hope. I love this image. God will come and dwell among us. God will wipe away our tears. Death will be no more. Pain will be no more. Why? Because God has come. The Synoptic Gospels give special emphasis to the coming of the kingdom of God. John the Baptist proclaimed the coming of Jesus, and Jesus proclaimed the coming of the kingdom. For centuries scholars equated the kingdom of God with the church. Wrong. Then the kingdom was equated with a badly needed reform of existing institutions. Wrong. Then C. H. Dodd coined the term "realized eschatology" and claimed that God's kingdom is here already. Not altogether true. The Jesus Seminar refuses to recognize any of the future-oriented passages as even being authentic. Problematic. Gee, what's a poor preacher to do?

Jesus taught us to pray: "Your kingdom come. Your will be done, on earth as it is in heaven" (Matthew 6:10). The connection is made and it is binding. You see, I believe we are allowed glimpses of God's imminent kingdom. We are allowed glimpses but only that. A cynic would say "teasers," but I prefer "glimpses" that are actually reassurances that the kingdom will eventually come. In Revelation 21:2, we are told that the New Jerusalem will come like a bride adorned for her husband. How many weddings have taken place in our sanctuaries? How many beautiful brides have made their way down the church's aisle? I've never seen a bride in a wedding that didn't give off an aura of beauty. We have seen grooms standing right there with an air of expectancy, joy, a feeling of being overwhelmed by the goodness of the moment. That's what we should feel as we think of the glory of God's kingdom.

Another basis of our hope is to be found in the strengths of diversity. God chose to create us different from one another and that can be a strength. The Dallas Mavericks basketball team had been a laughingstock of professional sports for years. Coach Don Nelson couldn't seem to get anything going until he started doing something very unusual in the NBA. He started looking around the world for talent. Everyone knows the best basketball in the world is found right here in the United States, but Nelson found Wang Zhizhi from China, Dirk Nowitzki from Germany, and Eduardo Najera from Mexico and blended them with American players. Coach Nelson discovered something pretty basic and actually quite theological: God spread goodness all over the world. God creates talented people all over the world. So the quest for ultimate excellence dictates that we include the global community! Diversity reflects the kingdom of God.

Finally, we can never forget that God is still creating. Creation is not just something that happened eons ago. Pictures from the Hubble Telescope remind us of this. Jubilant astronomers have unveiled some of humankind's most spectacular views of the universe, courtesy of NASA's Hubble Space Telescope as it peered into a celestial maternity ward called the Omega Nebula or M17. This remarkable view revealed a watercolor fantasy-world of glowing gases, where stars and perhaps embryonic planetary systems are still forming. In other words, the universe remains a dynamic place because the Creator is still creating—and the kingdom is still coming. We study these images and we are in awe of our Creator who is still creating and bringing about God's kingdom.

The other evening I walked out into our front yard after the sun had gone down and I saw it: that archetypal gleaming that triggers a series of childhood summer memories. I saw a lightning bug for just a moment. There was a greenish-yellow glow and then nothing. Now let me ask you something. When the bright glow stops, does that mean the bug ceases to exist? Does that mean it's no longer there? No. It just means you can't see it for a while—until you get the next glimpse. My experience of the kingdom of God is a lot like that. I wander dazzled from glimpse to glimpse. Indeed, it is addictive. Intoxicated by the glorious glimpses, one can put up with a lot of brokenness and absurdity because the glimpse makes it all worthwhile. All the loose ends are connected. Our lives seem to make sense. We feel attuned to the ever-expanding universe. At peak moments the Creator embraces us ... and then we go pick up the dry cleaning. And then we go get the car inspected. And then mundane life yanks us down and sends us on our way. But when we have glimpsed the glory of God's great scheme, we can endure much. For we have hope. (John Fiedler)

Worship Aids

Call to Worship

> Leader: Then I saw a new heaven and a new earth; for the first heaven and the first earth had passed away.
>
> **People: The world is a turbulent place.**
>
> Leader: He will wipe every tear from their eyes. Death will be no more.
>
> **People: Lord, you are still creating. Make all things new.**

Prayer

O God, our Creator, there is so much in the world that is discouraging and hurtful. We confess that there are days when we threaten to give up hope and become converts of brokenness. Lord, instill in us your vision for your great kingdom and let our hope lie in the Christ who did proclaim it. Amen.

Benediction

Go forth from this place and know yourselves to be cocreators with a God who is still creating. Where you see hatred, give love. Where you see suffering, give aid. Where you see injustice, be a force for right. For the kingdom of God is coming. Amen. (John Fiedler)

MAY 14, 2006

❦❦❦

Fifth Sunday of Easter

Readings: Acts 8:26-40; Psalm 22:25-31; 1 John 4:7-21; John 15:1-8

The Heart of It All
1 John 4:7-21

"Cut to the chase." A quick search on the Internet reveals that this saying goes back a long way, back to moviemaking in the 1920s. The saying refers to moving from a dramatic scene to an action scene. There are times in life when we want to say, "Cut to the chase," aren't there? When a story has gone on too long, for example. When a sermon has gone on too long, for example! When it seems we're dealing with peripheral matters when we have no time to waste, we want to say, "Cut to the chase. Get to the point."

Sometimes we are under such pressure and need desperately to know some answers and get some help that we know we don't have time or energy to wade through a lot of trivialities. We're facing a crisis and we want help. We've received a diagnosis about our health or someone else's and suddenly a lot of the issues we thought were important aren't important any longer. We face some decision that will affect our lives radically. Life has gotten down to the basics for us in some way and we feel we don't have time left for anything but getting to the point.

This passage is "the point." It's "the chase." It's the focus of so much of what we want to know about life and how life is to be lived. Here's what it tells us about what we might call, "the heart of it all."

This passage tells us what the bedrock of life is like when it tells us what God is like. It says that God is love. Maybe you've never wondered about this, but many of us have wondered whether there is indeed a God and what that God is like. It makes all the difference whether there is truly a God or we're alone, completely alone, living an essentially meaningless existence that is going nowhere, with that little hyphen between the date of our birth and the date of our death all there is. It matters, too, what this God is like. Is God distant and uncaring, ignoring us? Is God distant and unable to help, with no strength to enter into our lives? Is God mean and out to get us?

Those three little words, "God is love," get to the heart of it all. They cut to the chase. They tell us that God is pure self-giving love. God cares. Indeed, God cares deeply.

What a reality to build a life on! We are not alone, neglected, orphaned. God is love.

How do we know this? Of course, it's a matter of faith, but the reality to which John points is that God "sent his only Son into the world." God did not keep his distance from us. Any parent knows how precious his or her children are. God's sending his Son shows us unmistakably how much God loves us. There's more, of course. God "sent his Son to be the atoning sacrifice for our sins." God sent his Son to rescue us from the mess we are in, although much of it is our own fault.

How do we know that God loves us and that this little statement, "God is love," is not just syrupy sentiment, a deep-seated wish, or a figment of our imagination? Here, too, we are at the heart of it all. God in Christ has entered into our experience, our drudgery, our crises, and our need.

Have you ever flown directly over your home community, the place where your own family lives? As others looked out the airplane windows, perhaps they could make out roads and see the dots of houses. You, however, saw that and more. You saw places familiar to you and knew that people who loved you and whom you loved lived there. You had an attachment to that place that others on the plane didn't have. You'd been there. Well, God's been here. Indeed, in God's Spirit, God—this God who is love—*is* here, right where you and I live. God has "sent his Son" and "given us of his Spirit." The God who is love did that for us.

So how does this affect our lives? All of life is changed when we live on the basis that God is love. Living on the bedrock belief that God is love helps us "cut to the chase."

The heart of it all is that knowing, truly knowing, that God is love gives us confidence. No longer do we need to be afraid or uncertain about facing life—or death. We can count on the reality that God is love. God's been here, right here, right where we wonder about life, face threats and hardships, and worry about what might happen, has happened, or is happening. We can count on the God who is love.

This great truth affects our lives in yet another way. You see, if God is love and indeed loves us, then that has to affect our relationship with our fellow human beings. How can we ignore our fellow human beings if we know and worship a God like this—a God who is love? How can we harm our fellow human beings if we know and worship a God like this—a God who is love? How can we fear our fellow human beings or anything else if we have confidence in a God like this—a God who is love? Indeed, since we serve a God who has structured the universe so that love is what is most important, our only proper response is to live with love ourselves and love other people just as God has loved us. To love a God who is love means that we must love our brothers and sisters, all our fellow human beings, also. That's the heart of it all. (Ross West)

When Death Is Yesterday's News

First in a Series of Three: Vital Lessons from the Early Church

John 11:1-4, 14-44; John 20:19

Today's sermon begins a three-part series addressing three vital lessons that are a legacy of the early church. The themes of death and resurrection, the cost of faith, and the necessity of love are among the most important messages that Jesus shared with those who had ears to hear. Each of these themes may be historical to our faith, but there is nonetheless a mystery to this history. These ideas of faith have been so preached, published, and indoctrinated into the Christian tradition that we gloss over how radical they must have seemed to those who first heard. We are not unlike the person who takes electricity for granted and cannot understand why a primitive tribe would be fearful or fascinated by such a discovery. Still today, when our Volunteer in Mission teams visit remote areas of third-world countries, someone takes along a Polaroid camera. Such technology always captivates the people with whom they work and serves as a great "icebreaker" to establish rapport with the hosts.

This series will allow us to revisit these texts and the lessons they convey. We do so looking deeper into the experience of early believers and examining our own, lest we become so accustomed to doctrine that we ignore the truth and experience of God in which our faith is rooted.

Today we consider two texts about resurrection. The Gospel of John gives us both an account of Jesus' raising of Lazarus, as well as Jesus' postresurrection appearance to the disciples in the house where they were gathered. Historically, there have been stories and theories that have attempted to discredit both of these resurrection accounts. John's accounts help dispel these arguments. John gives us such detail, names the many witnesses, and even reminds us in John 12:9-11 that there was a plot to kill Lazarus. Why would such a plot be considered? The religious leaders were attempting to stop the hemorrhage of Jews converting to the teachings of Jesus as a result of Lazarus' resurrection. There is no question that many people believed that God had done something singularly different than they had ever experienced before.

They believed because they either had witnessed the resurrection of Jesus or Lazarus, heard firsthand from those who were there, had personally experienced spiritual resurrection in their own life, or had heard the witness of another whose life was resurrected from sin and despair by the saving love of Christ. The same can be said for us today. Death, the truth of our own mortality, is the one unstoppable force that no human endeavor alone can totally overcome. We may slow the aging process, but that does not stop death. We may use cryogenics to preserve a loved one and hope for a means of reviving them one day, but we really have no power to stop death altogether.

The early followers of Jesus shared that same powerless feeling in their own life. John 20:19 paints a portrait of fear and hiding. The betrayal, arrest, and crucifixion of Jesus was the most devastating blow they could ever have imagined. Behind locked doors and barred windows they huddled in fear of the religious authorities. They had seen what had happened to Jesus. Could that same fate await them? The first century was not a very hospitable place for diverse views, especially those that differed from established local religious practice or Roman decree.

Just when we think there is no hope, God appears. Just when the disciples felt that their faith had been in vain, they discovered that hope never dies when God is involved. A bit later in the scriptures, the Acts of the Apostles will record how these same sequestered and trembling people turned defeat into a demonstration of faith. At the day of Pentecost, their witness would convert thousands and those thousands would reach thousands more.

Resurrection is not simply about saving our body for eternal life, but is about saving our soul for eternal relationship. The gift of life, which Christ brings, is a gift for here and now as well as the hereafter. We need not focus on resurrection as a sign of only that which lies ahead. Resurrection faith is also a sign of what life can be when we claim the power that God gives to all who believe. We can share in Paul's own conversion and in his great proclamation, "I can do all things through [Christ] who strengthens me" (Philippians 4:13).

For it is true, "We know that all things work together for good for those who love God" (Romans 8:28a).

When death becomes yesterday's news instead of today's headlines, that is something worth sharing, celebrating, and believing. (Gary G. Kindley)

Worship Aids

Call to Worship

Whatever place your find yourself, wait. The third day is coming!
Whatever darkness overwhelms you, look. The third day is coming!
Whatever troubles darken your soul, take heart. The third day is coming!
People of God, hear the good news: Jesus Christ resurrects souls, hearts, and minds.
Thanks be to God for the resurrection faith! Amen.

Prayer

What a wondrous time is this season of life! There is so much joy and beauty in the world around us. Let us not be stuck in the darkness. Let us be a people of the light. Let us not be pulled down by troubles. Let us be a people of the light. Let our hearts be filled with gladness at the gift of life that knows no end. Let us be a people of the light. It is the light of Christ that opens tombs, brightens lives, and redeems souls. Amen.

Benediction

He is not here, for he is risen! Tell those who are wondering and those who are afraid. Tell those who are troubled and those in whom doubt lingers. Jesus Christ has saved you and his love can save all who accept it. Live Christ's love each day! Amen. (Gary G. Kindley)

MAY 21, 2006

❧❧❧

Sixth Sunday of Easter

Readings: Acts 10:44-48; Psalm 98; 1 John 5:1-6; John 15:9-17

Surprise! There's Room for You Too!
Acts 10:44-48

Have you ever been surprised by God? You expected God to work one way and God did the opposite, the unexpected? In the New Testament, God is constantly pulling surprises: God loves the most unlikely people, and shows up in the most unexpected places.

This is the message of today's text from the Acts of the Apostles. Perhaps a short Bible study will help us appreciate what is going on in today's reading. In the second chapter of Acts, we are confronted with the story of the birth of the church. We call it the Pentecost story. On the day of the Jewish festival of Pentecost something happened that no one expected. The Holy Spirit blew through the gathered community and caused quite a stir as people found themselves speaking in various languages and yet were able to understand what everyone was saying. It is a marvelous moment. Diverse groups of people are brought together through an unexpected visitation of the Holy Spirit and community is created.

However, this experience is a limited one. The gathered community is a community of Jews, the chosen people of God. It is Pentecost and the church has been fashioned by God's spirit. We celebrate this day every year in the liturgical cycle of the church.

A lot happens after this dramatic visitation of God's spirit. The story is thrilling and I encourage you to read it for yourself in this early history of the church that we call the Acts of the Apostles.

In the tenth chapter of this book a different kind of Pentecost occurs. It has been called the "Gentile Pentecost" because here we have a record of the Holy Spirit visiting Gentiles, the non-Jews of that world.

Now this is a surprise! No one expects God to act in this way. God is the God of the Jews. God's love is reserved for them. They are the people with the great faith tradition that begins with Abraham and continues through the exodus and the kings and prophets of the Old Testament. It would be only fitting that on the day of Pentecost God would do a special work like bringing the Spirit on the believers gathered at the sacred site of Jerusalem.

But God's spirit is always larger than our expectations. In Acts 10, that spirit confirms that God loves Gentiles too. The community of the excluded is included. The ones regarded as a "nonpeople" are elevated to the status of God's children. It is a surprise of monumental proportions! The early church is confronted with God's view and has to open its life and doors to all the people of the world. No longer can the church live in the comfort of fellowship with it's own. Now it must make room for all. It is a challenge and a blessing all at the same time.

Such is the story of the New Testament. Reading the Gospels and the Letters of this sacred text one becomes aware of one fact above all others: Jesus Christ is the friend of sinners, sufferers, and Samaritans! Just think about who gets noticed, who gets included in the story: Bartimaeus, the ten lepers, a man born blind, Zacchaeus, a hemorrhaging woman, an insane man living in a graveyard. Their names are legion. No "brightest and best" in this group. No power brokers, no names that graced the local social register, none of the king's palace advisors. These are the marginalized, the forgotten, and the overlooked. And God loves them all! This is the message of our text for today.

It is a reminder to us that Jesus is constantly moving toward those from whom others are moving away. And it is the good news that you, too, are included in the fellowship of the redeemed! No wonder we call this the gospel, which means, literally, "good news."

So here we are at church. We are an interesting group. We are the well behaved and the rebels. We are the righteous and the lost. We are the consistent and the inconsistent, the saints and the sinners. And, we all belong! Such is the grace of God that God's spirit of love reaches all.

I remember making a call many years ago to acknowledge someone's presence at our church. A woman had attended worship along with her children. I visited her home the following Monday hoping to see her and talk to her about our church. I wanted to invite her to come again and consider joining this community of faith. The woman was not at home, but her husband was. He and I had a pleasant visit at the front door. He told me his name was Bill. His wife's name was Betty. As I concluded my visit with Bill, I said, "Please tell Betty that we would love to have her visit our church again." And Bill said that he would. And then, as I turned to walk away, Bill called out, "And me too." And I said, "Of course . . . and you, too, Bill."

That scene has remained with me. "And you too, Bill." That is God's way. That is Jesus' example. That is the church when it is at its fullest with the inclusive spirit of the living God! Today the message comes to all of us: And you too! Surprise! There's room for you, too, in this place of sacred love. No wonder we call this the "good news" place! (Chris Andrews)

Faith Costs Something

Second in a Series of Three: Vital Lessons from the Early Church

Acts 7:51-60

Faith costs something. Depending upon your perspective, that is either such an obvious statement that it may seem trite, or a powerful reminder that discipleship is not without a price. Last Sunday we addressed the resurrection of Christ as a defining event in the Christian faith. Both the raising of Lazarus and the resurrection of Jesus served as witness to God's acting in human history. Such events cause some to stumble, for the idea of the miraculous carries different meaning for different people. A miracle is a sign or wonder that points to God, yet many of the miracles that we encounter each day may seem only miraculous to the believer and not the observer. Jesus' resurrection, a miracle that transcends our understanding of death, medical science, and physics, is certainly an idea that requires faith to grasp and to accept. Either you believe or you do not. Whenever you believe, faith costs something.

The first four hundred years of the Christian church were some of the most difficult, dangerous, and demanding times for believers. In the days of Christ and on through the time of Paul and the destruction of the Herodian temple in 70 C.E., religious persecution by Jewish leaders was a primary concern. Also very real was the derision Christians received from Greco-Roman culture, pagan cults, and other groups, which made discipleship perilous. Beyond this time, many Roman emperors fueled the increase of Christian persecution, such that it was more or less routine until the fifth century under the influence of Constantine. Some, like Nero, found Christians to be easy scapegoats or merely cheap entertainment for the Colosseum.

Today's text is the account from Acts of the stoning of Stephen, who is considered the first Christian martyr. Many of us may enjoy being first in line, first in a race, or first to be promoted, but few of us wish to place first in martyrdom. That seems too costly a price to pay for faith.

Acts tells the story in the style of great legends, and although we may not know how the writer embellished it before being recorded for our reading, it is clear that Stephen was a person of bold faith. It was his bold faith and unwavering conviction that led to the confrontation that ended with his death. This account has all of the elements of a Hollywood classic where a hero-figure is the object of injustice and evil. Waiting in the wings stands another protagonist who, unknowingly or even reluctantly, is about to bring redemption to the story. Saul is such a figure. Saul witnesses the price that Stephen paid for his conviction, yet the next chapter begins with these chilling words, "And Saul approved of their killing him" (Acts 8:1).

Depending on where you live, such persecution is still very real today. In 1999, Hindu extremists attacked an Australian Christian missionary and his eight- and ten-year-old sons, burning them alive in their car where they had been sleeping. In China, Bibles have had to be smuggled into some regions and many outspoken Christians have been censured or imprisoned.

No matter where you live, faith costs something. Faith in Christ involves commitment, service, humility, and sacrifice. It is not a dour faith, for there is joy and grace to fill a lifetime with blessings. Yet, when we respond to any great love, commitment demands our time and energy, as well as our money and resources. Just as any significant relationship can stretch us and challenge us to grow as a person, so does our faith relationship stretch us as disciples of Christ.

What do you expect to happen when you come to worship? Do you expect to be comforted but not challenged? Commended but not called to serve? Encouraged but not exhorted? Inspired but not stretched? At the same service I had a person moved to make a large gift to support a mission of the church, another volunteered to serve as a Sunday school teacher, whereas another person criticized the sermon and the music and challenged me to reconsider how our church worships. What do you think each of these persons expected out of worship? Who was listening, and to whom?

Christian discipleship that is rooted in love and grows through faith compels us to move out of the shallow waters of daily living and into the depths of true life in Christ. The abundance of life that Jesus offers is of a character and quality that no storm can overwhelm and no war can disquiet. There is a peace that squelches the raging turmoil of anxiety that robs us of joy. Life is not made easier by being a Christian disciple; it is made more fulfilling and given a foundation that is unshakable. (Gary G. Kindley)

Worship Aids

Pastoral Prayer

We wish to be a faithful people, O God. Faith is such an elusive thing. We cannot grasp it, and yet it can grasp us. We discover it when we let go and place our trust in it. We wish to be a faithful people, O God. Help us move from wishing for faith, to being faithful. May our love and our life be grounded in the grace that you so freely give. In the name of the Holy One we pray. Amen.

Unison Invocation

Holy God, we come to worship today with many different expectations. Some of us are celebrating a wonderful week and countless blessings, and we are here to offer you praise and gratitude. Some of us are at a difficult time in our lives, and things are not unfolding exactly as we planned. We are here for strength, courage, and direction. Then there are those of us, God, who are wondering where you are. We are lost, adrift, and wandering through life. Our doubts seem to outweigh our faith. Help us all, O Lord, come to an awareness of your presence. To be in your presence is enough. Amen.

Benediction

Go out into the world as a disciple of Jesus Christ. Go out into the world and witness to your faith. Go out into the world and be the church. In the name of the Creator, Sustainer, and Redeemer, Amen. (Gary G. Kindley)

MAY 28, 2006

❧❧❧

Seventh Sunday of Easter

Readings: Acts 1:15-17, 21-26; Psalm 1; 1 John 5:9-13; John 17:6-19

God's Gift: Eternal Life
1 John 5:9-13

In the world in which we live, there are very few things in life that we can be sure of, that we can count on. Material possessions wear out, our bodies falter, promises are broken, and life deals to us blows that overwhelm us. It's enough to cause us to ask, Is there anything we can rely on?

We can rely on God's word. Once we turn our attention to the word of God, we find it is filled with promises that sustain us and give us hope when hope seems impossible. We know from God's word that God loves us, and there is nothing we could ever do to go beyond God's reach. We know from God's word that there is indeed a place called heaven and a place called hell. We know also that we will spend all of eternity in one of those two places depending on what we believe about Jesus Christ. "God has given us eternal life, and this life is in his Son. He who has the Son has life; he who does not have the Son of God does not have life" (1 John 5:11b-12 NIV).

John spent a great deal of time with the Lord during John's ministry, and experienced firsthand the love and compassion that Jesus demonstrated on a daily basis to those around him. John writes this letter to proclaim the eternal life that is with the Father, and so we might fellowship with him and one another in the light (1:7). If we are in fellowship with God, we will confess our sins, and God will forgive us and purify us. We will also love our brothers and sisters in Christ, recognizing that God is love, and that "whoever lives in love lives in God and God lives in him" (4:16b GNT). God is light, God is love, and ultimately God is life through Jesus Christ.

John wants us to understand the promise and assurance of eternal life, given to us, not because of anything we have done, but because of God's grace and mercy. Our confidence is not founded upon human witness or people's opinion. Our confidence in eternal life is founded upon God's word. Because we know that "all Scripture is given by inspiration of God" (2 Timothy 3:16 KJV), we can also know God's heart. God is "not willing that any should perish, but that all should come to repentance" (2 Peter 3:9 KJV). "For whosoever shall call upon the name of the Lord shall be saved" (Romans 10:13 KJV).

John wants us to learn four valuable truths from our text today. First, John says the witness of God is greater than the witness of men. The witness of people may or may not be true. The witness of people may change tomorrow. The witness of people may be good for one person and not for another. But the witness of God will not falter. The witness of God is grounded in the testimony of God's only begotten Son, and that testimony does not fail. The witness of God is grounded in truth, it is grounded in love, and it is grounded in God's sovereignty. People are emotional; God is constant. Human words are subjective and fallible; God's word is objective and our standard. The witness of God is greater than the witness of human beings.

Second, John assures us God's witness separates those who believe from those who do not believe. We were told in verse 9 that the witness of God is in his Son, and John then says that "anyone who believes" is in direct contrast to "anyone who does not believe." Those who believe have the witness in their hearts. Those who believe can be identified outwardly by that which is in their hearts. Those who have not yet believed are by their actions denying the witness of God. John goes so far as to say that those who have not believed make God a liar. The distinction is clear— the witness of God separates the wheat from the chaff, the saved from the lost, and the sheep from the wolves. The question we might ask is this: Is the witness of God evident in my life?

John makes a transition from a warning to a promise. Beginning in verse 11, John tells us that God's witness gives us eternal life, and that this life is found only in and through God's Son, Jesus Christ. I daresay it could not be stated more clearly than when John writes, "He who has the Son has life; he who does not have the Son of God does not have life" (NIV).

Finally, John wants his readers to know that they have eternal life. The witness of God begins with salvation and is a progression that never ends. When we believe the witness of God, we believe in the Son. When we believe in the Son, we have life. When we receive life, we receive eternal life. When we receive eternal life, we have nothing to fear, for heaven is just a breath away and death can never harm us—all because of the witness of God and his amazing grace. (Jimmy McNeil)

Sharing Love and Joy Is Better than Acting Religious

Third in a Series of Three: Vital Lessons from the Early Church

John 3:16; Acts 2:43-47

The concept of a powerful divine presence that could easily destroy or alter the course of creation, and yet chooses, instead, to offer unconditional love is a story of truly amazing grace. It is such extravagant grace that liberates the soul and brings hope to the most desperate of lives. Of course, we human beings, the wayward, fickle, self-centered, ignorant, judgmental, closeminded, and skeptical lot that we are, take what is wondrous and amazing—the grace of God—and mess it up.

If I were to make parallels to our mishandling of God's incredible gift using mundane analogies, I might offer a few suggestions. God gives us indoor plumbing, and we build an outhouse. God gives us electricity, and we rip out the wires to replace them with wicks and flame. God offers us glimpses into other galaxies, and we watch movies where zombies come back to life and eat the flesh of the living. God gives us one another with a capacity to love, and we focus on ourselves and look at others with jealousy, envy, or disdain.

Sharing love and joy is better than being religious, not because religion is of itself bad. Religion is an expression of faith and the diverse human perspectives of God and the spiritual realm. Religion, like money, is not inherently evil or bad. It is what we do with religion that gives religion its character and value. We build religions that may focus more on ritual and doctrine than on service and love. We allow judgmental attitudes to give rise to mean-spirited actions. We debate hierarchy while ignoring the hungry, and preach piety while passing by the impoverished. The church is, at times, not unlike the dysfunctional family that has been living with destructive behavior for so long that their behavior becomes both normal and acceptable to them. At our best, we remember who we really are and who we are called to be. At our worst, we have lost sight of the vision of community that Christ shows us. We repeatedly miss the mark in being a community of love, justice, and service.

This is not a sermon about bashing the church or throwing out religion, but rather a plea to point us to the true message of the Christ. God is love. God loves us despite our sin and brokenness. God loves life so much that it is shared with us as a gift. God desires us to share in the celebration of life and to offer love and joy to others. Making disciples is to be in the seed-planting, good-news-sharing business. We offer the potential of a better way, a better life, a more satisfying journey. We invite people to consider our experience of God and to join us in the experience of grace. Being faithful is our calling. Religion is merely the framework of carrying out that faith in community, because we really do need one another.

Today's text from Acts is a snapshot of the early church sharing community together. It is an instructive lesson in how community in the Christian tradition is meant to be. They take meals in common, for there is little else more satisfying than breaking the bread of life with those you love. They share their possessions and resources. There is no need. There is no want. There is no one left out. There is no one alone. There is no one not welcome at the table. There is always room for one more. This is the kingdom of God!

The kingdom of heaven is not some abstract place up above. The kingdom of heaven is God's kingdom whenever and wherever two or more of the faithful are there. In foxholes and fancy sanctuaries, the kingdom of heaven can be in our midst. If we say that heaven means so much to us, then let us live today as we say we will live then. If the community of faith is so important, then let us make it a central part of our lives and band together with people who share the vision of love, justice, and service. When we do, amazing things begin to happen!

A young man was knocking on the glass doors of the church early one Tuesday morning. A senior adult happened to be inside setting up for a women's meeting, but she went to the door to talk to the man. Being alone, she did not wish to let him in, so she asked what he needed and discerned that he was in spiritual and emotional pain and in need of the pastor. She summoned me to the church and I learned that I needed a translator to speak to him. I found one, and we sat with the young man as he poured out the pain of his story.

Being from another country, he did not know anyone here except some immoral coworkers who had been a very bad influence upon him. His mother had told him that whenever he needed help he should go to a church, so he stopped when he saw the cross on our building. Problems are not resolved overnight, but as the weeks unfolded we connected the man to a Spanish-speaking church near his home. He was baptized, and soon after answered a call to ordained ministry. He is now enrolled in seminary and is excited about what God has done and is doing in his life.

So many things could have stood in the way of this young man's salvation. A senior adult could have chosen not to be bothered by a persistent visitor knocking on a locked door before office hours. I could have told him to come back another time. The translator could have said he was too busy at work. The pastor to whom we referred him could have chosen not to devote the time required at this critical point of his spiritual journey. Because people chose to respond in kind—to respond with the same grace and faith that God gave each one of us—a life was touched and changed.

The heart of the church of Jesus Christ is not rules but relationships. We all are a part of the body of Christ and each of us has a role that is so very important. Sharing love and joy is so much more important than act-ing religious. After all, it is the Christlike thing to do. (Gary G. Kindley)

Worship Aids

Call to Worship

> **People: God.**
>
> Leader: Which God?
>
> **People: The God who loved.**
>
> Leader: Whom did God love?
>
> **People: God so loved the world.**
>
> Leader: How do we know?
>
> **People: God gave his only Son so that the world might be saved.**
>
> **All: Let us love one another as God has loved us! Amen.**

Prayer

Gracious and loving God, your gift of creation humbles and awes us as we consider the complexity of this world. The beauty and intricacy of the human eye, through which we behold your handiwork, is by itself mirac-ulous. The touch of the human hand upon the face of a child brings joy, contentment, and tenderness. Who could imagine how skin and nerves could yield such simple pleasure? All the technology ever created cannot match the intricacy of the hummingbird; the capabilities of the human body; or the alluring fragrance, gentle texture, and visual delight of the rose. Bless us as we partake of your greatest gifts of life, love, and joy. In your wondrous name we pray. Amen.

Benediction

Be bearers of the love of God, the joy of life in the Spirit, and the peace that comes from knowing. Live out your faith with glad and generous hearts. In the name of the Father, Son, and Holy Spirit, Amen. (Gary G. Kindley)

JUNE 4, 2006

❧❧❧❧

Day of Pentecost

Readings: Acts 2:1-21; Psalm 104:24-34, 35*b*; Romans 8:22-27; John 15:26-27; 16:4*b*-15

The Lord God Made Them All
Psalm 104:24-34, 35*b*

For true reconciliation between the Native Americans and the non-Native peoples of the United States, a genuine understanding of the formal and legal relationship between the tribes and the federal government is needed. A respect for who the indigenous peoples are and what they have contributed is also essential. These verses from Psalm 104 reflect Native Americans' attitudes toward Mother Earth and creation, long in place before immigrants came to this continent. In a time when ecological issues such as nuclear waste, dependence upon nonrenewable resources, and global warming dominate the ecological forefront, what better time to foster an understanding of Native stewardship?

For most Native nations, the idea of land ownership was completely foreign in 1492. Each nation had its own territory, which they protected and defended, but they knew they did not own it. The land belonged to Creator; we were merely stewards. As Diné (Navajo), our land boundaries were the four sacred mountains. We had no surveyors or fences. Our identity is bound with the land. When the United States War Department of the 1800s determined the boundaries of the reservation, the Diné did not understand these limitations. In the early 1960s, the oil and gas companies came in and "bought" land from the Native people not living within those unseen bounds of the reservation. Never mind that the price those companies paid for one hundred acres of mineral-rich land was a pickup truck; the original inhabitants didn't understand that now they couldn't use the land for their sheep herd. Their hogans were torn down to make room for equipment or mining. The land they had responsibility for was now gone and many were left homeless. Even now, as individuals, we do not own land if we live on the reservation. Families pay for hundred-year leases. Our worldview and practice does not encompass the idea of ownership of the land.

Most of our cultures are interwoven with the land. The crafts we are known for use the gifts Creator made available to us. The Hopi craft their pottery from the earth. Baskets of the northeastern tribes use the plants in their domain. The Diné weave rugs made from the wool of their sheep and dyed with the local plants. The sandcast molds for their silverwork is made from the sandstone formations common on the reservation. The nations of Oklahoma are known for their bead and leatherwork, sewed on skins of their kill. With each piece of work, whether art or culinary, Creator is acknowledged and thanked.

Our "native" foods reflect the resources Creator gave us. Yakima have salmon; the Plains Indians had the buffalo, and the Pueblo communities had their corn dishes. The romanticized picture of the Native American is hunting for buffalo, but many were farmers. Both the hunters and the farmers had something in common; before the hunt and before the planting season, each gave thanks to Creator for their livelihood. Many of the dances are actually a prayer for a safe and successful season, or in gratitude for the same. In a hunt, a prayer is given to the animal who will die to feed and clothe the People. Likewise, the farmer offers a prayer to the earth for giving of herself for the People.

Llano, Texas, deer capitol of Texas, is in the middle of the Hill Country. Nestled among the oak trees with the Llano River running through it, the locals of Gillespie County are dependent upon deer season. Deer season starts the first weekend of September, but hunters are setting up camp and their favorite spot for several weeks before the opening day. The hunters come, with their four-wheelers, their trailers, their gear, and their beer. I remember the first time I visited Llano during deer season. I drove by a roadside park with black garbage bags overflowing the trash cans in several directions. Raccoons had ripped bags open so trash was everywhere. A deer's torso jutted out of one bag. The hunter had taken the rack and the best cut of meat and thrown the rest away. What a waste! What a shame! Perhaps the dominant society can still learn from the Native American.

Most creation stories of the different nations recognize that there is a Supreme Being, a Holy Mystery, who created the world. The nations' theology believes that God created the world precisely and exactly to support life of the two-leggeds. Is that not what Genesis and science teaches also? If it were just a little bit closer to the sun or if the atmosphere were to change by too much, planet earth could not support human life.

The psalmist praises Creator and creation with almost reckless abandon. Everywhere he looks, he sees evidence of Creator's majesty, power, and imagination. With so much available to us at discount stores, grocery stores, and restaurants, are we in danger of overlooking what Creator has given us? Native Americans are adapting to a different lifestyle, yet the dances and the ceremonies serve as reminders that we are here for just a short while, and we really "own" nothing. In the celebration of Pentecost, we are reminded of the gift of the Holy Spirit. May we also be reminded that everything we have is from God. (Raquel Mull)

The Gift of God's Spirit: Suddenly!

First in a Series of Four: The Holy Spirit

Acts 2:1-2

It had been a difficult eight months: a change in leadership of the ministry where I work, a move to a new home, a son leaving home for college, the loss of two staff members, and the hiring of two new ones to replace them. Needless to say, a lot of changes took place, and in the midst of all these changes was me. I became overwhelmed with all that was being asked of me. I began to focus on the demands of such change and began to feel out of control. I became the focus. After it all transpired, I was exhausted, struggling, self-centered, and hurt. Although the changes were good ones, I was not coping well with so much so fast. During the week of Martin Luther King, Jr.'s birthday my staff and I decided to challenge our students in a worship service to commit themselves to using their God-given gifts to strengthen our community. Our community had been struggling with some issues and in this service we wanted to confront our students with that reality. We wanted to challenge them to do something like King and like others who had strengthened their communities. We opened the altar at the end of the service and invited students forward to make those decisions, to talk with staff if they needed to, and to come to the altar to pray. The response from our students was powerful. They began to pour out of the pews. You could sense that life-giving gift of God's spirit present and working its powerful way with the hearts of our community. You could see it, sense it, feel it, know it, and behold its movement among our staff and students.

The scripture tells us that as they were all together in one place "suddenly from heaven there came a sound like the rush of a violent wind, and it filled the entire house where they were sitting." I like that word, *suddenly*. It identifies so well how the gift of God's spirit comes to us— suddenly. Without warning, without time to prepare, without a plan, without any sense of when it is going to come or what it is going to do, suddenly the spirit just comes. Isn't that just like this God of mystery? Isn't that just like this God who comes in his own time, in his own way, and in his own place of choice? This powerful story lets us know right from the beginning that the community of faith, the church, has every-thing to do with God and little to do with us. The church's birth narra-tive seeks to be clear on one point: we know not the time or the place or the way in which God seeks to move and work.

Mostly we don't care too much for this unexpected, unpredictable movement of God. We like being in control. We want to know. We are much more comfortable with a timetable, with plans, with being in on what is going on, and when it is going to happen. It seems to be human nature to be consumed with knowing. The author of Genesis reminds us in the creation story that it was this whole idea of knowing that got humankind into trouble in the first place. It seems as if God wants us to realize that what God is doing and when God will do it has little to do with us knowing much about anything. Perhaps part of what this story is trying to tell us is that God is moving, God is working, God's spirit is alive in our lives and world. That movement has little to do with you or me. It is entirely dependent on God's time, on God's sense of life and history, on God's perspective, and on God's understanding of the bigger picture.

Those sudden moments in our lives when we realize God's spirit mov-ing and working among us should provide us with a sense that God knows what God does. Jesus told those who gathered that day that this day of birthing would come. And maybe that is what it comes down to for us. The faith that we must have in what God in Christ has said will be done. It is strange in the Gospel stories that when God's promises in Christ, such as the resurrection or the coming of the Holy Spirit, do happen there is always such surprise and awe. Suddenly, God comes, God works, the spirit of God breaks through, and life is never the same again.

It is amazing what God does in the midst of community. It was not by accident that they were all together in one place. God calls us to be such a community. When the community gathers, who knows what God might do among us? One Wednesday evening, overwhelmed by life, frustrated by change, focusing on me, the community gathered. Suddenly, the spirit of God moved and everything changed. "Suddenly" brings with it a new perspective and a new way of seeing. Suddenly, thank God for suddenly. (Travis Franklin)

Worship Aids

Call to Worship (Isaiah 43:1)

Leader: But now says the LORD,

People: He who created you, O Jacob,

Leader: He who formed you, O Israel: Do not fear,

People: For I have redeemed you;

Leader: I have called you by name,

All: You are mine!

Pastoral Prayer

We come before you, Lord, as a sinful people. We come here today knowing that we are less than you have made us to be. Forgive us we pray in this time of worship. Pardon us from all that would keep us from you and from your will for our lives. Help us move beyond ourselves that we might be courageous in our witness to your love as we seek to be your heart, your hands, and your feet. Empower us to trust your most Holy Spirit as it seeks to lead us to do what we don't want to do in places we fear to go. Thank you for this marvelous gift of life. In the name of the risen Christ we pray. Amen. (Travis Franklin)

JUNE 11, 2006

First Sunday after Pentecost

Readings: 1 Samuel 8:4-11, (12-15), 16-20, (11:14-15); Psalm 138;
2 Corinthians 4:13–5:1; Mark 3:20-35

Of Cabbages and Kings
1 Samuel 8:4-11, (12-15), 16-20, (11:14-15)

In Lewis Carroll's *Through the Looking-Glass*, the sequel to *Alice's Adventures in Wonderland*, we discover this charming, whimsical bit of verse:

> "The time has come," the Walrus said,
> "To talk of many things:
> Of shoes—and ships—and sealing wax—
> Of cabbages—and kings—
> And why the sea is boiling hot—
> And whether pigs have wings."

Although Carroll was writing primarily for the amusement of his friends' children, he was also a master of satire, poking fun at culture and convention. He aimed one of the sharpest barbs at the inconsistency and irrelevance in his society's attitudes.

The Walrus, for instance, represents those who place the same value on trifles and treasures, on mundane things and ultimate issues. In the same conversation, with equal importance, he wants to talk of shoes, ships, and sealing wax; of cabbage and kings; why the sea is boiling hot; and whether pigs have wings.

It's too bad the Israelites didn't have Lewis Carroll around when they started demanding of Samuel, "Give us a king, give us a king!" He could so easily have shot holes in their foolish reasoning for their demand. It was clear that they didn't have the maturity to know the difference between cabbages and kings.

For centuries they thrived as a theocracy (rule by God). The nation with its covenant was responsible to God directly, not through a regal house. As a result, they could say, "What great nation is there that has God so near to it, as the LORD our God is to us? . . . And what great nation is there that has such statutes and righteous judgments?" (Deuteronomy 4:7-8 NKJV).

But evidently this was not enough for Israel. A poor prophet in a rustic mantle, although conversant with the Almighty, was embarrassingly unstylish among the neighboring nations. But a king in a purple robe and glittering crown, with his guards and officers of state, would look superb.

They didn't say, "Give us a king who is wise and good, and will rule with justice and mercy." They simply wanted a king "like the other nations," anybody would do who could cut a good figure. Israel obviously didn't know the difference between cabbages and kings.

When Samuel expressed displeasure, the people's polite request turned to a riotous demand: "Give us a king!" Foolish ambitions have a way of entrenching themselves when challenged. When the Westminster Assembly met in 1643 to reform the English Church, it was led in prayer by a self-willed divine whose petition was, "Lord, we beseech thee that thou wilt guide us aright, for we are very determined."

The Israelites had been a people chosen of God, a God who had led them from slavery to freedom and who had bound himself to them by a covenant. This gave them a unique status among nations. What eventually enabled Israel to make its unique contribution to religion was not that it had a king like other nations, but that it had prophets, as other nations did not.

As they stood before Samuel with their demands for a monarchy, they were clamoring, as we do to this day, to "keep up with the Joneses." How much of our praying is for what we need or for what our neighbors have?

The people thought they had really won the day when Samuel told them that God was going to let them have their king. What they learned so bitterly, as many of us have, is that God is often serving us better by refusing our prayers than by granting them.

Even as Samuel told the people they could have their king, he told them what it would cost them. Their sons and daughters would become virtual slaves to provide the royal retinue; to equip and feed a standing army; to give up their lands and vineyards to the king's favorites; to be burdened with heavy taxes to support the royal magnificence.

Their reply to Samuel was an even more vehement demand, "No, but we will have a king over us, that we also may be like all the nations, and that our king may judge us and go out before us and fight our battles"

(1 Samuel 8:20 NKJV). Now they present a new argument—they needed a king to fight their battles.

Had they forgotten so soon the great victory wrought by Samuel's prayer and God's thunder (7:10)? Ironically, their first king (Saul) was slain in a battle, which none of their judges ever were. They were not the first people, or the last, to forsake the Lord to their own peril.

But even when the people are obstinate and self-willed, God is patient and waits for them to discover the difference between cabbages and kings. Henry van Dyke once put in a few simple verses this roundabout, patient way of God.

> GOD said, "I am tired of kings"—
> But that was a long while ago!
> And meantime man said, "No,—
> I like their looks in their robes and rings."
> So he crowned a few more,
> And they went on playing the game as before,
> Fighting and spoiling things.
>
> Man said, "I am tired of kings!
> Sons of the robber-chiefs of yore,
> They make me pay for their lust and their war;
> I am the puppet, they pull the strings;
> The blood of my heart is the wine they drink.
> I will govern myself for awhile I think,
> And see what that brings!"
>
> Then God, who made the first remark,
> Smiled in the dark.
> (Henry van Dyke, "Remarks about Kings," in
> *The Poems of Henry van Dyke* [New York:
> Charles Scribner's Sons, 1920], 376)

(Bill Austin)

The Work of God's Spirit: Filled!

Second in a Series of Four: The Holy Spirit

Acts 2:3-4

Scripture tells us that as the community gathered and the spirit of God moved among them, a sign of the presence of God's Spirit rested on them like tongues of fire. The work of fire in the Gospels is that of purification. Luke wants us to know that part of the coming of the Holy Spirit is to purify us. The Holy Spirit refines us and readies us. The nature of fire is not only to refine or purify, but also to consume or to burn away. God's spirit in the life of this community is to strip away all that is unnecessary. It seeks to refine the community so that they are ready to do what it is the spirit of God leads them to do. I am reminded of Isaiah's experience in the temple as recorded in the sixth chapter of Isaiah. When Isaiah saw the vision of God he saw himself and his community as they really were, as a people of unclean lips. God sought to refine the impurities of Isaiah with a burning coal from the fire. Then Isaiah became ready for God's work among the people. The tongues of fire represent this refining work of God's spirit as part of a process that purifies and readies God's person and people for the work God calls them to do.

After the tongues of fire rested on each of them, the scripture tells us that they were "filled with the Holy Spirit." It is interesting to note that not just some of them were filled, but all of them were filled. In the midst of this community on this particular day, as God sought to begin and create this new expression of life, he left no one on the sidelines. They were all filled with the Holy Spirit. A consistent theme throughout the Gospels is the concept that God invites everyone to the table. This theme remains consistent; Luke makes it clear that God filled them all.

The work of the Holy Spirit in this time and place was to fill the community. Once refined and purified, those gathered were then filled with the Holy Spirit. The image of filling something or someone is used to instruct: that which fills is then used and poured out. When I fill a pitcher with water it is for the purpose of pouring it out for others. When I fill my car with gas it is so that the gas will be used to power the engine of my car. This idea of these being filled with the Holy Spirit implies that the community filled for some reason other than simply to remain full. How can you talk about filling something up if you don't also imply the idea of being emptied? The point of being filled is to be emptied. In the church, we fall in love with the idea of being filled. We design worship to be inspirational. We go to Bible studies to be nourished by God's word. We go to Sunday school to learn and to grow. And yet, the follow-up to such activity must do something with the inspiration, must respond to the nourishment we receive, must allow our growth to affect who we are and what we do in life. God filled the community that day. There was a purpose for the filling they received.

The passage implies that the work of God's Spirit is to fill us. So many people cannot be filled because they are already full. They are full of hatred, full of anger, full of resentment, full of pity, full of self-importance, full of so much stuff. Is it any surprise that when we go to worship we leave disappointed? How can we be filled with anything of God when we are so full of so much? Perhaps one reason that God could fill them that day was that they were together in one place as a community of people who had emptied themselves of their fear, of their misgivings, of their disappointments, of their presumptions, of their anger, and of their self-importance so that there was room to be filled with what mattered most—God's most Holy Spirit. God's Spirit is seeking us out in order that we might be filled. (Travis Franklin)

Worship Aids

Invocation

Into your presence we come, O God of love and hope. Inspire us with the gift of your most Holy Spirit as we gather here today. Empower us with a sense of anticipation as to what it is you will be doing among us in the sacred time and at this sacred place. In the name and spirit of Christ our Lord we pray. Amen.

JUNE 18, 2006

Second Sunday after Pentecost

Readings: 1 Samuel 15:34–16:13; Psalm 20; 2 Corinthians 5:6-10 (11-13), 14-17; Mark 4:26-34

Little Things Are Big Things
1 Samuel 15:34–16:13; Mark 4:26-34

The prophet Samuel's life sums up what it means to live a life of faith. For Samuel faith is not intellectual agreement with certain theological propositions. Faith is trust that God is reliable no matter what. That is the life Samuel led. In today's lesson Samuel goes to Bethlehem to anoint David king. In this story we see hints of what the faith-filled life could be.

First this story tells us not to spend our lives in the past. The story opens noting that Samuel was grieving over having anointed Saul as king. From the perspective of his old age, the most significant thing that Samuel had done was, as God's representative, anoint Saul Israel's first king. Samuel perhaps thought this was the most significant deed of his lifetime, but Saul's rule did not turn out well and Samuel was grieved.

I have known people who spent their lives grieving over a failed marriage or a wayward child or a lost job. They could never let go and move on. Now don't misunderstand me: grief is essential and the past is important. But the purpose of grieving is to move us on. We don't grieve to stay stuck in the sadness. We grieve to heal and move ahead.

Karl Wallenda, the great patriarch of the Wallenda high-wire artists, died in a high-wire accident. He planned a spectacular stunt to walk a wire that was strung between two skyscrapers. When the day came for the stunt, the wind was blowing harder than he would have liked. People tried to persuade Wallenda not to walk, but his pride got the best of him. He walked out, grasping his balance pole, and made his way carefully across the wire. Then a gust of wind unsteadied him. Onlookers saw him fighting for his balance with his balance pole. But he toppled off the wire and fell to his death. His lifeless body was found with an almost unbreakable grip on the balance pole.

Wire-walking experts will tell you the balancing pole is life. An experienced walker can keep his or her balance with the aid of the pole. Those who understand wire-walking will also tell you that in rare circumstances one has to let go of the pole and grab the wire itself. Karl Wallenda couldn't let go of the pole and he died. How many people go through their lives unable to let go of someone or something, or some sadness or some event? People of faith do not spend their lives in the past.

A second lesson from this story is that God does not see the way we see. When Samuel arrived at Jesse's house like any father of that era, Jesse presented his oldest son to Samuel and said, "Surely this is the one." Samuel saw he was strong and heroic, and was about to anoint him king when God said to him, "Not that one." Down the list of sons he went from the oldest to the youngest until he finally got to the youngest one, the one who in that time would have been the least likely to be considered. God said, "That one. That's the one." The text reminds Samuel and us that God does not see as we see.

How many times in life has something happened that you thought was wonderful and it turned out tragic? How many times have your tragedies been the springboard to something new and better? God does not see the way we see. We think we have life figured out. But life teaches that God is at work in ways that we do not clearly perceive.

Life unfolds in unpredictable ways. Faith is trusting God no matter what. Faith is trusting God when things turn to our benefit and when they don't, because in the big picture, we do not have the big picture. Faith is trusting in the God who does.

Finally, this story reminds us that big things often start small. David was anointed in secret. Saul was still on the throne. This was not a great public coronation of the new king. Samuel came to this obscure town of Bethlehem and secretly anointed a new rival king. Something that started as small as a secret anointing became, in time, the glory days of Israel. For centuries after, the Israelites would say their best times were King David's time. "Oh, if we could only have another king like David," they would say. That which began in hiding grew to be the glory days.

One of Jesus' parables speaks of the kingdom of God starting small as a grain of mustard seed and growing into a plant housing the birds of the air. If we had been a rider on the city bus in Montgomery, Alabama, when Rosa Parks refused to give up her seat, we could hardly have predicted her act of courage would start one of the most massive social changes in our country's history. Big things often start in small individual acts of justice, love, or mercy. We never know how God is going to use one small act. People of faith understand that even small things, like a mustard seed, can grow into a mighty shrub in which the birds of the air make their homes. So what small acts of love or mercy or justice or compassion are we doing?

Old Samuel, funny old sage and prophet, teaches us not to spend our whole lives in the past. He reminds us God does not see things the way we see them. He shows even the smallest acts of mercy and justice can become something big. When we live that way we discover what it means to be people of faith. Amen. (Carl L. Schenck)

The Gift of the Spirit: Purpose and Power!

Third in a Series of Four: The Holy Spirit

Acts 2:4

The heart and soul of the church's witness to faith is that of proclamation. The first action of the Holy Spirit as it fills these first followers is that of proclamation. As God initiates and begins to do God's work in the world, God first empowers the witness of proclamation. The scripture is quite clear as to the source of the church's proclamation of faith: the Holy Spirit of God.

It is this spirit of God that gave them this ability to proclaim. Proclamation in the church is always a gift from God's Spirit. Proclamation is not earned; it is not forced; it is not manipulated; nor is the source of its power anything less than God's Holy Spirit. Proclamation in the community of faith is from God. It comes as a gift of God and is given in the grace of God. It is given for a reason, as it was on that day, and it is given in the midst of community. Jews were gathered from all over the world in the Holy City of Jerusalem. The purpose behind this powerful gift of God's Holy Spirit was to empower the message of God's love into proclamation so that all gathered that day would hear what God was seeking to do among humankind. There is always a purpose behind what God is seeking to do through the gift and work of God's Holy Spirit. Without a sense of God's Spirit the church's proclamation would have no power or purpose.

God's purpose and God's power must be at the source of what the church seeks to proclaim. The early church began as a community founded upon the purpose and power of God's Holy Spirit. God's Holy Spirit thus became the source of the identity, the mission, and the birth of the early church. Such a foundation empowered the early church's identity, their proclamation, and their mission. The early church became the instrument through which the will of God's Holy Spirit sought expression. When the church witnesses, performs its mission, and has its source in the Holy Spirit, then the church fulfills its reason for being and doing.

This powerful passage reminds the church today what its identity, mission, and proclamation must be rooted in if it is to fulfill its legacy. The source of the church's identity, mission, and proclamation must be God's active, life-giving Holy Spirit. Only God's Holy Spirit can give the church the ability to be who the church needs to be and do what the church is led and called to do. I am reminded of the scripture that says, "Unless the LORD builds the house, those who build it labor in vain" (Psalm 127:1). At the center of who the church is and what the church seeks to do in its life and mission must be the gift and work of God's Holy Spirit. Without such a foundation the work of the church is done in vain. The church without the Holy Spirit is separated and cut off from its only source of identity, proclamation, and life.

The context of this passage identifies that the church was gathered that day in that place in response to Christ's instruction to the disciples to go to Jerusalem and wait for this gift of God's Spirit. What makes this story possible is the obedience of those first followers to the leadership and direction of the Christ. We must also keep in mind that those instructions were given by a risen Christ. The greatest news in all the world has just been experienced by these followers and now the word they have been given is to wait. It makes no sense in light of the empty tomb and a risen Jesus. And yet, Jesus says to them, "Go and wait." The early church was obedient to the instruction of Jesus.

Obedience is not a very popular word in today's culture. In the midst of a culture obsessed with independence and freedom, the word *obedience* is met with some suspicion. Outside of meaning and a sense of purpose, independence and freedom are both overrated. Obedience is behind this Pentecost experience. Through the disciple's obedience they find themselves at the time and place of God's choosing. Behold, the gift of the Spirit comes upon them, fills them, and breaks their lives wide open. This story reminds us as God's church that we are called to be an obedient people regardless of and despite how we feel about what God is seeking to lead us to do and God's claim upon us. As a community of faith we are to be faithful followers of a God who is seeking to lead us in ways that often we just simply do not understand. Understanding has never been a prerequisite to following God's lead and probably never will be. The church must learn to be obedient to God at any given moment regardless of appearances. Through the church's obedience to Christ's commands, the community was gathered where it needed to be; doing what it needed to do. Only there did God's Spirit break in upon them and something new was begun.

Today the church needs once again to be obedient to who God is calling it to be and to what God is calling it to do. The source of the church's identity, mission, and proclamation must be rooted and grounded in the gift and work of God's Holy Spirit. When the church fulfills its call to be and do according to the work of that life-giving spirit of God, its purpose will become clear and its work will be empowered in such a way that the world will be amazed and saved. (Travis Franklin)

Worship Aids

Invocation

O God, we gather together in this place seeking to know you. We gather together as a community of your people to know your will and way. Grant us the comfort and power of your presence. Accept us as we are, where we are, and lead us where you would have us go to do what you would have us do. In the name and Spirit of the risen Christ we pray. Amen. (Travis Franklin)

JUNE 25, 2006

❧❧❧

Third Sunday after Pentecost

Readings: 1 Samuel 17:(1a, 4-11, 19-23), 32-49; Psalm 9:9-20;
2 Corinthians 6:1-13; Mark 4:35-41

Faith or Fear?
Mark 4:35-41

I met a girl named Faith (not her real name). She and her grandfather came by to shoot basketball in the goal set up for our grandchildren. Faith was about ten years old. She was a very small girl but she could really shoot the basketball. She had a lot of confidence. Faith had a lot of faith!

There was another little girl who came to our church preschool program recently. Although I didn't know her name, it could have been "Fear," for she was afraid of everything. It broke my heart to see her so distressed. I have no idea what was going on at home or in her mind. Maybe it was just the first-day jitters of being away from Mom, but whatever, she was really fearful.

I began thinking about Fear and Faith. What makes a person have faith or be fearful? How can we encourage faith, for it is a desired emotional character trait, as over against fear? How can we dispel the debilitating effects of fear in our lives and the lives of our children?

One thing is certain, we live in a society that fosters fear rather than faith. Fear is everywhere. We fear for our safety in our homes and on the highways. We fear for our health. We fear for our security. We fear for our children in their schools.

The Bible recognizes the reality of fear, but it encourages faith as the intentional alternative choice for God's people.

Faith is one of the gifts of the spirit, which God is trying to give to us today. The Old Testament story of David and Goliath is the story of the faith of David. The Bible also tells about the twelve spies who went ahead of the Hebrews to explore the promised land. Only Joshua and Caleb reported out of a faith perspective.

There are the wonderful and powerful stories of Jesus exorcising the demons of disease and mental illness, and even the storm demon. How many of us deal with certain areas of our lives in which we are fearful, rather than believing and feeling confident that God will be with us and will see us through the storm? In the name of the living Christ, I command the demon of fear to come out of you and I pray that faith and confidence will move into the vacuum of your inner life that will now shape your emotions and your destiny.

One of the reasons we intentionally choose to place our families and ourselves in church is because here we encourage faith—not faith in ourselves but faith in God.

Here we seek to know and understand God's will. Here we reflect together on the meaning of God's word and read the word in worship: "God is our refuge and strength, / a very present help in trouble" (Psalm 46:1).

Here we are encouraged to live confidently in the center of the Creator's will despite whatever circumstances may occur in the world. Here we are encouraged to keep our eyes on Jesus. Jesus and Jesus alone is the center of our focus.

Here we learn and sing our songs of faith. In the 1970s just after the Vietnam War, I visited a refugee camp at Eglin Air Force Base in Florida. Hundreds of refugees were huddled under tents. Some learning English. Some filling out government forms. Some being taught to cook. Children playing games. In a temporary chapel, there was a group singing in their native tongue "Leaning on the Everlasting Arms." Here were people who had lost everything but their lives and their faith, and they were singing:

"What have I to dread, what have I to fear, leaning on the everlasting arms?"

Here we learn that through faith and love alone, God will see us through the bad times. Revenge won't do it. Human power and money won't do it. Fear won't do it. Only faith and love and hope; these three abide.

Let me make the following suggestions: First, claim a faith in something that is more dependable than the material things of this earth. Second, claim faith in God, for God will be with you as you live and as you die and even after you die.

When I was hit by a runaway car a few years ago and survived, and when my brother was hit by a runaway disease called cancer and did not survive, I realized on both occasions how tenuous and finite our lives really are. Death is one of the most certain of all certainties. We must face this fact and we can face it with fear or with faith. We can choose to face the storms of life, which will come to us with candor, courage, and faith.

In 1945 when Dietrich Bonhoeffer, a thirty-nine-year-old German Lutheran pastor who opposed Adolf Hitler, was taken away to be hanged in a Nazi prison, some said, "It is the end." Bonhoeffer said: "It is the beginning." Faith can enable you to face with confidence the challenge of living and dying.

Claim faith and strengthen your faith by practicing faithful living. For one day, believe that God is with you and will bless your life and will open up interesting opportunities for you to serve him. Pray and believe for one full week. Be a believing person rather than a suspicious person for one day, one week, and one month.

Claim faith and "when the storms of life are raging," God will stand by you. God will come to you in your time of greatest need. (Henry E. Roberts)

The Gift of God's Spirit: What Does This Mean?

Fourth in a Series of Four: The Holy Spirit

Acts 2:5-13

One of the amazing truths about the biblical witness of faith is its honesty. This passage from Acts is no different. This amazing story of the birth of the early church unfolds as the response of those who witness it is one of perplexity and amazement. The penetrating question this event elicits is a good one: "What does this mean?" This type of question often follows an expression of God's work and love among us. I am reminded of when Jesus calmed the storm on the Sea of Galilee. After this occasion the disciples wondered in amazement, "Who then is this, that he commands even the winds and the water, and they obey him?" (Luke 8:25). There is apparently nothing wrong with asking such questions. What is sometimes wrong is how we seek to answer the questions.

The passage states that all asked the question, "What does this mean?" but follows with an explanation by some, "They are all filled with new wine" (Acts 2:13). The nature of the human drama is that some just don't "get it." In the midst of events we don't understand, we regularly pass them off as some aberrant or unnatural expression of life. Such answers to life's mysteries seem to dismiss too easily that there are many experiences that go beyond simple explanations. Acts 2 is a powerful example of how

God seeks to work amid the ordinary and everyday experiences of life. God evidently moves among us, in us, with us, through us, and all around us. Such work by God makes some people uneasy. Rather than recognizing the mystery of life and God, and seeking to be open to what life might teach us or where God might lead us, our experiences of God become so much easier to write off as unnatural. Or we offer an explanation we understand but rarely fits. To dismiss the phenomenon that took place that day, by saying they must have been a little drunk, closes us to who God is and what God is seeking to do. We human beings are not that comfortable with those life experiences that defy what we seemingly think we know. Such a response, however, is irresponsible on our part and misses the point of how God seeks to work among us.

The very message God sought to bring was lost on those who responded with such an inappropriate explanation. When we stop to consider what was at stake for those who so easily explained away the obvious, the mystery of this experience was the very message they desperately needed to hear. This story, while splendid and exciting, also has a very tragic bent to it, as stated in verse 13. How many times in the life of the community of faith have we gotten so wrapped up in our own sense of what God was doing in our lives that we failed to sense that there were those who just didn't get it? The story refers to them as "those others." What we in the church must recognize and see is that in the midst of what God is doing, there are always those other persons. We have a responsibility to these others just as we do to those who do understand and who do see. We might remember that the whole reason the gift of proclamation was given that day in a variety of tongues was so that all could hear. The community of faith needs to take more responsibility for those others who so often just don't get it.

Our lesson today is followed by Peter's sense of responsibility for those others as he expounds on the experience just witnessed, with that same proclamation now focused on those who struggle to understand. It becomes so easy for the community of faith to just go with those who get it. To do so means that we have misunderstood the whole work of God's Spirit in the first place. If the community of faith is unwilling to meet people where they are with the questions they have, then we have become very irresponsible with all that God has entrusted to us.

"What does this mean?" becomes a relevant question that the church must wrestle with for those who dare ask it. If the God experiences of life cannot hold up to the honest questions posed by those who dare to ask them, then the church has failed to understand the very nature of what God is doing and how God seeks to do it. Such questioning in this story captures honestly for us just who people really are and how people really act when confronted with the mystery and power of this God who continues to move and work among us. (Travis Franklin)

Worship Aids

Call to Worship (Psalm 139:7-10)

Leader: Where can I go from your spirit?

People: Or where can I flee from your presence?

Leader: If I ascend to heaven, you are there;

People: If I make my bed in Sheol, you are there.

Leader: If I take the wings of the morning and settle at the farthest limits of the sea,

People: Even there your hand shall lead me,

Leader: And your right hand shall hold me fast.
(Travis Franklin)

JULY 2, 2006

❦❦❦

Fourth Sunday after Pentecost

Readings: 2 Samuel 1:1, 17-27; Psalm 130; 2 Corinthians 8:7-15; Mark 5:21-43

Out of the Trenches
Mark 5:21-43

I have often heard the expression you'll never find an atheist in a foxhole. That is to say that when someone is facing the possibility of death, there are few who will truly believe there is no God. I have never spent time in a foxhole, but I have spent quite a bit of time in hospitals as a pastoral care giver. I have observed that the foxhole statement is also true in times of health crisis and death. There are few who do not look up for answers when they find themselves flat on their backs. Today's text is a miracle narrative dealing with this very faith phenomenon. The great news of this Gospel text is Jesus' reaction to their desperation.

The chapters preceding Mark 5 deal primarily with early ministry events like the first healing, calling of disciples, and the reactions of the crowd to Jesus' early teaching. Chapter 5 delves into specific miracles of Jesus. It is important to remember that in Mark there is special consideration given to the faith of the nonapostles. Often in Mark the twelve disciples are the last to understand Jesus' words or actions. Instead, there are ordinary believers whose faith sets them apart. Jesus often uses these examples of faith as teachable moments for his disciples and his critics. Today's text deals with two examples of faith—individuals whose perhaps desperation-driven faith teaches an important lesson about Jesus. After delivering the demon-possessed man, Jesus crosses to the other side of the lake where a large crowd has gathered. There he is approached by a synagogue leader, Jairus, who humbly approaches Jesus, falls at his feet, and begs Jesus to come and heal his ailing daughter. From scripture, we well know that synagogue leaders were not often followers of Jesus, yet the desperation of this father led him to approach Jesus for healing.

Jesus is filled with compassion and agrees to go to the man's daughter. At the possibility of witnessing a miracle, the already assembled crowd presses on with Jesus and Jairus as they journey the street toward Jairus's home. The crowd must be so large and the street so narrow that they are practically arm-to-arm as they move. In the midst of that crowd a woman approaches and reaches to touch Jesus. This woman was also motivated to seek him through desperation, as she had been bleeding for twelve years—a condition causing not only physical suffering but also spiritual suffering as a Jew. She presumably cannot even get close enough to speak to him, but believes correctly that she may be healed if she can merely touch him. Even with the crowd so close, Jesus realized that he had been touched, and stopped to acknowledge her. Just as he finished speaking with the woman, some men came from Jairus's house reporting that the girl had died. Against the suggestion of these men, Jesus urges Jairus not to be afraid but to continue to believe. Upon entering the room with the girl's parents and the inner circle of the disciples, Jesus commands that the girl get up and she does.

Both Jairus and the nameless bleeding woman are desperate. Jairus feels the desperation of a parent losing a child and consequently is willing to do whatever it takes to restore her health. The woman feels the desperation of someone experiencing a chronic debilitating health problem and reaches to perhaps the last one that might provide her relief. Both reach out to Jesus in utter faith that Jesus is the answer to their desperate situations. Their faithfulness is particularly outstanding as told by Mark, since Jesus' own disciples and friends struggle to believe. I think that the most significant theological lesson to be learned from this text deals with Jesus' reaction to Jairus and the woman. In both situations, Jesus does more than heal. Jesus demonstrates that he is more than a magician or miracle man. Jesus acts out of his compassion. He embraces and blesses the individuals for their faith. He feels their desperation and demonstrates that his healing is more than physical. It is more than a magical or medicinal touch; it is a life-changing encounter.

We do not know the rest of the story for Jairus and the woman, but in most cases in the Gospels, those who experienced Jesus in this way became lifelong followers.

Some of us might find ourselves in actual foxholes (and God bless those who do)! Most of us will not. All of us, however, will find ourselves in a desperate situation at least once in our lives. Hopefully, this will not be when we reach for God for the first time. If it is, this text promises that God will respond to our touch. This text also promises that whenever we reach for Jesus, Christ will respond with compassion and understanding. We are not alone. We are not untouchable in our grief and suffering. We are not beyond hope. Jesus will always respond to our touch and cry for help. All we must remember is that Christ is there for us to call, whether we're in a foxhole, a physical crisis, or just need a touch from the Master. (Tracey Allred)

You're in Trouble if the Fire Goes Out

First in a Series of Three

Acts 2:14-21

For my thirtieth birthday my spouse surprised me with a hot-air balloon ride. Very early on a Saturday morning, we arrived at the launch site to see a beautiful hot-air balloon inflated and waiting for us to go. As a private pilot, I love to fly. I'd been up in many types of small aircraft but never in a hot-air balloon. This was a first. We climbed in the wicker basket and our pilot asked us if we were ready to go. With an affirmative answer, he told the balloon handler to cast off. Suddenly he pulled the trigger and a huge flame fired into the hot-air balloon. The noise was loud and shocked me. As the fire continued to burn, we soon lifted off the ground. When we got up to about one thousand feet, he turned off the fire and we floated along in a very eerie, strange silence. It was so beautiful and it gave us a whole new perspective of the world. You couldn't help but feel inspired and excited. After a while, however, we began to lose altitude and he had to turn on the fire again. We floated back up and the view was amazing. I asked our pilot, "What happens to us if the fire goes out?" He just looked at me for a moment and then he smiled and said, "You're in trouble. If there's no fire, we're going down."

The same thing is true about life. When we let the fire go out in our lives, when our spirits burn out, we go down. We get depressed, tired, and lethargic.

In our scripture lesson, we read about the day of Pentecost, the day when God poured out God's Holy Spirit on the disciples in Jerusalem. It's fascinating that Luke would describe that day by writing, "It was like God poured out tongues of fire on the disciples." The Holy Spirit was described as fire because the spirit lifted them up. It inspired them. It empowered them. And when that happened, they stood up to preach. Peter said to all, "When the Lord pours out spirit on all flesh you shall see visions and you shall dream dreams."

That was the power of the Holy Spirit. It enabled the disciples to stretch their minds, to think in new ways, and to be open to new ideas. Having seen the risen Christ, they were now open to new possibilities in life. They weren't going to set limits on what God could do. They were fired up.

To be normal means to conform to an accepted model, pattern, or standard. To be original means never having existed before, created independent of already existing ideas. When God poured out the Holy Spirit on the disciples in Jerusalem, God was not asking them to be normal, to live by an accepted model or standard. God was calling them to be original, created independent of already existing ideas. When we open our hearts and minds to experience the power of God's Holy Spirit then we, too, get fired up. We begin to look at life with new eyes and see new possibilities. We find ourselves inspired with a hope in the future and that gives us a new power in the present.

A number of years ago I had the opportunity to go to a church growth seminar in Orlando, Florida. My spouse went along with me because she said she wanted to go to Disney World. Neither one of us had ever been to either Disneyland or Disney World but to tell the truth, I wasn't really all that excited about it at the time. One day when we had a little free time, my spouse was adamant that we were going to go. Was I ever glad we made that decision! Disney World was one of the most incredible experiences I've ever had. I think my favorite ride was at Epcot. It was called "Journey into Imagination." If you've ever been on that ride, you'll remember how you get in a little car and it enters into a whole new world. You see a flying machine that looks half like an airplane and half like a hot-air balloon. The man who is flying it is called "Dreamfinder." As you meet Dreamfinder, suddenly out of this machine pops a purple dragon whose name is Figment—figment of your imagination. As you move along through the ride, Dreamfinder tells you about imagination and about people who have dreamed, and how imagination has changed the world. Dreamfinder and Figment keep telling you that if you dream it, you can do it. When we got off that ride, I couldn't help but think that one of the greatest gifts God has given human beings is the gift of imagination—the ability to ask, "What if?" "Why not?" and "Wouldn't it be great if ..." Too often we put limits on what God can do in our lives. We put limits on the dreams we allow ourselves to dream.

The disciples had been with Jesus. They saw him crucified, they saw him buried, and then they met the risen Christ, raised from the dead. They never dreamed that would happen in a million years. They came to realize that if God can raise Jesus from the dead, then why put limits on what God can do in our lives? They had no idea how God was going to lead them but they were open to the power of the Holy Spirit.

If you and I are not careful, the fire can go out and we become depressed, tired, lethargic, and we go down. The promise is that God will pour out the Holy Spirit on all flesh no matter how young or how old. God will pour out God's spirit to give us a vision, to give us new dreams, if we will open ourselves to possibilities. It is the power of the Holy Spirit that will give us hope in the future and power in the present day. (Robert E. Long)

Worship Aids

Call to Worship

Leader: The Lord is in God's holy temple. Let the people proclaim God's glory.

People: Praise God's holy name.

Leader: Jehovah, Our God, is with us—make God's name known.

People: To God belongs the glory. Praise God's holy name.

Pastoral Prayer

Now, O God, as we enter into thy presence, we desire your spirit and your power to rest on us today. May we as your people be unified in our desire to please you. May we be drawn together by the ties that bind us together. Amen.

Benediction

Our hearts have been stirred from the things our ears have heard. Now let us practice what has been preached. May we go forth and show God's love by our unity. Amen. (Jimmy McNeil)

JULY 9, 2006

❧❧❧

Fifth Sunday after Pentecost

Readings: 2 Samuel 5:1-5, 9-10; Psalm 48; 2 Corinthians 12:2-10; Mark 6:1-13

You Can't Go Home Again
Mark 6:1-13

One cannot read the Gospel accounts of Jesus' life without having a deep sense of longing and wonderment about what was going on with Jesus in those years between childhood and age thirty. These years that are lost to history have been the source of much speculation. Some speculate that Joseph died and left Mary with a house full of children, of whom Jesus was the eldest, and that Jesus' young manhood was spent supporting his mother and siblings. In the absence of any hard historical facts, this is certainly a reasonable supposition. No situation could have been more human for the Son of God than to have had the responsibility for the care of his mother and a house full of small children. Perhaps this is where Jesus developed his profound sensitivity about little children. Whatever may have happened during those years must have been preparation for what was to come. They were not wasted years, for in the "fullness of time" the signal came to Jesus that "now is the time."

After Jesus' baptism by John, Jesus' life is a continuous flurry of activity as he moves from one event to the next. The activity is broken only by the intentional efforts of Jesus to be alone for reflection and communication with the "Father." In Mark's account of the gospel, Jesus moves quickly from one occasion to the next. All are amazed at his miracles and the wisdom of his teaching. Jesus has selected the apostolic team and the ministry is making great headway. Then, Jesus suddenly has a very disappointing experience. He goes home to Nazareth where he is met with a combination of amazement, resentment, and open hostility.

This was obviously not a social visit where Jesus came to see old friends and family. He came as a rabbi, a teacher, with his disciples in tow. Jesus went to the synagogue, as an itinerant rabbi might do, and began to

177

teach. Mark reports that those who heard him were astonished at what he had to say. Then, like a typical group of hometown critics, they began with the usual disqualifying remarks: "Where did this man get all of this? What is this wisdom that has been given him? What deeds of power are being done by his hands?" You can just hear the critical rhetoric: "Hey, we've known this fellow since he was a kid. We know his mama and his brothers and sisters. He is just a carpenter. He is no better than we are. Where does he come off talking like that to us? We know him!" Mark says they took offense at him. Given the information in Mark, we might wonder why the people in Nazareth had such a strong reaction to Jesus.

It is Luke who enlightens us as to what this hometown boy said that made his old friends so angry. Luke reports that when Jesus came to the synagogue he was given the scroll of Isaiah, which he unrolled, to the place where it read: "The Spirit of the Lord is upon me, because he has anointed me to bring good news to the poor. He has sent me to proclaim release to the captives and recovery of sight to the blind, to let the oppressed go free, to proclaim the year of the Lord's favor" (Isaiah 61:1-2). Jesus handed the scroll back to the attendant, sat down, and began by saying to them: "Today this scripture has been fulfilled in your hearing." Jesus was clearly proclaiming himself as the Messiah. At the end of his discourse with the congregants they were not only amazed, but also enraged. They ran Jesus out of town and took him to the brow of the hill on which the town was built and would have hurled him off the cliff, "but he passed through the midst of them and went on his way" (Luke 4:16-29).

Surely Jesus and his disciples must have smarted under this stinging rebuke by people they had hoped would be supportive. Jesus' only response was to speak an axiom to them: "Prophets are not without honor, except in their hometown and among their own kin, and in their own house." Mark reports that Jesus could do no mighty works among them, except for healing a few sick people, because of their unbelief.

When one experiences rejection and threats (especially when it comes from those you thought would offer encouragement and support) there is a tendency to withdraw and lick your wounds, or reevaluate your situation. This was not the case with Jesus. He had a positive response before he came to Nazareth and he trusts he will have a positive response after he leaves. So, Jesus ratchets up his campaign. Up until this point the disciples have been observers. Now it is time for them to get actively involved. Jesus called the twelve together and gave them power over unclean spirits and the authority to heal. They were sent on a daunting mission. They had just witnessed a painful rejection. They might have been fearful of possible outcomes, but Jesus arms them with the one thing without which no disciple dares begin such an undertaking. Jesus gave them power and authority.

When we look at what needs to be done in our churches and think pensively, "I do not have the power to do this," we miss the core of the gospel message. What God calls us to do, God empowers us to do. If the only things that happen in our churches are the things we do in our own power, we have reason for concern. God calls. God empowers. The days and weeks in my ministry in which I have ended up in a state of frustration and emotional and physical exhaustion have been when I was operating out of my own power.

The disciples were sent on their mission without food, money, or even a change of clothing. They were to trust God to provide such as they needed through those to whom they were sent. They were not to stay at any place at which they were not welcome. If they were rejected they were to shake the dust off their feet and leave. The power and authority of Jesus did not forsake them. "They cast out many demons, and anointed with oil many who were sick and cured them."

Someone once said in my hearing that Jesus promised three things to those who followed him: "They would be absurdly happy, entirely fearless, and always in trouble." The first disciples have at this point in the journey experienced the first two. The latter is yet to come. (Thomas Lane Butts)

Building Bridges So That Others May Follow

Second in a Series of Three

Acts 3:1-10

I couldn't believe that it was time for my child to go off to college. That August the university had an orientation session for freshman students and their parents. As my child was learning about life in the dorms and class schedules, I was learning about how to pay for college. During part of our orientation, we heard from a man and his wife who were endowing a scholarship for students, and they explained why they were doing it. It turned out that the man was a successful physician. He had grown up in a family that was very poor. He said that his family gave him everything that was really important—they loved him, they encouraged him, and they helped him dream great dreams. They gave him everything that really mattered but they were not financially well off. When he got into high school, he decided he wanted a great education, so he applied to a private, elite university. He got back a letter stating he would be put on a waiting list. He was not accepted but he was not rejected, they simply said maybe. When it came September, he still had not heard from them. It was almost time to begin school, so the man decided to take matters into his own hands. This was in 1966. He packed up his bags, got on a train, and went to the big city. There he caught a taxicab and he went to a large hotel downtown. He went up to the front desk and said he needed a room. The front-desk manager looked at him and said, "Do you have a reservation?" The young man replied, "Can you do that?" The front-desk manager asked, "Where are you from, kid?" He said he didn't know you could make a reservation at a hotel. He had never traveled. The manager explained that this was Labor Day weekend and they didn't have any rooms but he said the young man could stay in the back with the bellman where they had a cot. He didn't want to see an eighteen-year-old kid from the country standing out on the street corners of downtown. The young man said he would never forget the kindness of that front-desk manager.

The next day he showed up at the admissions office to see the dean. He didn't have an appointment. He just announced that he wanted to see him and that he wasn't leaving until he did. He said all he wanted was an opportunity and he promised to excel if he was given that chance. The dean was so impressed with his tenacity that he looked up his file and said, "OK, you're in." The young man started school in the fall of 1966 and he did excel. He graduated, got into medical school, and went on to be a very successful physician. This young man, now in his 50s and reflecting on his life, said he had far fewer sunrises in front of him than he had behind him. He said, "I believe in life that first you learn, then you earn, then you return. It is important to build bridges so that others can come after you."

Now he and his wife wanted to build bridges, and that is why they wanted to establish a scholarship in honor of his mother and father, a front-desk manager of a hotel, and a dean. Then he made an interesting statement. He said, "I've always believed what the Bible says, 'To whom much has been given, much will be required.' "

That statement comes from Jesus and is found in Luke 12:48. Jesus tells Peter, "To whom much has been given, much will be required." Quite often when we read that statement we think about money. If someone has made a lot of money then he or she should give a lot of money. Although I believe this statement is true, I don't believe it is solely limited to that understanding.

What had the disciples received from Jesus? They certainly didn't receive money. Instead, they had the opportunity to see amazing things, they had experienced his unconditional love, and they felt forgiven and blessed. They had seen the risen Christ. They had been given much and now they had something to share. In the scripture lesson, we read about how after the resurrection Peter and John had gone up to the temple to pray. When they came to the temple there was a beggar asking for alms. They went and stood in front of him and Peter said, "Silver and gold I do not have, but what I do have I give to you: In the name of Jesus Christ of Nazareth, rise up and walk" (Acts 3:6 NKJV).

The man who spoke at my son's orientation said that he been blessed. He had made a lot of money and so he felt he needed to share that money to build bridges to help other kids get the same opportunity that he had. I believe that is good.

But I also think that all of us, individually and collectively as a church, have something important to offer. The disciples were given a message—a message about God's love and about God's amazing grace. It was a message that gave a lame beggar hope in the future and power for the present. It was a message that empowered him to get up and walk. It gave him a new beginning. The disciples went out to share the power of that message because they felt blessed by the grace of Christ, and built bridges so that others could come after them. Now it is our responsibility to keep building those bridges for others. We have received the message that gives us hope in the future and a power in the present, and to whom much has been given, much will be required. It's how we help change the world. (Robert E. Long)

Worship Aids

Prayer

Dear Heavenly Father, we thank you today for the gifts we receive. Help us use these gifts to build bridges so that others may have hope for their future and power in the present. (Robert E. Long)

Benediction

As you go from this holy place into a world that sees little as holy, may the spirit of God enable you to settle for nothing less than the highest and noblest values. Be wise and discerning, brave and kind, and make a difference because you know the difference. In the name of the Father, the Son, and the Holy Spirit, Amen. (Bill Austin)

JULY 16, 2006

Sixth Sunday after Pentecost

Readings: 2 Samuel 6:1-5, 12b-19; Psalm 24; Ephesians 1:3-14; Mark 6:14-29

In God We Trust, or Do We?
2 Samuel 6:1-5

How did you celebrate the Fourth of July? Did you picnic with friends? Did you pull out your red, white, and blue T-shirt and wear it to the parade? Did you spread out your quilt in the city park and lay back with your family to enjoy the fireworks? Did you hang your American flag beside the front door and join others singing "God Bless America"?

It is a good thing for us to celebrate our heritage, to be grateful for all the liberties that we enjoy, and to ask God to be with us. God is delighted when individuals and nations turn their hearts toward God in gratitude and in supplication for God's guidance in their lives together. However, our text this morning serves as a stark reminder that we must be very careful when we mix religion and politics.

But what's wrong with mixing politics and religion? Our country has always done that. "In God We Trust" is on our currency; we place one hand on the Bible when we take an oath in court; government meetings are often opened in prayer. In the last presidential election, many Americans believed it was important to know the faith tradition of the candidates, as well as how their faith (or lack of it) would affect their political leadership. In addition to asking, What's wrong with mixing religion and politics? you may be asking, How can we *not* mix the two? In our Old Testament text for today, King David certainly mixed the two.

The biblical story opens to a huge national celebration—picture thirty thousand people gathering with King David to bring the ark to Jerusalem. What is this ark and what's the big deal about bringing it to Jerusalem? First, remember this is the ark of the covenant, not Noah's ark. The ark of the covenant was seen as the embodiment of the presence of God among the people. It was said to lead the Israelites across the Jordan River into the promised land, and it represented Yahweh as a Divine Warrior who fought for Israel. The ark was seen as a unifying presence for the people. When we join the text for the day, the ark had been gone for twenty years—the Philistines captured it when they defeated Israel in battle. Its departure was described as the exiling of glory from Israel. And now, King David decides he is going to bring it home.

So off they go, David and all the people, to the house of Abinadab, to reclaim the ark and bring it to Jerusalem. They put it on a new cart and begin the journey dancing before the Lord, rejoicing and singing and playing instruments in the street. It is an enormous celebration. But then, in verses 6-12, something very strange happens. The ox cart hits a bump, the ark begins to sway, and Uzzah reaches out his hand to steady it. This is the ark. It must not fall. The anger of the Lord was kindled against Uzzah and God strikes him dead. And King David, who only moments before was dancing deliriously, becomes afraid. Suddenly, he decides he is not willing to take the ark into his care in Jerusalem, and he deposits it at the house of Obed-edom, the Gittite, where it remained for three months.

This is a strange turn of events indeed. Can you picture thirty thousand people, now with nothing to celebrate, dropping their instruments to their sides and dejectedly returning home, the ark still residing with foreigners? What happened?

The rest of the story, as you might guess, involves both politics and religion. Remember, before David became king, Israel was divided into two nations—Israel and Judah. David was first anointed king over Judah—only later is he anointed king over Israel as well. He is seeking to unite the two kingdoms, and he chooses to make Jerusalem the new capital. This is a big change for the Israelites, and David knows it. He realizes that bringing the ark to Jerusalem will send a strong message to the people: God is with us here in Jerusalem, unifying us together again under the reign of King David. The transfer of the ark links the kingship of God to the kingship of David. It tells the people that God's protection over them is now channeled through the protection of God's anointed king. It was a very savvy political move on David's part.

But wasn't David a man after God's own heart, God's anointed king? Didn't he truly want God's presence with him and with all of Israel? Yes, scholars believe that he did. But, they don't see God directing David to bring the ark, nor do they see David asking God's permission to reclaim it. At this point, they see a man very aware of the political power of his actions.

Three months later, after seeing how God is blessing the family who is keeping the ark, David decides to try again to bring the ark to Jerusalem. This time he is successful, and again there is great rejoicing, and dancing, and worship, and sacrifices. Everyone is happy except for David's wife, Michal, the daughter of Saul. Granted, she may have had her own agenda. She wanted the next king to be an heir of Saul, for the kingship to stay in her family, but this was not to be. But despite that, she had the courage to call David on his mixed motives; she voiced the danger of joining a religious symbol with political power.

The warning is a good one for us today as we reflect on our own national celebration. We say that we trust in God, but just as often we seek to coerce God's blessing or try to justify our actions by asserting that God is indeed with us. It seems that if our motives were pure and that God were with us, such political maneuvering wouldn't be necessary. In God we trust, or do we? (Tracy Hartman)

Tuning the Orchestra to A

Third in a Series of Three

Acts 6:1-6

My spouse and I love going to the theatre, and we especially love going to musicals. We had season tickets to the music hall when we lived in Houston and we were fortunate because we had second-row seats, dead center. I liked it because when the people performed on stage we could see the sweat on their brows. We could see them huffing and puffing as they were singing. We could see the expression in their eyes. I always enjoyed getting there early because we could look into the orchestra pit and see behind the scenes as people were showing up, getting their instruments, and warming up. When it was time, the first violinist stood up, called them to order, and then looked at the oboe to sound an A. I was talking about this with my staff when my children's director said that this was her job when she played the oboe in the university orchestra. She said everyone would tune to the A being played on her oboe and for a while you would hear chaos. Everyone was tuning up so it sounded like a bunch of noise. But then slowly it became more and more coherent until finally the conductor came out, rapped on the stand, and called everyone to order. It was time, and now they could make beautiful music because they were all tuned to the A.

The task of the church is to try to help people hear the same note; to hear the same message from Jesus; to tune our hearts to Jesus' heart. Once we all hear the same note, although we are all different, we can come together to make great music.

That is what the scripture lesson is really about. When the early church came into being, it quickly confronted many struggles. In this passage we see a multitude of people trying to come together to hear the same note; to get their hearts with Jesus' heart and to figure out who they're going to be. In the first line of our scripture lesson, Acts 6:1, it reads, "Now during those days, ... the disciples were increasing in number." That was good news but it also made circumstances difficult. It was hard enough to get twelve disciples on the same page, but now there were many more followers. Remember, Jesus had sent out the seventy to carry his message into the world. Then, of course, there were the women at the cross and the many who followed and funded Jesus' ministry. On the day of Pentecost when God poured out his Holy Spirit, three thousand were baptized. In Acts 2:47 we are told that people joined the church every day. Now the church needed to get organized. People had needs. The church had to discover what it meant to be a caring community of faith, how they would help the people find hope in the future through the good news in the resurrection and find a new power in the Holy Spirit for confronting their daily problems. The church had to get clear on their message and tune their hearts with the heart of Jesus. The church really believed that they could give people a hope in the future and power in the present through a faith in Jesus Christ. But to come together as a family of faith, they would first have to see everybody as a child of God. People were different, but each person had to be seen as equal in the eyes of God. Everybody had to be special.

In the early church we are told that when the people came together they had many needs. In the patriarchal society where men ruled, the people who had the most needs were women and children. If you became a widow, who was going to take care of you? If you were a child and lost your parents, who would take care of you? Women and children were at risk. The Jews understood that and made a commitment to take care of the widow and the poor and the orphan.

In the story of Naomi and Ruth, we remember how each had lost her husband and came back to Bethlehem. Ruth went into the field of Boaz and as he was harvesting the grain he said, "Let her glean even among the standing sheaves, and do not reproach her. You must also put out some handfuls for her from the bundles, and leave them for her to glean, and do not rebuke her" (Ruth 2:15-16). The Jews knew the needs of the widow and the poor and were committed to taking care of them.

In the earliest incarnation of the church everyone was Jewish, but we soon had different factions. For example, we had the Hellenist. Alexander the Great had conquered Israel years before and introduced the Greek culture. The Hellenist embraced this culture, spoke Greek, and became known as liberals. We also had the Hebrews. The Hebrews said no to the Greek culture and they spoke Aramaic. They held onto the Jewish traditions and were conservative. So we had the Hellenist Jews and the Hebrew Jews and now they were all trying to be followers of Christ. In the early church, the Hellenists complained that the Hebrew widows were getting more than they were—and it was probably true. The church struggled right at the beginning with the question, How are we going to treat people? Some things haven't changed in two thousand years. How easy it is to discriminate. How easy it is to be prejudiced. How easy it is to put labels on people—liberal or conservative; Democrat or Republican; gay or straight; Catholic or Baptist; Presbyterian, Lutheran, or Methodist; black, white, red, or brown. When we throw out labels we begin to treat people differently.

So what does it mean to say that we are all children of God? Until we can remove all the labels, until we stop automatically judging people, we can never become a family of faith. Here we see how the early church was trying to tune its heart to the heart of Jesus by hearing Jesus say, "By this everyone will know that you are my disciples, if you have love for one another" (John 13:35). The issue is not, "You are my follower if you have love for the Hellenist Jewish Christians, or if you have love for the Hebrew Jewish Christians, or if you love the liberal, or if you have love for the conservative." The statement is, "If you have love for one another then we are all God's children, and that means we can be a family of faith." The church has a message that can help people have hope in the future and find the power to live their lives today, but it is a message that only rings true when it is a message for everyone. (Robert E. Long)

Worship Aids

Call to Worship

Leader: Come before the Lord in holy worship.

People: We come asking that our lives be remade and our priorities reordered.

Leader: Open your hearts and God will open your lives to his way.

People: We are ready Lord. Make known to us your will.
(Chris Andrews)

Prayer

Gracious God, we ask your blessing about the church today. Help us remember that to be a family of faith we must love one another and remember we are all your children. Remind us, dear God, that if we tune our hearts to Jesus' heart, we will all hear the same note and come together to create a loving and kind world. In Jesus' name we pray. Amen. (Robert E. Long)

Benediction

Lord, you have promised to be with us today and in all our tomorrows and beyond. Help us go with you, without reluctance or fear, to live the life you call us to live. In Jesus' name, Amen. (Ross West)

JULY 23, 2006

❦❦❦

Seventh Sunday after Pentecost

Readings: 2 Samuel 7:1-14a; Psalm 89:20-37; Ephesians 2:11-22;
Mark 6:30-34, 53-56

The Last Best Hope?
2 Samuel 7:1-14a

I invite you to walk with me, at least in the mind's imaginative eye, to consider our national condition from three vantage points: first, the church's inherited teaching about war and peace; second, the judgment of modernity about war and peace; and third, a prospect for hope in a time of war and peace. As today's reading happily reminds us, we are from a deep, although intricately varied ethical tradition that enshrines selfless love, Christcentric love, cruciform love as the cherished ideal of human behavior. Jesus, of the house and lineage of David, could teach: As you wish others would do to you, do also to them.

Two basic understandings of war and peace have emerged in Christian thought. As you know, these roughly can be called the pacifist and just war understandings.

Pacifism preceded its sibling, and extends to all times the interim ethic of the New Testament: "To him who strikes you on the cheek, offer the other also." Remember that the Gospel of Luke, even though it was one of the later writings in the New Testament, expects the imminent return of the Lord to render all our ethical dilemmas moot, and therefore tends to err on the side of quietism and, in the case of violent conflict, pacifism.

The multiple theories of just war, or war as the least of all evil alternatives, have developed since the fourth century and the writings of Saint Augustine. Here the command to "be merciful, even as God is merciful" is understood tragically to include times when mercy for the lamb means armed opposition to the wolf. This position honors the New Testament apocalyptic frame and its interim, to be sure, but it supplements these with the historic experience of the church through the ages. Many saintly Christian people have honored this understanding with their selfless

188

commitment, including some present here today, and some who are not present because they gave their lives that others might live.

Just war thought includes several serious caveats: there must be a just cause in response to serious evil and a just intention for restoration of peace with justice; there can be no self-enrichment or desire for devastation; those prosecuting the war must use it as an utterly last resort, must possess legitimate authority, and must have a reasonable hope of success, given the constraints of "discrimination" and "proportionality" (usually understood as protection of non-combatants). Response, restoration, restraint, last resort, common authority: these are the guideposts through which we must navigate if a war is to be just.

These two venerable pillars of Christian thought—pacifism and just war—demarcate the limit of received Christian teaching, from scripture, tradition, reason, and experience.

In the winter of 2003, we Americans prosecuted a war upon Iraq. There are those who considered such an action a tragic necessity (a clear majority in my community and elsewhere) and others who considered it an unnecessary tragedy (a significant minority in my community and elsewhere, and a majority in many parts of the world). The church in which I serve has ministered with and prayed for many of our own younger women and men who continue to serve their neighbor by serving their country. We honor their courageous self-giving and continue to pray for their well-being. Neither the effectiveness of our military nor the personal courage and faith of our soldiers and sailors is in doubt.

But now that the dust of the desert has partly settled, I find myself compelled to ask what we have done. The answer I find to that question is that this war, in direct contrast to virtually ever other American conflict, was unabashedly prosecuted outside of inherited Christian ethical teaching. Of course, pacifism was discounted, but so, too, were the caveats of the just war theory. Our action was preemptive, not responsive; unilateral, not commonly authorized; a deliberate, but not a last, resort; and, for all the technological wizardry available, still brought death to thousands of unarmed civilians. Iraq 2003 is, to my view, America's first self-consciously post-Christian war.

What is darkly fascinating about the 2003 action is that the dilemma of leadership in which we Americans found ourselves was precisely rendered five hundred years ago. In the Italian Renaissance, the Florentine philosopher Niccolò Machiavelli quietly composed a frightful, but perhaps unconquerable, understanding of leadership and power, and thus of war and peace. He argued that the leader could be either effective or Christian, but not both at the same time. He would have to choose between effective, powerful, and sustainable leadership on the one hand and Christian virtue on the other. He could be successful or right, but not both at the same time. What Machiavelli most clearly stated has been the thorn in the flesh of Christian political ethics for the whole modern era. As Machiavelli predicted, none have been able or willing to fully face and finally solve his dilemma: As a leader, and particularly a military leader, you can be victorious or you can be Christian, you can be successful or you can be virtuous, you can survive or you can be good. But not both, argued Machiavelli.

Is this the best we can hope for? Are the horns of Machiavelli's dilemma unbreakable? For the country to survive are we forced to give up the application of our faith to matters of war and peace? Is this what our strategic future must now entail, unilateral preemption? Or is there a more hopeful path?

It was Abraham Lincoln who sang the praise of this great land as the last best hope of humanity. We as a people can, in some measure, live out Lincoln's majestic hope. We may be entering an epoch of American forbearance. You will remember something of forbearance, patient restraint, a great power for doing good. Sometimes it is better to exercise patience than raw power. If we can restrain ourselves, in the future, from making scapegoats of some in order furiously to retaliate against other hidden foes—that is, if we can *forbear*—we shall find that the community of peoples will see in us a last best hope. We may model, as a people, a path forward into a time of freedom, pluralism, toleration, compromise, and peace. How is one to find such power? Truly I see no other source than a confessional reliance on the Christ of Calvary; an epoch of forbearance. It was the genius of Lincoln that best bespoke this hope, especially in his annual message to Congress on December 1, 1862. Shall we live as the world's "last best hope"? (Robert Hill)

Who Knows What Evil Lurks in the Hearts of . . . ?

First in a Series of Four: How Sweet the Sound

Romans 7:13-25; Matthew 15:10-20

My daughter is home for the weekend, which means that the stations on my car radio will have been repositioned by Monday. But this is not new behavior. When my daughter was learning to talk, the first four words she assembled into a sentence were the words: "I get my station." Were it not for the car, I'd hardly listen to radio anymore. But there was a day when I would sit for hours and let the radio create marvelous pictures in my mind. Consider one of my favorite programs, *The Shadow.*

It took a long time before I could listen, given that the first thirty seconds of *The Shadow* scared the bejeebers out of me. First there was silence. Then footsteps ... slow, deliberate footsteps ... growing louder ... growing closer ... until they reached the door. It took fifteen seconds for that door to open, creaking every inch of the way. The sound was enough to make the hairs on my body stand at attention. Finally came the voice: "Who knows what evil lurks within the hearts of men?" Followed by the answer: "The Shadow knows." It was great theater, and it wasn't bad theology, either. For it goes without saying that there is a lot of evil lurking someplace.

There are those who claim that evil is lodged in only a few. This is the "bad apple" theory, vigorously argued by the mother of a boyhood chum. She had six kids, you see. Five of them were good. One of them was bad. Since 83 percent of her kids turned out perfectly, and since she had raised them all the same, it meant that one of her kids was a bad apple.

Working against the "bad apple" theory is Floyd Starr's (not his real name) theory. "There's no such thing as a bad boy," Floyd said. "But sometimes, the world takes good boys and messes 'em up. Therefore, such boys need to be taken to nice places with nice people who will unmess 'em and return 'em to their natural state of goodness."

Then we have the Flip Wilson, "Calvin and Hobbes" variation on the Floyd Starr theory. They argue: "Don't blame us. We're good boys. But something has taken hold of us over which we have absolutely no control." Flip was that funny man who would dress up as a woman named Geraldine. Then he would proclaim: "I didn't buy that dress. The devil made me buy that dress." To which Calvin added a new wrinkle. In one memorable series of strips, Calvin invented a duplicating machine that cloned six of him. Suddenly there were multiple Calvins running around doing bad stuff, for which the original Calvin was being blamed. "That wasn't really me," Calvin said. "It must have been someone who looked like me."

But none of these theories cuts it. To those who say that evil is none of us—a few rotten ones of us, something that possesses us, or masquerades as us—it still appears that a propensity for evil is intrinsic to all of us.

Read Matthew 15, where Jesus is scolded by the Pharisees for not properly washing his hands. To which Jesus says: "It's not what goes into a man's mouth that makes him unclean, but what comes out of his mouth."

For what comes out of his mouth comes from the heart. And from the heart come all sorts of things, such as evil intentions, murder, adultery, fornication, threat, perjury, and slander. Which leads one to wonder: "How do those things get into the heart in the first place?" Well, they originate there. They are a part of human nature. Not pretty, but true.

That evil has a name. Its name is "sin." To be more accurate, its name is "original sin." I remember doing a baptism and watching a grandmother hold a beautiful baby girl—a baby who hadn't spit up, cried, or wrinkled her pretty dress for at least an hour. And the grandmother said: "How can the church say that this child lives in sin? This child hasn't done anything bad in her life." And grandma was right. The child hadn't—and wouldn't—for at least an hour. But the propensity is there. It's in her nature.

And here's where the psychologists rescue the theologians. "You want another word for original sin?" they say. "Call it the Shadow." And what is the Shadow? "It is," says John Sanford, "the dark, feared, unwanted side of our personality ... the underside of what we have been taught and shaped to be." The Shadow is made up of the pieces that don't fit—the ones that don't belong in the picture. Or look at it another way. As we develop, we reject certain qualities we neither like nor want the world to see. Therefore, we deny them expression. But simply denying them expression does not mean they go away. They become the Shadow.

Consider the apostle Paul. He writes: "I cannot understand my own behavior. The things I love, I fail to do. The things I hate, I find myself doing. Instead of doing the good things I want, I carry out the sinful things I do not want. Wretched man that I am, who will deliver me from this body of death?" (Romans 7).

Consider a preteen girl, jealous of her older sister's popularity, spreading a vicious lie throughout the school about the sister and her boyfriend. Consider a collegiate male who is something of a loner, typing a fantasy about sexual indulgence, rape, and violence, and then entering it into the Internet. Consider a mother who catches her five-year-old son taking pennies from her purse. In order to teach him the evil of his ways, she holds his hand over the gas flame on the kitchen stove. Unfortunately, she miscalculates, holding it too close for too long, so that for the rest of his life that child will have one good hand and one withered claw. Consider a group of Boy Scouts, all with merit badges in animal husbandry. Then, on a campout, they cruelly dismember a squealing rabbit.

Consider a group of young soldiers, drilled about what to do in every military situation. Then they riddle a village with bullets, even though they have reason to believe that the village contains nothing but women and small children. Consider a television evangelist who preaches nightly against the lures of the flesh, only to lose his credibility in a succession of seedy motel rooms.

Are these bad people? Evil people? Possessed people? Rotten apples? Victims of mistaken identity? Of course not. What's going on? The Shadow.

Thirty years ago, Patty Hearst (that lovable debutante of San Francisco's society) was kidnapped and transformed into a gun-wielding, curse-spewing, bank-robbing member of the Symbionese Liberation Army. Following which, I said: "I do not fully understand brainwashing. But what I know is that given similar circumstances, stimuli, and opportunity, I would be capable of committing any of these acts."

Why am I bothering to raise it? Because a Shadow named is a Shadow on the way to being tamed. Once we understand something, we can begin to control it. But until we understand it, it controls us.

Denial is no answer. Repression is no answer. The goal is nothing less than the reconciliation of the Shadow with the remainder of the self. Consider this: most people love the prodigal son. I have preached his story from every angle, save one. What if the story is not about two brothers, but two sides of the same brother? What if the story is about the younger brother in us who would love to throw caution to the wind, hit the road, travel in the fast lane, push out the limits, and see what life is like in the far country, even as the older brother in us plays by the rules, conforms to the expectations, colors within the lines, and works every night until sundown? Which is Shadow? Which is real? You tell me! But if you read the story carefully, you cannot escape the conclusion that both brothers need each other desperately. Nor can you escape the conclusion that the Father will not be happy until both of the brothers are home. (William A. Ritter)

Worship Aids

Call to Worship

The psalmist said, "I will sing and make music. I will praise you, O Lord, among the nations; I will sing of you among the peoples." Let us heed these ancient words as we stand and sing God's praises.

Pastoral Prayer

Almighty God, source of all life and grace, we draw apart from the ordinary in the prayerful hope of connecting with the divine. We seek, especially in this hour, to receive the comfort and peace that only you can offer. We know deep inside that the pleasures and success symbols of this world will never satisfy our deepest hungers. Something cries within us for more. May these prayerful and reflective moments in worship help us separate the wheat from the chaff of life, so that we will not spend our lives on worthless baubles, but instead buy the pearl of great price. Amen.

Collect

Create pure hearts in us, O God, and renew our spirits. Purify us with your holy power and anoint us with your grace. Bring us into your presence that our lips might declare your praise. Lead us into paths of service, that our words might have legs, that our promises might have hands, that our creeds might have bodies. Amen. (Lance Moore)

JULY 30, 2006

❧❧❧❧

Eighth Sunday after Pentecost

Readings: 2 Samuel 11:1-15; Psalm 14; Ephesians 3:14-21; John 6:1-21

Strolling into Temptation
2 Samuel 11:1-15

The biblical writers were suspect with regard to public relations. They revealed most dirty secrets, foibles, and skeletons concerning major Bible characters. We read of Adam the liar, Jacob the cheat, Moses the murderer, and the mentally impaired Saul. Then we find David—brave shepherd boy, Israel's greatest king, God's favorite—caught in a steamy affair with the wife of Uriah. Proof of the Bible's veracity is that the dirty linen was rarely washed; the editors rarely censored the truth. We should be thankful. If we did not know the mistakes of the ancient Bible heroes, we would more likely repeat their errors. We might learn as much through the vice and failures of these characters as from their virtues and victories.

The story of David and Bathsheba, tragic as it was, reveals to us the subtle power of temptation and the step-by-step progression into deeper sin. Step one happens to all of us; temptation crosses our paths daily. For David, it was sexual temptation. For you, it may be something else. David had resisted the temptations of power, fame, and wealth. These "usual suspects" did not corrupt him. Temptation came at David's weak point: he was a romantic.

We regularly pray for God to "lead us not into temptation," knowing that temptation is a routine, unavoidable part of life. Even Jesus was tempted in the wilderness. It was not David's fault that Bathsheba was visible at her bath. Strolling on the rooftop, he had an innocent encounter that could happen to any of us. Here is what happened to me.

Years ago, we were staying overnight with my wife's family. I went to the bedroom we had been using and knocked. I heard my brother-in-law's voice reply, "Come in." I opened the door, and to my shock, there stood my sister-in-law in her underwear! She screamed, I closed the door and turned red. My brother-in-law, it turns out, was in the room next door; he thought I had knocked on *his* door so he invited me in. My sister-in-law, even in her unmentionables, was covered up better than the modern bikini, and we all had a good laugh. After all, it was her husband who had inadvertently invited me in!

We can understand how David's peeping might have been innocent. If David had simply said "oops" and turned away, he might have defeated temptation instantly. But he didn't. He stared. He examined this beautiful naked woman as animal instinct took over. David moved then from the first step of innocent temptation to the second: lust. Even President Jimmy Carter, the Baptist Sunday school teacher, admitted being guilty of lust. In our sex-crazed culture, it is difficult to avoid.

Sex is not the only ubiquitous temptation. We can't keep temptations from coming to mind, whether it be envy or covetousness or anger. But we can keep them from becoming obsessive. Martin Luther wrote: "You can't keep a bird from flying over your head; you can keep it from building a nest in your hair." Our attitude toward temptation should be something like my dad's attitude toward stray dogs. If a stray dog came into our yard, Dad would not allow us to feed it. He said if you feed a stray, it makes its home with you—you'll never be rid of it. If you feed an impure thought, sin will make its home with you.

This brings us back to David: he fed his lust. He went on to the third step. He inquired about his fantasy. He invited Bathsheba to his palace. Perhaps David still intended no harm. But from there, he took the final step: active sin, putting thoughts into action. David slept with Bathsheba.

So that we would not be hypocrites and Pharisees, Jesus warned us that even evil thoughts could be sinful. Nevertheless, once a sinful thought becomes an action, the damage is greater. God can easily forgive us for mental sins and free us from any harmful consequences. But actions always have costly consequences that forgiveness alone cannot undo.

For David and Bathsheba, their adultery had a serious consequence: pregnancy. Her husband, Uriah, was off at war. David could not contrive any way to make it look like the child was Uriah's. His secret sin would soon become public. This led to an even deeper sin: David conspired to have Uriah murdered!

How could this be possible? How could a godly man like David fall to such a low level of deceit and murder? The day he saw Bathsheba on the roof, he did not think: "I will break my marriage vow, enjoy that woman, and kill her husband." No, the sin began incrementally. This is how evil works. Evil weaves its temptations slowly, subtly, insidiously, and deceitfully. We fail to see how deeply we are entangled in sin until it is too late. We are blinded to the secondary costs of sin, the consequences upon ourselves and upon innocent others. Sin and temptation blur the facts; the fantasy is always more beautiful, easier, and less costly than reality. In our fantasy, no one gets hurt by sin; in reality, everyone is hurt.

Again, this is not a lesson just about adultery. The steps to sin revealed in David's sad story are universal. Your weak point, your emotional "hot spot," may be different; it may be a temptation to money, or power, or selfishness, or something else.

So what are we to do in the face of temptation? Simple. Turn away. An example: Three men being interviewed for a job as bus driver were each asked the same question: "How close could you drive to the edge of a cliff without losing control of the bus?" The first applicant said, "I could get within a foot of it without a problem." The second applicant boasted, "I have a strong, steady grip on the wheel. I could drive within four inches of the precipice." But the third one wisely said, "I don't know—I would never drive that close to danger." Would you like to guess who got the job?

When we toy with temptation, we are too close to the edge. Stay away from the precipice! Make a decision for love to reign. Keep your vows to God and to spouse. Stay strong in prayer, in Bible reading, in church attendance. Be honest with spouses and seek help from friends. We may, with God's help, have the strength to flee at sin's first appearance. As David later learned and wrote in what we believe was his seventy-third psalm, "My flesh and my heart may fail, but God is the strength of my heart and my portion forever" (73:26).

The final word from the life of King David is one of grace. Despite David's terrible sins, God forgave him. And God will forgive you and me. David also wrote, "You are forgiving and good, O Lord, abounding in love to all who call to you" (Psalm 86:5 NIV). Amen. (Lance Moore)

And You Think Your Feet Don't Smell

Second in a Series of Four: How Sweet the Sound

Romans 5:1-11

The year was 1960 when John Steinbeck outfitted his camper, pulled up stakes, and (with the companionship of an eleven-year-old French poodle) set off to find the real America. He writes:

Sunday morning, in a Vermont town. . . . I took my seat in the rear of the spotless, polished place of worship. The prayers were to the point, directing the attention of the Almighty to certain weaknesses and undivine tendencies I know to be mine and could only suppose were shared by others gathered there.

It had been long since I had heard such an approach. It is our practice now, at least in the large cities, to find from our psychiatric priesthood that our sins aren't really sins at all but accidents that are set in motion by forces beyond our control. There was no such nonsense in this church. The minister, a man of iron with tool-steel eyes and a delivery like a pneumatic drill, opened up with prayer and reassured us that we were a pretty sorry lot. . . . I began to feel good all over. For some years now God has been a pal to us, practicing togetherness, and that causes the same emptiness a father does playing softball with his son. But this Vermont God cared enough about me to go to a lot of trouble kicking the hell out of me.

I felt so revived in spirit that I put five dollars in the plate, and afterward, in front of the church, shook hands warmly with the minister and as many of the congregation as I could. . . . I even considered beating Charley to give him some satisfaction too, because Charley is only a little less sinful than I am. (John Steinbeck, *Travels with Charley: In Search of America* [New York: Viking Press, 1962], 77-79)

Now, I am not sure about you, but I liked that twenty-five years ago, and I like it even more today. In the early days of my ministry, I seldom talked about sin. I left that to the "fire and brimstone" boys. Then I mocked them. But sin is no longer a laughing matter. My apology for diminishing it is very much in order.

Actually, it took a psychiatrist to rediscover sin. The good doctor was the esteemed Karl Menninger who suggested that the problem (all along) might have been one of nomenclature. Sin never disappeared. We simply renamed it "sickness." People were no longer sinners so much as they were sick. Deviant behavior resulted from the fact that people were confused, hurt, rejecsted, misguided, dysfunctionally parented, improperly scripted, and the victims of everything from faulty toilet training to cultural deprivation.

Strangely enough, we began to like this way of looking at things. For whereas "sin" made us feel uncomfortable, "sickness" made us feel better. What's more, if there were no more "sinners," then we could rid our vocabulary of an equally unsettling term, namely, "salvation." For whereas sinners need "saving," all sick people need is "healing."

So where does one come by a theology of sin? Fortunately, my grandmother had one. Prior to her death at age ninety-seven, she was a lapsed Roman Catholic who had the sacred heart of Jesus in her bedroom and a crucifix in her hankie drawer. But she hadn't been to mass in sixty years. Nonetheless, a lengthy absence didn't keep her from articulating a theology of sin; for whenever anybody gave indication of thinking overly highly of themselves, the lady I affectionately called "the old Yugoslav" could be heard to mutter: "And you think your feet don't smell." Actually, she had an alternate version of the same saying. But in deference to her memory, I'm not going to tell you what it was.

From time to time, all feet stink. As a commentary on human nature, hers was the bottom line, the great leveler, not to mention the perfect pinprick in the balloon of all puffiness and pride. I once read that Peter Cartwright, that colorful preacher on the American frontier, used to come riding into settlements on his horse, reins in one hand, Bible in the other, shouting at the top of his lungs: "I smell hell here." Well, he could pick any village in any era and get a nose full. Sin stinks. It stinks to high heaven, which is probably why God smells it first. Sooner or later, however, it stinks closer to home, so that even lapsed Catholics like my grandmother can smell it next.

Frequently, pastors refer to Carroll Simcox's story when he recalls killing a robin with a slingshot he got in his Easter basket in his fifth North Dakota springtime. He felt instant remorse. He also remembered that the only explanation he could come up with was that he had done it "for the hell of it." "But you were only a child," they said to him when he recalled the painful event years later. "You were only five years old." "But," Simcox responded, "I did know better. And I did, indeed, do it just for the hell of it. And what is the hell of it? Hell is seeking one's own pleasure in ways that are contradictory to God's pleasure. And I knew, even at five years old, that God is displeased when I am heartless and cruel ... especially when I am heartless and cruel for no reason, save for the fact that cruelty can sometimes be quite pleasurable, and heartlessness quite exhilarating."

Once upon a time, I thought that people of faith were immune to such sordidness. But there is no immunity, even for Christians walking in the footsteps of Jesus. On a recent trek through Israel, most participants felt the high point to be our Communion service on the Sea of Galilee. No other buses. No other tourists. Just the sun, the breeze, the rippling waters of the lake, and the incredible memories of one who once walked its shoreline, who, in that moment, may very well have been walking it still.

But there was something about the loaf of bread I was holding in my hands. While eating breakfast, I realized we lacked bread. Then a loaf appeared on the buffet table. For what reason, I do not know. But knowing we needed it, I put a friend up to taking it. Which he did. Surreptitiously. Under his napkin. On the one hand, it was no big deal. The maître d' of the dining room may have been happy to give it to us. On the other hand, we didn't ask. We stole the Communion bread, for God's sake. And the fact that that was why we did it—for God's sake—didn't necessarily take the stain from our hands or the smell from our feet.

All of us have sinned and fallen short of the glory of God. But why rub our noses in it? Rather than answer that question, let me take you back to Steinbeck and his Vermont preacher. Why did that sermon make him "feel good all over"? The answer is simple. In that sermon, Steinbeck met a God who cared enough to take him seriously, which began by looking at him honestly.

If I matter to God, then I have got to believe that all of me matters to God. If our relationship—God's and mine—is ever going to get off the ground, my sins cannot be glossed over. How can I trust a God I can fool? The day God ceases to be interested in my sin is, I fear, the day God will cease being interested in me. Were I to sin against my marriage and my wife were to say, "Don't even bother to tell me about it, Ritter. I don't care what you do. It doesn't matter anymore," what would be clear is that it would be me who no longer mattered anymore.

It is a terrible thing, my friends, to stand in danger of the wrath of God. But there may be one thing worse, and that is not to stand in the danger of the wrath of God. For the day God ceases to hold me up against my sin, I fear (perchance) that God will cease to hold me. (William A. Ritter)

Worship Aids

Call to Worship

O Spirit of God, descend upon us now. Guide our worship, fill our mouths with praise and our hearts with love and gratitude.

Responsive Reading (adapted from Psalm 34:12-22 NIV)

Leader: Whoever of you loves life and desires to see many good days.

People: Keep your tongue from evil and your lips from speaking lies.

Leader: Turn from evil and do good; seek peace and pursue it.

People: The eyes of the LORD are on the righteous and his ears are attentive to their cry.

Leader: The righteous may have many troubles, but the LORD delivers them.

People: The LORD redeems his servants; no-one will be condemned who takes refuge in him.

Benediction

In the name of Christ, you are forgiven. Go now with joy but also with this charge: forgive your neighbor, as you would have God forgive you. In the name of God our Creator, Redeemer, and Guide, Amen. (Lance Moore)

AUGUST 6, 2006

Ninth Sunday after Pentecost

Readings: 2 Samuel 11:26–12:13*a*; Psalm 51:1-12; Ephesians 4:1-16; John 6:24-35

The Bread of Life
John 6:24-35

My friends, I invite you to a celebration and an adventure. You are invited to join a growing number of brothers and sisters all over this planet in celebrating the good news that the new age of God is literally transforming this present age! You are invited to join them in the unprecedented adventure of allowing God to use your life to change this world. You are invited to dare to believe that God is conspiring through your life and the lives of others like you to make a difference in his world.

God calls us to hope and to action. Our hope is based on the biblical faith that God is very much alive and is very much the Lord of history. God is, even now, working to bring God's new future into being.

Our action is made possible by the power of God's spirit working in our lives to change this world. We are part of that mysterious work that uses the small, the insignificant, the invisible, and the incomprehensible to change the world.

Now, to accept this invitation, you have to do a couple of things. First of all, you have to tune your ear so that you can hear the gospel. For example, in the text for today there are two levels of communication going on. This is characteristic of the Gospel of John, where there is always the message of the surface and then the message of the deeper level of the spirit. In today's lesson we read about the "bread of life." We know this is a message for the deeper part of us. Jesus is not talking about literal bread, but about that which satisfies the hunger of a soul.

And aren't our souls hungry? Is this hunger what lies behind the insatiable need to consume more and more?

At our home we receive a lot of catalogs advertising all sorts of things. I know you get them too. Have you "heard" the message of these catalogs with their attractive models and beautiful wares? Do you know what they are really saying to us? They're saying, "You're not happy. And you won't be happy until you have what we are selling. Look at us. Don't we look happy? We are happy! But, you're not, so place your order today!" And our garages and attics fill to the brim with stuff, and we numb ourselves with alcohol and drugs, all the while trying to satisfy the hunger of the soul!

This reality is what makes the text from the Gospel of John so incredibly relevant. Jesus is the bread of life. Jesus is not magic and neither is Jesus some form of insurance. Jesus is the bread of life that satisfies the hungry soul.

While preparing for this message, I turned to our hymnal and looked up the hymns listed under "Holy Communion." I found these lines that keep playing in my mind: "You satisfy the hungry heart with gift of finest wheat. Come, give to us, O saving Lord, the bread of life to eat" ("You Satisfy the Hungry Heart," *The United Methodist Hymnal* [Nashville: The United Methodist Publishing House, 1989], 629).

The spirit of those lines is captured in a little parable about a holy man who rested beneath a tree at the outskirts of a city. One day he was interrupted by a man who ran to him saying, "The stone! The stone! Please give me the stone!" He told how in a dream an angel had spoken to him of a man outside the city who would give him a stone and make him rich forever.

The holy man reached into his pocket and pulled out a large diamond. "Here," he said, "the angel probably spoke of this. I found it on my journey here. If you want it, you may have it."

The diamond was as big as his fist and perfect in every way. The man marveled at its beauty, clutched it eagerly, and walked away from the holy man. But that night he could not sleep, and before dawn he woke the holy man saying, "The wealth! The wealth! Give me the wealth that lets you so easily give away the diamond."

Jesus is the bread of life and in him we satisfy the hungry heart. Why do we come here for worship? Not to simply serve God. That is a pagan idea. We do not have to cajole God to be bounteous to us. God already is bounteous to us, because Jesus is the bread of life. We come to be served; to have Jesus put on the apron and spread a table before us. We come to be sensitized to what God has already given. We come to receive the wealth that lets us give away all our riches. We come for the bread of life. (Chris Andrews)

What if It All Piles Up?

Third in a Series of Four: How Sweet the Sound

Ephesians 2:1-10

One semester at the University of California, a student began strolling around the campus in the nude. Eventually, he was arrested and sent home. "Yes, we are a bastion of free expression," the university said. "But first and foremost, we are a bastion of higher education."

Over the years, I have met my share of weirdos in the hallowed halls of ivy. But none of them ever came to class undressed, although it was once permissible to walk around "naked and unashamed." I am speaking of Eden's first pair, who strolled through the garden *au naturel* until late that first afternoon when God arrived and our beloved twosome both hid from God's sight and covered themselves. Something about this fast-deteriorating situation no longer seemed as sweet and innocent as it had been before lunch, when Eve said, "How about a nice apple cobbler for dessert, my dear," and Adam said, "It would be sinful, sweet Eve, lip-smackingly sinful." In the Bible, being naked has more to do with being caught dead to rights than being caught with nothing in our closet.

The story is about sin: how easy to commit, how hard to deny. A father claims that his most vivid memory of raising children was when one of his offspring charged into the study and announced: "I didn't do anything bad in the dining room." Which led his father to ask: "And what bad thing in the dining room didn't you do?" All of which led this wise father to observe that God must occasionally feel like asking us would-be innocents: "And precisely what bad thing is it, my children, that you didn't do?" How is it that so many terrible things keep happening in the room next door, yet nobody seems to know how, why, or who did them?

That's the paradox of human existence. Professing the best does not always keep us from performing at our worst. One of the reasons we appear naked before God in the late afternoon is that when we go to our closets, there are skeletons hanging where our clothes ought to be. Over time, these skeletons keep multiplying, because, over time, our sins reproduce. Sin begets sin. It's the gynecology of corruption.

A fifth-grade boy steals a classmate's radio. When confronted, he lies about the theft ("Who, me? I didn't steal a radio"). When the radio is found in his locker, he lies about the motive ("I just wanted to see what size batteries it took"). When his motive is challenged, he lies about the lie ("I'm telling you the truth. What kind of teacher are you, if you don't even believe a kid who tells the truth?"). When he is punished, he lets the air out of his teacher's tires and beats up the safety patrol kid who catches him kneeling beside the teacher's wheel.

As Cornelius Platinga Jr. explains: "Youngsters soon discover what the wise have known for millennia. People rarely commit single sins." Which leads to the fear that as our moral slippages add up, their collective weight will drag us down.

I once referred (in a children's sermon) to the possibility of posting sins on the refrigerator door. After all, we post everything else there. What if (in our growing up years) every defection, indiscretion, omission, or fall from grace was printed on a little yellow sticky note and attached to the refrigerator?

Billy's sins for Wednesday:
- Forgot to feed cat
- Kicked cat
- Left milk glass in family room
- Blew off math assignment
- Was overheard using a four-letter word as a descriptive adjective for his sister

And if that wasn't bad enough, what if Thursday's sins were written out and attached to the bottom of the list from Wednesday? And what if Friday yielded its own list? Pretty soon there would be yellow sticky notes all over the refrigerator, with the paper trail of Billy's sinfulness doubled back against itself for all the world to see. And how many weeks would it take before Billy's sins would expand to cover the walls, the ceilings, the cabinet doors, and the closet where the canned goods are kept? Pretty soon Billy wouldn't want to come into the kitchen anymore, and would take to eating most of his meals out.

Make no mistake about it. When Paul talks about the "weight of sin," he is talking about Billy and the accumulative burden of Billy's record. What if it all piles up? What if none of it ever gets unstuck from the doors, walls, and closets of Billy's life? What if it all stays there and screams at him, day after day, in a bitter chorus of condemnation? It is frightening to realize how much is remembered, recorded, posted on the refrigerator, or pinned to the fringes of our reputation. For good or ill, most of us go through life dragging our "tales" behind us. And even if we escape the weight of sin individually, we carry the burden of it culturally.

What if none of it ever gets put to rest? What if the sins of the fathers and the grandfathers, not to mention the forefathers, keep reappearing every generation? What if we have to keep making payments, over and over again, for sins committed in Europe over the centuries, in England three hundred years ago, in Africa two hundred years ago, in the American South and its war between the states, and in Germany of seventy years ago? Carlyle Marney asks, "What if all of this agony piles up, so that our children's children have to keep suffering for atoning . . . for hurting . . . and dying for this mounting mound of moral stuff gone sour?"

What sense can we make out of all this tangled and troubled history? What will we do with this record of wrongs that is written on refrigerator doors; numbered in the chronicles of history; and kept alive in the collective memories of families, tribes, and nations? Will we ever get the problem fixed? The penance paid? The record expunged? The leftover eyes and teeth sorted out? The slate wiped clean? Or does it just get wider, deeper, and more burdensome by the day?

I can hear the prayer now: "O, for a means by which to wash it away." This is precisely what our faith offers, you see: a means by which to wash it away. Our sins don't have to keep piling up, getting higher and higher, deeper and deeper, greater and greater in number, hanging like paper chains across the walls and ceilings of our kitchens, or spilling into the third and fourth generations or our children's children. Our sins don't have to follow us to graduation day, dying day, or even judgment day; nor do they have to cling to us like barnacles on a boat's bottom, burrs on a pant leg, or gravy stains on an expensive necktie.

Our sins can be washed away. The waters of baptism, the wine of Communion, or the blood of the cross can wash them away. Imagery? Of course it's imagery. But grace-full imagery is always liquid imagery. Picture God's mercy trickling on down, washing on down, or even flooding on down. Or if you don't like that, picture the proverbial rain that falls on the just and the unjust. But remember that rain (biblically considered) is never considered to be a curse or an inconvenience, but a blessing and sign of grace. Or if you don't like that, picture, in the words of a beloved spiritual, "peace like a river," "love like an ocean," or "joy like a fountain" in your soul.

"O happy day, O happy day, When Jesus washed my sins away!" (William A. Ritter)

Worship Aids

Call to Worship

Leader: Come before the Lord in holy worship.

People: We come hungering and thirsting for good bread and fresh water.

Leader: The Lord of the banquet has spread a table.

People: In faith we gather to eat and drink. We have come to be fed.

Leader: God's grace is ready to feed us.

People: Let us celebrate the feast of his love.

Benediction

With thanksgiving for the nourishment of true bread, go forth to live for the praise and glory of Almighty God and God's Son, our Savior, Jesus Christ. Amen.

Invocation

Spread the banquet of your love before us, O Lord. We are hungry. We have tried many foods, and now come to your house and feed at your table that we might be nourished by the bread of life. In our worship this day may we find that which truly satisfies the hungry heart of each of us. Amen. (Chris Andrews)

AUGUST 13, 2006

❧❧❧

Tenth Sunday after Pentecost

Readings: 2 Samuel 18:5-9, 15, 31-33; Psalm 130; Ephesians 4:25–5:2; John 6:35, 41-51

The Bread from Heaven
John 6:35, 41-51

The aroma of fresh baked bread is one of the most delicious smells I have ever experienced. I can still close my eyes and conjure up the odor in the kitchen when my mother was baking homemade rolls, and when we drive by the local bakery we like to roll down the windows and let the aroma tantalize our taste buds. Many times over we have heard someone describe the smell and taste of bread as "heavenly" or "divine." Indeed, there seems to be something otherworldly about the pure sensual pleasure derived from feasting on plain, ordinary bread.

However, when Jesus called himself the bread from heaven, Jesus was not talking about the yummy smells and tastes of fresh baked bread. Why, then, did Jesus use such strange language? The context in which something is said invariably helps to understand the intent. Let's look at the context of Jesus' teaching.

Jesus had just fed the five thousand on the far side of the Sea of Galilee, and had returned to Capernaum. Some of the people went to Capernaum and sought him out, causing Jesus to accuse them of being more interested in a free meal than they were in the free grace of God.

The people asked Jesus what sign he could give to prove he was sent from God, and they reminded him that Moses had fed his ancestors with manna from heaven. Jesus corrected them, insisting that it was God, not Moses, who had given the people the manna. Then Jesus made this great claim: "I am the bread of life.... I am the bread that came down from heaven."

The Jews could neither understand nor accept these words of Jesus, whom they knew to be the son of Joseph and Mary. But Jesus went even further when he identified this bread of life with his own body and blood, which, he said, people must eat in order to enter into the life that death cannot touch.

The people had already alluded to the manna in the wilderness, and when Jesus called himself the bread from heaven, they were again reminded of that historical provision (Exodus 16:1-36). The story was deeply imprinted on the Jewish memory. In Nehemiah, the manna is even called "bread from heaven" (Nehemiah 9:15). It is called by the same name in Psalm 105:40; and in Psalm 78:24, 25, it is called the "grain of heaven" and the "bread of angels."

Thus to the Jew there was something mysteriously divine about the manna, and for Jesus to claim to be the bread from heaven was in itself a claim to be divine. In addition, when Jesus emphasized that it was God who gave the manna, and then insisted that it is he (Jesus) who gives the living bread, he was claiming in some sense to be God, or at least to be doing only what God could do.

This is the first startling revelation that is given with the title "bread from heaven"—that Jesus is divine. The second jarring word is that he invites us to participate in that divinity by consuming him—eating his flesh and drinking his blood.

Our Catholic friends interpret this admonition literally, arriving at their doctrine of transubstantiation, which teaches that the bread and wine at Communion actually become the body and blood of Jesus. Whereas most Protestants do not take the words literally, we do take them seriously. True believers must take Jesus Christ into their inmost being; Jesus must enter into us as does the food we eat and drink.

One of the most ancient religious ceremonies was a meal in a sacred place at which the circle of worshipers ate part of the meat that had been sacrificed. At such a feast the god himself was believed to be present and even to enter into the worshiper with the meat of the sacrifice.

Perhaps Jesus' audience knew of such traditions and would make the connection with Jesus' words. One thing is certain; John is certain that we can never know what life is until Jesus Christ enters into us. When Jesus said, "I am the bread of life," he was making one of his greatest claims and one of his greatest offers.

In Psalm 34:8, we are invited to "taste and see that the LORD is good" (NKJV). From the five senses of sight, hearing, smell, touch, and taste, it is taste that the psalmist selects to describe the religious experience. Consider the following aspects of tasting and how they compare with partaking of the Bread from Heaven:

Taste is the most personal of all the senses. All of the others can be shared outwardly and publicly, but taste is internal and individual.

Taste can be dangerous. Taking food into our bodies can poison us or make us sick. Those who risk taking food are vulnerable to its effect.

For good or bad, tasting and eating food changes us. We become like what we eat. Our weight, health, even our attitude can be changed by our choice of food.

Thus, partaking of food involves trust. We exercise such trust every day, often at the hands of strangers as we eat in restaurants. The second half of Psalm 34:8 reads, "Blessed is the [person] who trusts in Him!" (NKJV).

Although the experience of tasting is personal, the invitation to taste is universal. All must eat, no one can live without eating. All may eat, all are invited to the table of the Lord. All can eat, God has given each of us the capacity to dine upon his grace. "Oh, taste and see that the LORD is good!" (Bill Austin)

O Do Remember Me

Fourth in a Series of Four: How Sweet the Sound

Psalm 25:1-7; Luke 23:39-43

The phone rang late one night and I answered by saying, "Bill Ritter speaking," which was followed by another voice—higher, sweeter, and infinitely more teasing—saying: "I bet you don't remember who this is." I didn't., and admitted I didn't, which led to a second response: "I bet you don't forget all the girls from your past." And while I was still trying to figure out if I'd had a past—and if there were ever any unforgettable girls in it—she suddenly interrupted and asked who it was that I said I was upon answering the phone. She wasn't looking for me at all, which left her feeling embarrassed and me feeling old.

But my title comes not from my telephone conversation, but from my text. It is that marvelous little plea found in Psalm 25:7 (RSV). "Remember not the sins of my youth, or my transgressions; according to thy steadfast love remember me ... O LORD!" Actually, it is two phrases, juxtaposed in counterpoint. "Forget my sins. But don't forget me."

As I look through the rearview mirror, my youth was more boring than sinful. But that's not the way we picture things, "the sins of youth." What do you see? Many of us see sleazy dives and smoky rooms; all-night binges followed by aching heads; toga parties and chugging beer; fraternity basements and the backseats of automobiles. We see road trips, beer runs, and descents into the hell of God only knows where. In short, we see *Animal House* recreated in every sleepy college town in North America. This may be true for some of the young folk some of the time but is certainly not true for all of the young folk all of the time.

"O Lord, remember not the sins of my youth," not because they were among my worst, but because they were among my first. My sins, alas, have persisted. And my choices have not necessarily improved over time. My perversity leads me to seek my own way, swing to my own beat, and swim against the current of God's will (not to mention the river of God's righteousness). This leads me to recall the story of a man running frantically upstream beside a fast-flowing river. Someone called to him and asked, "Where are you going in such a hurry?" To which the man said, "My wife fell in the river and I'm trying to rescue her." "But why are you running upstream?" the bystander asked. "If your wife fell in that water, you ought to be searching downstream," which caused the husband to shout back, "You don't know how contrary my wife is."

Certainly God knows how contrary we are. And we know God knows. Hence, the cry: "Remember not the sins of my youth." Translated into confessional language this reads: "Our sins are ever before us, and the remembrance of them is grievous unto us."

Our initial petition, however, is far more personal. We wish that *we* could forget our sins. We wish that our past could be over and done with. But our past is never quite done with us. We are not the escape artists we pretend to be. In visiting with people pastorally, the most frequent suffering I encounter is suffering brought on by memory, which is usually well hidden. For while we fill our family rooms with the trophies, diplomas, brass rings, and blue ribbons that are the collective stuff of our good memories, we fill the corner closets of our souls with darker memories, drawn from those times in our lives when we were more deserving of chastisement than cheers.

Such things are difficult to forget, especially when one considers that those corner closets have direct pipelines, if not to our minds, then almost always to our digestive tracts. This is why guilt is an emotion often tasted before it is pondered. Besides, writes Henri Nouwen: "Burying our past is just another way of turning our backs on our best teacher."

All of this leads to a second formation of the psalmist's plea: "We wish, O God, that *others* could forget our sins." But they don't. They remember far too much for far too long. One of my colleagues recently attended his high school reunion. As the band was belting out oldies but goodies, a former female classmate came up to him and asked: "You weren't seriously thinking about ministry when we were in high school, were you?" My friend admitted that the ministry hadn't even crossed his mind in those years. "Good," she said. "That certainly makes me feel better." There's always somebody, you see, who remembers what we did on Saturday nights—or during the rest of the week as well. It's not so much that we keep finding our sins, but that the people who remember our sins keep finding us.

Our sins!

We wish that we could forget.

We wish that others could forget.

We wish that God could forget.

Does God have the memory of an elephant? If so, think of the pain that could cause us. Psalm 130:3 ponders: "If thou, O LORD, shouldst mark iniquities, Lord, who [among us] could stand?" (RSV).

A few years ago, I stumbled upon Paul Stucky's recurring dream about divine judgment. In Paul's dream, he is waiting in a long line (somewhat smugly) to have the content of his life reviewed by God. In order to kill time while waiting, he strikes up a conversation with the lady standing just ahead of him. Much to his surprise, he finds he is talking to Mother Teresa. But that surprise is mild compared to the shock of overhearing God say to the saintly sister: "All things considered, Teresa, I was really expecting a lot more from you." I don't know about you, but if I was standing there, hearing God say that to her, I'd start looking for people wanting to cut the line, giving me additional time to reassess my response. Sure, God knows I could have done worse—but God also knows I could have done better. Much better.

Think how painful such knowledge must be for God. If God really knows all this stuff—I mean, if God really sees everything, misses nothing, and carries it all around in his head—God must suffer terribly. What if God has to carry around not only the sum total of yesterday's meanness and cruelties but also the collective memory of who did what to whom at Auschwitz, Antietam, Appomattox, Belfast, Bosnia, and Baghdad; proceeding alphabetically past Mogadishu and Nagasaki; clean on through to Waterloo and Zaire? Could you carry the memory of all that stuff? Or, sooner or later, would you have to forget it, if not for the sake of others, then for yours? Nobody, even God—especially God—wants to carry all that junk around forever.

"Remember not the sins of my youth.... [But] according to thy stead-fast love remember me ... O LORD!" That's what we really want, isn't it? Not just to have our sins forgotten, but to have ourselves remembered, so that in considering us God will feel no need to call for our file, but will simply call for us. Hanging beside him on the cross, one thief mocked Jesus. The other said: "Don't you fear God? We're getting what we deserve. But this man has done nothing wrong." And then he said, "Jesus, remember me."

Remember me, not my sins. Our last and deepest prayer is that God will know us, in spite of all God knows about us, and that God will not turn his back on us, in spite of all that has come between us. For to be forgotten by God would be to be sentenced to the ultimate in homelessness, causing us to be numbered among the wild and wandering strays of the universe. Would God allow that to happen? Would God allow some to drift forever out of sight as a result of having been put forever out of mind? I think not, even as I pray not. For as a teenager who once knew fifty verses to the camp spiritual "Do Lord," it strikes me that I always sang the chorus with a smile on my face. (William A. Ritter)

Worship Aids

Call to Confession (using 1 John 3:1)

See what love the Father has given us, that we should be called children of God; and that is what we are. The reason the world does not know us is that we do not know him. Our sins keep us from knowing God fully. Let us confess our sins to God.

Assurance of Pardon (using 1 John 1:9 and 1 John 3:2-3)

Hear now the words of scripture. If we confess our sins, God is faithful and just to forgive us our sins and cleanse us from all unrighteousness. Beloved, we are God's children now; what we will be has not yet been revealed. What we do know is this: when God is revealed, we will be like God, for we will see God as God is. And all who have this hope in God purify themselves, just as God is pure. (Tracy Hartman)

AUGUST 20, 2006

❧❧❧

Eleventh Sunday after Pentecost

Readings: 1 Kings 2:10-12; 3:3-14; Psalm 111; Ephesians 5:15-20; John 6:51-58

Sing the Fullness
Ephesians 5:15-20

Partial 9/05

In five short verses Paul answers three weighty questions: How can we live wisely? How can we make the most of our time? How can we be filled with the Spirit?

Remarkably, Paul answers each question with the same quite surprising word: Sing! It is Paul's answer for how to be the counterculture called church. So let's consider singing—the power of singing, the transportation of our souls into another realm when good music sweeps over us. Let us consider how singing brings us into the fullness of God.

Have you ever gotten a tune in your head that would not let go of you? That happened to me a couple of weeks ago. We sang a song at the evening worship service called "Day Is Dying in the West." It is an old hymn that many of us learned to sing when evening worship services were still a normal part of Sunday's routine. The chorus stuck in my soul and mind and kept playing itself over and over:

> Holy, holy, holy, Lord God of Hosts!
> Heaven and earth are full of thee!
> Heaven and earth are praising thee,
> O Lord most high!
> ("Day Is Dying in the West," *The United
> Methodist Hymnal* [Nashville: The
> United Methodist Publishing House,
> 1989], 687)

It became a tune for the shower, for the car, for the early morning jog. It would not quit. "Holy, holy, holy...Heaven and earth are full of thee!...full of thee!" It has made for better days.

214

That is the power of singing and of music. For the most part, we humans have historically had a difficult time feeling like we are part of the party. The life-on-earth party, that is. We have bumbled through our million or so years of existence relating to the planet as if we were managers, regulators, consumers, or observers. We're outsiders looking in. We're strangers in a strange land. Seldom have we, as communities or nations, viewed ourselves as anything but earth's administrative staff. We're here to tame, train, torture, and tease the earth into satisfying our wants and needs.

Granted there have been a few cultures, such as those of indigenous peoples, who have behaved in a less superior manner. There have been people who have somehow realized that the earth is, truly, the Lord's and the fullness thereof. But for the most part, we humans have conducted ourselves like arrogant children. We have taken and looted and acted as if we can never have enough.

Maybe part of the problem is that we don't feel like we fit in. We live like fish out of water. When we speak of the beauty of creation, for example, we speak of clouds and trees, oceans and rivers, flowers and birds. Very seldom do we look in the mirror or at some other human and begin whistling "What a Wonderful World."

How many of us were taught that singing is the hallmark of wise living? Wasn't that what the foolish grasshopper did? He sang the summer away while the industrious ant kept quiet and worked. We weren't taught to make the most of our time by singing. No, we're supposed to be in bed early, and get up early, and make lists, and consult daily planners.

Paul wrote to people living in a dangerous world. And he said, "Sing." Simple? You bet. Simplistic? Not for a minute. To sing, to make melody to the Lord in your heart, is to live wisely and make the most of one's time.

Who is your favorite music maker? I have many, among whom I count the "man in black," Johnny Cash. A music critic once said of Johnny Cash, "He does make an honest attempt to hit every note." You know, that is all God asks of any of us—just an honest attempt to hit each note of the Lord's melody as we sing of the fullness of his love in our lives. (Chris Andrews)

Building the Church

First in a Series of Four: Life in the Church

1 Corinthians 14:1-12

Today we begin a series on life in the church. In this series, we will be exploring what it means to belong to this incredible institution, which can be for us the body of Christ in a very real way. We understand that Christ is the foundation upon which we build the church, but what does it take to build the church? What kind of community is it we are establishing? What difference does church membership make in our lives? Finally, what does it mean to belong to the body of Christ? These are questions we will be addressing together as we consider our common life in the church.

Many times when I perform in a wedding, I am asked to read 1 Corinthians 13. It is a beautiful passage on love, and it extols the power of love in a covenant relationship. What many people do not realize, however, is that 1 Corinthians 13 is nestled into a much larger section of scripture that has to do with spiritual gifts that are used to build up the church. Among these gifts we find faith, hope, and love (the greatest of them, of course, being self-giving love).

In 1 Corinthians 12, Paul describes for us what spiritual gifts are all about. Here is where we learn about gifts of teaching, healing, prophecy, and speaking in and interpreting other tongues. There are other gifts also, and Paul tells us that people possessing those gifts are all important. No person possesses a gift so great that that person can go solo without the need of other people possessing other gifts.

In the thirteenth chapter of 1 Corinthians, we hear about this gift of love that is foundational to the building of a community of so many people with so many diverse gifts. Then in the fourteenth chapter, Paul addresses a critical issue facing the Corinthian church. There were many people in the church in Corinth who had the gift of *glossolalia*, that is, the gift of speaking in tongues. Many of these people had decided that their gift, being more mystical in nature, was a greater gift than any other spiritual gifts. Some considered themselves better Christians with a higher calling than anyone else around them. Paul realized immediately that this smug, elite attitude was only destructive and could, in no way, build up the church. Paul's words are aimed at helping us understand the one fundamental truth about any and all spiritual gifts: the only valuable gift is the gift that builds up.

In my ministry, I have had the opportunity to be part of two major construction projects for churches I have served. In the time of planning and building, there are many choices to make. There are many things to be considered, and there are just as many opportunities to get sidetracked as there are to stay focused. I learned early in my ministry, whether constructing a building or planning a Bible study, to stop and reflect along the way and ask myself the question, "How is this going to help in the building of God's kingdom?" It is not unlike Dr. Zan Holmes, who, in my preaching class following each sermon, would make us answer the question, "So what?" What difference does it make? How does it build the kingdom?

There are many things that I think are important. There are many gifts that I have been given as a child of God, and if my guess is correct, every one of you is blessed with some special gift (or gifts) because you, too, are children of God. As we consider our life in the church, however, we are challenged to determine which of our gifts are more likely to build up the church and which of those are not. I know many ministers who are excellent golfers, and although I am certain that some of those ministers use their golf game to cultivate significant relationships, or even perhaps provide pastoral care or spend time discussing faith, most golfers I know simply use their golf skills as an outlet for fun. I am confident that God is not opposed to fun and fellowship on the golf course; however, I will not presume that any gifts I have for golf or any other sport can build up the church effectively. I also have been given the gifts of pastoral leadership, and those are the gifts that I consider will build the church more effectively than my golf game.

When I was a young boy, I remember spending time with my grandparents on their farm. I would spend my days playing around the farm, but what I really loved was spending time with my grandfather in his workshop. One day I was in the middle of a game of make-believe, and I was speaking to some imaginary person. My grandfather stopped what he was doing and asked what I said (presuming that I had spoken to him). When I told him that I was talking to no one, he replied, "Oh, you were just talking to the wind." I never knew that my grandfather was such a great biblical scholar, for that is exactly what Paul is explaining to the Corinthians. He explains that people who speak in tongues that cannot be interpreted or are otherwise unintelligible are just "speaking into the air" (1 Corinthians 14:9) or, as my grandfather put it, "just talking to the wind."

Consequently, the challenge for us as followers of Christ is to reflect upon the gifts we have received and to offer a true assessment of those gifts to determine which of them can most effectively build up the church. Then we are challenged to offer those gifts to the body of Christ, the church, that the church might be strong and that the work of Christ might be fulfilled. (Jeffrey Smith)

Worship Aids

Call to Worship

Leader: Let us sing of the beauty around us!

People: Let us sing of the beauty within!

Leader: O hear the earth tell that all shall be well!

People: All shall be well. In our bliss, in our sorrow, in the sun and in the rain, all shall be well.

Benediction

Go forth to sing. To dance. To share the music of God's love wherever you are and with whomever you meet. Go forth and sing your song!

Invocation

Put your music in our souls, O Lord. If we have lost our song, help us find it. If our joy has dried up, water us with the lyrics of your love. If our voices are flat, enliven us with the energy of life. O Lord, receive this our act of worship and praise, to the glory and honor of your name. Amen. (Chris Andrews)

AUGUST 27, 2006

😎😎😎

Twelfth Sunday after Pentecost

Readings: 1 Kings 8:(1, 6, 10-11), 22-30, 41-43; Psalm 84; Ephesians 6:10-20; John 6:56-69

Who Is Jesus?
John 6:56-69

Peter's question haunts us too. Peter asked, "To whom can we go?" The question came at the end of a long two days. The day before Peter asked his haunting question, a crowd had sought Jesus. Then, after Jesus had taught them, he had miraculously met their physical hunger by feeding this large crowd of five thousand with a boy's lunch of five loaves and two fish. So impressed was the crowd by Jesus' meeting their needs that they had wanted to "take him by force to make him king" (John 6:15). To avoid their plan, Jesus had gone away, by himself.

The next day found Jesus and his disciples across the lake, and the crowd came seeking him again. They would not give up. They wanted Jesus!

Or so they thought. After a series of interchanges with Jesus about who he was and what he did, the crowd dwindled. "Many of his disciples turned back and no longer went about with him." We get the feeling that Jesus' conversation with the Twelve in this text was to determine the depth of even their own commitment to him.

The crowd and even Jesus' closest disciples were struggling with what is easily the most important question of anyone's life—indeed, of all history: Who is Jesus?

Really, who is Jesus? It's a question that when seriously considered brings about a division in the ranks of every group who asks it. It even brings about a division within our own hearts. Who is Jesus?

The answers vary. For some, Jesus is the great teacher. He was a great individual with great ideas, who has contributed much by word and example. Jesus can be revered as one of the great teachers of history,

219

certainly alongside Aristotle, Plato, Buddha, and Moses. Jesus is to be respected and even loved.

For others, Jesus is the model person, the best person who ever lived, and we should strive to imitate Jesus—as long as we don't perhaps take it too far. This view of Jesus has often shaded toward simply attributing to Jesus the most popular values of current culture. Folks who hold this view often see Jesus as looking and acting a lot like they do.

For some, as in Jesus' day, Jesus is the Messiah, but a worldly Messiah, as Jesus was to the crowd on those two days described in John 6. They wanted him to solve their problems, both there and thereafter. They were impressed that, like Moses of old, Jesus had supplied them with food in the wilderness. "Hey, we can follow a guy like this!"

Of course, the overwhelming answer of the scriptures and of the church at its best through the centuries has been that Jesus is more than these descriptions or any others we might list. Who is Jesus? He is a human being, the person in whom God was uniquely present. Somehow, as Paul said, "In Christ God was reconciling the world to himself" (2 Corinthians 5:19). We may not be able to state the *how* of this truth very well, but we revel in its reality. Somehow, this person Jesus, who was flesh and blood, was the Person in whom the God of Israel and the universe was uniquely present.

Give a little more thought to this question: Who is Jesus? Jesus' contemporaries knew Jesus first as a human being. The scriptures affirm this part of Jesus' nature. He was human like us. Indeed, Jesus was fully human. In later writings of the New Testament, especially 1 John, the major issue was whether Jesus was fully human. That little letter begins with the affirmation that indeed Jesus was. The first verse states, "We declare to you what was from the beginning, what we have heard, what we have seen with our eyes, what we have looked at and touched with our hands" (1 John 1:1).

Sometimes it seems almost sacrilegious, even heretical, to think of Jesus as a human being who got thirsty, hungry, and tired. Jesus' closest disciples had no trouble seeing Jesus like that, however. Neither should we. One of the most astounding verses in the Bible is, "The Word became flesh and lived among us" (John 1:14). Flesh!

Who is Jesus? Jesus was a human being, fully a human being.

The scriptures also affirm Jesus as fully God. In ways we can only state and neither explain nor understand, the God of the universe was uniquely present in Jesus. This view of Jesus was no afterthought of the church after the days of the New Testament. It was not simply thought up and written down at a later church council. It is seen in the experiences of Jesus in the Gospels (see Matthew 16:16; Mark 1:11; 15:39). Also, it is seen in the reflections of Jesus' closest followers as they spoke and wrote of their experiences (John 20:31; Acts 2:32-33; Philippians 2:5-11; Colossians 1:15-18; Hebrews 1:1-4; 1 John 1:3; 2 Peter 3:18; Revelation 1:4-5).

So we return to Peter's question after Jesus had asked the disciples whether they would follow the crowd as they went away or follow him: "To whom shall we go?" Like the would-be followers of Jesus who were disturbed by Jesus' teachings, do we not sometimes say, "This teaching is difficult. Who can accept it?" It is not easy to be faithful to Jesus when who he is and what he wants us to do runs so counter to what our culture has told us all our lives. But when we consider who Jesus is, we can only come back to Peter's question, a question that is as much an affirmation of faith as it is a question (v. 68), "To whom can we go? You have the words of eternal life."

Who is Jesus? Let us join Peter in confessing that Jesus has the words of eternal life, and let us follow Jesus wherever he leads. (Ross West)

The New Community

Second in a Series of Four: Life in the Church

Acts 6:1-6

I was still in seminary, and I was serving as pastor in a small community. Following my first worship service, I was standing at the door greeting people, and I was so proud that I had finally arrived. I finally had my own pulpit. As I greeted the people, I felt someone tug on the sleeve of my robe. I turned to find a little girl, who was all of eight years old, anxiously trying to get my attention. I asked her what was wrong, and she told me that the upstairs toilet was running and would not stop. I told her that we would need to find someone to repair it, and in one of my more humbling experiences in ministry, she said, "No, my mom said that that's your job. You have to fix it." It was a long time before I moved from repairing toilets to providing the kind of pastoral leadership that empowered the trustees of the church to handle the toilets.

In the early days of the church, the apostles had to make that same kind of decision. One of the wonderful gifts that came to the church from our Jewish ancestry was the gift of caring for the poor, especially

221

the women who were widowed. It was not difficult for the apostles and all other followers of Jesus to become involved in these critical ministries of justice and peace. The problem, however, was that the Jewish followers were taking care of one another like they always had. Those who were poor and widowed were provided daily rations of food, and the apostles were right in the middle of the serving line along with everyone else. The Hellenists, however, had widows (and probably others who were poor) who were going without the daily food ration simply because the Hellenists were not organized to care for them like the Jewish followers.

The twelve apostles called together the whole community and began to organize them for ministry. In the process, they created the church's first ministry team. These were people who were set apart to organize this fractious band of believers into a new community designed to care for the least. Theirs was the task of cataloging the needs within the community and then organizing the community to meet those needs. The Greek word for this kind of servant ministry is *diakonos*, from which we get our words "deacon" and "diaconal."

As we consider our life in the church, it is important to remember that the church's entire ministry is founded upon servant ministry. The new community of faith is created only when we dedicate ourselves and organize ourselves for ministry with the poor, with those who are lost, with those who are suffering, and with those who are hopeless. Seven deacons were set apart to lead in that ministry.

The text tells us that the apostles themselves were then set apart for a different type of ministry. They devoted themselves "to prayer and to serving the word." As in most organizational structures, it may well appear that the apostles were moving up to something easier while they left the hard work for the deacons. Before we speak too harshly of the apostles, however, let us understand just how difficult the task of prayer and serving the word really are. As most people involved in upper management of any organization will attest, the job usually appears much easier than it really is.

As a young boy, I can remember hearing a preacher tell the story of a circuit rider who came across a farmer escaping the hot summer sun while resting under a tree. The circuit rider began with small talk, and he asked the farmer how his farming was going. The farmer looked up at the circuit rider, and he said, "I just wish I had it as easy as you. Here I am slaving away in the summer sun, but all you have to do is preach and pray."

The circuit rider assured the farmer that the business of the circuit rider was quite challenging. There were many things besides preaching and praying for which he was responsible. In addition, he informed the farmer that preaching and praying were themselves difficult tasks. The farmer replied, "Well, I don't know much about preaching, but I know I can pray without any problem."

The circuit rider offered a challenge. "When I ride from town to town, I spend much of my time completely in prayer. Sometimes that means I have to focus for one to two hours at a time praying without ceasing. If you can pray without ceasing for just five minutes, I'll give you my horse." The farmer stood up with a huge grin on his face. "You're on," he said. With that, he knelt down and started to pray.

The circuit rider glanced at his pocket watch. Thirty seconds passed . . . then sixty. About a minute and a half into the prayer, the farmer looked up from where he knelt and asked, "Say, Preacher, does the saddle come with that horse?"

The apostles' task of praying and serving the word is not as easy as we are prone to believe. What the apostles tell us through their words and actions is that, whereas servant ministry is foundational in the new community, prayer and preaching are vitally important to sustaining such servant ministry. The challenge for us as disciples of Jesus Christ is to organize ourselves for servant ministry that is sustained by earnest prayer and diligent preaching.

Many churches today are discovering such vital ministries. The people of God are rediscovering that mission and outreach empowered by prayer and proclamation are the essential elements of the new community of faith. May God empower your life in the church to reflect the life of Jesus. (Jeffrey Smith)

Worship Aids

Call to Worship

Come to him, a living stone, though rejected by mortals yet chosen and precious in God's sight, and like living stones, let yourselves be built into a spiritual house, to be a holy priesthood, to offer spiritual sacrifices acceptable to God through Jesus Christ (1 Peter 2:4-5).

Invocation

Come into our hearts today, O Lord, as we consider again who you are, what you mean to us, and how we will respond to your call to follow you and no other.

Benediction

God's blessing be on you today and in the coming days as you follow Jesus our Lord, who alone has the words of eternal life. In Jesus' name, Amen.

SEPTEMBER 3, 2006

෨෨෨෨

Thirteenth Sunday after Pentecost

Readings: Song of Solomon 2:8-13; Psalm 45:1-2, 6-9; James 1:17-27;
Mark 7:1-8, 14-15, 21-23

Listening Ears
James 1:17-27

We spend a lot of time in our family discussing good listening skills.
You see, we have a three-year-old daughter who is a regular chatterbox.
She talks from the time she gets up every morning until she goes to bed
at night. Her oral skills are marvelous, but her listening skills sometimes
leave something to be desired. And so we spend a lot of time talking
about "listening ears" and reminding one another to use them. The thing
about listening is that it is not a simple skill. Sometimes it is possible to
listen but not really hear what someone is saying. (We experience this
phenomenon quite a bit with our three year old.) The book of James
addresses the idea that fully living the Christian life requires action.
Although our faith is not based on works, the complete picture of what it
means to be a Christian includes action on our part. Actively living the
Christian life requires listening and understanding. Our passage today
specifically addresses this issue and sets the framework for the rest of
James's theological perspective.

The first chapter of James begins like many early Christian epistles.
James encourages the believers to stand firm amid persecution. This is a
common theme in the New Testament epistles as many first-century
Christians experienced persecution firsthand. The balance of the chapter
deals with the importance of really listening to the word. Verse 19 begins
with an admonition to be quick to listen and slow to speak and to anger.
There is perhaps no wiser practical verse in all scripture. The human tendency is to do just the opposite, it seems. Verse 22 continues with instruction not merely to listen but actually to do what the word says. "Doing"
is an important concept in James. For James, listening and even knowing
what it right is not enough. You must take your listening and knowing to

the next step and do what is right. In verse 26, the writer again cautions against the dangers of the tongue. We do not know much about James's situation or audience, but they must have been experiencing a reality that many churches experience. Outside persecution can threaten a body of believers, but inner strife, often caused by an untamed tongue, can damage the body.

What an important message for the church today! I have often thought that verse 19 should be etched above the doorway at the entryway to the sanctuary. There is not a better attitude for Christian living than that! Most church crises that I have observed or experienced have occurred because someone was talking much more than listening. There are several ways that this is destructive to the fellowship. First of all, since it is impossible to talk and listen at the same time, if you spend all of your time talking then you probably will not hear God's word for you. Talking busies our mind to the point that there is not much room for peaceful contemplation with the Lord. Talking can inhibit your relationship with Christ, which will in turn harm the fellowship of believers.

Second, talking can inhibit your relationship with other believers. No one wants to be in a relationship with someone who is not a good listener. When we fail to listen and do God's word, we often fail to follow God's important command to love one another in the way that Christ loved us. Third, a failure to control your tongue can harm your Christian witness. An effective witness is rarely one who says all the right things, but often one who listens and cares. A nonbeliever can actually be turned off to the gospel by one whose tongue is out of control and used to harm others. So, your unbridled tongue may even harm the growth of the fellowship.

The message of James for us personally is the same message that is preached in my home on a regular basis. Put on your listening ears! As believers we must be ready to listen and really hear God's word. To really listen, we must learn to control our tongues. This is an important discipline of our faith. If we cannot gain control of something so small but powerful, we have little hope for a productive, full Christian life. There is a second important part of this message. It is important with our daughter as well. "Listening ears" are not enough. If we listen to the word, but do not do what it says, then we wasted our listening. As a believer you can listen and know the right way but not follow through, which is as good as not knowing at all. James encourages believers that taking an active role in our faith is imperative. We must act on the word, and put our calling as Christians in motion. Listen and do! (Tracey Allred)

From Magic to Miracles

Third in a Series of Four: Life in the Church

Acts 8:4-13

I grew up loving and believing in magic. As a child, I watched the television series *Bewitched* with the hope that it was true that perhaps I was a warlock whose time had just not yet come. Even as an adult, I was captured by the charm of J. K. Rowling's *Harry Potter* books and movies. There is just something within many of us that wants us to believe that there is something "real" about this magic; however, at some point in our lives, we finally come to that place where we must distinguish between fact and fiction.

As wonderful as science is for our world, I am convinced that, deep within us, we want to think that we really do not have everything figured out. We want to know that there is something beyond ourselves that cannot be explained. We want to know that there is something greater than a formula, and we want to know that there is more to life than can be defined in scientific or mathematical terms. In short, we believe in magic because we need to know for sure that life is more than just the day-to-day drudgery it can become and that death really isn't the final word in this life.

In the story in Acts, Philip has gone to the region known as Samaria to proclaim the good news of Jesus Christ to any who would listen. Samaria, as you may recall, is the home of the Samaritans, an "impure" race of people descended from Jews who had married outside of Judaism. In many ways they worshiped as the Jews; however, their worship had developed apart from Jewish worship because they were unwelcome in Jewish life. It is in this setting that Simon the Magician is practicing his art. His magic is spellbinding, and he is considered to be the "power of God that is called Great." We do not know what kind of magic he practiced or what tricks he did. We just know that he was someone who captivated the people's attention.

The story tells us that Philip came proclaiming the good news and that people began to listen to him and turn away from Simon the Magician. Simon himself turned to see what message Philip brought, and it wasn't long before he became a believer himself. Then the story tells us that Simon "stayed constantly with Philip and was amazed when he saw the signs and great miracles that took place." Simon had moved from magic to miracles. He had gone from practicing illusions to practicing faith.

Many people are content with practicing magic, but life in the church means that we must learn to practice faith. In my childhood love of magic, I often used the words *hocus pocus* when conjuring up my pretend magic spells. I was amused as an adult to discover that *hocus pocus* might actually be an aberration of the Latin Mass. When the priest would offer the words of institution, he would say, "*Hoc est enim corpus meum*" (This is my body). The majority of people from the medieval period forward did not speak Latin, so they came up with words that sounded like what they heard. It was commonly assumed that the moment of the magical transubstantiation of the elements into the true body and blood of Christ happened at the moment that the priest said the "hocus pocus." The term refers, then, to the moment that the host and the wine become body and blood.

There are many times in my ministry when I have wished for the right incantation to make things happen. Whether in worship or the hospital room or committee meetings, I have often wished I could just chant some magic words that would make everything happen the right way. Unfortunately, the magic words never seemed to work. Ultimately, I had to learn to rely on God to work the miracles instead of relying on myself to work the magic.

Throughout my life, I have found that magic doesn't require much of me. It is merely entertaining and amusing. Magic is pretty much an end in itself. Miracles, however, point to something beyond themselves. I remember a college professor who ingrained in my brain that miracles are signs of the "inbreaking" kingdom of God. They point beyond themselves to God, who is in our midst. They are signs that God is here, and it is God's presence that invites us to respond in faith.

As a young associate pastor, I was discussing miracles with one of my mentors, the late Dr. Erwin Bohmfalk, who was known to many people only as "Bummie." Bummie and I were discussing the feeding of the multitudes, and I was really stuck on the idea that it wasn't a miracle unless the five loaves and two fish magically multiplied until there were twelve baskets full after everyone had eaten. Bummie challenged my thinking and said, "Perhaps they miraculously multiplied, as you say, but what would you think if people really had food with them? Then suppose that when it came time for dinner, Jesus asked who had food, and no one was willing to share. Now suppose that the little boy who gave everything inspired the people to do likewise. Then after the covered-dish feast was finished, there was plenty left over."

I was astounded. That would be no miracle at all. "Then you're saying it wasn't a miracle," I said. Bummie replied, "To me, it's pretty miraculous when selfish people are inspired to share. What do you think?" I had been looking for magic, and Bummie showed me a miracle.

Life in the church is a journey from magic to miracles. If you dare follow Jesus, then the miracle of faith will be yours. (Jeffrey Smith)

Worship Aids

Invocation

O God, we praise you for this day. We worship and adore you. We pray today for ears to listen and hearts to fully experience your love and grace. We thank you for your presence. May you receive all the glory and honor. Amen.

Benediction

May the message of James encourage us to listen more, talk less, and spend our energy doing your will and word. Amen.

Confession

O Lord, we cry out to you this day. For our sins of commission and omission, forgive us, O Lord. For the times that we fail to control our tongues, forgive us, O Lord. For not hearing or doing your word, forgive us, O Lord. Amen. (Tracey Allred)

SEPTEMBER 10, 2006

❧❧❧

Fourteenth Sunday after Pentecost

Readings: Proverbs 22:1-2, 8-9, 22-23; Psalm 125; James 2:1-10 (11-13), 14-17; Mark 7:24-37

His Love Knows No Limit
Mark 7:24-37

Sometimes people find it difficult to treat all people the same. We have a tendency to judge one another and treat others different according to their status in life. The car they drive, their color of skin, how they fit in socially, and even their physical appearance are measurements we use to judge people. What's true today was also true in the days of Jesus' earthly ministry.

In Mark 7, Jesus spends a significant amount of time teaching the people the dangers of principle; not fulfilling human-made laws. The Pharisees were judging the disciples because the disciples had eaten with unwashed (defiled) hands. Jesus responds by warning the Pharisees about obeying human commandments and ignoring God's commandments.

When traditions become the driving force of our lives, we find ourselves living in a dangerous place and we may lose our perspective if we are not careful. It has been well stated: "Tradition is the living faith of the dead; traditionalism is the dead faith of the living." Jesus said it this way: "This people honors me with their lips, but their hearts are far from me." Jesus also once said, "That which comes from within a person is that which defiles." Jesus not only taught by what he said, he went on to teach by example. In our text, verse 24 tells us that Jesus left and journeyed to the borders of Tyre and Sidon. What is significant is that Jesus left the Jewish communities and traveled to the Gentile areas of Tyre and Sidon. Jesus (who was clean) traveled to an area considered unclean to face and love unclean people.

When Jesus arrived at the edge of town, a woman from Syrian Phoenicia, a Greek woman, approached him on behalf of her sick daugh-

230

ter. Whereas the Pharisee's would not address her at all, Jesus responded to the woman's plea.

However, Jesus does not respond like we might expect. Jesus' response to her request is that she must wait until all the children have been attended to first. In other words, this Gentile woman came expecting to be treated like a Jew. Matthew gives us a little more insight into this account. The woman pleads with Jesus by saying, "Son of David," which was a Jewish reference. She approached Jesus with pretense and not in honesty. Jesus forced her to speak from the heart, out of her concern for her daughter. Jesus then healed her daughter, but not because of the woman's speech, or who she knew. Once she was honest and spoke from the heart, Jesus answered her request. When the woman arrived home, her daughter was well and the demon had left her.

It would seem somewhat a surprise that Jesus would deal with the woman in the manner he did initially. Jesus seemed somewhat abrupt. Yet, we understand that Jesus cared very much for this woman and her demon-possessed daughter. Jesus wanted to accomplish three things in this encounter.

Jesus wanted the people to understand that all people are worthy of our love and compassion. People are not unclean because of race or nationality. They are precious in God's sight and we should be reaching out toward these persons.

Jesus also wanted the woman to understand how much he cared about her, not because she spoke in Jewish terms. She didn't have to do that for Jesus to care about her. She needed to be transparent. She needed to come to Jesus as she was and let Jesus love her in that condition. God is not willing that any should perish but that all come to repentance. That promise includes us. We must come to God as we are and allow God to love and forgive us.

The third thing Jesus desired from this situation was that the woman's daughter might be healed. Jesus had every intention of healing the daughter. Jesus longs to see healing in our lives too. For the daughter, it was a demon that had her trapped. For us, it is sin. Jesus longs to free us of sin's grip. Sin will paralyze us; Jesus will set us free. Sin will attempt to defeat us; Jesus promises us victory over sin and the devil. We, too, can be free. We must put our trust in Jesus.

Jesus follows this miracle of healing the daughter with the healing of a deaf man. Jesus and the disciples travel to Galilee where a group who bring a deaf man to Jesus confronts them. Jesus responds by touching the man and opening the man's ears. Suddenly this man can both hear and speak. A miracle had taken place—that which had bound him was now gone. Can we relate? We, too, can be bound and gagged; we, too, can be left speechless by Satan the destroyer and by our own sin. But once Jesus moves into our lives, suddenly Satan is the one bound. He can't get to us. He can't control us. He cannot possess us.

It is a great and wonderful thing when Jesus moves into a life. It does not matter where you live or what your race. Your salary doesn't matter, nor does the kind of car you drive. Jesus loves you as you are. Jesus simply doesn't want you to stay bound. Jesus says, "We are free." Free from sin. Free from bondage. Let Jesus open your ears of understanding and you will then learn from him. And to know Jesus, in a personal way, is to be free forever and ever. (Jimmy McNeil)

The Peaceable Kingdom

Fourth in a Series of Four: Life in the Church

Isaiah 11:6-9

Many churches operate with a master plan. The church I currently pastor has the potential of growing more than 120 percent during the next fifteen years, and we are making plans to meet the various challenges of a growing church. Our church has a master plan for our church buildings in a new location. We also have a master plan for our staff, and we are planning for the staff to grow accordingly to meet the growing needs of the church family. We have a master plan for our program by which we are ensuring that our program is appropriately structured to see us well into the future. Master planning is critical. It is a road map designed to take us where we want to go in the future, and it is a deliberate effort on our part to keep us on the path we believe God intends for us.

From the age of twelve, I have had a vision of what I wanted to do with my life. Although I could not see the details, I had discovered early in my life that my calling was to the ordained ministry, and I just knew that I was supposed to fulfill a vocation in the church. That vision for my life has served as a master plan for how I would structure my education and training. The vision had implications for my wife and me in our planning for a family; further, it had implications for almost every area of my personal life from vacations to days off to hobbies. Everything had to be oriented to the vision. I knew early on that my relationship with God was dynamic and that the master plan could be altered throughout the course of my life to meet changing circumstances. However, I have also discovered that simply ignoring that master plan is not wise and usually leads to trouble.

The prophet Isaiah presents a master plan. Isaiah's image of the peaceable kingdom is a great master plan for us. It is a vision for how life in the kingdom ought to be. For Christians, it is a vision of what life in the church ought to reflect. It is an ideal vision of peace, and it asks the question of just how this vision compares with reality.

Current reality suggests that we are a long way from realizing this vision. Wolves and leopards still eat small goats and lambs. Bears still think of cows as delectable entrées. It's still not a good idea to keep calves, lions, and small children in the same pen. Terrorists still want to destroy human life. Enemies continue to kill one another. Dictators torture their citizens. War never ceases. How can we even consider this vision of a peaceable kingdom when reality suggests that the kingdoms in which we live seem to have no chance for peace?

One would think that, as I've grown older, I would have given up on idealism. Common wisdom maintains that, when you've been smitten by life a few times and when you've been hurt in the real world, you will finally come to your senses and begin to live with the harsh realities of life. I've had some people tell me that my idealism is sometimes like hiding my head in the sand, that I was in denial, and that I wasn't paying attention to the realities that define our world.

Isaiah would tell us, however, that if we give up on the ideal, then we give up the hope that our reality will ever improve. Reality will just continue to bite harder and harder until it finally destroys us.

Life in the church means that we are challenged to take up this new life in the kingdom of God. It is a kingdom where all are welcome and where strife and war will cease. It is a kingdom where neither the color of our skin nor our gender nor the shape of our bodies or who we are politically, theologically, or even sexually will matter. It is a kingdom where we and those who despise us and those whom we despise will somehow find a way to sit down together in peace. It is a kingdom where no one is cast out or left to despair. It is a kingdom where hope abounds and where laughter and love are the order of the day. It is a kingdom that we pray to enter when life here is done, but there are fools like me who continue to believe that it is a kingdom that can happen right now—where we live today!

In our world, there are two distinct categories of social justice. One is retributive justice and the other is restorative justice. Retributive justice is setting the record straight through acts of retribution. It is "getting even." Restorative justice, however, does not permit us to focus our energy upon "getting even" and asks us to focus, instead, upon restoring everyone involved back to relationship with one another. Isaiah is concerned primarily with restoration. Isaiah has little concern here with retribution.

Let the kingdom of peace be the master plan by which we live in the church. When we are in conflict with one another; when we are dealing with terror and fear in our world and in our individual lives; when we are put into the pen with the lion, the leopard, the wolf, and the bear; look around you and you will find a child.

This child is vaguely reminiscent of Jesus. This child is vulnerable and trusting. This child is full of hope and joy. This is the child who will show you what it means to live in perfect harmony even within those hostile surroundings. Follow the child, and you will discover a life of peace and joy awaiting you in the body of Christ. This is the life that God wills for us. (Jeffrey Smith)

Worship Aids

Pastoral Prayer

Our God, you are King of kings and Lord of lords. We thank you for the gift of eternal life that is available through the blood of Jesus. May the world know of your great love and may we be the ones who tell it. Amen.

Invocation

Our heavenly Father, as we enter this worship service, we ask for your divine guidance and presence to fall upon us. We need you every hour, and never more than now. Grant our request we pray. Amen.

Words of Assurance

"For God so loved the world." What could be said in our midst that would mean more? God loves us, and there is nothing we can ever do to change his love for us. May we never forget God's love. (Jimmy McNeil)

SEPTEMBER 17, 2006

୨ଌ ୨ଌ ୨ଌ

Fifteenth Sunday after Pentecost

Readings: Proverbs 1:20-33; Psalm 19; James 3:1-12; Mark 8:27-38

The Best-kept Secret in the World
Mark 8:27-38

It was a holy moment—a breakthrough for one of the disciples! It happened when Jesus went with his disciples to the village of Caesarea, Philippi. It came when Jesus asked, "Who do people say that I am?" That was the question that crystallized the answer in Simon Peter's mind: "You are the Messiah!"

Perhaps that breakthrough will come to you in some holy moment. May it be an experience that will change your life, your thinking, your habits, your relationships. Perhaps the breakthrough will come when you make your commitment to Jesus Christ—the moment when you say with Peter, "You are the Messiah, the Son of the living God" (Matthew 16:16).

Our understanding of God is wrapped up in Jesus. Jesus suggested that God is like a forgiving father, like a woman who seeks a lost coin, like the shepherd who secures the ninety-nine sheep but then cares enough to go out again to search for the one wayward sheep. Everything that matters in our Christian faith is wrapped up in our response to this basic question: "Who do you say that Jesus is?"

It has been said that "Jesus is the best photograph God ever had taken." Hundreds of people in our congregation have taken the *Disciple* Bible study course. For the first time many of them have read parts of the Old Testament and have discovered pictures of God where God is portrayed as vengeful and violent. They wonder to themselves, "Is this an accurate picture of God?" And the answer for us is no! In the fullness of time, God is revealed in Jesus of Nazareth. If you want to experience the fullness of God, then seek the mind and spirit of Jesus. Jesus Christ is the absolute standard by which we discern the nature of God.

Jesus is also the absolute standard by which we judge the nature of right living. If I can imagine Jesus doing what I am doing then my conduct is probably OK. But if in my wildest imagination I cannot picture the Son of God involved in what I am doing and thinking, then I am probably not doing the will of God. Some people criticize the bracelet with the letters WWJD, which stand for "What would Jesus do?" They say that we don't know enough about Jesus to be able to ask that question in every moral and ethical situation. Perhaps they are correct, but it is the best question we have. To ask ourselves, "What would Jesus do?" would probably keep our mouths shut when we are about to curse or criticize. I cannot image Jesus beating another person with a heavy stick, or firing a gun at another human being. Can you visualize Jesus stealing another person's property? I cannot image Jesus using another person for his personal advantage. Our problem is not in knowing enough about what Jesus would do; our problem is that we know too much and ignore what we do know.

Through Jesus comes the energy with which I live out the best that is within me. Yes, if there were a "Basic Christianity Exam," it would raise these issues: Who is Jesus? and What is my relationship to the Christ? Yes, Jesus is the means by which we live out the best that is within us. It is "in Christ" that we will experience fulfillment and meaning and hope and peace beyond understanding.

Does Jesus have a place in your life? Commit yourself to Jesus today and watch what happens in your life!

Members of our congregation completed a family-life survey form in which they ranked as the number one of ten recognized needs "the need for spiritual growth." Spiritual growth begins with a commitment to Jesus Christ. Thirty-one percent of those who completed the survey indicated they rarely if ever "share Christ." You might say, "Well, 69 percent do share Christ, and that is very good." But please, we are all the children of God; we are all the recipients of God's grace. There was a time when Jesus said: "Don't tell anyone." In Mark's Gospel that is called "the messianic secret." We believe the reason Jesus said, "Don't tell anyone" was that he was involved in his teaching ministry, and was trying not to attract the thrill seekers, or to be overwhelmed with the crowds of people who would come to him as a miracle worker. Jesus' instructions were for that day, not for this one. We have ignored his instructions concerning "giving the tithe," and "forgiving seventy times seven," and "praying for our enemies," but we have been faithful in his words to "tell no one about him." It's called selective obedience. Our faith is the best-kept secret in the world.

How long has it been since you said to your child, "God be with you!" Or to a friend going on a trip, "God bless you." Recently I was startled when a plumber said, "May God be in your home." Or when a hotel bag boy said, "God bless you on your trip" and a waitress said, "Thank you and may God bless you." It was their own unique way of making their witness of reflecting their covenant with God.

Jesus is Lord and Savior, God's Son. What we believe about Jesus shapes our lives and our understanding of God. When I have compromised Jesus as essential in my faith experience, I have diminished my faith and belittled my own potential. In Jesus we live and move and have our being. Jesus Christ is the best-kept secret of the Christian church. (Henry E. Roberts)

The Interesting Thing about Religion Is God

First in a Series of Six: Ephesians

Ephesians 1:3-14

The apostle Paul speaks in the first chapter of Ephesians, movingly and confessionally, about God. From the beginning, as we read this letter, our hearts and minds are given a new focus. The mystic Evelyn Underhill, writing to the archbishop of Canterbury in 1930, noted that "the interesting thing about religion is God."

Now this idea goes somewhat against our grain: church, spiritual life, and mission can become what we do—our activity, our action, our feelings, our preferences, our emotions, our beliefs. Ephesians orients us toward God. In the first chapter of the letter it is God who is at center stage. These verses are crammed with all that God has done for us.

God has blessed us in Christ; God has chosen us in Christ; God destined us for adoption; God's glorious grace has been freely bestowed on us; God has made known to us the mystery of God's will; God will gather up all things in Christ; God lavished his grace on us; God accomplishes all things according to his divine counsel and will.

This text is an inspired hymn of praise, a doxology to the God of the universe. Within these few verses we become aware of God's providence, God's watchful care. Do you remember the children's song "He's Got the Whole World in His Hands"? Do you believe that?

God provides. God is at work in our lives before we are aware, before we can respond. God has a plan for us, and that plan is rooted in John

Wesley's concept of preeminent grace, the grace that is prior to our response.

There is God's providence, and there is also God's power. We experience God's power as it makes us holy, whole, and blameless. We find the source of this power in the phrase "in Christ," which occurs ten times in these eleven verses. To live "in Christ" is to live to the praise of God's glory as we fulfill the mission of the Son who came to glorify his Father (John 17:1).

What meaning does the power of God have for you and me? At the end of the letter we read that Paul is an "ambassador in chains" (Ephesians 6:20). Even in prison, even awaiting trial, Paul could cling to and claim the power of God.

Some of us sense that we are powerless in this life, that we have lost control of our destinies, that our lives are closing in on us. The world has become smaller since September 11, 2001. Corporate decisions seem to have become removed from us, the challenges seem more immense, the needs greater, the resources fewer. Paul does not write from an ivory tower. Rather, Paul writes as one who is in bondage, and yet Paul knows the power and claims the power of God.

God provides for us. God's power is with us and for us. God has a purpose for us, that we might live "to the praise of his glory." At one time the church taught the faith through a series of questions and answers. The Westminster Confession poses the question: "What is the chief end of humanity?" The answer is: "Our chief end is to glorify God and to enjoy him forever."

What is our purpose? Why are we here? We discover answers to these questions as we worship God, the God of Ephesians 1, who gathers all things together in Christ. This God has a purpose for each and every one of us, and that purpose is always within the loving context of God's love for us. We come away from worship, we hope, wondering about that.

Consequently, worship is sheer gratitude, grace. On the other six days the world teaches us to view life from a particular perspective: the bottom line, what I can produce, how I appear, who I know, the family in which I grew up. On the seventh day, we worship God and we connect with something greater. We discover that the God who is out there—in the cosmos—is also the God who is also within us. This is the majesty and the intimacy of a relationship with the living God, who surpasses our understanding. Yet this God also numbers the hairs on our heads.

Some of us are listening to this message and we are anxious about the future; uncertain about the journey before us; apprehensive about how to move forward in relationships, at work, in life. Despite our anxiety, however, we can connect with a God who provides.

Some of us are listening to this message and we have failed, we have sinned, we have fallen short. We know that in our own strength we cannot please God. We cannot connect with a God whose power is at work in our lives, bringing about our salvation, our transformation, our healing.

Some of us simply know, deep in our gut, that there is more to life, that there is some reason we are here on this planet. We can connect with God's purpose that can help us make sense of who we are and why we are here.

Later, in Ephesians 3:20-21, there is a prayer that gathers up everything hinted at in the first chapter of the letter, and in this message. It is a benediction that speaks of providence, power, and purpose: "Now to [God] who by the power at work within us is able to accomplish abundantly far more than all we can ask or imagine, to [God] be the glory in the church and in Christ Jesus to all generations, forever and ever."

The interesting thing about religion is God. We connect with this God through our needs for providence, power, and purpose. May we come to know and worship God, in the name of the Father, the Son, and the Holy Spirit. Amen. (Kenneth Carter Jr.)

Worship Aids

Call To Worship

Blessed be the God and Father of our Lord Jesus Christ, who has blessed us in Christ with every spiritual blessing. God chose us in Christ before the foundation of the world to be holy and blameless before him in love. Let us worship God.

Words of Assurance

When you heard the word of truth, the gospel of your salvation, and believed, God marked you with the seal of the promised Holy Spirit. This is the pledge of our inheritance toward redemption as God's own people, to the praise of God's glory.

Benediction

Go forth to live as in the power, providence, and purpose of God. God is peace! (Kenneth Carter Jr.)

SEPTEMBER 24, 2006

❧❧❧❧

Sixteenth Sunday after Pentecost

Readings: Proverbs 31:10-31; Psalm 1; James 3:13–4:3, 7-8*a*; Mark 9:30-37

Ambition
James 3:13–4:3, 7-8*a*; Mark 9:30-37

Ambition fuels human behavior. Many events in people's lives are motivated by ambition. A shopkeeper strives to find new ways to display goods in the ambitious hope of being more prosperous. A scientist pushes back the frontiers of knowledge because of a love of knowledge. We all know students who burn the midnight oil. All are motivated by ambition.

Ambition is the fuel for many helpful human behaviors, but there is a dark side to ambition. How many people have wrecked their lives because their ambitions were so great that they sacrificed all other values on the altar of their ambitions? We have seen the human wreckage left behind by people who abandoned, manipulated, or abused their families by seeking their own ambitions. Ambition is a healthy motivator of good behavior and good activities, but it also has a more demonic side.

Henri Nouwen was a Catholic priest and academician. His academic pursuits took him to a teaching post at Harvard, a great accomplishment for anyone in the academic arena. Yet Nouwen reached a time in his life when he was not satisfied. He left his comfortable teaching post at Harvard, teaching some of the most brilliant students in the country, and became a worker at Daybreak, a home for adults who were mentally disabled. After Nouwen had been at Daybreak for a time, he wrote:

> Most of my past life has been built around the idea that my value depends on what I do.... I fought my way up to the lonely top of a little success, a little popularity, and a little power. But now, as I sit beside the slow and heavy-breathing Adam [a resident of Daybreak] I start seeing how violent that journey was, so filled with desires to be better than others, so marked by rivalry and competition, so pervaded with com-

pulsion and obsessions, so spotted with moments of suspicion, jealousy, resentment, and revenge. (Quoted in *Pulpit Resource*, November 12, 1990)

The Bible is skeptical about ambition. The book of James is a primer on practical Christianity. The writer says "selfish ambition" is earthly, unspiritual, and devilish. Hardly a recommendation, is it? James goes on to write that the primary results are disorder and wickedness.

Our gospel lesson speaks to this subject in tones gentle, yet powerful. The Gospel of Mark presents Jesus as the successful teacher and healer. Jesus attracts a large following. People who want to hear what Jesus has to say and want to see what he will do surround him. Then, just as Jesus' popularity is reaching a peak, Jesus turns his back on all of it. Jesus withdraws from the public arena; he goes into hiding with his disciples and instructs them about the way of the cross. Jesus turns his back on the successes of his early career. He sets his face toward Jerusalem and the cross.

One day Jesus hears his disciples arguing with one another. Jesus asks, "What were you arguing about on the road?" They are embarrassed to admit that they were disputing which of them was the greatest. Jesus says to the disciples, "If anyone wants to be first, he must be the very last, and the servant of all" (NIV). The disciples cannot seem to learn. I understand because I can't learn either. Can we really learn what it means to live this amazing paradox where those who would be first must be the very last and the servant of everyone? I don't want to learn it. I'd rather be first my way, wouldn't you?

In a wonderful Chinese folktale, a woman loses her only child in death. She goes to the holy man and asks him to bring her child back to life. He replies, "Search for the home that has never known sorrow, and, in that home, find the magic mustard seed and bring it to me. Then we will have the power to bring your child back." The woman's first stop is a great and luxurious palace. Thinking everything will be good and joyful there, she knocks on the door saying she is looking for a place without sorrow. "You have come to the wrong place," they reply, and recount all the sorrows that have come to that home of power and wealth. The woman says to herself, "Who is better able to help these people than I who have had such misfortune of my own?" She stays to comfort them, and later continues her search, which takes her to the hovels and the palaces of China. In each place she becomes so involved in ministering to other people's grief that she forgets her own. In her forgetfulness, she finds healing and peace.

Those who would find their life must lose it. Those who would be first must be last. This teaching runs so counter to our ambitious ways; but don't we have to admit that Jesus was right? Our ambitions are compulsive and suspicious and obsessive and jealous and resentful and full of revenge. The only ambition that truly gives life is the ambition to serve others—no matter what the cost. O Lord, make us ambitious to serve our neighbor. Amen. (Carl L. Schenck)

The Miracle of Being Included

Second in a Series of Six: Ephesians

Ephesians 2:11-22

As a child, I loved to play baseball. We would often gather at a field adjacent to an elementary school to play. We would bring bats and gloves, someone would also have a baseball. There was nothing organized about it. One of the older kids would devise some system for composing the teams. Captains would be identified, and then they would choose the players for their teams, alternating, one after the other. I remember standing, my hand pressed into the glove, waiting to hear my name; wondering if I would be included, if I would make one of the teams. Or would I instead be sitting under the shade, watching from the sidelines?

In life, there are insiders and outsiders. The welcome mat is placed for some and not for others. Some are accepted—others are rejected. Perhaps you have had the experience of being on the inside, of knowing acceptance. It is a secure feeling. Maybe you have also known rejection and exclusion. It can be frustrating and disillusioning.

What do these questions have to do with us, reading this letter to a strange place and to a people identified by the word "Ephesus," twenty centuries later? The answer, if I may be so bold to say it, is everything. The primary issues are our acceptance before God, our access to God, and our acceptance of one another. The good news, Paul confesses, is that there is "wideness in God's mercy." The good news, Paul insists, is that Jesus Christ has destroyed the distinctions between insider and outsider, accepted and rejected.

This is good news for us. You see, we are the outsider to whom Paul refers, we are the Gentiles, we are the ones who once were far off, but now have been brought near. There's wideness in God's mercy. This has happened through the blood of Jesus, through the blood of the cross—a cross that represents the peace that God has made with the world; a cross that represents all divisions; a cross that communicates God's desires for the world.

The wall of division was the wall of temple and law, which separated the holy people from the unclean; which prevented many people—most people—from God; which limited the access. God was hidden within the walls, but this could never be God's ultimate purpose, for it is true, there is wideness in God's mercy.

In Jesus Christ, God looks upon the multitudes and has compassion (Mark 6), and says, "You are included." In Jesus Christ, God looks upon the Gentile, and says, "You are included." In Jesus Christ, God looks upon the stranger, and says, "You are included." In Jesus Christ, God looks upon children, and says, "You are included." In Jesus Christ, God looks upon women and says, "You are included." God looks upon the prodigal (Luke 15) and says, "You are included." In Jesus Christ, God looks upon us, you and me, in all of our conditions, and says, "You are included."

This is the radical message of the gospel of Jesus Christ. There are no longer insiders and outsiders. There are no longer the accepted and the rejected. There are no longer the holy and the unclean (see Acts 10). There are no longer some who play the game and others who are banished to the sidelines! Jesus has broken down the dividing wall between these groups. The two groups have now become one.

We are included, and the visible sign of this inclusion is the cross of Jesus Christ. It is a reminder that nothing can separate us from his love. It is a reminder that we were bought with a price. It is a reminder that all have sinned and fallen short of the glory of God (Romans 3:23). It is a reminder that God's love is expressed to us in the miraculously good news that "while we were yet sinners, Christ died for us" (Romans 5:8 RSV).

What does it mean for us, then, that the excluded are now included? What does it mean for those on the inside and for those on the outside? For those on the inside—in the day of Jesus this would have referred to those who officiated in the temple and knew the laws—we open ourselves to the possibility that God is not confined to our traditions, codes, and formulas. The cross takes precedence over circumcision, in the inclusion now of Gentiles. The cross expresses the heart and character of a God whose covenant was intended for the blessing of all the families of the earth (Genesis 11). So then we broaden our circle a little, remembering that there is wideness in God's mercy.

For those on the outside, the cross can be good news, if it is embraced. Sometimes we become accustomed to being outsiders, standing apart, not taking our place in the circle. Yet the history of God's salvation continues, weaving together insider and outsider, offering new interpretations of law ("You have heard it said ... but I say to you"). The outsiders are welcomed, transformed into insiders. We become "one body through the cross." There are no longer two groups.

Jesus comes into our world to make peace, to unify, to integrate. This great work was accomplished in his body, on a cross, and continues in his body, the church. At times we forget, and we lapse into our comfortable divisions, looking toward those who look and think like us and turning away from those who are "strangers and aliens" to us.

This is never God's dream for the church. God wants something more. The miracle of being included, when it happens, is a foretaste of something greater. We know it when we see it. We rejoice when we experience it. There is a wideness in God's mercy. In Jesus Christ, fully divine and fully human, there is the creation of one new humanity. In a divided and conflicted world, this is surely good news! (Kenneth Carter Jr.)

Worship Aids

Call to Worship

For by grace we have been saved through faith. This is not our own doing; it is the gift of God. We were created in Christ Jesus for good works. O come, let us adore him!

Words of Assurance

Remember that you were at that time without Christ, being aliens from the commonwealth of Israel, and strangers to the covenants of promise, having no hope and without God in the world. But now in Christ Jesus you who once were far off have been brought near by the blood of Christ. (Ephesians 2:12-13)

Benediction

Let us go forth to proclaim peace to those who are far off and peace to those who are near, in the name of the Father, the Son, and the Holy Spirit. Amen. (Kenneth Carter Jr.)

OCTOBER 1, 2006

Seventeenth Sunday after Pentecost

Readings: Esther 7:1-6, 9-10; 9:20-22; Psalm 124; James 5:13-20; Mark 9:38-50

Do Not Forbid
Mark 9:38-50

It started early, that ugly, erosive, and persistent blight on Christianity. You might have thought it would take a generation or two before this selfish idea began to show itself, but here it is before Christianity is hardly out of the starting gate. John said to Jesus, "Teacher, we saw someone casting out demons in your name, and we tried to stop him, because he was not following us."

Perhaps we should not be too surprised. John and the other disciples came by it naturally. Their lives were marinated in exclusivism. They belonged to a religion and a culture whose main identity was that they were "God's chosen people." There is a certain legitimacy in the concept of "chosen-ness," particularly when it has to do with fulfilling a divine purpose, but there is an inherent danger also. The idea can degenerate from "chosen" to "different" to "better than," which is exactly what had happened in the religion as practiced and preached by the Scribes and Pharisees.

Perhaps John never thought about that slippery slope, but Jesus did. Jesus simply said, "Do not stop him." Jesus adds to this simple command a profound lesson on the psychology of inclusiveness: "For no one who does a deed of power in my name will be able soon afterward to speak evil of me. Whoever is not against us is for us."

Those who have studied the Gospels will quickly recall an occasion upon which Jesus said just the opposite: "Whoever is not with me is against me" (Matthew 12:30; Luke 11:23). Two things may be said about these conflicting statements that may be helpful to those for whom it is an obstacle. The first is that Jesus frequently used paradox as a means of stating truth. This was usually an occasion in which the opposing statements were in juxtaposition (for example, see Mark 8:35). Although there is no juxtaposition of these opposites, the statements are paradoxical. The second thing that may be said of these reverse statements is that the settings in which they were given are clearly different. In Mark, the strange exorcist is insinuating himself into the movement and using Jesus' name. He is joining the movement without giving previous notice. Jesus says the man is not against "us." On the other occasion stated in Matthew and Luke, he is speaking of people (religious establishment) who are actively against him to the extent that they accuse him of getting his power from "Beelzebul." Although explanations do not (and are not intended to) reconcile the opposites, they may give some insight as to how truth lies in and in between the two poles of paradox.

When seen in its larger context, there is some humor, if not irony, in the fact that the disciples are trying to prevent the alien exorcist from doing what they have just failed to do (Mark 9:18). The apostolic defensiveness suggests an element of embarrassment that an untrained and unauthorized stranger accomplishes what they have failed to accomplish. I have seen people from my own constituency genuinely converted and healed in unorthodox religious gatherings when nothing I could do seemed able to reach them. My rejoicing with them has almost always been tinged with a little bit of embarrassment. I have had to face up to the obvious fact that the power of God is not confined by the guidelines of practice in my denomination. To put an even finer point on this observation, I must confess that I have sometimes been surprised and a little professionally embarrassed when my successor in a local church has been able to effectively reach people who I had not been able to reach with my ministry. It happens! Get used to it. Learn to celebrate it.

The feeling expressed by John may not have been intended to promote a knee-jerk exclusiveness. He may well have felt a need to keep the kingdom message and practice uncorrupted by strange people and practices in order to maintain unity in the movement. Most institutionalized religious groups have a book of guidelines and order designed to regulate admission, practice, and interpretation. When does this become an impediment to the message? I do not know where the line is, but there is a line. Perhaps we should begin to look for the line when "the rulebook" becomes bigger than the Bible or when an inordinate percentage of the work force of a denomination is employed full-time as makers, inter-preters, and enforcers of rules, regulations, and guidelines.

It is clear that "do not forbid him" must be taken as a warning not only against exclusiveness, but also against an overemphasis on apostolic authority. Jesus wanted any boundaries to be drawn to include as many people as possible. It is all too easy to develop misplaced loyalties in which the means is more important than the end, and the organization becomes the object of our loyalty above the gospel it was created to serve. The power of God is always breaking through the boundaries that have been built by religious groups who have lost their focus. The great reform-ers, such as Martin Luther and John Wesley, whose work has enriched and enabled the promulgation of the Christian faith, lived and labored on the edge of heresy. They were "forbidden," but they went on their way, not counting the cost.

It was never intended that we build walls and close the circle in our practice and promotion of the Christian faith. Those who do the works of Jesus belong to him even if they do not belong to us. Remember the great hymn:

> There's a wideness in God's mercy
> like the wideness of the sea;
> . . . .
> For the love of God is broader
> than the measure of our mind
> ("There's a Wideness in God's Mercy," *The*
> *United Methodist Hymnal* [Nashville: The United
> Methodist Publishing House, 1989], 121)

We cannot fail to notice and make mention that this passage is set in the middle of Jesus' teaching about the importance of children. In a time in which women and children were given little or no regard, Jesus gave them high regard. In the next chapter (Mark 10:13-16), the disciples tried to turn away the little children who were being brought to Jesus. In a profound statement of inclusiveness of children, Jesus said: "Forbid them not." We often ignore and fail to see the potential of the children. Jesus never did.

Samuel Wesley was a devoted priest in the Church of England, in whose heart there burned a desire to see the church renewed and revived. One day he was studying and praying while his two small children, John and Charles, were playing on the stairway. Finally, he became so distracted by the noise that he rushed out of his study and cried out at them saying: "Go play elsewhere. I am trying to pray for a great revival to come upon the church, and your noise is disturbing me." Little did old Samuel know that the great awakening for which he was praying was running up and down those stairs, in the persons of his own small children, John and Charles Wesley.

Do not forbid the stranger who does the work of Jesus. Do not forbid the children he loved and blessed. In both there is infinite potential. Do not forbid! Do not forbid! Do not forbid! (Thomas Lane Butts)

Becoming a Grounded Person

Third in a Series of Six: Ephesians

Ephesians 3:14-21

It begins with an action, a posture. We humble ourselves before God. We get down our knees. In this way our faith is embodied. The writer of Ephesians has spoken, for two and a half chapters, about the power, providence, grace, and glory of God. We perceive God's revelation as cosmic and personal. We understand God's reconciliation as both accomplished and yet to be completed. It is a mystery that we comprehend only in part, and yet it moves us to thanksgiving and praise.

Therefore, we bow. This is not in our nature, if we are honest. We want to be respected. We wish to be acknowledged. We yearn to be honored. To bow before something, or someone, goes against the grain of our temperaments. Yet we sometimes find ourselves in the presence of the Holy. This One unto whom we bow is the Father "from whom every family in heaven and on earth takes its name." Many of the New Testament letters ascribed to Paul speak of congregational conflicts; leaders are named, situations are identified. We feel like we know the churches at Corinth and Philippi. Ephesians is a different letter. It reminds us that God is not only attentive to local matters; God is also interested in the planet.

For that reason we bow in humility before God. We confess our small part in the grand scheme of things. We say, with John the Baptist, "He must increase, but I must decrease" (John 3:30). We sing, with the swaying chorus, of an "awesome God." Our speech and our singing finds its way through our bodies and we discover that we are on our knees before God.

When was the last time you were on your knees?

On our knees, we find ourselves returning to the source. Sometimes we pray for others. Sometimes we pray for ourselves. Ephesians reminds us, "I pray that, according to the riches of his glory, he may grant that you may be strengthened in your inner being with power through his Spirit." We sometimes find ourselves on our knees because we come to the end of our own power, our own strength, and we confess a need for something more.

Listen to this parable:

A young pastor serves in a rural community, and one of the patriarchs of the congregation is a farmer, wise and powerful among his neighbors. Along the way the pastor comes into conflict with the patriarch and communication becomes difficult. The pastor makes a point, on occasion, to drive out to the farmer's home to keep the conversation going. The visits are never easy. There are always long silences and nothing tangible seems to be accomplished. As the pastor approaches the farm, she sees a sign that becomes a reminder to her: "Pavement ends."

When the pavement ends, the road becomes rough. When the pavement ends, the turbulence is greater. When the pavement ends, we depend on God.

Can you think of a time in your own life when the pavement ended: a financial crisis, a family tragedy, a church conflict, a health issue? When the pavement ends, we are forced to do things differently. We open ourselves to God, who, we discover, has already been reaching out to us. The gift is like a bequest of riches, which we had not known about or had forgotten, like an inheritance that we had ignored. The gift strengthens us, in our inner being, with power. We are encouraged. We are supported. We are uplifted.

Humility connects us with the uplifting power of God. As we become more grounded, we become more able to "rise up and walk," in the words of Jesus (Luke 5:23). In the Christian tradition, it is often noted that the deadliest of sins is pride. Pride is our inability to ask for help. Pride is our refusal to accept a gift. Pride is our rejection of God.

The removal of pride makes a space for something else, something greater: "I pray . . . that Christ may dwell in your hearts through faith, as you are being rooted and grounded in love." Christ takes the place of pride in our lives. The love of self gives way to the love of God and neighbor. The illusion of wanting to be in control is replaced by the image of the One "who loved [us] and gave himself for [us]" (Galatians 2:20). The arrogance of desiring first place is corrected by the great reversal of the gospel, where the last are now first.

In my pride, I might be tempted to drive at full speed, even when the pavement ends. In my pride, I reject the natural limits and boundaries that shape my life. In love, I give thanks for circumstances that ground me. In love, I praise God for creation and my place in it.

In pride, we claim more knowledge than we actually possess. In humility, we stand before a mystery. The writer continues, "I pray that you may have the power to comprehend, with all the saints, what is the breadth and length and height and depth, and to know the love of Christ that surpasses knowledge." We bow, finally, before a mystery. God creates, redeems, sustains, and sanctifies the world.

As we become more grounded, more humble, God draws near us. We come before this God in prayer and in worship, in adoration and praise. We ask for the knowledge to comprehend, in part, the riches of this holy and majestic God. And even beyond such knowledge, we pray for the gift of love. We love, because God first loved us (1 John 4:19).

Thus we bow, on our knees, grateful for the gift. May our lives be a living doxology, with the words at the chapter's conclusion: "Now to [God] who by the power at work within us is able to accomplish abundantly far more than all we can ask or imagine, to [God] be glory in the church and in Christ Jesus to all generations, forever and ever. Amen." (Kenneth Carter Jr.)

Worship Aids

Call to Worship

We gather to celebrate the boundless riches of Christ and to consider the mystery hidden for ages in God who created all things. With boldness and confidence let us worship the Lord. With faith and hope let us receive the grace of God.

Words of Assurance

God's grace and truth are available to those who are humble in spirit. Hear the good news: salvation is near to you. It is a gift. It is grace. Receive it and be thankful! Amen.

Benediction

"Now to [God] who by the power at work within us is able to accomplish abundantly far more than all we can ask or imagine, to [God] be glory in the church and in Christ Jesus to all generations, forever and ever. Amen." (Kenneth Carter Jr.)

OCTOBER 8, 2006

❧❧❧

Eighteenth Sunday after Pentecost

Readings: Job 1:1; 2:1-10; Psalm 26; Hebrews 1:1-4; 2:5-12; Mark 10:2-16

Touching the Fragile Things
Mark 10:2-16

In her book *Jesus CEO*, Laurie Beth Jones tells about her friend Willy, a talented artist and potter, who was having her first art show. Friends and family were invited to the pre-opening reception. Willy's five-year-old godchild, Megan, was led carefully through the gallery while her mother pointed out each piece, telling her not to touch anything, especially those that were marked, "Fragile. Do Not Touch." At the end of the day, Willy asked Megan if she saw anything she wanted. Megan leaned forward and whispered, "I want to touch the fragile things" (Laurie Beth Jones, *Jesus CEO* [New York: Hyperion, 1992], 223).

In the fullness of Jesus' popularity, Jesus was thronged by the mobs. They brought their little children to him that he might touch them, but his disciples rebuked them. Jesus became indignant over his disciples' attitude, and said, "Let the children come to me, do not hinder them; for to such belongs the kingdom of God. Truly, I say to you, whoever does not receive the kingdom of God like a child shall not enter it" (RSV). Then Jesus took the children in his arms and blessed them, laying his hands upon them.

Little vulnerable children represent the most fragile among us, and Jesus was eager to touch and even embrace the fragile children. It seems that Jesus had an uncanny way of recognizing and focusing on the fragile things. Jesus noticed the lilies swaying fragrantly in the field. Jesus noticed the baby sparrow that had fallen to the ground, and the number of fine gray hairs on an old man's head.

Jesus warned us about going through life and missing the fragile (and most valuable) things. Jesus cautioned us about looking for signs, and missing the breezes; about being scrupulous over such matters as tithing, and neglecting the weightier matters of justice and mercy; about washing the outside of the cup, and leaving the inside filthy; about gloating over how many sheep we have in the fold, and neglecting the lost sheep in the wilderness; about arguing over who is the greatest, and missing the chance for servanthood; about passing up a golden opportunity for service on the road to Jericho; about looking to do some great deed while ignoring "the least" of Christ's brethren.

The incident in the text was a very fragile moment between Jesus and his disciples, and they blew it. This instance was not the first or last fragile moment that the disciples wasted. When the woman anointed Jesus with the expensive perfume, the disciples argued about the appropriateness of her devotion, and thereby fumbled away that precious moment.

It was a fragile moment at the Last Supper when Jesus revealed that one of them would betray him and they began to argue. In the garden of Gethsemane, in that fragile moment when Jesus cried out to the Father, the disciples were sound asleep. When Jesus was arrested, they were given the opportunity to stand with him, but instead they all fled. When Peter was accused of being a follower, Peter shattered his moment for greatness by denying Jesus.

Why do we keep refusing to touch the fragile things and keep wasting the fragile moments? Is it because we are afraid of being fragile ourselves? Do we think we will break and shatter if we get too close to something or someone who is fragile and vulnerable?

We are afraid that the way of the Christ is a dangerous path, and we feel too fragile to be exposed to genuine Christianity. Thus we cannot afford to touch or get involved with the fragile people, the fragile causes, and the fragile moments of life. We think we will shatter when they do. Yet Christ made it plain that the fragile ones, like the little children, are the stuff that the kingdom of God is made of.

The disciples became irritated with the children and their pushy parents who kept interrupting Jesus. How many times have we heard or said, "Don't interrupt" to children who are trying to be heard or seen? Such interruptions often provide our most precious, although fragile, moments to minister and be ministered to.

I was preaching in a large church that had two morning worship services. During the first service the minister of youth displayed a tube of glue during the children's sermon, and asked the children what was the glue that made a church stick together. One bright-eyed youngster called out, "Love." The young minister stammered, "Yes, that's a good answer, but the real glue that keeps us together is prayer," and he delivered his little homily on the importance of prayer.

Between the two services I prayed that the young man would think about what had happened and realize that a little child had led us to a greater truth than his prepared remarks. But, during the second service, he didn't even ask the children what holds a church together. He just started on his little sermon about glue and prayer. It was a fragile moment that he squandered because he didn't want his plans to be interrupted.

Would you close your eyes for a moment and let your mind focus on the picture of the children, the disciples, and Jesus? Do you see the disciples trying to keep the children away from Jesus, ruining a fragile opportunity? Do you see Jesus embracing these fragile children with love and security?

Now, with your eyes still closed, call up the pictures of other fragile people in your community: those who are homeless, abused, and addicted; those in nursing homes, prisons, and mental institutions; those who are terminally ill, unemployed, or socially rejected. Do you know some of these fragile ones? Have you been afraid to touch them, let alone embrace them?

Visualize now the fragile moments of your life, when you have wasted a golden opportunity to show the spirit of Christ. Let us pray that God will give us more such moments and not find us wanting next time. (Bill Austin)

A Mature Church

Fourth in a Series of Six: Ephesians

Ephesians 4

I want to share a pattern of ministry that I am only beginning to embrace, to accept, and to feel comfortable with: that what I do with others, what I give to others, is more important than what I do myself. I have served churches where everything revolved around me. The problem, of course, is that a pastor moves on to a new setting of ministry. What happens then?

The pattern of ministry, the response to my question, is laid out for us in the scripture. "The gifts God gave were that some would be apostles, some prophets, some pastors and teachers, to equip the saints, to train Christians" (*The Message*) for the work of ministry, or the task of servanthood. This perspective takes the focus off me, as a preacher, and puts it appropriately on all the people. We are like a team—a team with a mission. The mission takes us into the exciting and dangerous world of spiritual gifts. We might play different positions, with different intensities, at different times, but we are called to be on this mission team, to use all the gifts of God for all of God's people. It is very difficult to achieve any kind of success when we use the gifts of only one person, or merely a few.

As a young adult I had a real passion for wanting people to come to faith in Jesus Christ, through a personal relationship. I was involved in witnessing in some pretty direct ways to those closest to me and to total strangers. At times I was spiritually arrogant. I have asked God to forgive me for some of the ways I interacted with people. I have come to discover that a core piece of the evangelical task is to call people to maturity in Jesus Christ. The equipping of the saints is for the maturing of the body of Christ, so that we are no longer tossed back and forth, getting tripped up by trivialities; so that we can speak the truth in love to one another; so that we can grow up into Jesus Christ, who is the head.

Those are the key words for me: "grow up." Sometimes we as a church are simply called to grow up! Now, we know how to do this with our children. We expect children to progress, to discover their identities, to blossom and flourish, and then, many would add, we expect them to leave home!

How does a church grow up? It becomes more like Jesus, whose roots are sunk deeply in prayer; whose life was invested profoundly in the calling of disciples; whose heart was with the last, the least, and the lost. This is our mission too—the mission of Jesus.

Paul focuses on growth—the church growing up into Jesus. With children, we focus on their strengths and on what they do that is positive, and we call that forth. And that has been a learning experience for me in the church. I do not focus, or dwell on, or become obsessed with what is wrong. I don't avoid conflict! Rather, my focus is on the signs of life and health; on the individuals and groups that are being led into the mission of Jesus that is within the church and beyond it; on those persons who are being knit together, promoting the growth of the body, building it up in love (Ephesians 2:16).

It is easy in parish ministry, or even in life, to focus on the pathology that is present in the church, in other people, and in us. It is more helpful to work toward the creation of a community that is becoming more Christlike, a body that is stronger, a people in love with God and one another. This is our necessary work as a maturing church.

The shifting pattern of ministry includes first the conviction that the ministry belongs to all of us, and second, the understanding that the focus is most helpfully on growth and maturity. A third essential learning from the fourth chapter of Ephesians is our continuing need for conversion.

I can recall the time and place when I made a commitment to accept Jesus Christ as Lord and Savior. I felt touched and convicted by the words of a preacher, which were very simple. It was a conversion. It was a call to leave the old life behind, and to enter into the new world. This was almost twenty-five years ago. Since then, I have had other conversions. Why? Because it is very difficult to leave the old life behind in its entirety.

Conversion is the difficult work of God within us, and we resist it! The grace of God that comes to us by faith (2:8-9) is therefore a work of continuing conversion. This new life is described in all too specific language in the latter portion of this fourth chapter of Ephesians: put away your former way of life, your obsessions with sex and money; be renewed, live faithfully, be holy, that is, live differently from the world; speak the truth in love in a way that shows your love for others; be honest, don't steal, work hard, so that you will have resources to help others; forgive, because after all Christ has forgiven you.

This is a rich description of a new life, and a vivid reminder of our need for continuing conversion.

The mission belongs to all of us, and effective participation in the mission will require the gifts of each one of us. God is calling us to grow up, to become more like Christ, as we are strengthened to be his body, the church. The Christian life is a process of lifelong conversion. We are being invited to leave the old life behind and enter a new world. Amen. (Kenneth Carter Jr.)

Worship Aids

Call to Worship

There is one body and one Spirit; there is one hope to which we are called; one Lord, one faith, one baptism, one God and Father of all, who is above all and through all and in all. In the unity of the Spirit, let us worship together!

Prayer of Confession

We confess, O God, that we have not always been open to your gifts. In our common life, we have not always spoken the truth in love. We have not always been generous with our possessions. We have not always been kind and forgiving to one another. Forgive us, and walk with us into the new life that is our destiny as your children, in the name of Jesus Christ.

Benediction

Go forth as saints, equipped for ministry, to be the body of Christ in the world. Amen. (Kenneth Carter Jr.)

OCTOBER 15, 2006

Nineteenth Sunday after Pentecost

Readings: Job 23:1-9, 16-17; Psalm 22:1-15; Hebrews 4:12-16; Mark 10:17-31

Do We Have to Talk about This?
Mark 10:17-31

The great poet and author Carl Sandburg was once asked by a reporter to name the ugliest word he knew. Sandburg is reported to have reflected for several minutes, pondering the question. And then he spoke, saying in effect that the ugliest word was *exclusive*. Now, don't you find that ironic? For most of our society the word *exclusive* is pretty. We like *exclusive*. We drive exclusive cars, wear exclusive clothes, and visit exclusive places. In the world for most of us, the more exclusive, the better. But Sandburg said it was an ugly word.

Here's another word for you. See what you think of it. The word is *intrusive*. How do you react to it? If you are like me, your reaction is not very positive. For most Americans the word *intrusive* is truly an ugly word. We love freedom, privacy, and autonomy. The greatest threat for many of us is that someone will intrude upon our cherished freedoms. We do not want the government, friends, or society to intrude.

Hold that thought for a moment and consider today's scripture lesson. A good man with a legitimate religious question approaches Jesus to talk about eternal destiny. The man knows and keeps the Commandments. He is faithful in his religious practices. The Bible says that he was a model of religious faithfulness and that Jesus loved him.

But the response of Jesus is so intrusive! It is almost harsh. The man is told to sell what he has and give it to the poor and come follow Jesus. It is too much for this earnest seeker and he walks away from the presence of Jesus. What follows is a word from Jesus about how difficult it is for a rich person to get into the kingdom of heaven.

Admittedly, this is not one of the more comforting gospel lessons. Does Jesus have the right to tell us what to do with our possessions? According to the New Testament, the answer is clearly yes.

So here we are, at a time of the year when we think about financial stewardship and our support of the church's ministry. Do we have to talk about this? Again, the Bible's answer is an emphatic yes.

Now it may seem that this text is about money, and it is. But it is not exclusively about money. It is about idolatry. It is about that which stands between a person and God. In the Bible there are consistent warnings about the danger of two things: a short memory and false worship. This text invites us to consider the second of these warnings.

The man in this encounter with Jesus is not sinful because he is wealthy. He is a sinner because he has a limited view of faith. The obstacle between this man and eternal life was not some blatant sin. Our idols are seldom that easily identified. Rather, his sin was about a value that he valued too much.

Jesus knew that there is something about riches that is spiritually hazardous. But the problem is not limited to money. Whatever we trust to save us is truly our God. It can be power, talent, beauty, intelligence, or a host of other things. We can give to these riches our heart and soul. We trust them, love them, pursue them, and promote them. They easily become the "one thing" that we may need to let go of in order to truly trust the Lord's grace.

The man in our story trusted money for his salvation. Many people in our society do the same thing. Psychologists call money the "last taboo." It is easier to tell a therapist about our sex lives than it is to tell our accountant about our finances. Money—not necessarily how much we have, but how we feel about it—governs the lives of some of us more than any other factor. Money and how we relate to it is important because behind money are very real spiritual forces that energize it and give it a life of its own. The rich young ruler's wealth was a rival god seeking his complete devotion. It had become an all-consuming idol and it had to be rejected totally.

Do we have to talk about this? Yes, we do, intrusive though it is. It is not for nothing that Jesus spoke about money as much as he spoke about the kingdom of God. Money is important, and how we relate to it can affect our spiritual destiny. A lot of people are in the faith up to the point of their money. Like the crusaders who baptized all of their bodies except the hand that wielded the sword, we, too, have our ways of holding back from God that which has become most precious to us.

The rich young ruler had given almost all he had to the service of God. He lacked one thing, and Jesus gave him very practical and concrete instruction as to what to do with that one thing. It was intrusive. It was instructive. Today's text invites us to get in touch with that which stands between God and us.

The Bible says Jesus loved the earnestly seeking rich man. It is this love Jesus feels for us that makes him intrude upon our carefully ordered ways of doing things. Jesus did not want the man to be poor; he wanted him to experience joy—the kind of joy that giving it all to God can bring to our lives.

And that, my dear friends, is why we have to talk about this; for we can know the price of everything and the value of nothing. This text is a good prescription for spiritual health. May it be for you the blessing that allows you to take stock and put away whatever it is that would stand between you and your Savior. (Chris Andrews)

Life as a Teachable Moment

Fifth in a Series of Six: Ephesians

Ephesians 4:29–5:2

We moved a few summers ago. We did a lot of packing and putting things in boxes. Some things we had accumulated and could throw away. Do you know what I mean? I was also amazed at some of the things I found. Some things I knew about, some I had forgotten. I have a fly-fishing rod that I asked for one Christmas. It has never been used. It is a reminder that I need to break away one afternoon. I have a baseball glove. As a teenager, baseball was my life. I used it to pitch in the state all-star game (we lost). Now the glove is stiff and hardened because I haven't picked it up in years. Still, I would never throw it away.

And then, in a box, I found some letters from my grandmother, most of them from when I was off at seminary, about twenty years ago. In some she was giving me advice. In some she was telling me about her life. In some she asked how I was doing. In some she told me what was going on at home. As I held those letters I remembered that she would often put money in them—maybe a one-dollar bill, maybe two dollars—not a large sum of money. I thought about that as I held those letters. They were always signed, "Love, Nanny."

We find strange things when we begin to look for them. That is true when we open boxes, and it is true when we open the Bible. The Bible also contains letters. I've heard it said that we can read the Bible like a newspaper, and we can read the Bible like a love letter. The news of the world hardens us; we stand apart from it. A love letter calls us into a relationship.

That's the spirit of Paul's Letter to the Ephesians. These letters call us to a way of life: do our words build others up? Are they grace to those who receive them? We put away an old life and take on a new life. We imitate God and live in love, remembering that Christ loved us and gave himself for us.

Paul speaks in this passage about gentleness. It is sometimes translated "tenderness" or "meekness." One of best meanings I have come across is this: gentleness is a teachable spirit. It is a life not hardened, like that baseball glove that is now stiff and inflexible. Gentleness is a life still being shaped and molded, like clay in the hands of a potter.

One sign that the Holy Spirit is growing in our lives is a basic quality of gentleness, of humility, a teachable spirit. We have something to learn. We are open to receiving. This is a sign that God is present in our lives because this is consistent with the very nature of God. This is the way God comes to us—in humility, in weakness, in vulnerability. Any relationship of love requires that we open ourselves to all kinds of things: love and joy, pain and suffering, delight and laughter, despair and tears.

It would be easy to shut all of that out, to say, "I don't need God," or, "I can figure life out on my own." And God could overpower us. But God speaks not with thunder and lightning but in a still small voice. God comes in meekness, in gentleness, in humility.

The power of God is weakness and humility. It is the core of the gospel, "Christ crucified, a stumbling block to Jews and foolishness to Gentiles, but to those who are called, both Jews and [Gentiles], Christ the power of God and the wisdom of God" (1 Corinthians 1:23-24). And Paul goes further: "God's foolishness is wiser than human wisdom, and God's weakness is stronger than human strength" (1 Corinthians 1:25).

The gentle power of God always comes to us as a gift, like a one-dollar bill inside an envelope, which communicates a profound truth: we are loved. We open this love letter and we are reminded that Christ loved us and gave himself for us, on a cross, the ultimate sign of weakness and humility.

A teachable spirit allows the reality of God's love to come into our lives. That changes us, and change is difficult. There is a lot about the old life we like. Maybe we like to be in control. Maybe we don't want to appear weak.

Perhaps we can't let go of a grudge or bitterness or anger or resentment. Maybe we've become hardened because it was the way we learned to survive. Maybe we are disappointed with God and we've built up a wall, and we intellectually believe, but if we are honest we're not sure if we trust.

A teachable spirit is like opening the window and allowing the wind to come in and move over us. There are a number of words for what this is like: surrender, yielding, trusting.

There is a power to help us surrender. There is a prayer in my own tradition that echoes the prayer of Jesus in the garden. These are the words: "I am no longer my own, but thine. Put me to what thou wilt, rank me with whom thou wilt; put me to doing; put me to suffering; let me be employed for thee or laid aside for thee, exalted for thee or brought low for thee; let me be full, let me be empty; let me have all things, let me have nothing; I freely and heartily yield all things to thy pleasure and disposal."*

"I am no longer my own, but thine." That is surrender. That is gentleness. That is a teachable spirit. When the spirit of gentleness is growing in our lives we care less and less about success or significance. We become living sacrifices, as Paul writes in Romans 12. We have been crucified with Christ, as Paul would later write to the Galatians, continuing, "It is no longer I who live, but it is Christ who lives in me" (Galatians 2:20*a*). That is a teachable spirit. (Kenneth Carter Jr.)

*The Book of Worship for Church and Home (Nashville: The Methodist Publishing House, 1964), 387.

Worship Aids

Call to Worship

Let our worship be an acceptable sacrifice to God, a fragrant offering to the Most High! Let us lift up our hearts unto the Lord. Let us worship in spirit and in truth.

Prayer of Confession

At times, O God, we have grieved your Holy Spirit. Our lives have lacked love, joy, and peace; patience, kindness, and goodness; faithfulness, gentleness, and self-control. We trust in your grace to produce the fruits of your Spirit in our lives. Forgive us, and in your mercy may we become a new creation.

Benediction

Go into the world to imitate Christ. Walk in love, even as Christ loved us and gave himself for us. Amen. (Kenneth Carter Jr.)

OCTOBER 22, 2006

☙☙☙

Twentieth Sunday after Pentecost

Readings: Job 38:1-7 (34-41); Psalm 104:1-9, 24, 35c; Hebrews 5:1-10; Mark 10:35-45

Are You God?
Job 38:1-7, (34-41)

Are you God? Not many of us would be bold enough to affirmatively answer that question. For religious people, the very thought of claiming to be God is blasphemous. This very claim is what directly led to the crucifixion of Christ. No, most of us would readily admit that we are definitely not God. Yet, it is not unusual to encounter individuals who believe that although they are not God, they do understand God's ways, actions, and plan. They freely interpret the world through the lens of God's will and way. Both ministers and laypersons fall into this spiritual trap. Probably every one of us has been guilty of claiming to understand God's ways. Whereas it is possible and preferable for believers to seek understanding through God, it is a careful balancing act to not overstep our bounds and possibility for understanding God. In today's text, Job struggled with this very balancing act.

Although there are few specific details surrounding the person and life of Job, Job's story is a familiar one. Job 1 describes Job's favored life as a successful businessperson with a loving family who feared God and lived a righteous life. Job is then tested as God allows Satan to attack Job and his family in order to see if Job will remain faithful. Job loses his livestock. His servants die, and his children also die. Job remains faithful. Job is then smitten with a painful physical condition that causes sores all over his body. Job remains faithful. Throughout the rest of this narrative, Job is counseled by his friends, who seek to give him theological advice. They all seek to give him answers for his plight. Their counsel does little to comfort or answer the concerns of Job as he endures his suffering.

After more than thirty chapters of conversation between Job and his friends, the Lord responds in chapter 38. Although Job has remained, as

262

he is characteristically described, patient, he has seemed to struggle mightily with understanding God's design in this tragedy that befell his family. In chapter 12, Job summarized God's design and purpose for the world as chaotic and destructive (Samuel E. Balentine, "Job," in *Mercer Commentary on the Bible* [Macon, Ga.: Mercer University Press, 1995], 426). In chapter 38, the Lord confronts Job's pretense that he would have knowledge comparable to God's. The Lord answers Job's assertion from chapter 12 with a series of rhetorical questions regarding God's creation and majestic involvement in nature. Through these questions, the Lord confronts Job. Although Job remained faithful through his suffering, the Lord seems to clarify that Job still does not understand God's plan and will for the world. On the contrary, Job understands very little about God's design and purpose. Chapter 38 is a reminder for Job that he does not have all the answers, and his faithfulness does not qualify him as one who has equal knowledge to God.

There are few of us who will ever experience suffering to the degree that Job suffered. Yet suffering is part of the human condition that we all will experience in some form or another. This text reminds us that even for the faithful, God is bigger than our understanding. Not one of us corners the market on understanding God. On the one hand, the idea that humans do not have the capacity to understand God's will and ways is scary. If our understanding of God is limited, then we are vulnerable and out of control. We must truly trust God's design and care for us. On the other hand, as scary as this seems, it is liberating. We are not in control. We do not have to understand it all and answer every question. There is mystery for which we are not responsible. God is the one in control. Our responsibility is to follow God and not to lay the plans.

This text challenges us on two fronts. First of all, we are challenged to accept the truth with which the Lord confronted Job. We do not fully understand God. God is bigger and more complicated than our human minds can comprehend. We no sooner could determine God's reasoning for suffering or pain than we could understand the methods of God's creation. Being a person of faith means that we accept our limited understanding and trust the Lord.

Second, because we cannot fully understand God's will and design, we should not try to answer for God. This is a wonderful reminder for Christians. So often as Christians we feel the need to defend God by explaining God's actions in every situation. In the parish setting, it is not unusual for pastors to walk in on a conversation in which one Christian is explaining another's tragedy or suffering. For some reason we are so uncomfortable with God's mystery that we feel the need to constantly explain God's ways. Yet, in my own life, I know that in times of suffering I have been most comforted when a fellow Christian has admitted not understanding God's actions, but has offered the inherent comfort promised and offered by God. This would have been just as powerful a reminder to Job and his friends as it is to us. On this day, let us embrace the wonderful news that we are not expected to have or give the answers. Glory to God for being a God of mystery and grace. (Tracey Allred)

Spiritual Warfare

Sixth in a Series of Six: Ephesians

Ephesians 6:10-20

The end of the Letter to the Ephesians connects to its beginning. In the first chapter we read of "the immeasurable greatness of his power for us who believe," a power displayed when "God . . . raised [Christ] from the dead and seated him at his right hand in the heavenly places, far above all rule and authority and power and dominion" (1:19, 20). Despite the triumph of Christ in the present age, however, it is necessary that we stay alert, even vigilant. The battle continues with "principalities and powers" (Ephesians 3:10).

For this reason, Paul writes of our need to put on the "whole armor of God." The battle for a Christian is against the forces of evil. I must confess that I am both drawn to and repelled by Paul's militaristic metaphor of the Christian life. We do live in a violent world—children are abused, the innocent are bombed, teenagers commit suicide as an act of martyrdom, random shootings fill the evening news reports. A part of us wants to ask for a different way of envisioning the Christian life—one that is more peaceful, more serene, more compassionate. Yet I also know that much is at stake and that evil is present in our world, and indeed in my own life. Paul writes about spiritual resistance, an act of faith that can take both passive and active forms.

The "armor of God" consists of the resources that are at our disposal in the battle against evil. These resources are identified as truth, peace, and faith. How can these resources help us as Christians?

First, we are truthful people. Our witness has integrity because it points to the truth. Jesus said, "I am the way, and the truth, and the life" (John 14:6), and Jesus confessed to his disciples, "You will know the truth, and the truth will make you free" (John 8:32). Often we are tempted to tell only a portion of the truth, or to distort the truth for some purpose that seems justifiable to us in the moment. However, truth is always the most powerful weapon; in time, lies and falsehoods come to light and the truth is disclosed. Those who speak the truth, through words and actions, possess great power in confronting evil.

Second, we are peaceful people. The prophet Isaiah announced the coming of the "prince of peace" (Isaiah 9:6); Zechariah spoke in the Gospel of Luke of a child who would "guide our feet into the way of peace" (Luke 1:79); and the beatitude of Jesus states simply, "Blessed are the peacemakers, for they will be called children of God" (Matthew 5:9). It seems paradoxical to speak of peace as a weapon, and still God always uses peace and love to overcome violence and hatred. The cycle of retribution and vengeance—responding to evil with evil—is not the will of God. I have heard it said, "An eye for an eye and a tooth for a tooth produces people who are blind and cannot eat!"

Third, we are a faithful people. "We are justified by faith," Paul writes (Romans 5:1). "By grace you have been saved through faith," we read earlier in Ephesians, "and this is not your own doing; it is the gift of God" (Ephesians 2:8). Faith is belief and trust, intellectual knowledge, and emotional risk. Faith is hearing the word of God and obediently following its meaning. Only faith allows us to trust in the unseen providence of God, which works within human events and beyond them. Only faith allows us to trust in the unmerited grace of God, which works alongside human efforts and in spite of them!

We are in a battle, and we do not engage in the spiritual warfare unequipped. We have been trained in the knowledge of truth, in the practice of peace, in the wisdom of faith. The "whole armor of God" includes each of these resources. Without any one of them, we place ourselves in danger. With the whole armor of truth, peace, and faith, we can "stand firm."

Every Christian comes to a moment in life when it is necessary to stand firm. We face a decision that seems like a compromise to us. We encounter racism in the workplace. We are exposed to values in the culture that are at odds with our Christian convictions. We need to set boundaries for our children. There are pressures in every facet of life that threaten to knock us off course.

If we are going to stand firm, we will need a strength that comes from beyond ourselves. Our friends in Alcoholics Anonymous refer to this as a "higher power." In the Letter to the Ephesians, the Christians are urged to "be strong in the Lord and in the strength of his power." The challenge for the Christian is to stand firm, to engage in acts of spiritual resistance. The comfort to the Christian is that God provides a way to do this. God equips us with the armor.

We become aware of the armor that we need, of course, as we read scripture, "the sword of the spirit, the word of God." We can only know ourselves—our strengths and our weaknesses, our gifts and our limitations—by reading the scripture. We can only know our world—its beauty and its terror, its goodness and its evil—by reading the scripture. We would not go into warfare without knowing as much as possible about our own resources and about the enemy. In the same way, we proceed in the spiritual life only as we avail ourselves of the resources God has given to us, and these are revealed to us in the Scriptures.

Let us stand firm in the faith. Let us live truthfully, peaceably, faithfully. Let us hear the word of God and obey it. Amen. (Kenneth Carter Jr.)

Worship Aids

Call to Worship

We draw strength from the Living God, our help in ages past, our hope for years to come. We draw strength from one another. We are not alone. Let us worship the God of power and might.

Words of Assurance

God is gracious and merciful. Even in our failures, God provides the resources we need to overcome sin and to resist temptation. In the name of Jesus Christ, and in his strength, you are being forgiven. Amen.

Benediction

Do not be conformed to this world, but be transformed by the renewing of your mind. Know that God goes with you, to strengthen you, to protect you, to give you peace. Amen. (Kenneth Carter Jr.)

OCTOBER 29, 2006

※※※※

Twenty-first Sunday after Pentecost

Readings: Job 42:1-6, 10-17; Psalm 34:1-8 (19-22); Hebrews 7:23-28; Mark 10:46-52

Without God

Job 42:1-6, 10-17

Have you ever met or been around someone who knows everything? I don't mean someone who is intelligent and has a high I.Q. I mean someone who thinks they know everything, someone whose confidence has grown beyond their own ability. We often use the old phrase "They are too big for their britches."

In the midst of Job's difficulties and the traumatic events that took place, he loses perspective, and over a period of time puts more confidence in himself and his own abilities than perhaps he should have. In Job 29, we find Job speaking about himself in a very confident way. His three friends Zophar, Eliphaz, and Elihu had confronted him and suggested that he look inside and find those things that were wrong. Job responded in a way that implied arrogance. Job had become "too big for his britches," so to speak. God had allowed the tragedies in Job's life because of Job's righteousness and God's confidence in his trustworthiness. But now that righteousness and trustworthiness had grown into arrogance that God would not allow.

In chapters 38–41, God confronts Job and helps him come back down to earth by asking questions that cannot be answered by anyone. "Where were you when I laid the foundation of the earth? Who determined its measurements?" On and on, God's questions came. When the Lord finished his questions, Job had been shocked back into reality.

As we come to chapter 42, our chosen text for today, Job's perspective has been adjusted. He now not only has a proper understanding of God, he also now understands more about himself and the limitations that we all have in common. Job says: "I know that you can do all things, and that no purpose of yours can be thwarted." For Job, it was a time of confession.

Job lost so much in his life, but he found himself. Job was forced to take a hard look in the mirror and he came to three valuable conclusions about God and himself. In the first six verses of chapter 42, Job reveals those conclusions.

First of all, he concludes that God is incredibly wise and strong. God can do as God wishes—anytime, anywhere, with anyone. There is absolutely nothing we can hide from God, neither our actions nor thoughts. God knows all things. We are reminded of this valuable truth in John 4 where Jesus approaches a woman who knew all too well about rejection in life. She had been married five times and was now living with a man. When Jesus told her to call her husband, she said she was not married. It was at that point that Jesus confronted her present condition. She was astonished. Jesus knew everything about her. Jesus knows everything about us. Jesus is wise and strong.

As the same time that Job learned what he did about God, he also learned something about humankind. Whereas God is strong and wise, people are both weak and unlearned. We cannot do as much as we'd like to think we can. Job said in verse 3, "I have uttered what I did not understand, things too wonderful for me, which I did not know." For the first time in a long time, maybe for the first time ever, Job saw humankind as we really are—helpless, defenseless, and hapless without God. Our knowledge is limited, our strength runs out, our patience wears thin, and our best falls short. We need something or someone to help us. We need someone to lift us up. God promises in his word that he would uphold us with his power. Jeremiah proclaimed that there is nothing too hard for God (Jeremiah 32:17). Job's response to this realization in his life was to hate himself, to repent with great remorse. We, too, need a hard look in the mirror and a deep look into God's word. They both will reveal to us what Job learned: God is God and we are not.

In addition to acknowledging God's strength and wisdom, Job also confessed that people are weak and unlearned. Surely we would come to the same conclusion. Without us, God is still everything, but without God, we are nothing. Noah, without God, would have simply been an old man. Moses would have been a young man in a foreign land miles away from home. Without God, the blind eyes of Bartamaeus could not have been opened, Lazarus would have remained dead, and the disciples would have never given up their professions. Without God, where would you be? Where would I be? Without God, we still would be in our sins, and we would have no hope of heaven. Praise the Lord, we will never have to face life or eternity without God. As Paul states in Romans 5:8 (KJV): "But God commendeth [or extended] his love toward us, in that, while we were yet sinners, Christ died for us" that we may have the opportunity to know God in a personal way; that one day we might receive Christ and know his great love. (Jimmy McNeil)

A Little Is Enough

First in a Series of Four: Generous Living

Mark 6:30-44

"You give them something to eat," said Jesus.

Jesus can be unreasonable. I mean that not as blasphemy but as an honest assessment of this passage. Consider an analogous situation: Your boss creates a situation of great demand needing immense resources but does nothing to provide for those needed resources. As people crowd forward demanding to be served, your boss simply turns to you and says, "You handle it."

Small wonder the disciples protested. "They said to [Jesus], 'Are we to go and buy two hundred denarii worth of bread, and give it to them to eat?'" We today would protest too. Their response cryptically translated is, "Are you crazy?" A reasonable person can readily identify with the disciples. They live with the syndrome I call "life in your face." Step back with me for a moment.

Jesus and the disciples have been engaged in the Master's ministry. They have heard the disheartening news of the cruel death of John the Baptist and withdrawn, perhaps, to be with their grief, possibly to compose themselves for the arduous task that lies ahead. Mark tells us, "They went away in the boat to a deserted place by themselves."

"Now many saw them going and recognized them, and they hurried there on foot from all the towns and arrived ahead of them." Sometimes life is like that. You need a moment to catch your breath, but people still come to you with issues, needs, and problems. The events and people of life demand of us, "Deal with me! I don't care how tired you are or how you feel!"

I remember a wonderful Christian couple telling me about raising their three children, then grown. The husband, a noted lawyer, recalled how it was when the children were young. He said that he would get home from work, and his wife would meet him at the door with a baby in her arms saying, "Here, you take him. I have to have a minute of peace!" He would mumble something like, "At least let me put my briefcase down," but she was not deterred. We all know that feeling, don't we? Here is where this lesson from the gospel intersects our lives.

Significantly, this is one of the few stories of Jesus' ministry that is reported by all four Gospels. Something important is transmitted in this teaching of Jesus. With life in our face, we tend to rush ahead and fixate on Jesus blessing and breaking the bread. We revel in the miracle of multiplication and the wonder of how God provides. However, in our haste, I believe we miss a profound truth that Jesus wishes us to know.

I remember a story I was once told about a mighty warrior mounted on a magnificent horse trotting down a road. Everyone, of course, made certain to get out of his way.

He noticed, however, directly in his path, in the very middle of the road, was a sparrow. The bird was lying on its back with its feet in the air.

The horseman drew in his reins, halted, and dismounted. He went to the sparrow and asked, "Are you dead? And if not, what are you doing in the middle of the road with your feet in the air?"

"No," answered the bird, "I'm not dead, but I heard the sky might fall down, and I'm helping to hold it up."

The warrior thundered and shook with laughter. He rolled on the ground and slapped his thighs. At last, he wiped the tears from his eyes and said, "You silly bird! Even if the sky did fall down, what difference could you possibly make with those puny, spindly little legs?"

"Well," explained the sparrow, "you do what you can do."

Generous living begins here; we do what we can do. The gospel story from Mark tells us the disciples ascertained how much food there was. Jesus took the food, blessed it and broke it, and gave it back to the disciples. Under his direction, they passed it out to the hungry crowd. They did what they could do. In the hands of Jesus, a little is enough.

Take any of the clutch of activities that might run under the rubric of faithful discipleship—our stewardship giving, our sharing of time and talents, teaching in Sunday school, perhaps volunteering to serve the poor, or possibly sharing in visitation ministry—faithfulness lives not in genius or great skill but in doing what you can do. In the mystery of faith, we who are engaged in doing what we can do, discover Christ's divine presence and blessing. In the hands of Jesus, a little is enough.

When I was a camp director in New England with the Hartford County YMCA, during one of the two-week sessions we had two inner-city kids in the same cabin. One was black and one was white. Both were nine years old. Jerry and Tim came from large, relatively poor families; and both knew what it was like to be hungry. At every meal the cook always put out a plate of bread and a large can of generic peanut butter. If you didn't like the meal or were still hungry, you could have a peanut butter sandwich. Jerry and Tim always ate peanut butter sandwiches, even after eating the regular meal.

One of the lessons those two boys taught the rest of us was the importance of passing the bread. They would loudly insist that you only took your share (two slices) and that, before you went on to feed yourself, you passed the bread to the others so that they could eat. Such is the way of faith. We share what we have, and in the hands of Jesus, it is transformed. (J. Michael Lowry)

Worship Aids

Call to Worship

Leader: In thee, O Lord, do I put my trust.

People: Let me never be ashamed.

Leader: For with God all things are possible.

People: Lord, I yield my life to you.

Prayer of Confession

We bow before you and confess that you, O Lord, are the greatest need we have. We need your strength. We need your wisdom. We need your touch. May we never stray so far from you that we forget who you are and what you have done. Amen.

Benediction

As we depart from this place it is our prayer, O God, that you would grant us your wisdom and sustain us with your power. We confess that without you we are hopeless and helpless. Give us your peace today. Amen. (Jimmy McNeil)

NOVEMBER 5, 2006

❧❧❧

Twenty-second Sunday after Pentecost

Readings: Ruth 1:1-18; Psalm 146; Hebrews 9:11-14; Mark 12:28-34

A Pre-Thanksgiving Sermon
Psalm 146

On occasion, some people stumble upon this profound theological insight: DOG is GOD spelled backward! Unfortunately, no theologian has ever made any sense of this ... until now. I have found the significance of this oddity: I am to God as my dog is to me! I'm serious. My mental ability to grasp the greatness and omniscience of God, and my limited appreciation of all that God does for me, is about the same as my dog's ability to know and appreciate me.

My dog Spot is not the brightest pup in the litter. If I go outside with a bag of trash, Spot thinks that I am coming out to play, for him alone. Never mind that my hands are full, Spot thinks that I should throw his ball. Likewise, I sometimes think that God's only agenda in the universe is to take care of *me*. Although I'm sure God loves me, God's universe does not circle around my ego any more than my ego circles around Spot's ego. Just as Spot doesn't understand all my amazing human abilities or realize all the things I do for him, so are we with God. We see only a fraction of God's grandeur and can never fully appreciate all that God does for us.

Nevertheless, we do well to try. Psalm 146 reminds us that God deserves our praise even if we can only scratch the surface of the Divine Glory.

We all know a wonderful prayer used as a child's blessing for meals: "God is great, God is good, let us thank him." This makes a simple but effective outline of what the psalmist is calling us to do.

God is great. Contemplate what an understatement this is. God is, as Paul Tillich put it, "the ground of all being." Luke wrote, "In him we live and move and have our being" (Acts 17:28). John 1:3a (NIV) states: "Through him all things were made." We speak of God as omnipotent and omniscient. Do we believe it? Whatever childish, mythical images humans have had in our heads about gods are simply inadequate. God is bigger than mighty Atlas shouldering the world; God is more powerful than Poseidon controlling the ocean waves; God is wiser than the Oracles of Delphi; God is more eternal than white-bearded Zeus. The entire pantheon of Greek and Roman gods cannot hold a candle to the God who is described so well by the prophet Amos (5:8 NIV): "He who made the Pleiades and Orion, who turns blackness into dawn and darkens day into night, who calls for the waters of the sea and pours them out over the face of the land—the LORD is his name." In Job we read (9:4, 10 NIV): "His wisdom is profound, his power is vast. . . . He performs wonders that cannot be fathomed." Job understood that God is beyond full human knowledge and perception. The best Job could do was look to the majesty of nature and see reflected in its beauty the face of the Creator. We, too, can glimpse the magnificence of God's handiwork. The fingerprint of the artist is impressed upon the art.

I recently visited a butterfly garden. The incredible variety of colors, shapes, and patterns on butterfly wings was awe inspiring, with hues of iridescent colors found nowhere else. God could have made every butterfly in the world look just the same. But instead, our Creator made millions of variegations—all stunningly beautiful—and certainly not an economy of design. The simple butterfly vividly trumpets God's genius of creativity and artistry.

Life in all its vast forms testifies to God's grandeur. We could literally cite a million examples of God's greatness in nature.

God is good. Cynics and atheists are quick to ask, "If God is so good, why do children die of hunger?" It is a tough question without an easy answer, a question more complex than I could convey in a thousand sermons. With the principle of free will in mind, we can at least say that divine goodness is not impugned by human badness.

The larger point is that even in the worst-case scenario—like the death of a child—God is still good. John 3:16 clearly suggests it. Death and tragedy exist, but our good God has done all that can be done to deal with the problem. What more can you ask God to do? Christ suffered torture and death on a cross in order to defeat death, the ultimate sacrifice, the ultimate altruism. Christ died purely because of God's love for us.

God could have enjoyed all of eternity in quiet heavenly bliss without the nuisance of pesky humans. Rather, God chose to abandon the comfort of the royal throne to become a peasant—to save us. Why? As John said, "God is love."

Virtuous individuals such as Mother Teresa and Albert Schweitzer remind us of God's goodness. However, no human other than Jesus has been able to constantly, unfailingly do good. Who can be totally altruistic, caring, loving, and unconcerned with self every minute? Again, God's goodness is so much greater than ours that we have about as much knowledge of it as my dog has of algebra.

Finally, what does the child's prayer tell us? "God is great, God is good, let us thank him." Our response to God's power, love, greatness, and goodness should be thanks and praise. God doesn't need our praise for a divine ego trip. Rather, praise and thanksgiving should be the natural consequence of meeting God. The more we contemplate the majesty of our Creator, the more we will overflow with feelings of awe and words of worship. Our English word *thankful* is a derivation from the Anglo-Saxon *thinkful*. To be thankful is to be mindful of a benefit received. To be truly full of thanks is to think fully of what God has done for us.

Give thanks! (Lance Moore)

The Gift of Giving

Second in a Series of Four: Generous Living

2 Corinthians 9:1-15

The recent revival of Victor Hugo's great novel *Les Miserables* on Broadway brings to mind a famous scene that takes place between Jean Valjean, the bishop, and the magistrate. Jean Valjean is befriended and given lodging by the bishop. Later he steals his candlesticks. The bishop reports the theft; a magistrate is brought in and questions Jean Valjean in the bishop's presence. As the scene unfolds, Valjean appears headed for jail. Surprisingly, the bishop retracts his charges and offers an excuse for the missing candlesticks. Jean Valjean is stunned. When he and the bishop are alone, he asks, "Why did you do that? You know I am guilty."

The bishop replies, "Life is for giving."

This is a great principle of generous living.

As Paul writes to the church at Corinth, he shares basic components of the Christian faith and instructs the church on how one lives as a Christian. In doing so, Paul lays out three elements, which engender the gift of giving.

The first element is a reminder of a basic law of life. "The point is this: the one who sows sparingly will also reap sparingly, and the one who sows bountifully will also reap bountifully." It is almost like saying two plus two equals four. Whether we agree with it, love it, or hate it, sooner or later this basic law of life will assert itself. Jesus says, "The measure you give will be the measure you get" (Matthew 7:2). Generous living reaps a harvest of love and kindness.

I suspect it is human nature to reject this truth. The lottery is based on the faint hope that, by sheer statistical improbability, we might reap what we haven't sowed. It is not so in life. Even those seemingly "lucky" breaks are the result of a huge amount of sowing. If we sow bountifully, we reap bountifully. In our more reflective moments, we know the elemental truth of this biblical phrase. Jesus put it this way: "Give, and it will be given to you. A good measure, pressed down, shaken together, running over, will be put into your lap; for the measure you give will be the measure you get back" (Luke 6:38).

The second element in the gift of giving is simple. God's love is poured out on those who are cheerful and joyous in their giving. It is a part of the gift! Giving enhances our joy! Jesus has said that he wants his joy to be in us and our joy to be complete or full. Thus, "God loves a cheerful giver."

While pastoring in Kerrville, Texas, I preached once a month at a retirement center and nursing home. The lay leader of the worship service was a resident. In his younger days, Van Gleeson (not his real name) had been a professional musician for some big bands. An exuberant joyful Christian, then in his eighties, Van still played his trombone—loudly (which was the way they liked it, because many were partially hearing impaired). It was great! There we were, me in my twenties and the rest them in their eighties, just rocking out. In his giving, Van's joy was infectious. It flowed out on us and back on him. When asked why he continued to play, Van would comment, "When I came to the Lord, I brought my trombone with me!" He lived a joyful life. It showed in his "alive-ness," not just for God, but with and for others. Life for Van was in the giving.

The blessing comes when the giving is joyous and willing. Paul cements his conviction that the gift of giving is inextricably linked to joy and cheerfulness by stressing that the decision to give is taken individually and without force. "Each of you must give as you have made up your mind, not reluctantly or under compulsion, for God loves a cheerful giver."

The gift of giving in cheerfulness or joy not only enhances the value of our gifts but also provides real worth for them. Whether it is large or small, a gift of friendship, support, money—you name it—rebounds back upon us. Cheerful, joyful giving leads us to a third element.

I find it interesting that it is here the Bible lesson gets pointed. It is as if Paul looks us in the eye and says, "Look, if you really trust God with all of what you are and all of what you have, God will both provide for you and pour out blessings upon you." To share in the gift of giving, we must live in trust.

Paul says, "You will be enriched in every way for your great generosity." Herb Miller writes: "Giving is not so much a matter an act of generosity as it is an act of trust. We do not feel secure financially because we have; we feel secure financially because we trust God to continue providing what we need" (Herb Miller, *Money Isn't Is Everything: What Jesus Said about the Spiritual Power of Money* [Nashville: Discipleship Resources, 1994], 15). The third element in the gift of giving is: God will provide.

I find such trusting difficult. It takes an act of courage and maturity of faith. Often God provides in ways that are not of my preference, but in ways I truly need. I have discovered and rediscovered that, every time I am willing to risk, God comes through. In the gift of giving, I receive blessings in abundance.

I have a close treasured friend. One year his wife gave him the assignment of providing entertainment for their seven-year-old son's birthday party. He sweated bullets about what to do and finally went out and hired a clown. He told me about watching that clown entertain the kids and enjoying their joy. My friend said, "That's the best money I ever spent." Joy came in the gift of giving. (J. Michael Lowry)

Worship Aids

Psalter/Responsive Reading (adapted from Psalm 100, NIV/KJV)

Leader: Shout for joy to the LORD, all the earth.

People: Worship the LORD with gladness; come before him with song.

Leader: We are his people, the sheep of his pasture.

People: Enter his gates with thanksgiving and come into his courts with praise.

All: For the LORD is good and his love endures for ever; his faithfulness to all generations.

Pastoral Prayer

O Lord our God, we come into your house to sing your praises, to lift up your name above all names and, in turn, to humble ourselves. We praise you for coming to our rescue when we are lost in our own petty interests, caught up in our toys, baubles, and possessions. Forgive us for our narcissism. Forgive us for seeking fulfillment in lesser things or in other relationships. Help us work not only for the food that perishes but also for the food that endures for eternal life. Give us the wisdom to know the difference. Guide us in following your will and living in your ways. Send us out with renewed thankfulness. Amen.

Benediction

Now may we go in gratitude, mindful of God's constant presence and love in our lives. So fill us with the joy of thankfulness that it overflows on those we encounter this week, in the name of the Father, Son, and Holy Spirit. Amen. (Lance Moore)

NOVEMBER 12, 2006

❧❧❧

Twenty-third Sunday after Pentecost

Readings: Ruth 3:1-5; 4:13-17; Psalm 127; Hebrews 9:24-28; Mark 12:38-44

A Famine of the Word?
Mark 12:38-44

The central concern of Mark 12:38-44 is justice, a theme of interest to Judaism for many centuries. The ancients knew about this. Amos fiercely predicts that all manner of calamity will befall his eighth-century B.C.E. countrymen. Amos saves the most horrific for last. There will come a time, he forecasts, given your wayward habits, given that so many so often are living a lie (this is sin, living a lie), when there will be no word. After which, as Jesus so often said, it is too late. Famine was the great scourge of antiquity, feared as today we fear nuclear holocaust. Amos said there is something worse: a holocaust of the word—when there is no word, no truth, no communication, no consort, no connection.

Has a famine of the word overtaken us? The great hopes with which television writing began, in the 1950s, have given way to waste, a beautiful bedazzling wasteland. And yet, there are exceptions, children of Rod Serling found in the magic box; here a little, there a little, even on television. We enter a new dimension, not of sight or of sound, but of mind and imagination.

Has a famine of the word overtaken us? Look at the Internet, a sprawling universe of chat, governed by e-mail. E-mail: immediate, global, indelible, irretrievable, reactive. It is the medium of choice today. Does it play to our penchant for control and our slothful introversion? Like aerial bombardment, it puts a distance between aggressor and victim. I guess I fear I will come to love it, even though it brings out less than the best in me, and yet there are exceptions: a carefully composed, thoughtful letter, kind and honest, only sent over the waves after three editings; a joyful e-note from Europe or Texas or Iraq.

278

Has a famine of the word overtaken us? Listen to our political discourse. We were led to war on the argument that prudence dictated immediate action, so we could act preemptively—though this was not our custom; unilaterally—though this was not our desire; imperially—though this was not our heritage; unforeseeably—though this was not our preference; so an ostensibly Christian country could be led to prosecute a post-Christian war because of the fear of weapons of mass destruction. Where are they? It is not fatal—for the government, or for the vast majority across our con-gregation, county, and country who have supported the war—if they are not found. We can survive that, as readily as we can their discovery. People know about mistakes, and thus about contrition, compunction, apology, and learning. The discovered atrocities within Iraq provide some cover and justification. But it needs saying, doesn't it? From the highest offices, doesn't it? Or are we beyond telling the truth? Just how broad and lasting is the word *famine*? Are we still in the era of questioning the meaning of words like *is* and *sex* and *good*? I thought we voted that out of office.

Has a famine of the word overtaken us? Listen to our church talk about gays. Why has this issue swallowed all others? I believe this issue is the identified patient in our dysfunctional family rhetoric. The perennially ill person in a family distracts (and protects) others from talking to one another, or about other things. A pastor learns to let the identified patient be, and to talk to the others, the so-called healthy family mem-bers. What (or who) does the patient's illness help others avoid? This issue helps liberals avoid other issues such as evangelism, abortion, and stewardship. This issue helps conservatives avoid other issues such as war, justice, and money. Really, homosexuality is the perfect scapegoat, both for liberals and for conservatives. It helps us in our daily preference of the anxiety of the known over the fear of the unknown. All you need is a willingness to let go of the truth.

Amos spoke eight hundred years before the birth of Christ. Amos mourned the bitter loss of an only son, before that phrase would trigger theological reflection, as it does for us. He foretold a darkness at noon before that phrase titled an account of Joseph Stalin's purge. Amos spoke of songs becoming laments before the poetry subsequent to 9/11. He comes before Jesus the Christ. Amos's prophecy about a famine of the word may fit most or some of our current experience. I wager it fits more than we care readily to admit. But this is not the last word! The word *famine* is not the last word now!

We trust our life and future to Jesus Christ! It is his *word*, finally, that carries us, and his role as prophet that means most for us. In Jesus, the voice of the prophet continues, even in a word famine, to speak to us. His word lives as spirit right now, right here among us.

The other cold day I sat at the streetlight noticing the temperature— minus two degrees Fahrenheit. Here is a strange reality. There are great gulfs crossed between gas to liquid and liquid to solid. But those gulfs are numerically unheralded. They are not known by great numbers such as one hundred degrees or zero degrees. No, they are found out on the arithmetical periphery, in forgotten minor numbers like 32 and 212. Celsius is so much more orderly. But Fahrenheit is peripheral like prophecy and lopsided like life. You find the word spoken in forgotten places—with Amos, in a little hamlet of Tekoa; with Jesus, up on the lakeshore; with John Wesley, in coal mines; with Martin Luther King, Jr., in the black church—voices, peripheral but clear.

The prophet gives voice to silent agony. The generations-deep hurt of people of color in the United States finally found full voice in the well-tempered homiletics of Martin Luther King, Jr. In Christ, the divine voice has taken full-throated residence in the heart of hurt. A voice to be heard needs loving connection with an addressable community. The prophet does not stand above or apart from his people. The prophet abides, dwells, tabernacles among the people.

Up then and let us wait for the word: waiting without idols; waiting without substitutes. People do not live by bread alone, but by every word that proceeds from the mouth of God. (Robert Hill)

The Blessing of Giving

Third in a Series of Four: Generous Living

Acts 20:32-38

A review of the teaching of Jesus could almost be summarized in one word: give. There is a blessing in giving. Consider the evidence in Holy Scripture. In Luke 6:38 Jesus says, "Give, and it will be given to you. A good measure, pressed down, shaken together, running over, will be put into your lap; for the measure you give will be the measure you get back." Or take Jesus' statement in Luke 14:13-14, "But when you give a banquet, invite the poor, the crippled, the lame, and the blind. And you will be blessed, because they cannot repay you, for you will be repaid at the resurrection of the righteous."

In today's Bible lesson taken from chapter 20 of the Acts of the Apostles, Paul echoes this seminal teaching of Jesus. The context is significant. It begins in verse 17 where the apostle Paul meets in Miletus with the elders of the church at Ephesus, which he helped establish. It is a sad farewell. Paul is bound for Rome for imprisonment, and perhaps eventual execution. Paul has taught them, raised them in the faith, and now offers a valedictory address.

It neatly breaks into three parts as this great Christian leader sets out expectations for the Christian leaders who will serve after him. In verse 28, he instructs them to feed the church. In verses 29 through 31, he warns them against various dangers facing the church. Finally in verses 33 through 35, he admonishes them not to be greedy for personal gain but to give for a blessing. Verse 35 closes with his echoing Jesus and sharing the instructions upon which Paul has based his life. "It is more blessed to give than to receive."

The biblical truth couldn't be plainer. A crucial step in living the life we've always wanted is to give. We are blessed in giving. Notice how Paul has framed this central teaching. In verse 32, he sets his whole farewell speech in the context of God's grace—freely forgiving love. "And now I commend you to God and to the message of his grace, a message that is able to build you up and to give you the inheritance among all who are sanctified." Did you catch that? It's able to build us up and give us an inheritance. He's telling us this is how you come to live the life you've always wanted.

In verses 33, 34, and the first part of verse 35, Paul cements his case by offering himself as an example. He hasn't coveted wealth or possessions. Paul has worked to support the weak. While others see a tear-stained future, the apostle Paul embraces great living. He comforts them and remembers the words of Jesus, "It is more blessed to give than to receive."

The problem with such a teaching is that we believe and yet almost simultaneously doubt its veracity. Why is that? Oh, we know the answer. We get captured by the cult of the mall. It is so easy to buy (pun intended) into the illusion that spending for something new can make us into something new. It is difficult to ignore these powerful false gods, which clamor for our adoration. Yet, instinctively, we know that great living comes in giving—giving of our time, our energy, or our possessions, including our money.

Contemporary research reveals through scientific study what Jesus knew through spiritual instinct. The six greatest needs of every human being are meaning and purpose, self-esteem, loving relationships, spiritual connection with God, security, and a sense of immortality. Why did Jesus talk so much about money? Why do so many of Jesus' parables discuss the appropriate and inappropriate use of money? Because money has the power to help or hinder people from meeting these six basic needs that determine the quality of our daily living. "Money cannot buy happiness," we say repeatedly. True! But the way we use our money directly influences how happy we are. (Herb Miller, *Money ~~Isn't~~ Is Everything: What Jesus Said about the Spiritual Power of Money* [Nashville: Discipleship Resources, 1994], 44)

Giving is one of the crucial steps in living the life we've always wanted.

There is an old cartoon where a pastor stands in the pulpit speaking to the congregation. He says, "I would like to remind you that what you are about to give is tax deductible, cannot be taken with you, and is considered by some to be the root of all evil" (Miller, *Money ~~Isn't~~ Is Everything*, 41). We all laugh, but there is a much more positive reason for giving. We are blessed in giving. We are enriched in giving. "John Wesley said that if you have poor giving habits, you are robbing God. Jesus went beyond that. He said that if you have poor giving habits, you rob yourself" (Miller, *Money ~~Isn't~~ Is Everything*, 41).

Soon, we as a congregation will once again have the opportunity to embrace the life we've always wanted. We will again have the chance to decide if we trust the Lord and believe his word. Paul speaks to us: "In all this I have given you an example that by such work we must support the weak, remembering the words of the Lord Jesus, for he himself said, 'It is more blessed to give than to receive.'" We are invited to an adventure in faith. This is the path in living the life we've always wanted. We are blessed in giving. Amen. (J. Michael Lowry)

Worship Aids

Call to Worship (from Psalm 48)

Leader: Praise the Lord!

People: Praise the Lord from the heavens, praise him from the heights!

Leader: Let us praise the name of the Lord, for his name alone is exalted.

All: For his glory is above heaven and earth.

Leader: Let us worship God.

Benediction (from Colossians 3:16-17)

May the word of Christ dwell in you richly, may you teach and admonish one another with gratitude in your hearts, and whatever you do, in word or deed, do everything in the name of the Lord Jesus, giving thanks to God the Father through him. Amen. (Tracy Hartman)

NOVEMBER 19, 2006

❧❧❧

Twenty-fourth Sunday after Pentecost

Readings: 1 Samuel 1:4-20; 1 Samuel 2:1-10; Hebrews 10:11-14 (15-18) 19-25; Mark 13:1-8

Let No One Lead You Astray
Mark 13:1-8

Christians are sojourners and wanderers on the earth. This theme is a thread that runs through the scriptures that invites us to think of ourselves as people who don't quite fit. Most of us look at our culture and world as belonging to us. We think of American culture as Christian and we think of ourselves as the major religious tradition. Note, however, that it is said there are more Muslims in America than Episcopalians. We live in a very diverse culture and mostly we live in a culture that's not very religious at all. In some very important respects we are different. We are aliens in a culture that is not ours. We live in a world where scores of children will die of hunger while we worship. We ought, perhaps, never feel at home in such a world. We ought never to feel like such a world is our kind of world as long as these tragedies occur. In some very profound ways the Christian is a nonconformist; in some profound ways a Christian is an alien, a nonresident, not really of this world.

Some of those differences may seem superficial. For example, the church of Jesus Christ has a calendar that is foreign to the common secular calendar. Now we might think, as many people do, that New Year's Day is January 1. However, in the church New Year's Day is December 3, the first Sunday of Advent. Now that is really marching to the beat of a different drummer, isn't it? Our church tradition goes back centuries and informs us that the first Sunday of Advent is the beginning of the year. We Christians are on a different clock, you see, and the annual cycle turns and comes to these last two weeks, today and next Sunday. In these last two weeks of the year the gospel lessons sound strange to our culture, but they fit into our larger Christian view of life. Christians end the year waiting for the reign of Christ, so we look at this odd text from Mark, which is about the end of the world. Mark 13 is one of several texts in the Bible that invites much misunderstanding and much mischief.

So I want us to think a little bit about the end of the world, the second coming, the close of the age, and then ask ourselves what this means to us and how it contributes to our alien nature in the world.

First, Jesus' words to the disciples ought to be our beginning watchword, that is, "Let no one lead you astray." Jesus begins with the statement "Don't be led astray." Predicting dates for the end of the world is one way many are led astray.

Thirty years ago everyone was reading Hal Lindsey's book *The Late Great Planet Earth*. He made a lot of money selling books and giving lectures predicting the end of the world until his timetables passed and the end didn't come. There's always some guru taking people, who have sold their homes and their businesses, off to a mountaintop to await the second coming. They are regularly disappointed.

Friends, the Bible is not a mysterious crystal ball through which you sift to find clues that give you the secret knowledge about when some catastrophic end is going to take place. Anyone who tells you that the Bible is that sort of book fundamentally misunderstands the Bible.

If these texts are not for pinpointing the date for the end of the world, what are they for? The biblical writers were trying to say to their generation and to ours that history has a godly destiny. The Bible sees history as a parade leading toward a great goal.

In many respects, the world doesn't get much better. Jesus could talk about wars and famines, and low and behold, if you open your eyes, we have the same thing today. The world doesn't, on the surface of it, seem to be headed anywhere in particular. But the church of Jesus Christ says that if you have a heart to believe you can see the destiny of the world is the rule of the love of Christ.

The storm clouds of war are not the last word. The hungry dying babies are not the last word. The trampling down of people because of their race or gender or age or religious beliefs does not have the last word. God has the last word. Trying to put schedules on it is futile, but believing that we are headed toward peace and justice and the rule of love makes all the difference. Living by God's hope for us makes us aliens in a world that seems to be ruled by violence, by hate, by power. We believe in a world ruled by love.

The end of the world. Don't try to schedule it, or describe it, or figure it out in any detail, but believe that we are headed somewhere good.

Believe human history is going in a direction, a direction that is good and invites goodness in us. God invites a witness from us to something that we believe is true even if the world seems to be rushing headlong over a cliff in the other direction. When we believe God will reign; when we believe Christ's love will one day be the deciding decisive reality, then we are aliens, but just the kind of strangers and aliens God wants us to be. Amen! (Carl L. Schenck)

Great Power and Great Grace

Fourth in a Series of Four: Generous Living

Acts 4:32-37

Over the years, I have gotten all kinds of phone calls. One of the strangest and most joyous calls came near Christmas about six years ago. It was at a time when the price of oil was devastating the local economy and causing a number of people to be laid off. Despite the fact that the church was growing in membership, many of the new members were without jobs, and the church was in financially bad straights. The phone call came from a man who had converted to Christ just a few years earlier. He was a new believer who was married to a woman who was a long-time Christian. When we got done exchanging pleasantries, he said, "Mike, I've been praying about this, and I want to give my wife a special Christmas gift." (I thought to myself, "That's fine. But, why would you call me about her Christmas gift?") He continued, "I totaled the amount of money that I spent on her Christmas last year. (They were fairly well off.) By my total, I spent about two thousand dollars. Well, I want to give her that Christmas gift this year by giving the church two thousand dollars in her name for you to use in the budget any place you see fit."

I was dumbfounded! His Christmas gift to his wife was going to be a two-thousand-dollar check to the church. "That's right," he said. "I don't think anything else would please her more." He requested that I draw up a little certificate for him to give her. He came by the next day to pick it up. The certificate wasn't anything fancy.

Early that January, she came into my office with that certificate. Her husband had framed the certificate, wrapped it up with a bright bow, and placed it under the tree. With tears in her eyes, she talked about how wonderful it was as a gift and how she had never received anything better at Christmas.

A scene of similar joy and generosity is found in Acts. They experienced great power and great grace. "There was not a needy person among them, for as many as owned lands or houses sold them and brought the proceeds of what was sold." When the family of Christ gathers together, generosity erupts! Generous living defines and shapes their relationships. This passage teaches us that the use of our financial resources is fundamentally a spiritual issue. A spiritual life anchored in God is intimately tied to generous living. Those who believed lived generously. They had great power and great grace precisely because the use of their possessions was freely surrendered to God's will, purpose, and desire.

To be a Christian is to be a part of a generous family. This is so because our leader, Jesus Christ, lived with an extravagant generosity that defined Jesus' life, death, and resurrection. God is generous! This is the basic reality of God, the provider of all good gifts. You and I cannot outgive God!

About a year and a half ago, I found myself standing in a hospital in front of the windows viewing newborn babies. The father, both sets of grandparents, and I were standing and gazing through the windows of the hospital nursery at this newborn child. As everybody beamed, smiled, cooed, and celebrated, one of the grandparents turned to his son and said, "He looks just like you." I thought to myself, "No he doesn't." But in a certain way the baby did. There was a family resemblance.

There is something special about the physical resemblance that identifies the oneness of the family. The child is identified with his father or his mother. Similarly, I believe that God is pleased when God sees a family resemblance in us though our actions and our attitudes.

The tough question for all of us is how. How do we take on a family resemblance and move into generous living through the giving of our resources and ourselves? Step one: Begin with prayer. Get honest with God in careful-listening prayer, and God will honor you with divine guidance. For years we tithed (gave 10 percent of our income for the work of the Lord) after taxes. I remember one year praying to God about what we should write down, and God said to me, "Look, stop fooling around. Trust me with the real 10 percent, not 10 percent after you've already taken out a number of things." God wants us in the family picture. Pray to God and listen for God's guidance. Generous living starts in prayer.

Step two: Give to God first. Proverbs 3:9 says, "Honor the LORD with your substance and with the first fruits of all your produce." Don't give God your leftovers. The joy of generous living comes through firstfruit giving.

Step three: Give of yourself. It is not enough just to write a check. The joy of generous living comes through serving. Great power and great grace belonged to the first Christ followers because they took care of those in need.

Step four is crucial: Make a public commitment to live generously. When we make something public, we bind ourselves to keep the commitment made. Periodically, I've had people ask me why they need to join the church. "Can't I just keep coming?" they will say. I ask them if they loved their husband or wife before they got married. Inevitably they respond, "Of course." "Why did you get married, then?" I'll ask. "What is gained in the wedding ceremony?" The answer is simple. The public commitment seals the bond before God and the congregation. It is instructive that not once, but twice in this brief passage we are told that they brought what they had and "laid it at the apostles' feet." They made a public commitment to live generously. We are to do the same. (J. Michael Lowry)

Worship Aids

Call to Worship

O give thanks to the LORD, for he is good; for his steadfast love endures forever (Psalm 106:1).

Invocation

God, you call us to what is important, away from the trivial. Lead us to focus our lives on the heart of it all, your great love for us; a love we see most clearly in your sending your Son. In Jesus' name, Amen.

Benediction

Lord, bless us as we go into our world. Help us focus more and more on what is truly at the heart of all of life, your love. Lead us to rely on your love and to let your love transform our lives. In Jesus' name, Amen. (Ross West)

NOVEMBER 23, 2006

❧❧❧

Thanksgiving Day

Readings: Joel 2:21-27; Psalm 126; 1 Timothy 2:1-7; Matthew 6:25-33

Can I Get a Witness?
Psalm 126

Who likes responsibility? The truth is almost no one. Most of us do not like the responsibility that befalls us in this life. We sometimes spend more time finding ways to escape responsibility than we do meeting our obligations.

What is true in everyday life is also true in the Christian world. Once we accept Christ, we find there are many responsibilities that await us. For example, we are responsible for maintaining our relationship with God. We must read God's word and spend time in consecrated prayer every day. It is our responsibility. We must also be obedient and obey the commands we find in scripture. It is our responsibility to attend church and fellowship with other believers. Time will not permit us to name all the responsibilities that are ours in Christ.

One of the greatest responsibilities we have is that of being a witness for the cause of Christ. How else will the world know who God is and what God can do unless we tell it, unless we show it?

In the midst of the book of Psalms, we find many psalms that challenge us in our responsibilities. One such psalm is our text for today, Psalm 126. Although its authorship is unknown, it is no doubt a psalm of ultimate praise for God's deliverance of his people in a time of captivity. The Babylonians had taken God's people captive and God had promised he would intervene and return them to their homeland (Jeremiah 29:14).

The first four verses of Psalm 126 give praise and honor to God for divine deliverance. The Israelites testify in verse 1 that being rescued from bondage was almost like a dream. It was as if they were imagining the entire thing. Yet they were not dreaming. God was at work in their behalf. There was laughing and there was singing. Even those who were outsiders (not Israelites) declared the greatness of God. In verse 2 the nations declare, "The LORD has done great things for them." It's a great thing when we sing about the goodness of God. We, too, have been in bondage and we, too, can sing of God's deliverance in our lives. What the nations said in verse 2, the Israelites now proclaim in verse 3. We are glad because God has done great things for us.

If it's not enough that they praise God for deliverance, they now give testimony of how sometimes we suffer wrong only to have opportunity in the end to sing praises. Today there may be tears, but as we sow in tears, we will reap in joy. No doubt for Israel, while in captivity there were many sleepless nights—nights of turmoil, days of uncertainty. Yet another psalm (30:5 NKJV) reminds us, "Weeping may endure for a night, but joy comes in the morning."

The nation of Israel was quite familiar with periods of weeping. It had been a long time ago, but forty years in the wilderness was part of their history, and in the early days, they were slaves in Egypt before God's deliverance. We, too, can testify of nights of weeping, years in bondage, and we, too, can testify of God's deliverance from the bondage and penalty of sin. This brings us to the final verse of this psalm.

It was stated at the outset that we have many responsibilities in the Christian life. To be a witness for Christ is one of our greatest. Verse 6 of our text tells us, "Those who go out weeping, bearing the seed for sowing, shall come home with shouts of joy, carrying their sheaves." The conditions of our fulfilling this responsibility are set forth in that one verse. There are two conditions that must be met and two results of obedience.

The first condition of obedience is that we must go and care. There is no possible way for us to witness for Christ unless we go. If we ever expect the world to know about Jesus, we must be the ones to tell about the Christ. The nations saw what God had done and gave glory to God on Israel's behalf.

The second condition of obedience is that we must tell the world the truth. It is our responsibility to tell the lost of God's love and Jesus' payment on Calvary, and how forgiveness is available if they will but receive it from Jesus. We are to "bear seeds for sowing." In Matthew 13 Jesus taught the "parable of the soils," and in the story, seeds were being scattered. Not all of the seeds brought forth fruit, but seeds were still scattered. Ours is the responsibility of scattering seed and letting the fruit grow. God will give the increase. God always does. The conditions of obedience are clearly laid out. Once the conditions are met, the same verse in Psalm 126 tells us of the outcome. There are results to our obedience and those results are twofold.

The first result of obedience is that we will see fruit. When one plants an orange tree, there is but one goal, to one day see oranges. When we as believers share the gospel with the world, we will see fruit from our labor. The "Great Commission" still applies today. "Go therefore and make disciples of all nations" (Matthew 28:19).

The second result of obedience is tied closely with the first. As we are the witness God has called us to be, we will see fruit and we will find ourselves rejoicing over the goodness of God. We will have something to sing about. Heaven's number will be increased. Satan will lose strongholds. Families will be saved. Marriages will survive. Children will be raised in godly homes. Why? All because of the obedience of God's people. God's question today is this: "Can I get a witness?" Will you be that one who will stand and obey and watch God do more than you could ever dream? We must act now! (Jimmy McNeil)

The Truth about Life

First in a Two-Part Series

Leviticus 23:9-14; Matthew 13:24-30

Because Thanksgiving was originally a harvest festival, today it is appropriate to explore an agricultural parable. This parable is not really about farming methods, although it offers a clever way of separating weeds and wheat. Jesus is not giving us a lesson about nature, but about the nature of life.

Whereas parables contain several messages, the message I see in this parable is: life is a mixture. Life is a mixture of weeds and wheat, of bad and good, of sorrow and joy, of pain and pleasure. This seems so obvious you're probably wondering why I'm writing it.

The reason I'm writing that life is a mixture is that I don't believe we really accept this truth. Much of the time we deny it, resist it, or even rebel against it.

M. Scott Peck in *The Road Less Traveled* (New York: Simon and Schuster, 1978) makes this point in his opening words: "Life is difficult."

> This is a great truth, one of the greatest truths. It is a great truth because once we truly see this truth, we transcend it.... Most do not fully see this truth that life is difficult. Instead, they moan more or less

incessantly, noisily or subtly, about the enormity of their problems, their burdens, and their difficulties, as if life should be easy. They voice their belief, noisily or subtly, that their difficulties represent a unique kind of affliction that should not be and that has somehow been especially visited upon them and not upon others. (page 15)

The difficulties of which M. Scott Peck writes are the "weeds" of life. He is right. There are always weeds: challenges, obstacles, disappointments, failures, problems, pains, and even tragedies. This is the truth.

I recently spoke with a woman whose mother had suffered from Alzheimer's disease for the past ten years. She had watched her mother retreat into a shell of silence. I asked her how she was doing. She said, "I'm angry. My mother was such a good person, such a good mother. She doesn't deserve this. It's so unfair!"

Life's unfairness is another way of saying that there are always weeds. On September 11, 2001, hundreds of persons who worked in the World Trade Center survived simply because they didn't go to work that day. Some were home sick or stayed home with a sick child. Some were traveling on business or vacations. Some simply missed the early train. Is it fair for such random events to determine who would live and who would die? Of course not. It's not fair.

I want to offer another metaphor to approach the message of the weeds among the wheat. This came to me while I was at the U.S. Open tennis tournament about fifteen years ago. I found myself standing next to a man with flowing white hair and a full gray beard. He looked familiar and I suspected he was famous (it wasn't Santa Claus!). Then I heard someone behind me whisper to a friend, "Look, that's Kenny Rogers."

Kenny Rogers, the country and western singer and sometime actor, had a hit song in the 1980s titled "The Gambler." This song offers a metaphor: life is a card game. We can't determine the hand we're dealt. The cards we're dealt are the "givens" of life: our genetic makeup, who our parents are, where we were raised, how we were raised. Life forces itself upon us without our consent.

There are also givens in the lives of those whom we love. Some of you have been dealt a child with a learning disability or an emotional problem. Some of you have been dealt an ill parent, spouse, sibling, or child.

We can't determine the hand we're dealt. All we can do is play our hands to the best of our abilities.

There are ways that we sabotage playing our hands well. First, we can refuse to accept the hand we've been dealt by railing against the unfairness of it. We can take on a victim mentality and blame someone else for our difficulties, including God. Second, we can hope for a "redeal." Have you ever coveted someone else's hand? I have. We can imagine that everyone else has a better hand than we do and feel sorry for ourselves.

The key question is: Will we accept the hand we've been dealt and be thankful for it?

One thing to keep in mind is that, within the givens, there are always choices. Søren Kierkegaard wrote about the "righteous sufferer" in *Purity of Heart*. He contends that, whereas most suffering happens by chance rather than choice, we always have one choice: we can choose to remain related to God.

How does our faith in God help us in playing our hands? Some people view God as the Divine Dealer, who doles out good cards to some and bad to others. I think this view of God is absolutely wrong. This makes God seem arbitrary and unfair. I see God as the Divine Guide, who gently guides us in playing our hands.

One final thought. When we're in the middle of the game, it's difficult to know which cards are good and which are bad. The cards that bring suffering and adversity often strengthen us and build character and compassion. At the time, suffering seems harmful and unfair. But, at the end of the game we can see that we were really playing a winning hand.

I'll leave you with a question borrowed from the end of the M. Scott Peck paragraph I quoted earlier: "Life is a series of problems. Do we want to moan about them or solve them?" (Bob Walker)

Worship Aids

Call to Worship

Leader: Come, you thankful people, come!

People: From God we have received everything we need for life.

Leader: Come, you thankful people, come!

People: We come in gratitude and thanksgiving for all of God's gifts!

Prayer of Confession

How arrogant of us to take one day a year and call it "Thanksgiving Day." The truth is that each and every day is an appropriate occasion for giving thanks to you. Too often we are so preoccupied with our problems, difficulties, and demands that we forget to say thank you. We are too self-absorbed to see, let alone be grateful for, the gifts that surround us. Forgive us our lack of gratitude and renew in us thankful hearts. In Jesus' name we pray. Amen.

Benediction

Go out into the world with glad and generous hearts, sowing the seeds of thanksgiving everywhere you go. (Bob Walker)

NOVEMBER 26, 2006

❧❧❧

Christ the King/Reign of Christ

Readings: 2 Samuel 23:1-7; Psalm 132:1-12 (13-18); John 18:33-37; Revelation 1:4*b*-8

How Old Is God?
Revelation 1:4*b*-8

How old do you think God is? Is God a baby? a child? a teenager? a young adult? a senior adult?

An old saying says there are no right answers to a wrong question. Of course, that is a wrong question to which there is no right answer. In the Revelation, God is spoken of as the One "who is and who was and who is to come." Indeed, the Lord God identified himself as "the Alpha and the Omega" in that same verse. Of course, alpha is the first letter of the Greek alphabet and omega is the last. God was saying that as far into the past as we can go and as far into the future as we can imagine, we'll find God there.

God is timeless, yet related always to every time, be it past, present, or future. Think about what this means, that God is, God was, and God is to come.

First, God is. God is active in the present. When we think of God's timelessness, I wonder whether we give enough attention to this thought. I wonder whether most of us do not simply think of God as being very, very old—eternally, endlessly, perpetually old. The danger is that we may come to think of God as sitting in a rocking chair, wringing his hands about the world, unable to do much if anything about it, and longing for the good old days that never were.

However, if God is timeless, we have as much basis for thinking of God as perpetually, eternally, endlessly young as for thinking of God as being very, very old. Whatever age we think of God as being, realizing that God is, is active now and with us now, is tremendously important. We need this recognition that God is, and we need it especially in the midst of a world of great change. Whatever happens in these days and whatever changes may occur in the near future, we have not left God behind, as if God is irrelevant to us and our changing world. God is.

Of course, the terms *eternally young* or *eternally old* are really unimportant, even wrong, as applied to God. What is truly important, however, is that we affirm that God is. God is with us and active in the now.

An equally important affirmation is that God was. This truth is what we see when we read of God's mighty acts in scripture, in both the Old Testament and the New, and supremely in God's Son Jesus, our Lord. God was active in the past. Note that we do not look back to God's past actions, however, simply to satisfy our interest in history, however great or meager that might be. Rather our purpose in looking back to God's acts in the past is to help us look up and in and to learn that this same God is with us today. As Paul wrote about past occurrences recorded in the Old Testament, "These things happened to them to serve as an example, and they were written down to instruct us" (1 Corinthians 10:11). Why do we study the Bible, this ancient book, if not because we believe that in the Bible we have the record of God's revelation of himself to humankind, coming finally to us to whom has been announced "things into which angels long to look" (1 Peter 1:12).

To know that God was gives stability, challenge, and hope for our present and future. As others counted on God, so can we. As others were challenged by God, so are we. As others knew the fulfillment of God's promises, so will we.

Another fact about God's age is that God is to come. If we could go into the farthest reaches of the future, we would find God there. The truth is these words that God "is to come" ought to give us encouragement and hope. If God is with us, we ought not be overly concerned about the future. We don't know the future, but we do know the God of the future. We know that that God is a match for anything that the future may hurl at us. Neither the distant future nor what may happen tomorrow or this week ought to discourage us. Neither holds any perils that God cannot master and overcome. As scripture affirms, "For I am convinced that neither death, nor life, nor angels, nor rulers, nor things present, nor things to come, nor powers, nor height, nor depth, nor anything else in all creation, will be able to separate us from the love of God in Christ Jesus our Lord" (Romans 8:38-39).

That God is the God of the future also challenges us to hear God's call to go into the future with him. We must learn from the past, but we must not live in it. We must not even live in the present, since it mysteriously slips away from us the moment we say we live in the present. Rather, the

God who "is to come" calls us to move into God's future right along with him. We must not slip backward or stagnate. We must not stop growing. When we move into the future right along with God, we will find that God will be continually meeting our needs and continually growing us to be all that God wants us to be.

When we commit ourselves to God in faith, God changes us continually. God continually engages us in relationship with him and continually grows us to be more like him. The God "who is and who was and who is to come" gives us a profound sense of his presence with us now, a due appreciation for God's acts in the past, and encouragement and challenge as we go with God into the future. (Ross West)

The Truth about Jesus

Second in a Two-Part Series

Isaiah 49:13–50:6; John 18:33-38

Thomas Cahill, the author of *How the Irish Saved Civilization*, *The Gifts of the Jews*, and *Desire of the Everlasting Hills*, refers to this series of books as "the hinges of history." In each of these books, he looks at turning points in human civilization that changed the course of history.

Today is a "hinge" Sunday. This is the final Sunday in the six-month-long season of Pentecost; Advent begins next Sunday. We call this Sunday "Christ the King." It's a time to celebrate the sovereignty of God's love in our lives and world. And, it is also a time to look forward to Christ's coming reign.

In the gospel lesson, we encounter Pilate's interrogation of Jesus. The fact that Pontius Pilate is the only name other than Jesus mentioned in the Apostles' Creed points to the important role he played in the Gospel of John's passion drama.

Pilate begins by asking Jesus directly, "Are you the King of the Jews?" Jesus responds in a way consistent with his answers throughout the Gospel of John: Jesus answers a question with a question. Then Jesus reminds Pilate that his kingdom is not an earthly kingdom.

Pilate won't let go of his original question and presses, "So you are a king?" Jesus then baits Pilate, just as he did with Nicodemus in chapter 4 of John, saying, "I came into the world, to testify to the truth."

Pilate takes the bait and asks his famous question, "What is truth?" I've often wondered how Pilate asked this question. Did he ask it sarcastically? Disdainfully? Mockingly? Inquiringly? Sincerely? We know that Pilate was a cruel and often brutal Roman governor. He was merciless in putting down Jewish uprisings against Roman rule; crucifixion was his most favored method of punishment. Yet, in his encounter with Jesus he seems curious, even mildly sympathetic.

Again, Jesus doesn't give Pilate an answer. This time Jesus responds with silence. Is this because we, the readers, are expected to know the answer? Jesus has said earlier in the Gospel of John, "I am the way, and the truth, and the life" (14:6a).

How would you answer Pilate's question?

Buddhism answers this question with "The Four Noble Truths." These are: (1) life is suffering; (2) the cause of suffering is desire; (3) desire can be overcome; (4) the way to overcome desire is by following the teachings of the Buddha called "The Eightfold Path."

Most of us would agree that life involves suffering. To live is to endure pain, difficulties, disappointment, and failure. Yet, deep down, do we really accept this truth? Have you ever found yourself saying, "This shouldn't be happening to me!" or, "I'm a good person and don't deserve this"?

Our refusal to accept the inevitability of suffering can prevent us from overcoming the difficulties that invariably come our way. In seminary, I spent a semester in clinical pastoral education at a large hospital in Dallas. I was assigned to the "cancer floor" as a chaplain, and talked and prayed with persons suffering from various kinds of cancer. After that semester, I came to a conclusion: there are two kinds of cancer patients—those who accept the reality of their disease and fight to overcome it and those who live in denial of their cancer. The latter group didn't seem as happy, or as healthy, as those who acknowledged their illness.

If suffering is the truth about us, what is the truth about Jesus, the King of the Jews?

Jesus never was a king in any recognizable sense. He had no kingly trappings. Jesus' crown was made of thorns. Jesus' throne was a cross.

Yet, the Gospels present Jesus as a king. How is this possible? Jesus is a king only when we are loyal subjects. It is only when we obey Jesus and worship him that we truly understand the nature of his sovereignty.

Jesus said to Pilate, "My kingdom is not from this world." Jesus' kingdom is not political or geographical, but spiritual. The kingdom of God proclaimed and ushered in by Jesus is the reign of God's love, justice, and peace. We are part of this kingdom when we follow the demands of a Savior who lives and dies for us.

In Jesus' time, many Jews were hoping for a messiah/king who would lead their nation in defeating the Romans, who were an occupying force in Palestine. They were looking for a strong warrior who would establish a theocracy and usher in a new age of peace. However, Jesus didn't fulfill these messianic expectations.

Instead, Jesus fulfilled the messianic role of "suffering servant" as described in Isaiah chapters 40–55. These chapters contain four "servant songs" that describe how God's servant suffers willingly and obediently. The early church, including the gospel writers, understood Jesus' messianic role in terms of this "suffering servant."

This is good news for us! In Jesus Christ, we see a God who isn't a remote, distant sovereign, but God-with-us. Jesus suffered physical and emotional agonies during his passion. By so doing, he reveals a God who knows our suffering, and shares it.

When I am in pain I, too, want a warrior/king who will come into my life and instantly take away the causes of my suffering. Yet, what we are offered is the "true" King who eases our suffering by sharing it.

As a parent, I've often had to witness the pain of our sons. When my younger son was hit in the forehead with a baseball, I wanted to take away his pain. But there are many pains that a parent cannot remove and this was one of them. However, what I did was to take him in my arms and hold him. That was all I could do, but it was enough.

In Jesus Christ we see the Sovereign of Love, who shares our pain. What is truth? Jesus is the truth, the way, and the life. Amen. (Bob Walker)

Worship Aids

Call to Worship

Leader: Rejoice! Christ is King!

People: We gather to worship our Sovereign God.

Leader: Christ comes to reign over us.

People: We promise to follow Christ in the way that leads to abundant life.

Prayer of Confession

We find it more appealing to follow a triumphant King that to obey the commands of a dying Savior. We are more interested in getting immediate gratification than we are in committing ourselves to the disciplines of Christian living. Forgive our weakness of will and shallowness of commitment. Strengthen our resolve to recommit ourselves to living as loyal subjects of Christ our King. Amen.

Benediction

Go out from this place following in the way of the True King, Jesus Christ! (Bob Walker)

DECEMBER 3, 2006

❧❧❧

First Sunday of Advent

Readings: Jeremiah 33:14-16; Psalm 25:1-10; 1 Thessalonians 3:9-13;
Luke 21:25-36

Interpreters of Circumstances
Luke 21:25-36

These verses in Luke's Gospel tell of the cosmic signs predicting the coming of redemption and advent of the Son of Man. They also tell of the promised doom of the end times. Some people get caught up in the signs reading newspapers and watching television, trying to fit the events of the day into the foretold doom. Rather than focusing on the promise of the "Son of Man coming in a cloud with power and great glory," these people read with great relish of wars and earthquakes. Most of us also forget the rest of the story. *The New Interpreter's Study Bible* describes it as: "Jesus moves from prophetic warnings to pastoral counsel. His followers are to be able interpreters of the events around them and through prayer and watchfulness to maintain faithful readiness" (Joel B. Green, *The New Interpreter's Study Bible* [Nashville: Abingdon, 2003], 1895). How do we rate as interpreters? Do we detect God's presence in our circumstances? Can we accurately interpret events in others' lives, in our community or the world?

God does use circumstances to speak to us or show us God's will. In some circumstances we can see God's hand clearly. My twin brother and I are adopted and we searched for our biological family decades ago. Recently, through a very bizarre set of circumstances, we were reunited with our birth family. They had been looking for us constantly since we were taken from a hospital many years ago. Only now did we find one another. Any other time, it would have been too expensive and complicated to arrange visits. Now, at this point in time, I was ready emotionally and spiritually to embrace new family members. With a new appointment to Native people, it was advantageous to have connections to the reservation where my family lives. God's timing was perfect and I could clearly see God working throughout these events.

Sometimes our circumstances may seem "bad" and we may question, "Why is this happening to me? Where is God in this mess?" A biblical example is Job. Everything Job owned was destroyed. His children were killed and then he got sick. He did not know what was going on. His friends thought they knew God's perspective and advised Job to confess his sins. Job searched his own life and heart and could find no unrighteousness. We probably could not make the same claim although we struggle with understanding God's perspective dealing with terminal illness, divorce, the death of a child, bankruptcy, rape, war—the list could go on and on. Yet the question remains, Are we able to be interpreters of God's presence in all circumstances?

God's perspective is crucial to interpreting all situations. It is so difficult to see God from the middle of our own circumstances. We may see another's problem with spiritual clarity. With great confidence, we can proclaim, "God is teaching you patience or God is using this incident to draw you closer to God." Yet, from the midst of our very own problems, one tends to have a distorted understanding of God. We may find ourselves saying, "God is not fair" or "God doesn't love me."

Another common response is the questioning of God's wisdom. We may even try to blame God for our decisions and choices, "I thought I was following your will and doing the right thing. If this was wrong, why didn't you stop me?"

The Gospel lesson from Luke reminds us that we must be prayerful and watchful. If you find yourself in the middle of difficult circumstances, pray. First, not as the last resort, pray. Ask God to show you God's perspective on your circumstances. Use the heart of God to understand your situation. Trust that the Holy Spirit will reveal the truth about your circumstances and help you understand God's perspective. Look back, and with brutal honesty, determine how you got in the circumstance. What were your decisions? Who did you go to for advice or help? What was your motivation? What were your expectations?

We all face "bad" circumstances that are not of our own making. This process toward understanding is just as important, perhaps more so, at this time. Instead of being overwhelmed or discouraged, we can continue to glorify God at all times. To be able to see from God's perspective increases our faith and our witness to God's omnipresence. God did not tell Job what to do, but Job acknowledged God's sovereignty and love. A crucial part, and a difficult stage, of the process is praising God—especially when we do not feel like it.

If, during your process, you discern God's working, then you must adapt your life to join God. Obedience. What must you change in your lifestyle and your attitude to be in line with God's perspective?

Finally, I believe one must know God's word. How can one properly interpret if one does not know God's vocabulary, God's heart? At the United Methodist 2004 General Conference, a record number of translators registered to help Central Conference delegates understand the procedures and legislation through translation and interpretation. Translators could translate the words, but the process occasionally bogged down because words represented ideas and those ideas required some interpretation. Not only did translators need to understand "United Methodese," they needed to understand *Robert's Rules of Order*, and have knowledge of existing church policies to explain the changes. We, as Christians, need to have a solid understanding of God's word to interpret circumstances for ourselves as well as others.

The Son of Man is coming! This Advent season reminds us of our hope and expectations for the coming kingdom—a kingdom where peace, love, righteousness, and justice reign. Scripture offers these promises, as well as earthquakes, cosmic signs, and times of distress. Are you willing and able to accept and offer the Messiah's peace and hope to a world in despair and fear? Can you, with confidence, interpret the circumstances and events to others, always, like Jesus, showing how God ceaselessly works for us, God's beloved children? (Raquel Mull)

Preparing the Way

First in a Series of Four: Advent

Luke 1:5-25, 57-66

A man walked into a store seeking a product with which he thought he was familiar. He went to the appropriate section of the market, looked high and low, but could not spot the desired item. He inquired of a clerk, who immediately plucked the item from the very shelf where the man had been searching. Why couldn't the man see it himself? Because the packaging had been changed, that's why. It did not have the "look" he had been expecting.

That is precisely what happened when the long-anticipated Messiah arrived. The people did not recognize the Messiah because he did not have the "look" they had been expecting. What was needed was someone who would come ahead of the Messiah to point out differences between what they were expecting and what God was sending. That was the role played by John the Baptizer. And that is the role the season of Advent may play for us, preparing us to recognize the One whom God is sending.

People had been conditioned to expect a royal figure, a David-like figure who would be a kingly sort and a warrior who would lead them into battle, defeat the Romans, and who would assume the throne and restore Israel to her once and former glory. What they were being sent was a lowly humble baby, born in a manger, who would walk among them and tell stories to them; who would give them a glimpse of the Father; and who would tell them that the kingdom of God was already present among them and in them. No wonder they needed someone to prepare them, correct their theology, and show them a new paradigm.

Who was John? How would readers of the scriptures today know that they should pay attention to John? How should the people in John's day have known that they should pay attention to him? The answers to these questions are all wrapped up in the story of John's birth. It happened like this:

Zechariah and Elizabeth were of advanced years, but had no children. They had wanted children, but Elizabeth remained barren. Their life was not completely without fulfillment, for Zechariah was a priest serving the Lord. Once while serving at the temple, he was selected to burn the incense in the sanctuary. While alone in the Lord's presence, an angel of the Lord appeared to him and announced that his longing would be answered. He and Elizabeth would have a son.

Zechariah doubted the angel, pointing out that they were old, well beyond childbearing years. The angel seemed insulted that the divine word would be disputed, and told Zechariah that he would not be able to speak until these things had come to pass.

When Zechariah came out of the sanctuary, it was clear that something had happened to him. He had a dazed look and could not speak. When his duties ended, he and Elizabeth went home, and sure enough, Elizabeth was soon with child.

When their baby was born and it was time to circumcise and name him, everyone assumed the boy would be named after his father. But Elizabeth said, "No. His name is John." Zechariah's people argued with her, until Zechariah signaled for a writing tablet and spelled out, "His name is John." With that, his tongue was loosed, and Zechariah explained all that the angel had said.

The student of the scripture will recognize immediately that John is someone special. John is a special messenger sent from God. The people in John's day should have recognized the signs as well.

The first sign that invites our attention is the sign of people who are old and childless giving birth. In Genesis 12, we meet Abraham and Sarah, a childless couple advanced in years, who in chapter 21, give birth to Isaac; and the nation of Israel has its beginning. First Samuel opens with Hannah and Elkanah, a childless couple advanced in years, giving birth to Samuel, who becomes the new prophet of the Lord God, the one who will anoint Saul and later David to be Israel's first two kings. Luke begins his story with Zechariah and Elizabeth, a childless couple advanced in years, giving birth to John, who would prepare the way for the Lord. Each time we find in the scriptures a childless couple advanced in years giving birth, we can be sure God is at work. Pay attention, for God is breaking into history.

The second sign that should make us sit up and take notice is a new name being introduced into the story line. In Bible times, the firstborn male child would often be given the father's name. That would be the expectation especially when the child was long awaited, arriving after all hope had been abandoned that there would be any children. Therefore, when Abraham and Sarah finally had a child, one would not have expected the child to be named Isaac. When Elkanah and Hannah finally had a child, one would not have expected the child to be named Samuel. When Zechariah and Elizabeth finally had a child, one would not have expected the child to be named John. The introduction of a new name into the story line is a sign that God is at work and that we are to pay attention.

John bears watching. Pay attention to this one. God is breaking into history. John's role is to pave the way for the One who is coming. God is breaking into history in the person of John to give the people a "heads up" so they will recognize the One God is sending to them, even the Savior of the world. This is Advent, a season of preparation. Even God is making preparations.

In the remaining three weeks of Advent, we will examine John's preaching, trying to discern the nature of the One who is to come so that we will not miss him. (Douglas Mullins)

Worship Aids

Call to Worship

We have been seeking signs of your presence all of our lives. Open our eyes, open our ears, open our hearts to receive some word of hope as we anticipate the coming of the One whom you are sending.

Prayer of Confession

O Lord God, as we begin to prepare our hearts to receive the One whom you are sending, forgive us for all the times we have missed seeing you in our midst, for all the times we have doubted your presence, and for all the times we have failed to help others find their way. Forgive us, in the name of Jesus, the One who is coming. Amen.

Benediction

As we go forth from this holy place, let us look for signs of your coming, and let us be messengers, preparing the way for the One whom you are sending. In the name of the Father, and of the Son, and of the Holy Spirit, Amen. (Douglas Mullins)

DECEMBER 10, 2006

Second Sunday of Advent

Readings: Malachi 3:1-4; Luke 1:68-79; Philippians 1:3-11; Luke 3:1-6

Anticipating the Advent
Luke 1:68-79

Anticipation. You may remember the old ketchup commercial where Carly Simon sings the song "Anticipation" while the ketchup slowly hangs in midair. Anticipation should be a joyful feeling, not the feeling of anxiety and dread. But the feelings are similar in that whatever we expect, whether good or bad, is often surprising.

One of my favorite jokes illustrates the connection between anticipation and surprise. Back in the wild West, a stranger stands at a saloon bar. Suddenly a cowboy runs in screaming, "Hey, everybody, Big Bad John is coming to town." Several others exclaim: "Big Bad John is the meanest, toughest, biggest outlaw in the West. Let's run for it." Everyone heads for the door except the stranger and the bartender. The bartender says, "Are you deaf, mister? Big Bad John is coming!" The stranger replies, "I don't know who he is, but he can't be all that big and bad. I'm not afraid." So the stranger and the bartender wait. Soon the saloon doors fly off their hinges, and a mountain of a man stomps through the door. Covered with scars and sporting a scowl, he demands a drink. The bartender meekly complies. The stranger nervously thinks to himself, "Now I wish I had run away; this guy is the biggest, meanest-looking outlaw I've ever seen." The outlaw downs the drink in one gulp, slams it down on the bar, then turns and looks the stranger coldly in the eye to announce, "I don't know about you, stranger, but I'm gettin' outta here. I don't wanna be here when Big Bad John comes in!"

Anticipation is usually followed with surprise! Most jokes have that same structure: anticipation, then surprise. We know something is coming but then it was not what we expected. There is something delightful about the formula. Children know it. That's why they love opening

Christmas presents. They must look at those wrapped gifts for weeks of suspense, and only on Christmas morning do they receive the surprise.

If only we adults could reclaim some of the anticipation and surprise, the excitement and wonder, of a child's Christmas ... or of the very first Christmas. Admittedly, we know what is coming. We feel no anticipation about the coming of Christ; Christmas for some people is just another holiday, that same old time of year where we fight our way through stores, unpack our ornaments, and eat too much.

So we must work at it if we wish to reclaim the excitement of Advent. Paradoxically, one must prepare to be surprised. Pause for a moment and consider the hope, anticipation, and surprise of that first Christmas.

Consider Jewish history. From the days of Samuel, the event was predicted by the prophets and anticipated by the people. King David sang about the coming of the Messiah in the psalms; Isaiah wrote poetry about a Savior, a Prince of Peace; Jeremiah preached in the streets about the "righteous Branch," which would "sprout from David's line" (Jeremiah 31:15). The Israelites had been waiting centuries for a powerful liberator, redeemer, and healer. They anticipated—they prepared for—a great sign from God.

That sign came first to Elizabeth and Zechariah. Elizabeth was to be the mother of John the Baptist, who in turn would prepare the way for Christ. She was a faithful Jew, and she anticipated the coming of a Savior. Thus, when Zechariah told her she would have a baby—despite that she had been barren for years—she didn't doubt him. It was a surprise, and yet it had been anticipated. It was something wondrous and unexpected, and yet she was prepared. Elizabeth had anticipated something miraculous, just as the prophets had said.

This is true of the other characters in the Christmas story: Joseph, Mary, Simeon, the shepherds, and the magi. They all had made preparations, albeit with some angelic prodding, and thus, like Elizabeth and Zechariah, they were surprised yet prepared. The cast of the first Christmas drama had this in common: they all had anticipated the unexpected; they had hoped for the miraculous and by faith they had prepared. By the time John the Baptist cried out, "Prepare the way of the Lord," it was a family tradition!

So I'm asking you in this Advent season to shift your perspective. Don't view Christmas as a mundane or repetitious holiday. Don't expect the "same old, same old." Don't rule out the miraculous and the startling; prepare your mind for the serendipitous joy of new insights, liberation, and the fulfillment of hope. Prepare to be surprised.

We should move toward Christmas with wide eyes and an open heart, but too many of us face it with dread. Some folk still view Christmas as a chore—like the woman who had waited until the last minute to send Christmas cards. She rushed into a store and hurriedly bought a package of fifty Christmas cards without giving them a second look. In a panic to beat the post office closing, she addressed forty-nine of the fifty and signed them, never stopping to actually read the preprinted message inside. On Christmas Day, when things had quieted down, she chanced upon the leftover card and finally read the message that she had sent to forty-nine of her friends. Much to her dismay, it read: "This card is just to say, a big gift is on the way!" Suddenly she realized that forty-nine of her friends were anticipating a big gift from her–a gift that would never come!

A big gift is indeed on its way to you–the biggest and best in all human history. The gift of Christ at Christmas has come, and will come again. Anticipate that gift. Prepare for it. Don't let it get buried underneath the packages and tree trimmings. Don't walk past the eternal, oblivious in your worries of the temporal. Open your eyes. Watch for the signs. Bare and prepare your heart. The miracle is coming! (Lance Moore)

Out of the Wilderness

Second in a Series of Four: Advent

Luke 3:1-6

On the first Sunday of Advent, with the illustration of a man looking for a particular item in the store and being unable to locate it because it was not packaged in the way he was expecting, we discovered that if one is looking for the wrong thing, one may not recognize the right thing. If we are to recognize the Savior when he comes into our lives, it behooves us to be prepared. That was precisely the message of John the Baptizer as he stepped out of the wilderness.

John was a sight to behold. From the moment the angel of the Lord had informed Zechariah that he was going to have a son, John was dedicated to the Lord. In his special role, John would not cut his hair, he would live in the wild, he would eat off the land and dress with whatever he could find to wear. Accordingly, when John stepped out of the wilderness he was wearing some sort of garment made from a camel skin, he was unshorn and unshaven, and remnants of his "natural" diet (wild honey and bits of locust parts) lingered in his beard. It was not a pretty sight, but in those days it did inform those who saw John that he was a holy man of God.

In addition to John having been the firstborn child of aging parents and having been given a name new to the story, stepping out of the wilderness is something of a biblical sign that we are to sit up and take notice. When Moses arrived in Egypt to free God's people, he was stepping out of the wilderness. When Jesus began his ministry of teaching and healing, he stepped out of the wilderness (after facing temptations). Here we see John stepping out of the wilderness to begin his ministry of preaching and baptizing. We are to pay attention, for God is at work here.

John was sent into the world to prepare the way for the One who is coming. He would do that by challenging the *status quo*. At the outset we are told that there were powers to be challenged. Note the opening verses of today's text. Luke tells us that there were powers both political and religious. There were political rulers such as Emperor Tiberius, Pontius Pilate, Herod, Herod's brother Philip, and Lysanias. And there were religious powers, notably Annas and Caiaphas, the high priests. There are those who would claim that the only reason Luke listed all these names is to help us pinpoint the exact time John stepped out of the wilderness. Whereas it is true that naming those who were in power was a way of recording time, two or three names should have sufficed if that was all Luke had in mind. But no, Luke lists seven names. I think the reason he did so was to impress us with the formidable powers that John and later Jesus would face.

To this day, there are political powers without and religious powers within that must be challenged. Prayer in schools has fallen by the wayside. Religious symbols in public places are disappearing. And all the while, the media is making sordid behavior look commonplace.

Within the church we face powers that would limit our effectiveness as Christian witnesses. There is complacency. People are so comfortable with the way things are that they do not see any reason to challenge them. We hear the detractors saying, "It can't be done." Others will say, "But we've always done it this way." Still, others will counsel, "Don't rock the boat." There are also those who narrowly interpret the gospel and would restrict others' freedom of thought.

John stepped out of the wilderness to challenge great and powerful persons and institutions, and in doing so, provided us with a model of courage. "Speak the truth," John would tell us, "and when you do, stand up straight and tall, shout out your message no matter what the consequences." John would say, "When you speak the truth, never whisper, never let your head hang low, and never mumble." Note that when John stepped out of the wilderness to be an agent of change, he did not choose as his weapon a sword, but rather the word. Never underestimate the power of the spoken word.

Learn from John, and note further that the scriptures invite us to speak out, indeed, command us to speak out. The scriptures invite us to choose our words carefully, for our words may comfort, heal, soothe, work for justice, bring peace. To be sure, our actions are crucial to an effective witness. Our example is a powerful teacher. Still, a word inviting a neighbor to church may change a life. A word spoken in someone's defense may right an injustice. A word about Jesus may save a soul.

In the face of awesome power, armed with no weapon other than the spoken word, John began to preach. He reached back into scripture and singled out a word from the prophet Isaiah: "Prepare the way of the Lord." Translation? "Get ready. The One who is to come is almost here." We must be ready. We must make straight the paths of our lives. The roughest places in our lives are to be made smooth. We are to prepare for the arrival of the One who is to come by cleaning up our act.

You and I are up against powerful influences. There are those who would oppress and lead many astray. Lest we lose heart, let us pay attention to John the Baptizer, who would step out of the wilderness, and with nothing more than the spoken word would seek to set people on the straight and narrow. Let us prepare for the One who is coming by making smooth the rough places in our lives. (Douglas Mullins)

Worship Aids

Call to Worship

Leader: We come to prepare for the One who is to come.

People: Let us make straight the pathways of our lives.

Leader: Let us make smooth the roughest places in our lives.

People: Let us boldly speak words of comfort and peace and justice.

311

Prayer of Confession

O Lord God, we confess that our lives are not as clean and pure as we would wish them to be. We are not the people you have called us to be. Give us the courage to clean up our act that we may be ready to greet the One whom you are sending. Forgive us for failing to speak out when we might have made a difference. Grant us your peace, in the name of Jesus your Son. Amen.

Benediction

As we go forth from this holy place, let us go forth boldly to proclaim the good news that you are coming to redeem the world. In the name of the Father, and of the Son, and of the Holy Spirit, Amen. (Douglas Mullins)

DECEMBER 17, 2006

Third Sunday of Advent

Readings: Zephaniah 3:14-20; Isaiah 12:2-6; Philippians 4:4-7; Luke 3:7-18

The Tipping Point
Luke 3:7-18

Malcom Gladwell wrote a book titled *The Tipping Point*. "A tipping point," he says, "is a magic moment when an idea, trend, or social behavior crosses a threshold, tips the scales and spreads like wildfire."

The day that John baptized Jesus in the Jordan River was a "tipping point" for all of history. John called people to a new way of life. Luke writes, "John called on those whom he baptized to produce fruit in keeping with repentance." The people asked, "What should we do?" And John answered: "Whoever has two coats must share with anyone who has none; and whoever has food must do likewise.... Do not extort money from anyone by threats or false accusation, and be satisfied with your wages" (Luke 3:11, 14).

A tipping point is a magic moment, like when a person moves into a new and exciting phase of his or her life. It is an idea or a trend, which causes old tired churches smoldering in the ashes of past fires to ignite again and burst into flames.

Just as a single sick person with a cough can start an epidemic of the flu, so also can a small but precisely targeted push cause a fashion. For example, Brittany Spears appeared on stage one night early in her adolescent career in the 1990s with her midriff showing. Within a six-month period, kids all over America had taken scissors to their well-fitting shirts and were showing their navels to aghast parents. It was a tipping point, a watershed moment in the fashion industry. I'm not characterizing it as a wonderful moment, because now it seems it has led to showing it all, and how silly that looks.

Sometimes these tipping points can lead to great things and sometimes they lead to evil. I have wondered if maybe our nation is at a tipping point with regard to words like *integrity* and *honesty* and *right*. National

Public Radio recently carried an interview with a mom and her teenage son about downloading music from the Internet. The boy had downloaded thousands of songs without paying for them. His mother saw nothing wrong with the practice. She said: "If he were going to burn them to CDs and sell them, that would be inappropriate." Notice she did not say that would be wrong, but it would be "inappropriate." Do you see the problem here? The trend? Have we passed a "tipping point"? Are we now to begin to reap the destructive benefits of trends that have weakened such character traits as honesty, truthfulness, faithfulness, and integrity?

In 2003, my wife and I were in New York City during the blackout. I was impressed with the helpfulness of the New Yorkers in that time of uncertainty. In the 1970s a similar blackout led to muggings, looting of stores, and even murder on the street. But this time everybody pitched in to help everyone else. Ordinary citizens were directing traffic and helping older people. At first I thought that it was because of the emotions of post–September 11, when the evil side of human beings was so dramatically seen, but since then I have discovered another significant factor in the cultural shift that had occurred in New York.

In the 1980s crime escalated everywhere, but especially in New York City. By 1992, there were 2,154 murders and 626,000 other serious crimes in the city. But the situation tipped and by 1995 the crime rate had fallen by almost half. What happened that changed the culture of the city or tipped the scales of an escalating crime scene? Mayor Giuliani points to the "broken windows" theory: In the late 1980s criminologists were hired as consultants by the city, and they proposed that the city start fixing up broken windows that marked many buildings. If a window is broken and left unrepaired, people walking by will conclude that no one cares. Soon, more windows will be broken and the message goes out that anything goes. Thus broken windows, graffiti, and panhandling invite more serious crimes. It is a theory that an epidemic can be reversed, can be tipped, by tinkering with the smallest details of the immediate environment.

Jesus' life and ministry was a tipping point. Judaism had become an old tired religion of laws and rules. And Jesus said: "I have come not to abolish but to fulfill.... You have heard that it was said to those of ancient times, 'You shall not murder.' ... But I say to you ... first be reconciled to your brother or sister.... You have heard that it was said, 'An eye for an eye and a tooth for a tooth.' But I say to you, ... if anyone strikes you on the right cheek, turn the other also; ... and if anyone forces you to go one mile, go also the second mile.... You have heard that it was said, 'You shall love your neighbor and hate your enemy.' But I say to you, Love your enemies."

Assuming that in some ways we all recognize the magic possibilities of tipping points when we live a godly life, let me suggest the following:

Commit your life to Jesus Christ.

No change can be lasting without Jesus.

Let Christ into the center of your life.

Having committed your life to Jesus Christ and seeking to be obedient to his example of godly living, you will begin to see hardships as challenges, obstacles as opportunities, and impossible problems as new possibilities. Some of you might leave the familiar comfort zones of your lives and enter into some new phase of ministry. You might go to Zimbabwe. You might go to the neighbor just down the street. You might go to the person in the office down the hall.

Open your mind and heart today to God and the Holy Spirit and see if there will not be a magic moment of change, a tipping point, for you and for us all. Be baptized in the waters of possibility! (Henry E. Roberts)

The Things That Matter

Third in a Series of Four: Advent

Luke 3:7-14

John was the firstborn child of parents who were "getting on in years," as Luke so delicately put it. The name "John" was introduced as a new name in the story line. John stepped out of the wilderness to begin his ministry of preaching and baptizing. All of these signs tell us that God is at work. We can surely learn some lessons here.

John would prepare the way for the One who is coming by preaching. After suggesting that all persons would do well to put their lives in order, smooth out the rough places, walk the straight and narrow, John quickly focused on what was wrong with the religious establishment of his day.

John had about as much tact as he had grooming. We discover in today's text that when the people, his congregation if you will, had gathered at the river, he looked them in the eye for a long moment and then said in a loud voice, "You snakes!" Well, what Luke writes is that John said, "You brood of vipers!" Either way, it's not a sermon introduction designed to win converts. The amazing thing to me is that John got to preach the rest of his sermon. I'm surprised that anyone stayed around to hear what else he had to say. Perhaps they stayed because like so many people in our pews today they were certain he was speaking about someone else.

What followed was John's claim that the religious establishment was wrongly functioning on the basis of position and family or ancestry. John implied that God cares very little about hierarchy. God is not impressed with position or rank. What interests God, said John, is whether or not you are faithfully doing what you are supposed to be doing. If you are a bishop that means nothing unless you are being the very best bishop you can be. If you are a pastor, you are called to be the very best pastor you can be. If you are a lay leader or a caretaker of church property, it means doing your very best at your assigned task. People who rest on their laurels or pull rank to demonstrate their power or get their way hold no sway in the kingdom. God loves each one of us and when the judgment comes it is not based on position but on faithfulness.

Power and position don't work and neither does family heritage. John was confronting people who believed they were closer to God because they came from a people who had once been close to God. It doesn't work that way. Once you come of age you cannot ride on the strength of a former generation. We should probably breathe a sigh of relief over that. Whereas it might be nice to be blessed by someone's earlier accomplishment, it is good to hear John say that, the psalmist's lament aside, the sins of the father (or the virtues of the father) are not necessarily visited on children's children. That's not how it works. Each generation must stand on its own. We must claim responsibility for our own words and for our own actions. John preached that neither position nor ancestry matter in the kingdom. God's mercy belongs to all people. No one arbitrarily has an edge.

John preached that the kingdom of God is at hand. We should waste no time making ready. It's not about what your people did in the past; it's about what we are doing in the present time. Once John's audience understood that they would stand or fall on their own merits, they raised the question, "What are we to do?"

We may not rest on our laurels. It will not do to simply go through the motions of being religious. It will not do to blame someone else. We should ask, as John's congregation asked, "What are we to do?"

John said, "Whoever has two coats must share with anyone who has none; and whoever has food must do likewise." Of course, this isn't just about coats and food. It's about a spirit of generosity, about caring and sharing and compassion. This is about looking around and being aware of the needs of others, looking at ourselves and noting the manifold ways we have been blessed, and then sharing what we have. John told his audience that they were to be a generous people.

To the tax collectors in the congregation, John said, "Collect no more than the amount prescribed for you." Of course this isn't only about tax collecting. This is for everyone. John was telling anyone who would listen that we are to be honest in all our dealings. Honesty, trustworthiness, truthfulness are demanded by God. This is to be the way of God's people.

To the soldiers in the congregation, John said, "Do not extort money from anyone by threats or false accusation, and be satisfied with your wages." Of course, this isn't just for soldiers. This is for everyone. We are to treat others fairly and we are to be content with what God has given us. We are not to envy what others have. Do not steal what belongs to others. Be fair; be content.

The word is clear. John stepped out of the wilderness with a message from God. It is a message for people who think they are religious. Do not rely on position. Do not rely on family or ancestry. Do not rely on the past. Prepare yourself to greet the One who is coming by living in this present day, as God would have you live. Be generous, be honest, be fair, be content with what you have and with the role God has given you to play. May we be the kind of persons God would have us be and thereby be prepared when the One who is coming gets here. (Douglas Mullins)

Worship Aids

Call to Worship

Leader: The One who is coming draws near.

People: The kingdom of God is at hand.

Leader: Repent, and make the rough places in your lives smooth.

People: Let us walk the straight and narrow path.

Prayer of Confession

O Lord God, the day is growing closer. Still there is work to do. We are not the people you would have us be. We have not always spoken the truth. We have not always treated others with compassion and kindness.

We have not always cared enough. Forgive us, in the name of Jesus, the One who is coming. Amen.

Benediction

As we go forth, let us prepare for his coming by being generous, honest, and kindly people, that the world may be a better place, and that others may come to know you. In the name of the Father, and of the Son, and of the Holy Spirit, Amen. (Douglas Mullins)

DECEMBER 24, 2006

❧❧❧

Fourth Sunday of Advent

Readings: Micah 5:2-5a; Luke 1:47-55; Hebrews 10:5-10; Luke 1:39-45, (46-55)

The Time Has Come
Luke 1:39-45, (46-55)

The birth of Jesus is, no doubt, the most joyous and celebrated of all holidays in our culture. Families get together, gifts are exchanged, and a good time is usually had by all. Even people who know or believe little or nothing about Jesus celebrate his birth. Most people think of Christmas as a singular event. It just hangs out there by itself and when it is over, it is over until the same time next year.

Although the birth of Jesus was a momentous event, it was not a singular event. Jesus' coming has deep roots in the religious and cultural tradition of the Jewish people; and the fact that he came has had ever widening ramifications that show no sign of abating even after two thousand years.

Who was this Galilean peasant, whose obscure beginnings got connected with so much from the past, and whose brief life has so profoundly influenced so many for so long? Who was this stranger from Galilee about whom we know so much, and so little? Why is it that what he said and did has given so much hope to so many regarding this life and life in the world to come?

The Messiah had been expected for a long time. As a nation, and as individuals, the Jews had been hoping and praying for his appearance for hundreds of years. Ever since the Jewish people got into so much trouble that they realized their condition was beyond human help, they had been expecting divine intervention into human affairs in the form of a messiah. Their expectation of a coming messiah was about as intense as an unrealized intangible could be. Mothers prayed that their unborn would be a male child, and that he would be the Messiah. The expectation was not casual.

When times were good the expectation was less intense. Like most of us they did not feel the need for divine assistance when they were getting on quite well by themselves. The intensity of expectation was in direct proportion to the degree of national and personal difficulty they were experiencing at any given time. But, the expectation was always there, albeit at times in the background. When times were tough, they expected the imminent arrival of divine help. Like present-day Christians, when in trouble, the first words out of their mouths were: "Dear God, where are you?" It became increasingly obvious to them, as it does to us, that God's timetable does not necessarily correspond with our timetable.

Crises came and went and no messiah. False messiahs came and went. In every age there are religious charlatans who exploit for their own selfish purposes the simple faith of the naive and desperate. There is always a following. People who live in the zone of desperation will grasp at any straw of hope and help. They are blind to the incongruity of religious leaders who drive expensive cars, own airplanes, and live in million-dollar houses while they tell the story of a man who had no place to lay his head. The principle is the same in every age. Only the setting is different. There were disappointments and dashed hopes, but the false prophets in any age usually have enough support to make the next payment or move to the next town.

There were many widely divergent concepts of what the Messiah would be like when he came. For the most part their hopes and dreams tended toward a political and religious "strong man," a warrior-like messiah who would destroy the enemies of Israel and restore Israel to the power and splendor of the reign of David. They never dreamed that the Messiah would come when and as he did. Only Isaiah came close with his "suffering servant" who would be a light to all nations, and this was a fragmented glimpse that had little ideological support by the Jewish people (Isaiah 53). The Messiah is on his way! The time is drawing near that the hope of the ages will be fulfilled, but in a most unexpected manner.

The epicenter of Christmas is the birth of Jesus. Even those who know nothing but the solitary fact of his birth can be blessed by the event, but blessing and insight await those who know how it all came to pass. No one puts it all together in such a fetching story as Luke. Luke takes the loose ends of strange and obscure events occurring in the lives of the most unlikely people and leads us unerringly to Bethlehem, a stable, and the manger in which the newborn Messiah was laid by a wide-eyed teenage mother as a puzzled, but faithful, Joseph looked on.

It started in this fashion. An old priest named Zechariah whose wife, Elizabeth, was barren, drew the honored duty of burning incense to the Lord. While performing this duty the angel Gabriel appeared to Zechariah and informed him that his wife, though advanced in age, would bear a son who was to be named John. Because Zechariah doubted this promise he was struck speechless until "the day these things came to pass."

In the sixth month of Elizabeth's pregnancy (which she had kept secret), an angel appeared to a teenage girl named Mary and informed her that she would bear a son without benefit of an earthly father, who was to be called "Jesus." The angel informed Mary of the pregnancy of Elizabeth, her kin. So, in the sixth month of Elizabeth's pregnancy, Mary came to visit. When Mary greeted Elizabeth the baby leaped in her womb and Elizabeth was filled with the Holy Spirit. The unborn babe is prophetically aware of the unborn Messiah. The future mother of the forerunner then recognizes the future mother of the Messiah. Elizabeth said to Mary: "Blessed are you among women, and blessed is the fruit of your womb." These two women share a secret that the world has waited long to know. As they revel in what they have come to know, Mary speaks a song of praise that has more to do with her unborn son than herself. It is Mary's song. We call it "The Magnificat," from its Latin name.

The song thanks and praises God for including her in this unfolding divine drama. As Mary sings of the power of God, we can read what she says to be the power to be exercised by her unborn son. It portends a revolution and a reversal of present reality. This is the most comprehensive statement of liberation theology in the Bible:

> He has shown strength with his arm;
> he has scattered the proud in the thoughts of their hearts.
> He has brought down the powerful from their thrones,
> and lifted up the lowly;
> he has filled the hungry with good things,
> and sent the rich away empty.
> He has helped his servant Israel,
> in remembrance of his mercy,
> according to the promise he made to our ancestors,
> to Abraham and to his descendants forever. (Luke 1:51-55)

On which side of this revolution do you wish to be when it comes to pass? (Thomas Lane Butts)

Someone Greater Is Coming

Fourth in a Series of Four: Advent

Luke 3:15-18

All the signs tell us that John the Baptizer is to be watched. God is at work in him. God is breaking into history. However, although John was sent by God, John is not the main attraction. He is the forerunner. He is the one who comes to prepare the way for the One who is coming. John is the one who will preach a message designed to prepare people to recognize and greet the Messiah when he shall appear. John preached a sermon that, if a title had to be printed in a worship folder, would have been called, "Someone Greater Is Coming."

John's audience, which seemed so attentive at first, turned out not to be paying attention at all. In the Fourth Gospel (John 1:19-28), we find the Jews sending messengers to John asking, "Who are you?" Isn't that rich? John was the messenger sent by God and the Jews were sending messengers asking John who he was. Had they been paying attention they would have remembered the words of Isaiah, who said, "A voice cries out: 'In the wilderness prepare the way of the LORD, make straight in the desert a highway for our God'" (Isaiah 40:3). John was only echoing their own prophet.

John was the messenger who cried out in the wilderness, telling them to prepare the way for the Lord. And they sent messengers asking, "Who are you anyway? Are you the one for whom we have been waiting? Are you the Messiah?" John, with just a hint of mirth in his eyes said, "No," as if to say, "Guess again." "No," said John. "I am not the one for whom you have been waiting. Someone greater is coming; I am not even good enough to bend down and untie his sandals." So, if we were to contrast John with the one who is coming, how do they differ? How is Jesus greater than John?

For one thing, John would baptize with water. He would invite people into the river, and would splash water on them as if to rinse off some of the dirt from the past. But Jesus would baptize with the Spirit and with fire. The fire, like a refiner's fire, would burn away every blemish and would purify. This cleansing would not be superficial, but would clean through and through. It would be as if we had never sinned. And Jesus' baptism would bring the gift of the Spirit, God present with us to guide us and comfort us. Truly, Jesus is Emmanuel, which means, "God is with us."

A second contrast hinges on the manner of John and Jesus. John stepped out of the wilderness and in a loud voice said, "Repent!" This sounded a lot like, "Repent, or else." John would seem to be trying to frighten or badger people into the kingdom. Jesus would take us by the hand and gently lead us into the kingdom. Jesus would be like a shepherd whose sheep know his voice and would follow when he gently calls, "Come, come."

In the third place, John was going to change the world by speaking to the individual, washing clean the individual, preparing the individual to greet the one who is coming. Although Jesus came offering people a personal relationship with the Father, he also offered them something more. He offered fellowship one with another. Jesus knew that salvation is not only an individual thing, but a social thing as well. He surrounds us with a supporting group "the church" where we can worship together, encourage one another, and pray for one another. Jesus would even call nations to be accountable for their faithfulness. Whole nations are to fall on their knees and become followers of him. Jesus would send people out to make disciples of all people, seeming to make us responsible for the welfare of one another.

A fourth difference in the way of John versus Jesus has to do with John's demand for repentance now. Jesus realized that great results do not often come suddenly. Reaching goals may take time, lots of time. The immediate question, as the apostle Paul would later clarify, is not, "Are you saved?" as so many ask today; but rather, "Are you *being* saved?" John Wesley, the founder of the Methodist societies, would never have asked, "Are you perfect?" But he did ask, "Are you *going on to* perfection?" What matters, Jesus would say, is whether you are a better person today than you were a year ago, or last week, or yesterday. Perfection is elusive. Salvation is a process. Do not worry so much about your flaws, but do ask if you are making progress.

Luke, as illustrated in John's preaching, wants you to expect the right things. Our expectations always color what we see. If we enter the hospital with some condition, but expect that everything will be just fine, our chances of everything coming out just fine are increased tenfold. When, as a college student, I sold shirts in a department store, everyone who came through the door looked like a customer. When I became a store detective, everyone who came through the door looked like a thief. What you expect makes a difference.

Whether you expect to meet the Christ this season or think that none of this makes any difference and that this is all just one more "ho-hum" tour through the seasons of the church year, you are correct. John was expecting the One who is coming. John was begging us to expect the One who is coming.

Do you expect to discover the Christ in fresh new ways in your life as these days of Advent give way to the celebration of the nativity? If so, you won't be disappointed. You will know that someone greater has come. May his peace be yours. (Douglas Mullins)

Worship Aids

Call to Worship

Leader: We have been making our preparations.

People: They are preparations of our homes and our hearts.

Leader: Our anticipation is mounting as we await his coming.

People: Come, Lord Jesus!

Prayer of Confession

O Lord God, purify our thoughts; they are never as pure as we would wish. Cleanse our minds; they are never as clean as you demand. Open our hearts; we need to make room for the coming of your Son. Forgive all that has stood in the way of fully welcoming him as the Lord of our lives. Forgive us in the name of the One who is coming. Amen.

Benediction

As we go forth, let us expect great things to happen in our lives and in our world, for the One who is coming as the Savior of all is almost here. In the name of the Father, and of the Son, and of the Holy Spirit, Amen. (Douglas Mullins)

DECEMBER 31, 2006

First Sunday after Christmas Day

Readings: 1 Samuel 2:18-20, 26; Psalm 148; Colossians 3:12-17; Luke 2:41-52

Who Are Those Remarkable Children?
1 Samuel 2:18-20; Luke 2:41-52

Picture in your mind a child you know who is remarkable. It can be your own child, or someone else's—but focus your mind's eye on a remarkable child. What makes that boy or girl so special? Is he or she a gifted musician or student or athlete? Is he or she particularly mature for his or her age? Is he or she sensitive and articulate or easygoing and a pleasure to be around?

Our Old Testament and gospel lessons this morning invite us to focus on two remarkable children in scripture, Samuel and Jesus. Samuel was the first son of Hannah and Elkanah. Like some couples you may know, Hannah and Elkanah were unable to have children, and this grieved them deeply. Hannah was even taunted for her barrenness. Finally, one year, when they had traveled to Shiloh for the yearly sacrifice, Hannah reached the breaking point. She became so distraught that she couldn't eat, and she couldn't stop weeping. Finally, she decided that she would present herself before the Lord, where she poured out all of her grief and pain to God. Hannah pledged that if God would give her a son, she would return the child to God's service as a Nazirite priest. God heard Hannah's prayer that day and granted her a son. And Hannah kept her word. As soon as Hannah weaned the child she brought him to the temple for the priests to raise and train.

When our story opens today, Hannah and Elkanah have once again arrived in Shiloh for the yearly sacrifice. Oh, how they must have looked forward to those trips—for the chance to hold their beloved son and visit with him. Hannah had worked diligently beforehand, making clothing to give Samuel—and I'll bet there were other gifts as well. Imagine the parent's pride as they watched their remarkable child ministering before the Lord.

Most of us are probably more familiar with Jesus' story. The particular narrative we heard earlier is significant because it is the only story we have about Jesus between his birth and his baptism nearly thirty years later. In this story, Jesus' family, like Samuel's, had traveled for a significant holiday. As we join the text, Jesus' family had traveled with a large caravan from Nazareth to the temple in Jerusalem to celebrate the Passover. After the festivities, the group began the long journey home. Although it seems strange to us that it took Mary and Joseph a whole day to miss Jesus, this would not have been unusual in his time. It was not uncommon for children to visit or travel with other families in the same caravan, and Jesus' parents would not have been neglectful to assume that Jesus was among the group.

We can all imagine Mary and Joseph's panic when they discovered that Jesus was missing. All of us who have temporarily lost a child can remember the fear that grips our hearts and the adrenaline rush that compels us to search frantically for our child. Mary and Joseph leave the caravan and rush back to Jerusalem, where it takes them three days of diligent searching to finally find Jesus. While they had been madly searching, Jesus had been sitting in the temple, absorbing the teaching of the rabbis. Luke tells us that all who observed Jesus were amazed at his level of understanding and at the depth of the questions and answers Jesus shared with the teachers. But Jesus' parents were not amused or impressed. Understandably, they scolded him for the great anxiety he had caused them. Jesus, who does not appear to have been willfully disobedient, seemed nonplussed. "Why were you searching for me? Did you not know that I must be in my Father's house?" Jesus asked.

Scholars observe that up to this point, all the signs of Jesus' special nature or mission have been to or through others—the angel, Mary, Elizabeth and Zachariah, the shepherds. But now, Jesus is beginning to have his own awareness. There were, in Jesus, vague stirrings of his own identity, if not his vocation. Jesus was a remarkable child.

But were Jesus and Samuel really so remarkable in this regard? Of course, Jesus was truly remarkable. He was God's Son, as an adult he was both fully human and fully divine, the One who came to be God with us and our redeemer. But at this point in Jesus' childhood, and in Samuel's, are these events so unusual? Perhaps we are in error in believing that they are.

If we are honest, in most of our congregations we don't have very high expectations for our children. Instead of working to incorporate them into the full life of the body of Christ, instead of allowing them to minister before the Lord as Samuel did, we let them light the candles, we have the children's choir sing occasionally, and we let them participate in the annual Christmas pageant. We don't expect them to be able to accomplish much more. Instead of allowing them to have in-depth dialogue with the rabbis and teachers as Jesus did, we whisk them out to children's church because we don't expect them to be able to sit through "the real sermon."

Church-growth folk tell us that for every three ministers who are retiring, there is only one young person entering the ministry. Although there are many reasons for this, a significant one is that in many of our churches, we no longer expect God to call and we no longer expect or encourage our young people to hear and respond when God speaks. Jesus and Samuel had special callings, but they did not hear them in a vacuum. They were surrounded by wise and discerning adults who helped them listen and respond. When was the last time a member of our congregation experienced a call to ministry? When was the last time we listened and encouraged? Stop and get a picture in your mind with me. Who are those remarkable children in our midst? (Tracy Hartman)

Do We Believe in Promises Anymore?
Acts 2:38-40

A faithful Roman Catholic friend, poking fun at contemporary worship practices, told me the story of a young priest whose promise got him into trouble. He promised the leaders of his congregation that he would increase attendance if they would allow him to make some changes. Tempted by such a promise, they agreed with a mixture of hesitancy and expectation. First, the priest removed the front pews and replaced them with comfortable theater seating to encourage people to sit at the front. Next, he dismissed the choir and added upbeat vocalists and a praise band. Finally, the change that got him into real trouble was his addition of a drive-through confessional. The leaders could tolerate the concept, especially when it was noted that the number of confessions had doubled. It was the sign outside near the driveway that disturbed them. It read, "Stop and tell or go to hell!"

Promises can bring hope or sorrow. Some may read today's text as merely an account of the first converts to the Christian faith. I think that there is also an important word here about the integrity of God's promise of salvation, and what that says to us about the promises we make and the promises we keep.

Genuine promises are realistic. It is absurd to make a promise that one cannot possibly hope to fulfill. Such promises deliver false hope and ultimate disappointment. They rob genuine promises of their true power and expectation. The first year I began serving as pastor of a large church, there was a man who submitted an enormously generous pledge card in support of the church budget campaign. I was thrilled! I thought that we had put our budget goal well over the top! A church financial leader told me not to get my hopes up. "He turns that in every year," the leader told me, "yet he gives less than some of our poor widows." How sad that this man had become known not for his service or his gifts but for his empty promises. Promises that are unrealistic do not take into consideration the effort and resources necessary to fulfill them.

In this passage from the Acts of the Apostles, Peter proclaims the promise of God to save those who turn to God. This is a passionate statement testifying to a powerful God. God always keeps God's promise! God can do it, so God promises. Genuine promises are realistic. This promise is so wondrous because it points to God's ability to redeem us with immeasurable hope that is rooted in unconditional love.

In his admonition, Peter exhorts the potential converts to "Save yourselves from this corrupt generation." Why did Peter consider the generation corrupt? It was a time when people focused on religious legalism rather than grace and faith. Love was lacking in the practice of faith. Religious leadership was generally self-serving rather than selfless. Religious piety and exacting religious legalism were given far more importance than a life of grace. All of this missed the true mark of God's faithful—the love of others. People were missing the true nature of God's promise. When the promises of God become obscured by our own shadowy practices, truth is buried. What is left behind is dead religion and empty faith.

Genuine promises are realistic. God promised because God can and does deliver. The lesson for us is plain: don't promise more than you can deliver.

Genuine promises have value. Genuine promises truly mean something, so those making them take them seriously. I have told my youngest son that I plan to be at each of his basketball games barring a significant unforeseen conflict. I do not wish to disappoint my son, so I work to keep the promise that I made. There have been many circumstances where I might have broken the promise. I have missed some meetings, refused free tickets to another event, and declined to officiate at the wedding of a former parishioner. My promise has cost something. There was some sacrifice involved not only for me but also for others influenced by my choice to make the promise. I made it realistically. I did not promise to attend every game; I promised to attend every game that I reasonably could. Still, in order for the promise to have value, exceptions must be rare and with true merit.

When you think of a significant promise or vow, you are likely to think of wedding vows. Both the church and society places value on relationships, yet the rate of divorce leaves many fearful for the integrity of marriage. Because we value something, we take care of it. Because we value relationships, we must be willing to work to make them strong.

Genuine promises cause growth. Genuine promises stretch us just a bit. They may lead us out of our comfort zones into an area where discomfort yields great reward. We start a new year with resolutions or goals. Perhaps you have made a serious soul-searching assessment of your life. You want to go somewhere, be something, do something, change something, aspire to something. This need not be an idle wish but an active desire. You can make a promise to yourself that is realistic (but don't expect to be a surgeon if you faint at the sight of blood). You develop a plan to fulfill that promise, and you follow up on your action plan. This is where the fruits of growth are realized. Years of study and sacrifice yield educational credentials and career opportunities. Sacrifice and wise stewardship yield financial objectives and economic health.

A young couple stands before a congregation with their newborn child. They promise to raise the child in a Christian home and live in the way of the gospel. They promise to pray for and with the child that this little one might one day accept the gift of salvation. It is a genuine promise, but how can anyone know fully the consequences such a bold promise might entail? This is why promises are made as an act of faith and trust. We are mortal beings pursuing an immortal journey. We have been given great gifts and possibilities. God's promises are true. Claim them. Celebrate them. The promise of God reminds us of what genuine promises are meant to be. (Gary G. Kindley)

Worship Aids

Call to Worship

Leader: We gather for worship and to claim the promises of God.

People: We come to be reminded of the grace that sustains and the mercy that forgives.

Leader: We come to renew our covenant as followers of the Christ.

People: Blessed is the name of the Lord and greatly to be praised! Amen.

Unison Invocation

We have come today, O God, seeking your grace and claiming your healing power. We have journeyed through another week of life, with both its joys and blessings, and its hardship and trials. Wash us with your Holy Spirit and renew us for the journey of life in the name of the Christ. Amen.

Benediction

Go forth as a people of promise, claiming the power God gives you. Live a life of grace, mercy, and justice in the name of Jesus Christ. Amen. (Gary G. Kindley)

III. APPENDIX

SPECIAL SERVICES

Funerals

General

Greeting

Dear friends, we have gathered here to worship God and to witness to our faith as we celebrate the life of (Name). We come together in grief, acknowledging our human loss, but also in gratitude, thankful to God for the gift of (Name's) life in our lives. In this hour, may God the Holy Spirit search our hearts and tend our souls, that in our pain we may find comfort, in our sorrow hope, and in the face of death experience more deeply than ever before the abiding assurance of resurrection through Jesus Christ our Lord. Amen.

Greeting

Dear friends, we are here today to praise God, and to witness to our faith as we celebrate the life of (Name), who has gone the way of all the earth. Brothers and sisters, let your hearts be large today, for they must hold many things: lament and thanksgiving, anguish and comfort, regret and surrender. Let your hearts be large, for they must feel at once the sting of death and the hope and promise of resurrection, both for this one we have loved and lost and for ourselves.

For the promise of the gospel is for us and for all, that God's love is greater than death by far, and that those who are lost from us are never lost from God but held forever in God's love and care.

Let your hearts be large today, and in the midst of sorrow find your voice for singing together a song of faith.

Gathering Prayer

O God, who gave us birth and walks with us through all our years, we trust that you also meet us at the time of death, when the shadows lengthen, and the busy world is hushed, and we draw our final breath.

Grant us to know your presence in this hour, that as we shrink before the silencing mystery of death, we may sense the light of your grace leading us to everlasting life.

Speak to us once more your solemn and comforting message of life and death and life beyond death, and let us hear once more your enduring promise that nothing in life or in death will be able to separate us or those we love from your great love in Christ Jesus our Lord. Amen.

John 14

These words from John 14 are Jesus' last words with his disciples before his departure, before the cross, before his ascension to God in the resurrection. This section of John has long been known as the "farewell discourse." It is appropriately named when we consider the literal meaning of that first word: fare well.

The farewell discourse of Jesus is more than just "good-bye," "so long," "see you around." Jesus' words are intended to give assurance to his disciples, to help them to *fare well* in the face of what is coming, which is, in this instance, his going away from them. Three assurances are given in his words to these disciples, soon to be bereft of their teacher and friend. These are assurances we might well overhear ourselves and, at a time of saying good-bye to a loved one in death, take as our own.

First, you will fare well because "the Advocate, the Holy Spirit, whom the Father will send in my name, will teach you everything." In Greek, the comforter is the *parakaleo*, literally, the "side-caller." The Spirit will provide you comfort and a peace deeper than any peace the world can give. I like to think of that otherworldly peace as a sort of surrender, a sense that in spite of what has happened, in spite of this grief, in spite of the fact that one I love has gone away, all shall be well.

Second, you will fare well because you will remember. Jesus says the Spirit will "remind you of all that I have said to you"; remind us of the assurances of Scripture, remind us of the presence of the living Christ through this and every circumstance; and yes, remind us of the one we have loved and lost, the gifts of her life to us and to the world.

Sometimes we recall a life only in strained or painful ways, having to fetch short pieces of string from here or there in our mixed memories, then tie them together to make any sense of that person's life, to see it whole. At other times, we have a wealth of tender and beautiful memories with which to weave into a tapestry of remembrance and affection. In either instance, the Spirit will bring your loved one to your remembrance and help you to come to terms with her life, and with her death.

Finally, you will fare well because there is a place that is prepared for us, a place of rest, of joy. As Tolkien once put it, "beyond the walls of this world." "And if I go and prepare a place for you, Jesus says, I will come again and will take you to myself, that where I am, there you may also be." When I hear these words, I remember those of John Greenleaf Whittier: "Life is ever lord of Death, / And Love can never lose its own!" ("Snow-Bound" in *The Complete Poetical Works of Whittier* [Cambridge Edition; Boston: Houghton Mifflin, 1894], 401).

And so we say, fare well to you, *(Name)*. And fare well to you, her loved ones. The Spirit is with us to comfort and encourage, to mend and to heal. The memories we knit together from a lifetime shared will sustain and hearten us. And the life of the one we cherish—and our own—will be held forever in God's eternal love.

Prayer of Thanksgiving

God of love, we thank you for all with which you have blessed us to this day: for the gift of joy and days of health and strength, and for the gifts of your abiding presence and promise in days of pain and grief. We praise you for home and friends and loved ones, and for *(Name)*, loving wife, devoted mother, dedicated teacher, sister of the church, daughter of the kingdom. Above all we thank you for Jesus, who knew our griefs as well as our joys, who died our death and rose for our sake, and holds forth to us the promise of our own resurrection.

Into your hands, O merciful Savior, we commend your servant, *(Name)*. Acknowledge, we pray, a sheep of your own fold, a lamb of your own flock, a child of your own redeeming. Receive her into the arms of your mercy. Raise her on the wings of eagles, bear her on the breath of dawn, make her to shine like the sun, and hold her in the palm of your hand. This we pray through Christ our risen Lord. Amen.

Death of a Child

Prayer

Loving God, we call upon you, our eternal parent, who has designed us and created us in your image. We come to you today in great sorrow for the life that we had so anticipated sharing for years to come. We ask you to know the sadness of your children gathered in this room today. Hearts are burdened as these friends assemble to comfort parents, brothers, sisters, grandparents, and one another. We are aware of your unfaltering love for us even as we release this child from our presence into your loving and welcoming arms.

We are comforted to know that your arms surround (*Child's Name*) just as your Spirit surrounds us in this hour of grief. Parent God, be with the parents and family members who have learned to love (*Child's Name*) so deeply. Comfort them in their pain. Extend your comforting hand, dear God, and bring strength and courage to all of us gathered in your presence today. We seek your guidance to help endure this loss. Let us see the vision of hope beyond our current sense of hopelessness. In the name of Jesus, the great comforter and teacher, we pray. Amen.

Scripture Suggestions

Matthew 18:3-4, 10, 14
Matthew 19:14
Psalm 23
Romans 8:35, 37-39
Revelation 7:17

Sermon

Friends, we are God's children and today we gather to worship him. We are here to witness to our faith even as we mourn the death of (*Child's Name*). All of us stand beside (*Parent's Names*), the loving parents who grieve this loss. We are also here to celebrate the brief time we enjoyed (*Child's Name*) and are comforted by the Gospel writer Mark who described the love of Jesus for children when he said, "And he took them up in his arms, laid his hands on them, and blessed them" (Mark 10:16).

It is that very descriptive picture that provides the comfort of knowing that (*Child's Name*) stands courageously before God and is blessed by God. It is a picture that assures us that we have a reason to grieve, and we have a reason to celebrate. Friends, we are to move beyond the grief that weighs on our hearts this moment and rejoice as (*Child's Name*) is welcomed into heaven. All of you are witnesses to the love of God and to the eternal life we will each treasure together in God's presence one day.

It is important that we allow ourselves the freedom to grieve the void that is left in the midst of all who love (*Child's Name*).

- Some of you may feel some resentment toward God for allowing this to happen. It is normal to feel resentment.
- Some of you will say that you do not understand why (*Child's Name*) has died. It is normal to sense a lack of understanding.
- Others will secretly question God as to why he did not take your life instead of (*Child's Name*). It is normal to question.

All the things that are normal in the grieving process can only be overcome by the realization that God has given us free will. As a result of that gift, we know that life comes and goes, and life moves on the absence of those we love.

Be assured that God does not love (*Child's Name*) more or less than any of us who worship him here. This death affirms that God has granted humankind a freedom to choose the ways we react to events—good or bad—that occur in our mental pictures of God's creation.

We must all believe that God was with (*Child's Name*) when he walked through the "shadow of the valley of death." God comforted this child in the shadowed valley, and God comforts this child in his gracious presence now.

We would not grieve if we had not experienced the joy of being with (*Child's Name*) during the eyeblink of time. Because we had (*Child's Name*) among us, we celebrate his life as a gift from God. We will praise God for the gift that was wrapped so preciously at birth, opened by the awe of the world around him, and placed in the memories of all who enjoyed the wonder of childhood laughter and the quest for knowing.

Today Jesus is celebrating a homecoming even as we say good-bye. We find comfort in the fact that we are welcomed into eternal happiness just as (*Child's Name*) is welcomed into the presence of our heavenly parent, God. It is in the middle of all the grief and lack of understanding that we find our God, who comforts us.

God makes a promise to us all. John writes about that promise in the book of Revelation saying

> The Lamb at the center of the throne will be their shepherd,
>   and he will guide them to springs of the water of life,
>   and God will wipe away every tear from their eyes.
> (Revelation 7:17)

Let it be so for all of us who celebrate the life of (*Child's Name*).

Prayer

God, who gives life and receives life into your presence, hear our prayer. Send your comfort to the family and friends who worship you even as they say farewell to (*Child's Name*). Allow them to feel the comfort provided as you wrap loving arms around them. Welcome this child into your presence and let us know that your love and faithfulness to us endures forever. In the name of Jesus the Christ we pray. Amen. (Ted L. McIlvain)

Unexpected or Difficult Death/Suicide

Call to Worship

Worship the Lord in the Lord's holy place. We come as mortals to find life's meaning in the midst of meaninglessness. O God, help us now in our hour of need. Let us hear the life-giving word that you alone offer. Amen.

Scripture Lessons (Two or more may be used)

Jeremiah 15:15-21
Psalm 13 (principal reading)
Revelation 21:1-7
John 16:19-28

Pastoral Prayer

Let us pray: Gracious God, we have tried to be as faithful as we can, but being faithful in the world is a difficult task. Now that we have entered a time of wilderness, our faith is shaken. So we return to you this day, O Creator, you who have created us and given the boundaries within which we find our life's deepest purpose. Help us now, for you alone are our refuge and strength.

Grant us your blessing in this hour, and help us put our trust and confidence in your wisdom alone. Grant us the ability to move through this desert time and come out on the far side with our faith renewed and our belief intact. Heal us in our pain, through Jesus Christ our Lord. Amen.

Sermon

Sisters and brothers we have gathered here to say our earthly good-byes to *(Name)*, whom we have all loved well. His departure from earthly reality will leave a void in all our lives, but we gather to draw from the faith the church baptized him into and from which we may all draw strength. Listen to the word of the psalter with glad and generous hearts.

How long, O LORD? Will you forget me forever?
How long will you hide your face from me?
How long must I bear pain in my soul,
and have sorrow in my heart all day long?
How long shall my enemy be exalted over me?
Consider and answer me, O LORD my God!
Give light to my eyes, or I will sleep the sleep of death,
and my enemy will say, "I have prevailed";

> my foes will rejoice because I am shaken.
> But I trusted in your steadfast love;
>   my heart shall rejoice in your salvation.
> I will sing to the LORD,
>   because he has dealt bountifully with me. (Psalm 13)

Psalm 13 begins with a series of rhetorical questions. The psalmist asked these questions not so much for an answer but rather to make a statement. From the psalmist's perspective, Yahweh causes the petitioner's predicament. The psalmist experiences disorientation when God is absent. Life appears as a bundle of tribulations and the psalmist holds Yahweh responsible. It may shock us in the pietistic tradition that a prayer could produce such outpourings of anger and wrath toward God. If a person carefully reads the individual lament Psalms, however, he or she soon discovers just how angry a pious Jew can be when addressing God. Without relationship there exists no such thing as anger. The screaming and vigorous outpouring toward Yahweh suggests that the pray-er is serious about his relationship with the Almighty.

I want to suggest that there are not a few of us here who feel this way. We are angry, disappointed, and frustrated about our friend, (Name); cut down in the prime of life by something we cannot yet understand. We are, in a sense, overwhelmed by the thought of a good and faithful person plucked from our midst for no particularly good or logical reason. Most of us are a little too wary of the wrath of God to admit that we are angry with God. Yet, deep down within our beating hearts a subtle but insistent voice cries out: Why? Essentially, this is what the psalmist cries out, and, if you are feeling like me right now, you, too, have this same cry stuck sideways somewhere down in your throat!

Many pastors know the experience of curling our toes over the edge of a six-foot deep hole in an unfamiliar cemetery, searching for words to comfort a grieving family. Too often, however, church folk and we pastors are far removed emotionally from the experience.

We have had a lot of time since last Thursday afternoon to think about (Name) and his untimely death. When I got the call, like many of you, I simply sat down and wondered how such news could be possible. You know and I know, however, that (Name)'s death is not a death many of us can dodge emotionally. A death like this one hits home with an unusual piercing wound—or perhaps a stony thud. This is interesting to me, because in my experience, (Name) was about as objective and logical about life as anyone I have ever known. Yet, (*Name*)'s death strikes us with an emotionally odd ruthlessness. I don't even know what to feel.

In our honest moments we do know that we are now a bundle of conflicted emotions that we can barely identify, but identify them we must. Perhaps we feel varying degrees of fear, anxiety, remorse, separation, dread, anger, regret, depression, confusion, and, perhaps, even withdrawal. These feelings are natural. God gives us these feelings, for none of us can think our way through moments like these, as much as we must feel our way through them with prayer and supplication to God. We seek comfort, and we seek peace. But most of all, we seek a hope that does not disappoint us.

The gospel has a word for us now. Paul writes the word to the church at Thessalonica:

> But we do not want you to be uninformed, brothers and sisters, about those who have died, so that you may not grieve as others do who have no hope. For since we believe that Jesus died and rose again, even so, through Jesus, God will bring with him those who have died. (1 Thessalonians 4:13-14)

We need hope, and we need it now—at this very hour. We need God's assurance that God has not abandoned us. For this reason we gather to worship the God we can't explain or even begin to understand. Our limited human perspective leaves us with only our inarticulate minds and our faltering tongues.

Whatever passions and dreams (*Name*) had during his life, whatever disappointments and heartaches he may have experienced, I join with all of you in praying and wishing for him the peace that may have eluded him at times and a rest from his labors. (*Name*) touched many lives throughout his time here. We are a better church and better people for having (*Name*) pass our way. But theological questions still haunt us nonetheless.

Theodicy is a big fancy theological word that basically has to do with the justice of God in an apparently unjust world. And you might be surprised that the word *theodicy* describes more average run-of-the-mill theology undertaken by ordinary people than all other questions about God put together and multiplied by ten. Questions about theodicy usually sound like: What did I do to deserve this? Or, why did this happen to me or us? Why now? Why?

Theodicy is the doctrine that validates God's justice in a world where evil truly exists. We ask these kinds of questions about God, and to God, in funeral homes and hospitals. I've spent a lot of time the last twenty-five years thinking about and trying to answer such questions, but truthfully, there are few satisfactory answers. Since September 11, 2001, I suppose, more Americans have been doing theological thinking about theodicy than they have done in a good long time—some good, much dreadful.

Preachers (and I believe this is an occupational hazard) naturally encounter such questions constantly: Why did our friend get cancer? Why couldn't my children stay married? Why do children have to go to bed hungry? Why is there war? What did I do to deserve this? Why did this happen to us?

Like most of you, I am guilty of asking these kinds of questions about the way things are. We want to know why the good suffer. We want to know why bad things happen to good people, and worse, why do good things happen to bad people? The psalmist speaks for us all when he writes:

> But as for me, my feet had almost stumbled;
>   my steps had nearly slipped.
> For I was envious of the arrogant;
>   I saw the prosperity of the wicked. (Psalm 73:2-3)

Technically Psalm 13 is not a question, but realistically it is a question: What did I do to deserve this? Why did this happen to me?

This is a good question for us today. Certainly, we can ask why did this happen to (Name) or us. We can shake our fist at God with the psalmist and do so on good biblical grounds. We can fall into the despair created by grief and mourning. Yet, if I knew (Name)—and I did and I do—he had enough faith, through our questions and beyond all our doubts, to ask us to take a good look at our lives. He would want all of us to get right with our families and with our God. (Name) would want us to push through the pain and get on with the task of living. Today, I think, (Name) would tell us that the *why* question will always be with human beings, and he himself asked them often enough. But (Name) would also want us to ask a larger question: what do I do with my life today and tomorrow? Ultimately this is the real question of faith because it is the only question that we can help answer to our satisfaction.

The authentic question is: how do we live our life before God in a faithful way? The *why* questions too often form a blockade to keep us from continuing on our journey of faith that carries us to the end. Our end will be in God. So I pose for you another question on this bright and beautiful October afternoon. Instead of asking God why, could we not try asking instead, God, what must I do in this circumstance to be a person of faith and integrity? God, what must I do in my pain and grief and disappointment to be someone who cares for all of God's children? These are questions that will put us back on the path of our journey toward faithfulness.

It is fitting that we say good-bye to (*Name*) in this magnificent church's sanctuary. *Sanctuary* is a good word for us to depart on. (*Name*) has finally found that elusive eternal sanctuary that God promises all of us who have the good sense to accept God's amazing grace in Jesus Christ. May God bless us in this midst of our tragic loss but redeem us as God's chosen people in the process. Amen. (David Mosser)

Weddings/Renewing the Vows

Wedding Prayer

Loving God, you have formed us in your image of love and made for us relationships with one another. On this day, we come to praise and thank you for the love between (*Name*) and (*Name*). We ask for your blessings upon them as they begin their journey of marriage together. Allow them to experience your grace and love as they strive to keep the covenant they will make here today. Be present with us as a worshiping congregation that we may experience your love for us this day. In Christ's Holy name we pray, Amen.

Scripture Suggestions

Genesis 2:4b-7, 15-24
John 15:9-17
1 Corinthians 13

Wedding Homily

Have you noticed that love is sometimes easier than at other times? If not, you will. Today, as you stand here in this beautiful setting, surrounded by your loving friends and family, looking into each other's eyes, love seems pretty easy. Everything feels right. Unfortunately, this day will end. On many days, you will not feel like you or your partner is quite as pretty or handsome as you were on your wedding day. There will not always be friends and family so close to support and encourage you. You will not always feel this happy to see each other.

Now, for the good news. The vows and promises that you make here today are not dependent upon any of these things. The Scriptures describe love as rising above all the imperfections of life in order to accept a person just as God has made him or her. This is why the rest of us can gain so much from your wedding ceremony. The love we see between the two of you is merely a reflection of the love God has for each of us. Weddings have been connected to the church for years, so God's people have a tangible example of what God's love is like.

In 1 Corinthians 13 we hear a description of love that is a great example for a husband and wife to follow. It is a true description of how God loves us as well. We have a God who looks at us some days and probably wonders why we deserve grace and forgiveness, yet God is always willing to offer it to us. (*Name*) and (*Name*), you will not always want to love each other, but the fact that you promise to rise above those temporary emotions and strive to love unconditionally helps us understand how God puts up with who we are. As you exchange your vows and promise to love each other for better or worse, you are promising to love the unlovable some days. You are willing to make this promise because you know the inherent God-given value and goodness of your soon-to-be spouse.

God makes the same promise to us all. God loves us no matter what we look like in the morning. God loves us when we are in a bad mood. God loves us when the day has just been really hard. God is always there for us. In your marriage find strength by knowing that God is always there for you. God will never stop loving you individually. God will not stop loving you as a couple. God will not stop loving us as gathered friends and family. We worship together and take hope in the knowledge that God's love for us is as committed as the love you share here today. We give God thanks for your marriage, and we also give God thanks for loving us all.

Blessing of the Marriage

Creating, Redeeming, and Sustaining God, send your blessings upon (Name) and (Name) that they may know your love and sacrifice for them. Allow them to keep their promise made here today so their home may be built upon a foundation of peace and love. Grant each of us the courage to live as your partner in ministry to the world. In the loving name of Jesus we pray, Amen. (Chris J. Hayes)

Teacher Dedication

Greeting

Teach your children well. Teach them the stories of the faith, the songs of the ages, the friendship of Christ, the ways of God.

Keep the words of Scripture in your heart.

Recite them to your children,

and talk about them when you are at home

and when you are away.

Bind the promises of God to your daily lives

as though they were a sign on your hand,

a symbol on your forehead,

a mark on your front door.

The Lord your God, and God alone,

You shall honor and serve and love.

Mark 4:26-29

We often speak of the role of the Sunday school teacher as one of making disciples through teaching, of forming persons in faithful living. Yet how exactly do we "make" disciples for Jesus Christ? Is it like "making" a widget, with an assembly line of heavy presses and stamps and lathes, the outcome being precise and predictable? How do we form people into the community of those seeking to be faithful to God in their lives and in their life together? Is it like forming clay into the shape of a pizza or an earthworm?

This parable of Jesus suggests otherwise. It seems to suggest that the way we make disciples, the way we form children, youth, and adults in holy living is more like the way a gardener grows a garden. We plow, plant, water, weed, and then scratch our heads—not with frustration but in wonder.

If you plant seeds as teachers, those seeds may sprout and yield their fruit tomorrow, or next year, or sometime in the next century, or perhaps, hard as it is to fathom, a millenium from now. But if the parable has it right, they will do so in their own time, not in ours. If we see those fruits right away, that's wonderful. If we don't, that's where trust comes in. Hidden within the gardener's sweeping gesture of scattering seed is a pledge of surrendering to God the outcome of the work. The seed sprouts and grows, yet the gardener "does not know how."

I was in the fifth grade when my Sunday school teacher asked us to memorize the 23rd Psalm. I was a pretty quick study; I was back the next week with my assignment completed. A year later, I'm sure I hadn't thought of that psalm a single time since having learned it. Three years later, when I thought about my teacher, it was only in reference to his teenage daughter, who was too old to be interested in me but not too old for me to be interested in her. Ten years later, I was buried in seminary studies, learning about Barth, Tillich, Julian of Norwich, and church history—I had little opportunity to revisit the "Shepherd's psalm." However, fifteen years later, I was standing at gravesides on a regular basis, reciting, sometimes alone, sometimes in unison with a bereaved family, the psalm my teacher had taught me way back in the fifth grade: *The Lord is my shepherd; I shall not want.*

Nearly every time I think of that psalm now or pray it at a funeral or a hospital bedside, I whisper a prayer of thanks for my teacher, who first invited me to learn it by heart thirty-five years ago. I wonder who is whispering your name in thanksgiving because of the Sunday school teacher you were thirty-five years ago, or ten, or five, or just last year. I wonder who, thirty-five years from now, or five, or one, will be whispering your name in thanks because of the Sunday school teacher you are going to be this year.

We never know when the seeds we plant in the minds and hearts of children, youth, and adults will bear fruit for the kingdom of God. We only know the way in which, according to Jesus, the kingdom happens: in ways beyond our knowing. Albert Outler used to speak of having "the patience to see the slow growth of seeds." With characteristic wit he poses an oxymoron, which contains within it a kernel of truth: of course we cannot "see" the growth of seeds—they are buried in the ground, hidden from view. If there is any way in which we can actually see a seed's slow growth, it must be with the gardener's eyes, with Jesus' eyes, with the good teacher's eyes; it must be with eyes of faith.

A Litany for the Dedication of Sunday School Teachers

(*Those who have taught previously are called by name and asked to stand and read as follows:*)

Teachers: We have responded to God's call and have served the church by teaching the children, youth, and adults of our church family. Through our teaching ministries we have been vessels of God's love, blessed in our teaching, learning even as we have taught.

Congregation and Pastor: We affirm you for the work you have done and will continue to do among us. We take this opportunity to recognize and thank you for having taught us and our children throughout this past year. We are grateful for your faithful service.
(*Current teachers are called by name and asked to come to the front of the sanctuary.*)

Teachers: We have been called to serve God and one another by giving ourselves as an opportunity to claim and share our faith. With God's help, and your blessing, we can accept our calling to teach the children, youth, and adults of our church.

Congregation and Minister: We pledge to you our loyalty, our support, and our love.

Litany of Thanksgiving

Today we pray in gratitude for those who teach and those who learn. Guide, O God, our teachers to present your good news, through word and example, to all those entrusted to them.

Grant wisdom and understanding to all who teach.

Lead them as they seek to give direction through the confusion of conflicting values and questions of faith.

Grant our teachers your inspiration and strength.

Give them enthusiasm and patience, loving discipline and creativity, and a sense of humor.

Grant, O God, the joy born of your Spirit to all those who learn.

Impart to them inquiring minds, listening ears, and receptive hearts free from distraction and fear.

Grant that your Word may take root in them.

Satisfy their hunger and thirst with your life-giving Spirit.

Grant wisdom and openness to each of us—teachers and learners all.

Let us remember and affirm that we are all called to grow as disciples of Jesus Christ.

Grant us insight to support one another in our faith, in our teaching, and in our learning. These things we pray in the name of Jesus, the one true Teacher. Amen.

Graduation/Baccalaureate Service

Prayer

Loving God, it is pleasing, these moments you have given us to gather and to celebrate. Your presence in this place is comforting, and we are grateful. These young men and women have completed a course that leads them to this place in time. We pray for your blessings on them as they set a new course for the rest of their lives. Grant them, O God, the wisdom and the courage to be the leaders in both civil and spiritual arenas. Present them with good judgment to make the decisions that will influence the people they will touch in community, country, and world. Bestow on them a peace and understanding about their role in this world and give them the nerve to assume their place in society. These things we pray in the name of Jesus, the great teacher and our Lord. Amen.

Scripture Suggestions

Jeremiah 1:4-8
1 Peter 2:21

Sermon

Graduates, we are here today to honor you for your great accomplishment. You have demonstrated commitment and resolve that now sets the standard for the rest of your lives. Other people may tell you that the next steps will not be easy. Perhaps life will be only as complicated as you allow it to be. It is evident that you are already successful. That knowledge should be used as a foundation for the next success you can expect. The apostle Peter makes us aware of a foundation based on the perfect example from Jesus, "For to this you have been called, because Christ also suffered for you, leaving you an example, so that you should follow in his steps" (1 Peter 2:21).

We have read the passage of scripture from Jeremiah. God had selected him before he was born to be a prophet who would lead nations. Imagine the emotions that must have been churning in his mind as Jeremiah was informed in this poetic passage about God's plan for him. Jeremiah said, "Ah, Lord GOD! Truly I do not know how to speak, for I am only a boy" (Jeremiah 1:6).

It has long intrigued me that people can find an excuse not to do things that causes them anxiety. The fact that Jeremiah used the words "I do not know how to speak" means that he would have been among the vast majority of people in our society today. The fear of speaking is more prominent than the fear of snakes, spiders, heights, or dark roads near a cemetery. The interesting thing is that God offered the assurance that God would give Jeremiah the words and that he should not fear. I believe God was saying to Jeremiah, get past your petty panic, go speak to the people, and get better with practice and time. God was adamant that Jeremiah should understand that God is present for him in this brief weakness. "Do not be afraid of them, / for I am with you to deliver you, says the LORD" (Jeremiah 1:8). I believe the Lord stands by you and me to deliver us from ourselves. We must simply pray for his presence, ask his blessings, and work hard to do his will and please him. In so doing, you will surely please yourself.

In addition to facing up to the fears, we are expected by our family, friends, the church, society, and by God to have a purpose in life. Graduates, you are in a position to plan a strategy that will influence you for a lifetime, however long it may be. Having a life objective is important to the decisions you make as you embark on this new voyage. Purpose comes from knowing where you want to go, knowing what you want to be, and knowing that you don't know all the answers that will take you to your goal.

I watched the Olympics and was intrigued by the men and women who were interviewed. It seemed to me that each winner looked into the camera and clearly left the impression that they knew from a very early age that they were going to be gold medal winners in the Olympics someday. They remained focused on the mental image they had of standing on the platform and bending forward to receive the medal around their neck—just as they had dreamed it many years before.

You also have dreams that can be accomplished when you get your mind and body in motion to do all that is necessary to reach your goals. A great archer is still a great archer even if he is blindfolded. But, because he cannot see his target, he will surely fail. Knowing what the target in your life will be is critical to having the insight and vision to help you achieve.

The strength of this message is knowing that you do not have to do it alone. Look around you and you look into the faces of people who support you now and who will support you throughout your life. Look inside you and you will find that there is comfort in knowing that God is also with you. Just as surely as God assured Jeremiah, he also assures you. God said to Jeremiah and he says to you, "Do not be afraid of them, / for I am with you to deliver you" (Jeremiah 1:8).

May God's blessings be upon you as you set your sights on new adventure and many successes.

Closing Prayer

Eternal God and loving teacher, surround these young men and women with your presence. Help them feel you in their lives. Grant them courage and strength to be the great leaders of tomorrow. Grant the wisdom to lead through focused attention to your desires and to the needs of humankind. In the name of Jesus, the greatest teacher, I pray. Amen. (Ted L. McIlvain)

Dedication of a Sanctuary

Greeting

Unless the Lord builds the house,

they who build it labor in vain.

Unless the Lord watches over the city,

they who watch over it stay awake in vain.

From God above comes every good and perfect gift;

to God be the glory, now and forever. Amen.

Sermon

1 Kings 8:22-30

We are here today to dedicate a new sanctuary to the glory of God. We're not the first to do so, of course. It was some three thousand years ago that King Solomon stood at the front altar of the newly completed temple at Jerusalem to dedicate that sanctuary to God. It had to have been an exhilarating moment in the history of the people of Israel. Slaves in Egypt for four hundred years; wanderers in the wilderness for forty more; established finally in the promised land, this moment was the fulfillment of generations of hopes, dreams, and aspirations on the part of the Hebrew people: to live in a land they could call their own; to build a temple for their God.

It must have been an electric moment when the doors of that new temple were opened for the first time, and King Solomon in all his glory began to pray:

> O LORD, God of Israel, there is no God like you in heaven above or on earth beneath, keeping covenant and steadfast love for your servants who walk before you with all their heart, the covenant that you kept for your servant my father David as you declared to him; you promised with your mouth and have this day fulfilled with your hand. (8:23-24)

Then Solomon said something in his prayer the wisdom of which has endured through the ages. It was one of those things that you would say was true not only for that moment but for all time: "But will God indeed dwell on the earth? Even heaven, and the highest heaven cannot contain you, much less this house that I have built!"

It was a profoundly unorthodox statement for a royal sovereign to make in reference to his greatest architectural achievement. With those words, Solomon demonstrated that he had the humility to know, the faith to know, the wisdom to know that as beautiful as that new temple was and as much as a source of pride and accomplishment it was for him and the nation of Israel, it could never, ever contain God and must never, ever become God.

Solomon must have known that idols come in all shapes and sizes. Buildings can become idols as easily as golden calves—maybe, to Western, "enlightened" minds, more easily.

And so his prayer, with remarkable simplicity, expresses that as great as a building may be, God is always greater—greater than our buildings, our words, our songs, our prayers. And the best sanctuaries remind us of that truth; they are merely symbols pointing beyond themselves to a reality they can never themselves contain.

Frank Lloyd Wright once claimed that every building is a missionary. If that is so, then every sanctuary, and this sanctuary, has one message to convey: the majesty of God.

From this day forward, may this sanctuary always serve its missionary purpose of pointing beyond itself, toward something far greater, toward a God whose greatness is unsearchable, and so lead us to confess our devotion to the God whose glory is contained neither by a sanctuary, nor the earth, nor all the heights of heaven.

Litany for the Dedication of a New Sanctuary

To us has been given the high calling of being the church of Jesus Christ in this time and place. To that end we have given our best resources—our financial gifts, our skills and abilities, our hopes and dreams—to build a sanctuary to the glory of God.

May God be praised for these gifts and for their good use.

Many have given generously to this work—time and talents, love and prayers, heart and soul. These persons have served us well, and we have been blessed by their labors of love.

May God be praised for these gifts and for their good use.

As a congregation we have trusted our leaders and workers, prayed for them in their plans and preparations, worked and waited patiently beside them, and celebrated their achievements on our behalf.

May God be praised for these gifts and for their good use.

The Lord has been gracious to us and blessed us. God has given us the gift of a new future in this place we now call our church home, and so we dedicate this sanctuary as a place of worship and a house of prayer for all God's people.

We dedicate this sanctuary, O God, made beautiful by the love and labors of so many. Let it be made holy by your presence and your blessing, and as it is sanctified so, too, may we be, to your glory, now and forever. Amen.

Church Anniversary

Litany of Praise

Blessed are you, Sovereign God, creator of the universe, giver of life, source of love and joy in every congregation and in this church.

You have given us beauty and space, color and promise, table, cross, and candles, Christ the Light of the world.

You have blessed us with your Word and nestled our church's story into the folds of your eternal story of redeeming love.

You have lent to us song and dance, music and worship, and by your Spirit filled our circle with babies and children and youth and adults, wise ones and young ones, dreamers and doers, prophets and pray-ers.

A warm heart you have given us, and a willing hand, to love and serve you here and in the world.

Blessed are you, Sovereign God, from whose hand have come all these good gifts of the Spirit, through Jesus Christ. Amen.

A Golden Key
Revelation 3:14-22

G. K. Chesterton, a British author known best for his Father Brown mysteries, had only vague memories from his own childhood of his father, but those memories were very precious. Chesterton remembers his father having a toy theater in which all the characters were cutouts in cardboard. One of those cutout characters was a man with a golden key. The man with a golden key would unlock a certain door in the theater, and a story would unfold from there. Reflecting years later on that childhood experience with his father, Chesterton said, "In my mind I connected my father with that character—my father was the man with a golden key, opening to me all kinds of wonderful and thrilling stories, adventures, dramas, and mysteries."

What if we were to borrow that key from Chesterton's father today, a golden key in our anniversary year as a congregation? Where would we turn with it? What locks would we unlock? What doors could we open?

With that key we could unlock our congregation's past, rich with stories of courage, vision, and faith, from which to grow in our own faith, fruit from the tree of whom we have been, fruit that is ours to touch, let down in hand, and savor. There are funny stories, touching stories, inspiring stories, and ordinary stories. If with that golden key in our anniversary year we were to unlock the past, there's a lot we could learn there.

Or, we could take that golden key and look ahead, unlocking the future. What would we see ten years from now, or fifty, or a hundred? In an interview, Woody Allen was once asked what he'd like people to say about him in a hundred years. Woody Allen answered, "I'd like them to say, 'He looks pretty good for his age.'"

In that span of time, or even less—in the next twenty years, or ten— how will we look for our age? What great things will we have attempted for God and the gospel? Who will we have sent into the world in mission? What lives will have been touched, healed, renewed by the labors of our congregation, our children, our grandchildren?

Who will have been led by the Spirit to new avenues of ministry and service, gifted in ways we cannot even begin to imagine for the great work of God as it unfolds in the future?

What children that we cradle now in our arms, coddle in our nurseries, teach and sing with around the circle of Sunday school will be emerging as leaders of our churches, cities, schools, hospitals; leaders of our country, and in the world; children who first learned within these very walls, from you and from me, the first and the last lesson of the faith: "Jesus loves me, this I know"?

If that golden key could unlock the future, fifty years from now, or five, or one, or even next Sunday, will we be found faithful to the call of God to follow Jesus through the thick and thin of our days and years and to invite others to share that journey with us? May it be so.

For what shall we use the golden key in this anniversary year? To unlock the past? the future? We could unlock the present. Who are we, church, not yesterday, not tomorrow, but *today*? From Revelation, we hear the words of the living Christ: Not "I once stood at the door and knocked," or "Someday I will stand at the door and knock," but "Behold, I stand at the door and knock" (Revelation 3:20). The living Christ seeks entry *now*; not yesterday and not tomorrow. *Today.* This is the living Christ who, if we open to him, will feast with us, and lead us into God's future. For the golden key, finally, belongs not to us but to the Christ, who alone can sanctify our past, bring meaning and purpose to our present, and guide us into a future alive with promise as the people of God in this place.

Litany of Thanksgiving and Dedication

From the prayers of many, and the gifts and labors of many more, a church was born, an infant congregation with no name, no place, no home, only a song to sing and good news to share.

Glory to God in the highest heaven, and peace to the world God loves!

Week after week this fledgling group kept the ancient rhythm of the saints—gathered to worship, went forth to serve; gathered to celebrate, went forth to share; gathered to pray, went forth to invite others to the welcome table.

Glory to God in the highest heaven, and peace to the world God loves!

Their labors were long, their progress slow. They tilled, planted, and watered. They watched, waited, and prayed. In due time, God gave the increase: new plans, new projects, new outreach, new fields for harvesting. Their numbers grew, their vision broadened, and their hearts were lifted up.

Glory to God in the highest heaven, and peace to the world God loves!

In tenderness they raised their young on the stories of the faith; in boldness they sent out their missioners by the Spirit's power. In delight they gathered to praise God, to study the Scriptures, to enjoy the beloved community of the church; in compassion they looked upon the world in its need and stepped through their doors to be the church beyond their walls.

Glory to God in the highest heaven, and peace to the world God loves!

Through many and various seasons our mothers and fathers in the faith have tended this place, mined its treasure, shared it with the world. And in these days, we remember their stories and honor their faithfulness. We would take upon ourselves their tenderness toward the young and their boldness in mission. We pledge ourselves to carry into new frontiers the ancient rhythm that calls us together for the glory of God and sends us out for the peace of the world.

Glory to God in the highest heaven, and peace to the world God loves!

Hallelujah! Amen!

TWO CLASSIC SERMONS

The Great Expectation
An Old-Year Sermon

by Phillips Brooks

"Let your moderation be known unto all men. The Lord is at hand."—
PHILIPPIANS 4:4

It is not easy to decide just what the apostles expected with reference to the second coming of the Lord. Sometimes it seemed as if they looked almost immediately to see the opening sky and the descending chariot. At other times, with a more general faith, they seemed to anticipate what has come to pass, the slow and spiritual occupation of the standards and purposes of human life by the spirit of Jesus, to be quickened at some future day and brought to some great consummation which it is impossible to describe beforehand, but which, when it comes, will centre about him and crown him as the Master of the world. Sometimes one of these thoughts, sometimes the other seems to represent St. Paul's anticipation. But, whatever was the form which their expectation more or less definitely assumed, the great fact about him and the other disciples was that they always were expecting. Their look was always forward; and they found abundant clearness and abundant inspiration in their expectancy when they described the thing which they expected as a "coming of the Lord." "Maranatha." "The Lord will come." It was one of their customs to greet one another with that salutation.

We cannot probably imagine how complete this habit of expectation had possession of their lives. It must have given color and meaning to everything they did. Every step they took in life brought them a little nearer to that great end and purpose. They set out on a voyage, and as they turned their eyes away from the fading shore and looked across the broad waters, they seemed to be sailing out to meet the coming Lord. Two of them parted from each other, not knowing when they were to meet again, and they said to themselves. Whenever it is it will be in some nearer presence of the Lord. One of them moved to a new dwelling, and, as he entered into the door of what was to be his future home, its rooms became sacred to him because in them he was to witness the approach of Christ; in them Christ was to be nearer to him than ever in the house which he had left behind. "Now is our salvation nearer than when we first believed." Those words which once came from the apostle's lips, expressed the feeling and the power which was always in all the apostles' hearts.

And it has been this expectation of a coming of the Lord which, ever since the time of the apostles, has always been the inspiration of the Christian world. The noblest souls always have believed that humanity was capable of containing, and was sure sooner or later to receive, a larger and deeper infusion of divinity. The promise of Christianity is as yet but half fulfilled. All that has been done yet in all the Christian centuries is only the sketch and prelude of what is yet to be done. This has been the faith of every Christian reformer. This is what has made it easy for souls which loved the dear associations of the past as much as any others, to cut loose from them and sail out on unknown seas. It has not been mere wilfulness. It has been really the profoundest faith. It has dared to think of human history not as a great flat plain on which men wandered pleasantly but aimlessly, always coming back at last to the dead camp-fires where they had slept before, but as a flight of shining stairs up which men were to struggle toilsomely but eagerly toward a day of the Lord, a kingdom of heaven which was waiting for them at the top.

And as the noblest souls have thought of the world's history, so the most earnest men and women have always thought of their own lives. The power of any life lies in its expectancy. "What do you hope for? What do you expect?" The answer to these questions is the measure of the degree in which a man is living. He who can answer these questions by the declaration, "The Lord is at hand: I am expecting a higher, deeper, more pervading mastery of Christ"—we know that he is thoroughly alive.

And, as I have already intimated, one of the great signs of how strong life is in such a man will be the way in which he leaves his past. What a difference there is in men about that! Some men are always driven out of their past and leave it only because they cannot stay there. Other men go forth from their past because they have grown weary and disgusted with it, and are willing to flee from it for pure love of change. Other men leave their past full of honor for it, full of gratitude for the equipment which it has given them for their future life, but full also of the attraction of the future in which the equipment which their past has given them is to be used. Here on a ship's deck which goes sailing out of port some day there are three men together. All of them are leaving the home-land. Behind all three alike, standing on the same deck, the same land fades away and is lost out of sight.

But is it the same thing to all of them? Has leaving home for all of them the same meaning? One is an exile, who, having committed flagrant crime, is permitted to live only on condition that he shall leave his country and never come back to it again. One is an idler, who, having exhausted the surface of the land where he belongs, is sailing now to feed his restlessness in mere change, in the mere sight of things he never saw before. The third is a discoverer, who has gathered all the knowledge and character which he could gain at home, and is now set to use them in reading the secret of some hidden country and making the world larger for mankind. How different they are! with what different eyes they see the familiar shore sink down into the sea! But they are not more different than are three men who leave any one period of life behind them and go out into a new one, one of them simply with the feeling that he cannot help himself, another with the vague sense that the past has grown tame and the future will offer something new, and the third with the eager hope that the Lord is at hand, that in the larger circumstances and with the maturer powers he will come nearer to and know more of Christ.

You know of course why I have thus begun to speak to you to-day. It is the last Sunday of 1884. The year which came to us twelve months ago, all fresh and young, is old and weary. Before next Sunday a new year will come to crowd him from his place. On such a Sunday it is not a mere habit, it is a natural and healthy instinct, which makes us stand between the new year and the old, between the living and the dead, and listen to them as they speak to one another. Can we not almost hear the words they say, and is not their deepest burden something like this which I have tried to express? The old year says to the new year, "Take this man and show him greater things than I have been able to show him. You must be for him a richer, fuller day of the Lord than I could be." The new year says to the old, "I will take him and do for him the best that I can do. But all that I can do for him will be possible only in virtue of the preparation which you have made, only because of what you have done for him already."

We want to think then about men going forward to greater things, leaving the past, in hope and expectation of a greater future. As I announce that subject, I can almost hear some cynical bystander say, "You may spare yourself the trouble of that sermon. For one half of your hearers it will be needless. For the other half it will be useless. The young people know without your telling them, know better than you can tell them, that the future is very great and glorious and splendid; and you will not convince the people who are no longer young that the future will be in any great way different from the past. Perhaps there are a few just trembling between youth and age, not having wholly lost the vision of the one nor gained the insight of the other, whom you may persuade to cling to their illusions a little longer; but is that really worth your while? By-and-by the eyes must open and the vision disappear, and then the monotony of life must be accepted, and the man give up all expectation of anything except running the same round of routine till he dies."

I want at least to bear a protest against the mockery of such words as those, and to assert that that cry, "The Lord is at hand," may and ought to be in the ears of every man as he goes from the old year to the new.

There are really two divisions of our subject. We may think first of the way in which a man becomes more conscious of the God who is already close to him, and second of the way in which God actually comes closer to him, year by year. They are what the philosophers would call the subjective and the objective thoughts of God's nearness. And we start with that which must be true, the assertion that the more varied and manifold a man's experiences have become, the more he has the chance to know of God, the more chance God has to show Himself to him. Every new experience is a new opportunity of knowing God. Every experience is like a jewel set into the texture of our life, on which God shines and makes interpretation and revelation of himself. You hang a great rich dark cloth up into the sunlight, and the sun shines on it and shows the broad general color that is there. Then one by one you sew great precious stones upon the cloth, and each one, as you set it there, catches the sunlight and pours it forth in a flood of peculiar glory. A diamond here, an emerald there, an opal there, the sun seems to rejoice as he finds each moment a new interpreter of his splendor, until at last the whole jewelled cloth is burning and blazing with the gorgeous revelation.

Now a much-living life, a life of manifold experiences, is like a robe which bursts forth of itself to jewels. They are sewn on from the outside. They burn out of its substance as the stars burn out of the heart of the night. And God shines with new revelation upon every one. And the man who feels himself going out of a dying year with these jewels of experience which have burned forth from his life during its months, and knowing that God in the New Year will shine upon them and reveal Himself by them, may well go full of expectation, saying, "The Lord is at hand."

Life may be always expecting new sight of God, because life is always acquiring new experiences on which, through which, God may declare His nearness and His love. We may, if we will, turn the jewelled cloth away from the sun, but if we let him shine upon it, he must make himself known. To most of you—shall I not say to all of you?—have come in this past year, some new experiences, some things which you have never known before. Some of you have known for the first time what it is to be poor. Perhaps some of you have known for the first time what it is to be rich. Some of you have had your first sickness. Some of you have felt for the first time the keenest suffering in the death of your best beloved. Some of you have begun the new joy of family life. Some of you have become fathers or mothers. Some of you with yet deeper changes, which bore no outside witness of themselves, have laid hold upon new and inspiring ideas. Some of you have given yourselves up to a profession; some of you have made a new friend; some of you have entered into the communion of the Church and put on Jesus Christ. These are the jewels on the cloth of gold of your life. As you go forth, knowing that God must have something new of himself to show to you through these experiences as they become more and more set and fastened in your life as its habits and possessions, can you help being full of expectation? Can you help saying to yourself: "The Lord is at hand"?

Is there not something of the same kind when in the midst of some great experience you look forward to meeting again, with the power of that new experience in you, your most noble and many-sided friend? "It may be," you say to yourself, "that this experience will be the key which I have needed to unlock that closed chamber of his nature, before which I have so often stood and wondered." You see him coming to you, and new light streams forth from him. You have gained a new power of reflecting him. Henceforth your whole life with him is going to be a richer, deeper thing. Make this mutual; let each of two friends with multiplying experience, gain new power to reflect the other's light; and have you not the whole philosophy of deepening friendship, of the way in which those who are true friends become more and more to each other every year, the longer that they live?

A soul goes forth from this world and enters into heaven. Surely a part of that intensified and deepened sight of God which is to be its privilege and glory there, will lie in the abundance of experience which it has accumulated here, and which will belong to it forever. Every treasured experience will be to it like an eye with which to gaze on God. We shall know him better forever and forever, because of that success or this disappointment, because this friend played us false, or because the market turned just as our fortune was on the point of being made. Could anything make the events which happen to us here on earth seem more interesting and significant than such a truth as that?

Thus much we say of the way in which the Lord is constantly coming by the ever increasing capacity, the ever multiplying experience of man, to discover and display more and more fully how near He is already. But this subjective interpretation is not all. There is the other, the objective side. We must pass to that. In these days man is so conscious of himself, so large a portion of his time and thought is given to the consideration of himself, he is so aware of the fact of his own activity, that sometimes it seems as if God were wholly passive, standing off there and waiting for man to come to Him; and meanwhile only making revelation of Himself to man as man turns to Him this or that side of his reflecting nature. Other times have been full of the truth of the activity of God. The Old Testament is all alive with that idea, and constantly in history there have recurred ages full of the spirit of the Old Testament, which think of God as He was thought of in those vigorous and stirring books. That God is seeking after man, changing His methods of treatment according to man's behavior, actually coming nearer to or going farther off from man, not simply making Himself known as near or far, but actually changing from near to far, from far to near, that is the Old Testament truth; and the New Testament, with the Incarnation for its light and glory, evidently has not lost or thrown away that truth.

No religion can live and be thoroughly strong unless it keeps that truth of the activity of God. Some religions, like Calvinism, have kept it so strongly that they have lost or made little of the other truth, of the activity of man. In our time, as I said, man is so aware of himself, and of what he has to do, that there is sometimes danger lest he forget—sometimes he certainly has forgotten—the activity of God.

Let us remember that great truth, and then, does not man's expectation of the future lift itself up and become wonderfully enlarged? Not merely, I shall grow so that I shall be able to understand vastly more of what God is and of what He is doing. God also will be ever doing new things. He is forever active. He has purposes concerning me which He has not yet unfolded. Therefore each year grows sacred with wondering expectation. Therefore I and the world may go forth from each old year into the new which follows it, certain that in that new year God will have for us some new treatment which will open for us some novel life.

The world, as it looks back upon the past years, knows that God's active care for it has proved itself abundantly in all his various treatments. One year He lifted the curtain from a hidden continent, and gave his children a whole new world in which to carry out His purposes. Another year He revealed to them a strange, simple, little invention which made the treasured knowledge of the few to be the free heritage of all. Another year He touched the solid frame of a great spiritual despotism, and it trembled and quaked, and thousands of its slaves came forth free men. Another year, in our own time, in our own land, He sent the message of liberty to a nation of bondmen, and the fetters fell off from their limbs. We call these events of history. They have a right to be called the comings of the Lord. They all are echoes and illustrations of that great coming of the Lord from which they who have known of it agree by instinctive consent to date their history, the birth of the child of Bethlehem, the Man of Nazareth and Calvary, into the world.

When we once think thus of the events of history as the activities of God, as the comings of the Lord to man, then there comes a great vitality into the story of mankind. It is all alive. And then we stand before the yet unopened history of a new year, and say, "What will God do?" Something of what he will do we can guess, as a child can guess something of the future actions of the wisest man by intuitions of his character; but what we guess is very little and very vague. Still there is enough left on which to feed our wonder. What will God do this year? How will he come near to man? It may be, O that it might be! that he will break up this awful sluggishness of Christendom, this terrible torpidity of the Christian Church, and give us a great, true revival of religion. It may be that he will speak some great imperious command to the brutal and terrible spirit of war, and will open the gate upon a bright period of peace throughout the world. It may be that he will draw back the curtain and throw some of his light upon the question, of how the poor and the rich may live together in more cordial brotherhood. It may be that he will lead up from the depths of their common faith in a power of unity into the sects of a divided Christendom. Perhaps he will smite this selfishness of fashionable life, and make it earnest. Perhaps by some terrible catastrophe he will teach the nation that corruption is ruin, and that nothing but integrity can make any nation strong. Perhaps this! perhaps that! We make our guesses, and no man can truly say. Only we know that with a world that needs so much, and with a God who knows its needs and who loves it and pities it so tenderly, there must be in the long year some approach of His life to its life, some coming of the Lord!

And if we know this of the world, shall we not also know it of ourselves? For us too God is certainly active. We look forward into the opening months and we say, Yes, no doubt something will happen, some change will come. It may be one thing or another. It may be fuller life; it may be death. It may be what we wish or what we dread. When we are young men we try to anticipate what is coming. As we grow to be older men we are very apt to give that up in hopelessness and merely wonder what will come. If we have no religion (or do not use the religion which we have, as many religious men do not), we think of what will happen as the falling of accidents or as the maturing of self-ripening processes. If we think of it at all religiously, we talk about God sending messages to us. If our religion is a real life thing, we feel God actually coming to us Himself, in all the unknown things which are to happen to us before another New Year's day. Ah, after all, that is everything. To know that there is no accident. To know that indeed there is no such thing as a mere message of God. To know that He is always coming to us. To know that there is nothing happening to us which is not His coming. To know all that, is to find the most trivial life made solemn, the most cruel life made kind, the most sad and gloomy life made rich and beautiful.

These are the two ways then in which the Lord comes, is always coming, to His servants. He opens their eyes to see how near He is already, and He does actually draw nearer to their lives. And now I must say a little about the other words of St. Paul in this text of ours, in which he describes what ought to be the result of this expectation of the coming of the Lord upon a man's life. "Let your moderation be known unto all men. The Lord is at hand." Moderation! Is not the word almost strange at first? Does it not almost chill us? Moderation! we cry. Nay, but in him whose soul is full of glorious expectation will not enthusiasm be the great condition? Will not his soul expand and claim its larger heritage? Will not those other words of Paul describe him to himself: "All things are yours!" Who shall talk to him of moderation? What a hard, cold word it is!

But this word moderation—forbearance, the new version renders it—is one of St. Paul's great words. Men are known by their favorite words. And as Paul uses this word it has more meaning in it than we can put into any one single word by which we can translate it. Indeed it is one of those words descriptive of character, which have no hope of being understood except as they find a conception of the character which they try to describe already present in the mind of him to whom the description is given, and are able to point to it and to say: "That is what I mean." It is self-restraint, it is self-possession.

There is—all man's self-knowledge has borne witness to it—there is somewhere in the human mind an image of human character in which all wayward impulses are restrained, not by outside compulsion, but by the firm grasp of a power which holds everything into obedience from within by the central purpose of the life. Thus character dreads fury and excitement as signs of feebleness. It hates exaggeration of statement, because exaggeration of statement means weakness of belief. It shrinks from self-display just in proportion as it accepts the responsibilities of selfhood. It is patient because it is powerful. It is tolerant because it is sure. It is hopeful for every man because it has found solid ground in the midst of the great turmoil for itself to stand on, and believes that all other men have the same right to solid ground to stand on as itself. It is this character, I think, which St. Paul calls by his great word moderation. It is self-possession. It is the self found and possessed in God. It is the sweet reasonableness which was in Jesus, of whom it was written that he should not strive nor cry, neither should his voice be heard in the streets; that he should not break the bruised reed, and the smoking flax he should not quench until he sent forth judgment unto victory. In these words I think we have the true description of what St. Paul means by moderation.

In the midst of eager and sometimes frantic struggles after virtue and after power, is there not something very great and refreshing in this setting up of moderation as the perfection of life? Be yourself in God, it seems to say, and virtue and power will take care of themselves.

And St. Paul says that this great self-possession in God must come to any man who really expects the coming of the Lord. O, my dear friends, if you knew that in the most evident of all ways, which is by death, the Lord were coming to you to-morrow, and if you could be perfectly free from all base feeling, from fear and flurry, from defiance and from dread, from exaggerations and depressions belonging to that awful moment, if so you could calmly lie and listen while the great, quiet footsteps came nearer and nearer to your door, what would be the condition which it would make in you? Would it be anything like this which I have tried to describe? Would it be any elevation, refinement, solemnity, and broadening of life? Would it be the calming of frivolity, the release of charity, the kindling of hope? Would it not be all of these?

Not yet for us does that great solemn footfall sound outside the door. But none the less is the Lord at hand. I have preached to you in vain to-day unless I have made you feel that He is always at hand. All expectation may be expectation of Him. All expectation then ought, if Paul is right, to be the birthplace of this lofty character of moderation. And is it not? Tell me, what would you like to do for any friend of yours, or for your son, who was foolishly exuberant, overrunning into frivolities and quarrels and silly theories of life, into petulant discontent and all the base ambitions of the hour? What would you like to do to save him? Would you not be sure that if you only could set a noble expectation before him, and give it dominion over his whole soul, he would certainly be saved?

That is St. Paul's doctrine! There is salvation for us all. Oh friends, the old year is fast slipping back behind us. We cannot stay in it if we would. We must go forth and leave our past. Let us go forth nobly. Let us go as those whom greater thoughts, and greater deeds await beyond. Let us go humbly, solemnly, bravely, as those must go who go to meet the Lord. With firm, quiet, serious steps, full of faith, full of hope, let us go to meet Him who will certainly judge us when we meet him, but who loves us while he judges us, and who, if we are only obedient, will make us by the discipline of all the years, fit for the everlasting world, where life shall count itself by years no longer.

Phillips Brooks, *Twenty Sermons* (New York: E. P. Dutton & Company, 1886), 353-69.

Exposition on Psalm 123

by Saint Augustine

1....Let this singer ascend; and let this man sing from the heart of each of you, and let each of you be this man, for when each of you saith this, since ye are all one in Christ, one man saith this; and saith not, "Unto Thee, O Lord, have" we "lift up" our "eyes;" but, "Unto Thee, O Lord, have I lift up mine eyes" (ver. 1). Ye ought indeed to imagine that every one of you is speaking; but that One in an especial sense speaketh, who is also spread abroad over the whole world....

What maketh the heart of a Christian heavy? Because he is a pilgrim, and longeth for his country. If thy heart be heavy on this score, although thou hast been prosperous in the world, still thou dost groan: and if all things combine to render thee prosperous, and this world smile upon thee on every side, thou nevertheless groanest, because thou seest that thou art set in a pilgrimage; and feelest that thou hast indeed happiness in the eyes of fools, but not as yet after the promise of Christ: this thou seekest with groans, this thou seekest with longings, and by longing ascendest, and while thou ascendest dost sing the Song of Degrees.

2....Where then are the ladders? For we behold so great an interval between heaven and earth, there is so wide a separation, and so great a space of regions between: we wish to climb thither, we see no ladder; do we deceive ourselves, because we sing the Song of Degrees, that is, the Song of ascent? We ascend unto heaven, if we think of God, who hath made ascending steps in the heart. What is to ascend in heart? To advance towards God. As every man who faileth, doth not descend, but falleth: so every one who profiteth doth ascend: but if he so profit, as to avoid pride: if he so ascend as not to fall: but if while he profiteth he become proud, in ascending he again falleth. But that he may not be proud, what ought he to do? Let him lift up his eyes unto Him who dwelleth in heaven, let him not heed himself....

3.... If, my brethren, we understand by heaven the firmament which we see with our bodily eyes, we shall indeed so err, as to imagine that we cannot ascend thither without ladders, or some scaling machines: but if we ascend spiritually, we ought to understand heaven spiritually: if the ascent be in affection, heaven is in righteousness. What is then the heaven of God? All holy souls, all righteous souls. For the Apostles also, although they were on earth in the flesh, were heaven; for the Lord, enthroned in them, traversed the whole world. He then dwelleth in heaven. How?...How long are they the temple according to faith? As long as Christ dwelleth in them through faith; as the Apostle saith, "That Christ may dwell in your hearts through faith." But they are already heaven in whom God already dwelleth visibly, who see Him face to face; all the holy Apostles, all the holy Virtues, Powers, Thrones, Lordships, that heavenly Jerusalem, wanderers from whence we groan, and for which we pray with longing; and there God dwelleth. Thither hath the Psalmist lifted up his faith, thither he riseth in affection, with longing hopes: and this very longing causeth the soul to purge off the filth of sins, and to be cleansed from every stain, that itself also may become heaven; because it hath lifted up its eyes unto Him who dwelleth in heaven. For if we have determined that that heaven which we see with our bodily eyes is the dwelling of God, the dwelling of God will pass away; for "heaven and earth will pass away." Then, before God created heaven and earth, where did He dwell? But some one saith: and before God made the Saints, where did He dwell? God dwelt in Himself, he dwelt with Himself, and God is with Himself. And when He deigneth to dwell in the Saints, the Saints are not the house of God in such wise, as that God should fall when it is withdrawn. For we dwell in a house in one way, in another way God dwelleth in the Saints. Thou dwellest in a house: if it be withdrawn, thou fallest: but God so dwelleth in the Saints, that if He should Himself depart, they fall....

4.... What then followeth, since he hath said, "Unto Thee do I lift up mine eyes"? (ver. 2). How hast thou lifted up thine eyes? "Behold, even as the eyes of servants look unto the hand of their masters, and as the eyes of a maiden unto the hand of her mistress: even so our eyes wait upon the Lord our God, until He have mercy upon us." We are both servants, and a handmaiden: He is both our Master and our Mistress. What do these words mean? What do these similitudes mean? It is not wonderful if we are servants, and He our Master; but it is wonderful if we are a maiden, and He our Mistress. But not even our being a maiden is wonderful; for we are the Church: nor is it wonderful that He is our Mistress; for He is the Power and the Wisdom of God.... When therefore thou hearest Christ, lift up thine eyes to the hands of thy Master; when thou hearest the Power of God and the Wisdom of God, lift up thine eyes to the hands of thy Mistress; for thou art both servant and handmaiden; servant, for thou art a people; handmaiden, for thou art the Church. But this maiden hath found great dignity with God; she hath been made a wife. But until she come unto those spiritual embraces, where she may without apprehension enjoy Him whom she hath loved, and for whom she hath sighed in this tedious pilgrimage, she is betrothed: and hath received a mighty pledge, the blood of the Spouse for whom she sigheth without fear. Nor is it said unto her, Do not love; as it is sometimes said to any betrothed virgin, not as yet married: and is justly said, Do not love; when thou hast become a wife, then love: it is rightly said, because it is a precipitate and preposterous thing, and not a chaste desire, to love one whom she knoweth not whether she shall marry. For it may happen that one man may be betrothed to her, and another man marry her. But as there is no one else who can be preferred to Christ, let her love without apprehension: and before she is joined unto Him, let her love, and sigh from a distance and from her far pilgrimage....

5. "For we have been much filled with contempt" (ver. 3). All that will live piously according to Christ, must needs suffer reproof, must needs be despised by those who do not choose to live piously, all whose happiness is earthly. They are derided who call that happiness which they cannot see with their eyes, and it is said to them, What believest thou, madman? Dost thou see what thou believest? Hath any one returned from the world below, and reported to thee what is going on there? Behold I see and enjoy what I love. Thou art scorned, because thou dost hope for what thou seest not; and he who seemeth to hold what he seeth, scorneth thee. Consider well if he doth really hold it.... I have my house, he hath boasted himself. Thou askest, what house of his own? That which my father left me. And whence did he derive this house? My grandfather left it him. Go back even to his great grandfather, then to his great grand-father's father, and he can no longer tell their names. Art thou not rather terrified by this thought, that thou seest many have passed through this house, and that none of them hath carried it away with him to his everlasting home? Thy father left it: he passed through it: thus thou also wilt pass by. If therefore thou hast a mere passing stay in thy house, it is an inn for passing guests, not an habitation for permanent abode. Yet since we hope for those things which are to come, and sigh for future happiness, and since it hath not yet appeared what we shall be, although we are already "sons of God;" for "our life is hidden with Christ in God:" "we are utterly despised," by those who seek or enjoy happiness in this world.

6. "Our soul is filled exceedingly; a reproach to the wealthy, and a contempt to the proud" (ver. 4). We were asking who were "the wealthy:" he hath expounded to thee, in that he hath said, "the proud." "Reproach"

and "contempt" are the same: and "wealthy" is the same with "proud." It is a repetition of the sentence, "a reproach to the wealthy, and a contempt to the proud." Why are the proud wealthy? Because they wish to be happy here. Why? since they themselves too are miserable, are they wealthy? But perhaps when they are miserable, they do not mock us. Listen, my beloved. Then perchance they mock when they are happy, when they boast themselves in the pomp of their riches! when they boast themselves in the inflated state of false honours: then they mock us, and seem to say, Behold, it is well with me: I enjoy the good things before me: let those who promise what they cannot show depart from me: what I see, I hold; what I see, I enjoy; may I fare well in this life. Be thou more secure; for Christ hath risen again, and hath taught thee what He will give in another life: be assured that He giveth it. But that man mocketh thee, because he holdeth what he hath. Bear with his mockeries, and thou wilt laugh at his groans: for afterwards there will come a season when these very persons will say, "This was he whom we had sometimes in derision." . . .

7. To this we must add, that sometimes those also who are beneath the scourge of temporal unhappiness, mock us. . . . Did not the robber mock, who was crucified with our crucified Lord? If therefore they who are not wealthy mock us, why doth the Psalm say, "A reproach to the wealthy"? If we carefully sift the matter, even these (the unfortunate) are wealthy. How are they wealthy? Yea; for if they were not wealthy, they would not be proud. For one man is wealthy in money, and proud on that score: another is wealthy in honours, and is proud on that account: another imagines himself wealthy in righteousness, and hence his pride, which is worse. They who seem not to be wealthy in money, seem to themselves to be wealthy in righteousness towards God; and when calamity overtakes them, they justify themselves, accuse God, and say, What wrong have I been guilty of, or, what have I done? Thou repliest: Look back, call to mind thy sins, see if thou hast done nothing. He is somewhat touched in conscience, and returneth to himself, and thinketh of his evil deeds; and when he hath thought of his evil deeds, not even then doth he choose to confess that he deserves his sufferings; but saith, Behold, I have clearly done many things; but I see that many have done worse, and suffer no evil. He is righteous against God. He also therefore is wealthy: he hath his breast puffed out with righteousness; since God seemeth to him to do ill, and he seemeth to himself to suffer unjustly. And if thou gavest him a vessel to pilot, he would be shipwrecked with it: yet he wishes to deprive God of the government of this world, and himself to hold the helm of Creation, and

to distribute among all men pains and pleasures, punishments and rewards. Miserable soul! yet why do ye wonder? He is wealthy, but wealthy in iniquity, wealthy in malignity; but is more wealthy in iniquity, in proportion as he seemeth to himself to be wealthy in righteousness.

8. But a Christian ought not to be wealthy, but ought to acknowledge himself poor; and if he hath riches, he ought to know that they are not true riches, so that he may desire others.... And what is the wealth of our righteousness? How much soever righteousness there may be in us, it is a sort of dew compared to that fountain: compared to that plenteousness it is as a few drops, which may soften our life, and relax our hard iniquity. Let us only desire to be filled with the full fountain of righteousness, let us long to be filled with that abundant richness, of which it is said in the Psalm, "They shall be satisfied with the plenteousness of Thy house: and Thou shalt give them drink out of the torrent of Thy pleasure." But while we are here, let us understand ourselves to be destitute and in want; not only in respect of those riches which are not the true riches, but of salvation itself. And when we are whole, let us understand that we are weak. For as long as this body hungers and thirsts, as long as this body is weary with watching, weary with standing, weary with walking, weary with sitting, weary with eating; whithersoever it turneth itself for a relief from weariness, there it discovereth another source of fatigue: there is therefore no perfect soundness, not even in the body itself. Those riches are then not riches, but beggary; for the more they abound, the more doth destitution and avarice increase.... Let then our whole hunger, our whole thirst, be for true riches, and true health, and true righteousness. What are true riches? That heavenly abode in Jerusalem. For who is called rich on this earth? When a rich man is praised, what is meant? He is very rich: nothing is wanting to him. That surely is the praise of him that praiseth the other: for it is not this, when it is said, He wants nothing. Consider if he really want nothing. If he desires nothing, he wants nothing: but if he still desires more than what he hath, his riches have increased in such wise, that his wants have increased also. But in that City there will be true riches, because there will be nothing wanting to us there; for we shall not be in need of anything, and there will be true health....

Saint Augustine, "Psalm 123," *Saint Augustin: Expositions on the Book of Psalms* (trans. A. Cleveland Coxe; vol. 8 of *A Select Library of the Nicene and Post-Nicene Fathers of the Christian Church,* ed. Philip Schaff; Grand Rapids: Eerdmans, 1956), 596-98.

CONTRIBUTORS

Tracey Allred
Durham Memorial Baptist Church
521 Crossview Lane
Durham, NC 27703

Chris Andrews
First United Methodist Church
930 North Boulevard
Baton Rouge, LA 70802-5728

Bill Austin
9300 Country Lake Drive
Waco, TX 76708

Brian K. Bauknight
Christ United Methodist Church
44 Highland Road
Bethel Park, PA 15102

Tim K. Bruster
First United Methodist Church
800 W. 5th Street
Fort Worth, TX 76102

Thomas Lane Butts
First United Methodist Church
324 Pineville Road
Monroeville, AL 36460

Kenneth Carter Jr.
Providence United Methodist
  Church
2810 Providence Road
Charlotte, NC 28211

John Fiedler
First United Methodist Church
1928 Ross Avenue
Dallas, TX 75201

Dan L. Flanagan
Saint Paul's United Methodist
  Church
324 S. Jackson Street
Papillion, NE 68046

Travis Franklin
1111 Herring Avenue
Waco, TX 76708

Tracy Hartman
Baptist Theological Seminary
3400 Brook Road
Richmond, VA 23227

Chris J. Hayes
First United Methodist Church
  Arlington
313 North Center Street
Arlington, TX 76011-7593

Robert Hill
Asbury First United Methodist
  Church
1050 East Avenue
Rochester, NY 14607

Gary G. Kindley
First United Methodist Church
5601 Pleasant Run Road
Colleyville, TX 76034

Robert E. Long
St. Luke's United Methodist Church
222 NW 15th Street
Oklahoma City, OK 73103-3598

J. Michael Lowry
University United Methodist
  Church
5084 DeZavala Road
San Antonio, TX 78249

Ted L. McIlvain
First United Methodist Church
  Arlington
313 North Center Street
Arlington, TX 76011-7593

Jimmy McNeil
1405 Orchid Lane
Kissimmee, FL 34744

Lance Moore
First United Methodist Church
324 Pineville Road
Monroeville, AL 36460

David Mosser
First United Methodist Church
313 North Center Street
Arlington, TX 76011

Raquel Mull
2220 Utah N.E.
Albuquerque, NM 87110

Douglas Mullins
7771 Meadowcreek Drive
Cincinnati, OH 45244

William A. Ritter
1589 W. Maple Road
Birmingham, MI 48008

Henry E. Roberts
First United Methodist Church
6 E. Wright Street
Pensacola, FL 32501

Carl L. Schenck
Manchester United Methodist
  Church
129 Woods Mill Road
Manchester, MO 63011-4339

Jeffrey Smith
Woodway First United Methodist
  Church
9191 Woodway Drive
Waco, TX 76712

Robert Martin Walker
9 McCrea Lane
Darien, CT 06820

Ross West
Positive Difference
  Communications
100 Martha Drive
Rome, GA 30165-4138

INDEX

❧❧❧❧

OLD TESTAMENT

NEW TESTAMENT

A must for traditional and contemporary worship! "As pastors, we recognize that few worship planners have as much time and creative energy to spend planning their services of worship as we would like. . . . *The Abingdon Worship Annual* provides pastors and worship planners the liturgical elements to put a complete service of worship together," say Mary J. Scifres and B. J. Beu in the 2006 volume of *The Abingdon Worship Annual*. Although a plethora of resources are readily available for sermon, worship, and music planning, scant few provide assistance for creating coordinated and moving worship for traditional and contemporary worship experiences. Designed with this need in mind, *The Abingdon Worship Annual 2006* offers:
· weekly lectionary readings for each Sunday · calls to worship
· praise sentences and gathering words · pastoral and congregational prayers · benedictions and blessings. *The Abingdon Worship Annual 2006* is a must-have sourcebook offering countless opportunities for meaningful and insightful worship.

0687062497; $20.00

 **Abingdon Press**